POP! GOES THE WITCH

the disinformation guide
to 21st century witchcraft

edited by fiona horne

This collection Copyright © 2004 The Disinformation Company Ltd.

All of the articles in this book are Copyright © by their respective authors and/or original publishers, except as specified herein, and we note and thank them for their kind permission.

Published by The Disinformation Company Ltd.
163 Third Avenue, Suite 108
New York, NY 10003
Tel.: +1.212.691.1605
Fax: +1.212.473.8096
www.disinfo.com

Design & Layout: Leen Al-Bassam
Front cover photo: Randee St. Nicholas

Library of Congress Control Number: 2003113895

ISBN 0-9729529-5-0

Printed in USA

Distributed in the USA and Canada by:
Consortium Book Sales and Distribution
1045 Westgate Drive, Suite 90
St Paul, MN 55114
Toll Free: +1.800.283.3572
Local: +1.651.221.9035
Fax: +1.651.221.0124
www.cbsd.com

Distributed in the United Kingdom and Eire by:
Turnaround Publisher Services Ltd.
Unit 3, Olympia Trading Estate
Coburg Road
London, N22 6TZ
Tel.: +44.(0)20.8829.3000
Fax: +44.(0)20.8881.5088
www.turnaround-uk.com

Attention colleges and universities, corporations and other organizations: Quantity discounts are available on bulk purchases of this book for educational training purposes, fund-raising, or gift giving. Special books, booklets, or book excerpts can also be created to fit your specific needs. For information contact Marketing Department of The Disinformation Company Ltd.

Disinformation® is a registered trademark of The Disinformation Company Ltd.

enormous thanks to

Liam Cyfrin
Everyone who contributed so generously to POP! Goes The Witch
Disinformation
You!

table of contents

6 introduction

10 blessed be

STEPPING OUT OF THE SHADOWS: Where We Came From and Where We're Going

16 The Wicked Witch is Dead: Bad Witches are Out; Good Witches are In by Phyllis Curott

18 Witches, Witches Everywhere by Brenna Fey

20 Fire-light and Moon-Shadows: A Summary of Wiccan Lore by Morning Glory Zell-Ravenheart

28 A History of Wicca In England: 1939 to Present Day by Julia Phillips

42 Wicca and Satanism: A Case of Confused Identity by Nevill Drury

47 Frequently Avoided Questions by Liam Cyfrin

CHANT THE SPELL AND BE IT DONE: A Sprinkling of Practical Magick

56 How Spells Work (and a Stack of my Favorites) by Fiona Horne

74 Street Magicks by Rhea Loader

78 Birds, Bugs and Spiritual Growth: Totem Animals and the Witch by Scaerie Faerie

83 Child Magic: Creating Child Friendly Spells by Anton and Mina Adams

89 Divination and Space/Time Magick by Taylor Ellwood

93 The Oracle Tarot: Clearing the Karma of this Sacred Witches' Tool by Lucy Cavendish

THE HOLISTIC WITCH: Integrating the Magick of Body and Soul

100 The Everyday Life of a Modern Witch by Carmela Leone

107 Who What Wear: Dress with Intent by Francesca Gentille

109 I Feel Good: Healing Self-Esteem Issues with Witchcraft by Lucy Cavendish

114 How to be a Happy Hag: Three Lessons from the Queen of Witches by Kayt Davies

118 Closer to my Divine Craft by Serene Conneeley

124 Mending Ways: Keeping the Healing Traditions Alive by Rev. Dylan Masson

127 A Sense of Magick by Rhea Loader

132 Barefoot in the Soul by Phil Brucato

134 The Raw Food Revolution by David Wolfe

BETTER IT BE WHEN THE MOON IS FULL: Creating the Magickal Community

142 Neophytes in the Nest: Starting out in Witchcraft by Scaerie Faerie

147 The Breath and its Parts by Tri Johns

152 Herding Cats: Practical Ritual Writing by Gabrielle Cleary

159 The Religious Rights of Wiccans and Pagans in America by Phyllis Curott

INTERMISSION

A Poetic Interlude by Janet and Stewart Farrar 169

MULTIMEDIA MAGIC: Pop Culture Paganism

The Mad Mad House (and what I did in it) by Fiona Horne 182

Invoking Buffy: How to Use Pop Culture Icons as God-Forms by Taylor Ellwood 184

The Magickal Purpose of Horror: A Feast of the Powers of Darkness Stalking the Dark Archetype in 188
Mainstream Media by Anatha Wolfekeepe

PARALLEL PATHS: Other Kinds of Magick

Wicca and Christians: Some Mutual Challenges by Philip Johnson 196

Living in the Land of Aboriginal Magic by Janine Roberts 203

Bali Magic: The Enchanted Isle by Odyle Knight 210

Voodoo Queens and Goddesses: Feminine Healers of the African Diaspora by Iya Ta'Shia Asanti Karade 216

GENDER BLENDING: Love, Sex, Choice and Freedom

When a Witch Falls in Love with a Guy who Isn't by Lucy Cavendish 220

Calling the Great God Pan: The Horned God in Witchcraft Today by Caroline Tully 225

Never Mind the Warlocks: XY Chromosomes and the Craft by Liam Cyfrin 230

Coming Out of Two Closets: The Path of the Gay Witch by Christopher Penczak 234

A Queer Situation: Queering the Craft the Wiccan Way by Mitchell Coombes 239

The Wide Wild World of Magickal Sex by Francesca Gentille 242

You Sexy Witch! by Fiona Horne 245

THE WORDS OF THE WITCHES: Some Individual Voices from the Craft

A Somewhat Radical Revisioning of Contemporary Witchcraft by Phyllis Curott 250

The Way of the Goddess: A Profile of Ly De Angeles by Fiona Horne 254

The Meaning of Witchcraft to Me by Raymond Buckland 263

Ruling the Roost: Interview with Wendy Rule by Fiona Horne 267

Remembering Roie, the Witch of Kings Cross by Nevill Drury 275

Iron by Phil Brucato 279

THE UNBROKEN CIRCLE: Making Contact

Index of Influential Wiccan and Pagan Traditions by Oberon Zell-Ravenheart 282

Additional Websites, Contacts and Resources by Fiona Horne 295

Recommended Reading by Fiona Horne 298

Glossary by Liam Cyfrin and Fiona Horne 307

Hi! It occurs to me that, even though I have written many books on Witchcraft released in varying order and at various times around the world over the last six years and have popped up on radio and TV a fair bit, this may be the first time some of you and I have met. Also as this is the first book I have had a hand in creating in America, my new home, it feels right to tell you a bit about myself and explain what brought me here.

Courtesy of Kevin Foley/SCI FI Channel

I have been a practicing Witch for seventeen years. During part of that time I sang in an Australian electronic rock group called Def FX. For seven years we released successful albums, toured Australia and America many times, both as a headlining act and playing alongside bands like No Doubt, the Smashing Pumpkins, Soundgarden and the Beastie Boys. MTV played our videos, we were on the Billboard charts, and we were carving out quite a nice career for ourselves until we broke up in a rather untimely fashion. The aftermath was a really sad and difficult time for me.

During my career with the band I had been practicing Witchcraft, but I never came out about it publicly, apart from wearing my Pentagram necklace on a couple of CD covers! My song lyrics did suggest my esoteric interests and I was pretty wild and free onstage, but that was about as magickal as I let the public know my life was. So, when the band ended, part of the healing process involved me "coming out of the broom-closet" so to speak. I wrote a book. At the same time I guess the performer in me still needed an outlet to let off creative steam, so I started to channel all the energy from my onstage performances directly into working in television and radio, as well as my writing.

My first book, *Witch – A Personal Journey*, created quite a splash in Australia, partly because I was the first well-known person in Australia to come out as Wiccan. I think it helped to open a lot of people's eyes as to what modern Witchcraft is and isn't, and helped to dispel a lot of the negative stereotypes associated with the Craft. I also started hosting my own television show and appearing on a popular morning radio show providing "magickal solutions" for call-in listeners – that is, I prescribed spells (anchored with some practical advice) for everyday dilemmas.

I began to find that what had once been an intensely private spiritual pursuit started to blend strongly with my career. I grappled with this for a while, wondering if it was appropriate to be so open about what is essentially an occult spiritual tradition (by dictionary definition occult means "hidden and secret"). I wondered whether I was contributing to the dissolution of its essence – making it too available and even trivializing it? But my concerns were quashed as I received more and more positive feedback, from both the Pagan and the Craft community and newcomers who were applauding my efforts in opening up access to spiritual knowledge that people wanted and even needed.

tainly not on a crusade to convert the Western world to Witchcraft, but I do want to help people feel good about themselves and I do want to help people feel happy and fulfilled. Sharing my experiences about life as a Witch in my books *Witch – A Magickal Journey*, *Witchin' A Handbook for Teen Witches*, *7 Days to a Magickal New You*, and *Magickal Sex – A Witch's Guide to Beds, Knobs and Broomsticks* – and being prepared to answer questions and provide reliable information on the Craft is a way for me to do that.

When I came to this conclusion, it immediately felt right to move to the USA. Australia

Heaven is here on Earth and there are many ways to experience that magick and invoke even more into your life.

At the same time a proliferation of books started to appear and soon Wicca/Witchcraft was being credited as the "fastest growing spiritual path in the Western world." The more lectures and appearances I did in Australia and on trips to the United Kingdom and the United States as my books were released internationally, the more Witches – both old and new – I met. This made me realize that what I am doing (along with other "out" public Witches) is contributing to a rapid phase of spiritual evolution in the human species. And a big part of doing this means embracing modern methods of communication and expression. It all became very clear the day I realized that if Jesus was around now he would probably have his own TV show, his own website and a series of bestselling books. It's all just a sign of the times.

I stopped holding back and decided to dive right in and really let my career and spirituality fuel and enhance each other. I decided I wanted to see how far I could go and how much good I could do. In saying this I am cer-

is a beautiful, uncrowded, geographically isolated, *easy* place to reside. By contrast the US is the obvious hub of the Western world and a challenging, powerful environment. The country is also unique in the way it welcomes immigrants – especially if you work in the arts. I think America is a country of phenomenal opportunity if you are prepared to work hard and can stay focused and committed to the task. So, I decided to move to America and weave together all my creative work and create a television and radio show based on my books and life as a Witch and entertainer, and do as much good as I possibly could. I knew that Los Angeles was the place I should be based, as it is the birthing place of most television shows – and the sun shines pretty much all year round!

I knew that if I could launch a successful show in America, then the opportunity to positively open up the world of the Craft to those who chose to explore it would be to maximum effect.

However, it was a pretty big deal to decide to pack up a very comfortable and successful life in Australia and make the move to another country – especially the overwhelming and monolithic United States of America. I think that if I'd had any inkling of how hard it was going to be – to leave a loving relationship, a beautiful home, great friends, close family and comfortable work that I loved – I would probably never have left. But I felt drawn to the US, and not just because of dreams and goals I'd had since I was a young girl wanting to live a "big" life. There was something far more subtle and profound going on too. It just felt right and was something I had to do.

The day I rocked up to LA I had to pretty much start again from scratch. It was like establishing a new identity: I had no rental history, no credit, nothing. I didn't even have a driver's licence! I only started to drive when I moved to Los Angeles – before that a taxi or a broomstick was good enough! But now, a year down the track, I've got a good home, great new friends and I feel happy and fulfilled. And a big part of that fulfillment is created by the wonderful experience that was the *Mad Mad House*, the SCI FI Channel's television show I starred in that highlighted my life as a Witch and cemented my career here in the USA.

POP! Goes the Witch is the first book I have edited, and it was exciting to be able to contact my many friends, heroines and heroes of the Witchy world to be a part of it. At first the task seemed quite daunting as there are so many brilliant lights in the Pagan/ Wiccan/ Witchcraft universe, but in the end I realized that my best strategy was to try to include some of the lights that shone on me as I have forged my Witchcraft over the last seventeen years.

Being the "international" Witch that I am, the contributors come from the four corners of the planet as they are all people who have enriched my path, whether by the one-on-one time I have spent with them or by the writing and work they have done that played an integral role in the evolution of my personal Craft.

In the section called "Blessed Be" I speak at length about my individual relationships with the contributors to *POP!* and I hope you will find this section an entertaining and enlightening experience as I welcome you into my world.

At this point it seems appropriate to explain this book's title! Wicca and Witchcraft have achieved much more widespread popularity and acceptance in recent years – so there's the *pop* part explained for you. It's also notable that one of the pervading aspects of contemporary Craft is its ability to take itself seriously without falling into the pomposity of many other spiritual paths. "Let there be beauty and strength, power and compassion, honor and humility, mirth and reverence within you …" – Doreen Valiente's "Charge of the Goddess" says it all. For those reasons, a title like *POP! Goes the Witch* embraces the Craft's modern explosion. I have always felt that a little bit of humor goes along way to conveying a positive message that on face value may seem confronting. (Check out some of the chapter titles of my books on Witchcraft and you will see what I mean!)

As you read *POP! Goes the Witch* you will see this book is not only about Witchcraft but also about magick – the magick of life – the idea that Heaven is here on Earth and there are many ways to experience that magick and invoke even more into your life. One of most beautiful aspects of Paganism, the earth honoring heart of the Craft is (as Philip Heselton very wisely observes in his introduction to his *Wiccan Roots* (Capall Bann, 2000) that, unlike the majority of world religions that are based around the words of men and would cease to exist if all knowledge of them disappeared from human society, it would be born again and again upon a human gazing upon the lustrous beauty of a full moon or marveling at the budding blossoms of spring or gazing into a mirrored lake and sensing deep within themselves the divine magick of the sacred world in which we live.

I know the modern movement of Witchcraft will continue the evolution of what is at its core an ancient and innate way of experiencing and expressing our spirituality. We 21st century Witches are forging new magickal paths but under the same magickal sky as our ancestors!

You'll also find a wide range of voices in this anthology, since the Craft and other Pagan paths are rich in both tolerance and diversity. While some writers might speak of Wicca as Goddess or women's religion, others will discuss the magic that results from a true balance between God and Goddess and men and women. Some will focus on Wicca as a religion and others on Witchcraft *as* a craft; some will speak of the Witches' way as a mass spiritual movement and others of journeys of uniquely experienced magical exploration. Words and phrases such as Pagan, Wicca, Witch and Goddess Spirituality will be used in different ways by different contributors. This freely expressed individualism is at the heart of the Craft and is what makes the Craft so dynamic and relevant an expression of the human spirit in this modern age. But just in case things get a bit confusing, there's always the Glossary!

After seventeen years as a practicing Witch, I am excited as I see the individual means of expression within the Craft adding up to something ultimately greater than the sum of its parts. In editing together a diverse book like this I hope to specifically encourage those of you drawn to the Craft to break out and do it your way.

Make magick in your life by enjoying and honoring nature both in yourself and the world around you, and any time you feel cut off from a sense of personal peace or disillusioned and overwhelmed by the pressure of this hectic age, just let go, sit on a beach and watch a sunset, hug someone you love, smile at a stranger, read an inspiring article in *POP!* and let the world come to you revealing itself as the divinely magickal miracle that it is. Do this and you'll always be where you want to be.

Blessed Be*

Fiona Horne is the best selling author of seven books, a television presenter/producer, radio personality, singer and practicing Witch of seventeen years. In late 2001 she moved from Australia to America to further pursue her career in television and publishing. In 2004 she starred in SCI FI Channel's hit show, *Mad Mad House* and is now casting her spell over Hollywood.

To find out more visit www.fionahorne.com

Also by Fiona Horne:

Witch – A Magickal Journey
Witchin' A Handbook for Teen Witches
7 Days to a Magickal New You
Magickal Sex – A Witch's Guide to Beds, Knobs and Broomsticks

(published by Thorsons/ Element/HarperCollins)

I would like to introduce you to all the amazing people that have contributed to *POP! Goes the Witch*, and in doing so, give you an insight into my relationship with them that led them to being a part of this book. The list that follows is in alphabetical order, since these very magical people are impossible to list as favorites!)

Anton and Mina Adams: One of several pen names used by two very good magical friends of mine. The multi-talented "Mina" is a pillar of support to both the Artist Hardly Ever Known as "Anton" and to me, and in her many literary guises is one of the most savvy, unpretentious and reader-friendly writers on the Craft around, as well as being one of the most prolific.

Phil Brucato: A new friend that I met online through Francesca Gentille. Phil is an incredibly accomplished and motivated Pagan with a proud and sensitive male voice in such a female dominated community!

Raymond Buckland: It's a major thrill to have a Witch as well respected and influential as Ray being part of this collection. His "Big Blue" book – *Buckland's Guide to Witchcraft* – was an essential handbook for me seventeen years ago, and I still refer to my battered old copy today sometimes! Being able to email Ray and have him contribute a first person account for *POP!* is one of the highlights of my life.

Lucy Cavendish: I have known Lucy for about seven years now. We first met when she was editor of the feisty women's magazine, *Australian Women's Forum*. She is a bright soul and a dear friend. Her articles in *POP!*

really speak to the urban young lady juggling her palm pilot, mobile phone and athame! Lucy is ultra-cool and ultra-magickal and it is an honor to feature her advice on making love and magick work in the 21st century.

Gabrielle Cleary: I have wonderful memories of when I first met Gabby over a decade ago at a Coven meeting. Over the years we have shared special magickal times together, one of my favorites being Wemoon – the women's-only gathering that I write about in my book, *Witch: A Magickal Journey*. She is an experienced and charismatic High Priestess, and you will find her article on Training Groups in Ritual educational and fun.

Serene Conneeley: A long-time friend, Serene is someone who inspires me with her focus and dedication to evolving as an individual and sharing her gifts and lessons with the world around her.

Mitchell Coombes: Sweet sixteen (at the time of writing) and a more accomplished Witch than some thirty-year-old Wiccans I know! Mitchell has a wonderful bright soul and shares his enthusiasm for the Craft generously with everyone he comes into contact with. His article about being an out-and-proud Witch and young gay man is informative and inspiring.

Phyllis Curott: My very dear friend and one of the most charismatic and inspirational Witches in the world, not only to me but to thousands and thousands of others who have read her books and attended her lectures and workshops. Phyllis is like my cool big sister and I love her heaps! I am grateful for all the work she has done in her capacity as a lawyer and Wiccan activist to pave the way in America for me to be able to practice my Craft without fearing persecution!

Liam Cyfrin: Well, profound gratitude is actually in order here! I honestly couldn't have completed this book without his editorial advice, assistance and magickal good vibes! He and his myriad alter-egos have been a part of my Wicca-ed life since Day One when I discovered in a Witchy bookstore in Sydney a little magazine called *Shadowplay* of which he was co-editor and a major contributor. He's a very learned Witch who has been on board as an advisor and contributor to nearly all my books, usually managing to be as frivolous as possible while making some very potent points. He's also a dear, dear friend. I love him like a brother.

Welcome to my world of the Craft!

Kayt Davies: I met Kayt when she invited me last year to be the cover girl of the magazine she edits, *Vital*. And then as we exchanged emails we realized we have quite a bit in common. As soon as I see her again, we are going to sit down and trace our respective Witchy her-stories together to explore all the places where they cross over! Kayt wrote a terrific piece about Crone Goddess consciousness for *POP!* that can be appreciated by all – old, young, female and male.

Ly de Angeles: Ly is like my original High Priestess as one of her books was the very first I bought on the Craft and used to self-initiate. *POP!* features an interview I conducted with her a few years ago, and I am honored to share my intense experience of meeting her face to face after her words had made such an important impact on my life and Craft.

Nevill Drury: I bought Nevill's seminal work *Other Temples, Other Gods* (co-authored with Gregory Tillett, Methuen, 1980) in a truck stop

in the outback of Australia when my band was touring in the very early 90s! Somehow this juicy insight into the Occult in Australia spirited its way there to significantly enhance my life, and years along Nevill is a friend as well as a hero. He is so incredibly knowledgeable and he personally knew Rosaleen Norton, the most notorious and bravest Witch to ever come out of the broom-closet in Australia. Nevill shares his memories of Roie in *POP!* and in another piece makes it very clear why Witches do not worship Satan!

Taylor Ellwood: I first was introduced to Taylor through his provocative article "Invoking Buffy" published in *newWitch* magazine (I buy every issue!). It was a great day when he emailed me back and said I could publish it in *POP!* along with another typically fascinating piece on Tarot divination.

Scaerie Faerie: Scaerie (or Faye as she signs of most of her emails to me) was a frequent visitor to the forum on my website, and I was always impressed by her strong personality and fresh views on the Craft. I invited her to write a first person account for *POP!* and she also contributed a piece about animal totems – she is a veterinary nurse after all!

Janet and Stewart Farrar: A heroine and hero of mine – and of countless Wiccans the world over! Very few writers on the Craft have done more to cut through the illusions and pretensions that often clutter the Craft, and liberate its magickal essence. To have the previously unpublished words of these groundbreaking luminaries in *POP!* is a ridiculously huge honor!

Brenna Fey: I met Brenna through Phyllis Curott, and I have had some lovely times with her, both magickal and practical from lunches in New York Irish Pubs to May Pole dancing in Central Park! Brenna is a vibrant voice in the modern Wiccan community and a good Jewish girl too!

Francesca Gentille: Francesca is a new online buddy of mine that I met through Oberon Zell-Ravenheart. He signed me up to her online newsletter and I loved her writing so much that I asked her if she would agree to be in *POP!* – and she did! Her sensual, sacred personality radiates through her words and breathes the breath of the Goddess onto these pages.

Philip Johnson: Philip attended a book launch of mine a few years back and I remember thinking then that he was a positive bridge between the world of Wicca and Christianity. His pieces here are essential reading for Wiccans and Christians – we have a lot more in common than we are given credit for!

Tri Johns: My dear Coven member! I am so glad I managed to squeeze this out of Tri – and, believe me, she really pushed the deadline! She has so many talents, both magickal and practical (hmm, is there really a difference?), and her article in *POP!* is her debut published piece – and it's bloody good! Let's raise a glass of mead to her!

Iya Ta'Shia Asanti Karade: Iya starred in *Mad Mad House* with me. Meeting her and having the privilege of living with her was very enriching spiritually and emotionally. She is a truly beautiful and evolved human being and an inspired Priestess in the African-American Voudon tradition. In the *Mad Mad House* she paid me the greatest honor by formally recognizing me as a fellow Priestess and my soul is still singing!

Odyle Knight: I met Odyle at a book launch many years ago. She enthralled me with her stories of Bali – one of the most mystical places in the world and my absolutely favorite place to visit. When the tragedy of the Bali bombing occurred, Odyle was in the front line, and the piece she has contributed to *POP!* shows that in the face of such sadness and devastation the magickal heart of Bali beats strong and pure.

Carmela Leone: My dear friend and one of the purest and most committed Witches I know, Carmela has generously allowed me to share her life's journey in three of my books now, and her first person account in *POP!* beautifully demonstrates how the ancient heart of Paganism can beat so strongly in a modern girl's breast.

Rhea Loader: Rhea was Liam Cyfrin's co-editor and magickal partner in the *Shadowplay* magazine days (which live on at www.shadowplayzine.com) and this is how I was introduced to her. A clear and potent voice in the Craft with unique and integrative ideas on redefining and enhancing personal Craft practice, the effervescent, self-confessed "madly corrupt Pict" is one of Australia's most highly valued exports to the US Wiccan community!

Rev. Dylan Masson: Dylan is something of a soul mate I think, and one day I will actually meet him and his wife Cheryl in person now that we live on the same continent! I had a remarkable "remote healing" experience with Dylan and his Coven a few years ago when I was in Australia and had a bad back injury. US-based Dylan and many of his immediate and "hived out" Coven members sent me healing energy one night and I was back on my feet the next day – after being bed ridden for two weeks. I can attest to his extraordinary powers as a healer and as a dynamic, motivating High Priest! You will greatly enjoy his insights into healing in his article.

Christopher Penczak: I first saw an article by Christopher in *newWitch* magazine and emailed him inviting him to share his experiences as a gay Witch in *POP!* Christopher is a prolific writer of books on the Craft – both for queer and straight Witches alike. He is also a brilliant musician and his passion for the Craft shines though in all his creative work.

Julia Phillips: Again I am falling over myself as I say how privileged I am to have Julia contribute to *POP!* Her piece on the history of Wicca could be considered the jewel in the crown of *POP!* as the revised edition she created especially for these pages is one of the most comprehensive and accurately researched piece on our nebulous history ever. Her work as editor of the early Occult publications, *Children of Sekmet* and *Web of Wyrd,* and her role in co-writing *The Witches of Oz* had an enormous positive influence on me as I took my early Witchy steps in the world – so she is a heroine of mine too.

Janine Roberts: Gary Baddeley of Disinformation introduced me to Jani through her extraordinary book that they published in 2003, *Glitter and Greed.* It blows the lid off the diamond trade, showing the many human and environmental rights abuses of the De Beers cartel – and it is fascinating and alarming. Her piece in *POP!* documents some of her experiences during her time spent working for the Australian Aboriginal land rights organizations and is an inspiring insight into their spirituality – the very spirit that I connected with so greatly as a child growing up in the Australian bush.

Wendy Rule: Interviewing Wendy, a supreme songstress and living Goddess, was not only fun for me but spiritually enriching. Her music is that of the spheres – she is one of the most gifted Witches performing on the stages of the world today and I am privileged to be able to share some of her most beautiful song lyrics with you on these pages. She is also an adept astrologer, scholar of myth and mother. We can all learn a lot from Wendy!

Caroline Tully: Caroline is the news and events editor and a regular contributor to Australia's *Witchcraft* magazine. An independent, deeply committed and completely magickal member of the Oz Wiccan community, the lovely Cazz is also a very wise and articulate voice in the international Witchy community. Her piece on honoring Pan is a great balancing piece for women looking to identify with the masculine within.

David Wolfe: My beloved "Avocado" and fellow cast mate of *Mad Mad House*, David has played an incredibly significant role in my life by expanding my eating from vegan organic to raw vegan organic food. The shift that has occurred in my life physically, mentally, emotionally and spiritually from embracing raw living has been one of the most important in my life. I urge you all to experience the raw revolution.

Anatha Wolfkeepe: I visited Anatha about eight years ago to interview her for an article I was writing on Witchcraft for *Marie Claire* magazine. Face to face, she is a powerful force and this presence comes through in her brilliantly independent writing. It is a great privilege to have her piece on magick, music and horror featured in *POP!*

Oberon and Morning Glory Zell-Ravenheart: Another long-time hero and heroine of mine, I am proud to say I can count these two remarkable people as friends. My altar is graced by one of their extraordinary Mythic Images creations – a ripe green Goddess statue of the Millennial Gaia that is empowered with the intense creative energy of these two leading lights in the Pagan/Craft world.

SO FINALLY…

Welcome to my world of the Craft! I hope you have a blast exploring it.

AND REMEMBER…

Everyday is the best day ever. (Thanks for that line, Avocado!)

stepping out
of the shadows
where we came from and
where we're going

the wicked witch is dead
bad witches are out; good witches are in
Phyllis Curott

Can you imagine Cybill Shepherd, Roseanne, Olympia Dukakis, Tori Amos, Stevie Nicks, Chrissie Hynde, Sarah McLachlan, Marianne Williamson, Deepak Chopra, Erica Jong and Camille Paglia standing in a circle together beneath a gorgeous full moon? I can.

Why? Because they are among some of America's most prominent celebrities, authors and performers who have discovered the Goddess. Goddess spirituality is now the fastest growing spiritual practice in America and popular artists are openly and enthusiastically bringing this ancient wisdom to the attention of the media and the American public. And where they go, their audiences are sure to follow.

grown up with countless fairy tales about the wicked Witch with deadly powers. The hags of Shakespeare's *Macbeth* have convinced generations that Witches conjure our darkest natures with noxious eye of newt. Durer's woodcuts show her to be ugly and misshapen. But where did this vision come from?

In the late 1400's, worship of the Goddess was branded satanic by the Catholic Church. Though there is no devil in the Old Religion of the Goddess and Witches do not worship him, hundreds of thousands were tortured and killed. Almost 90 percent of these victims were women and those who survived lost nearly all legal rights, became chattel, and were prohibited from owning or inheriting

> Witches know that magic is not about commanding and controlling, but about consciousness and communion.

While Goddess spirituality takes many forms, the most popular is the contemporary revival of Witchcraft. America is discovering that behind the mask of the wicked Witch is the beautiful face of the Goddess. Witchcraft, also called Wicca, is actually the ancient, pre-Christian spirituality of the Goddess.

Unfortunately, the word "Witch" also evokes the image of a green-faced hag riding a broomstick and brewing evil potions, a stereotype vividly brought to life by actress Margaret Hamilton in *The Wizard of Oz* (1939), Bette Midler in *Hocus Pocus* (1993) and *The Blair Witch Project* (1999). This gender-based stereotype points us in the direction of the hideous hag's origins and her persistent presence in popular culture. We've all

property, receiving an education, practicing medicine or the Goddess's religion.

This prolonged period of persecution, known as the Witch craze, assured the domination of the stereotype of the wicked Witch. And over the centuries, the hag came to personify the culture's shadow and its fear of women – their powers to give birth, their sexuality, and their spirituality. Fairytales, plays, illustrations and sermons perpetuated this vision.

Times are changing and the Goddess is returning. In the past 40 years, pop culture provided at least one good Witch a decade: Glinda, the Good Witch of the North, Veronica Lake in *I Married a Witch* (1942), Kim Novak in *Bell, Book and Candle* (1958), and

Elizabeth Montgomery in *Bewitched* (1964-1972). Today, good Witches are everywhere, with Hollywood at the forefront of a radical shift in public perception. Nicole Kidman and Sandra Bullock portrayed sister Witches in *Practical Magic* (1998), which captured the number one spot at the box office when it opened. When Sandra explains that "there is no devil in the Craft" and "there's more to magic than spells and potions," millions heard important messages that hopefully will enable real Witches to practice their religion in peace and safety and with public acceptance.

different problem arises. These Witches tend to fall into a gender stereotype; that is, they are exclusively female. In fact, there have always been male Witches (not warlocks), and their numbers are rapidly increasing.

Witchcraft is also increasingly receiving serious attention from the "hard" media. In recent years, the release of my first book, *Book of Shadows*, it's follow-up, *Witchcrafting* and the presence of Witches in the military prompted respectful stories about Witchcraft as a Goddess religion in every major daily news-

America is discovering that behind the mask of the wicked Witch is the beautiful face of the Goddess.

On television, two new shows, *Sabrina, the Teenage Witch* and *Charmed* feature strong, independent young women who are Witches; a character on an afternoon soap opera regularly exclaimed "Oh my Goddess!" and conducted charming Goddess rituals as part of the plot; and the NBC sitcom, *Friends*, devoted an entire show to the female characters discovering their inner Goddesses. But while these shows and films portray positive characters, they rely on silly special effects that perpetuate the stereotype of Witches having supernatural powers (like freezing time or making objects move). The powers that Witches cultivate are not supernatural; they are completely natural, divine gifts latent in all of us. From spiritual practice, Witches know that magic is not about commanding and controlling, but about consciousness and communion. They have discovered that by living in harmony with nature, they live in harmony with the divine, and that real magic flows from our connection to that divinity.

In television shows, including *Picket Fences*, *Buffy the Vampire Slayer* and *Judging Amy*, that present Witches as sympathetic, realistic characters who practice a bona fide religion, a

paper, in major magazines, and on top television shows in the US and abroad.

According to the *New York Times*, Wicca is also the fastest growing, most lucrative subject in the publishing field. Witchcraft, at this moment, is undergoing a major transformation – stories about Witches are increasingly becoming stories by Witches. No longer confined to the broom-closet, Witches are increasingly public and confident in the exercise of their rights to express themselves and the truth about their religion. But more importantly, the Witch is once again retrieving her and his role as the culture's shaman, the teller of myths that are our collective dreams. The Witch is again telling sacred stories that chronicle and inspire our encounter with divinity.

Marginal religions are no longer the territory of hippies and self-styled weirdos. Far from the days of dark, secret meetings in the shadows, today's Witches are roaming the halls of some of the country's biggest businesses. I personally know two Witches who work for magazines, one financial consultant, and one in a publishing house. A practitioner for over a decade, I can count lawyers, editors, computer technicians, social workers, and schoolteachers among my Covenmates. Surprised? Don't be. Recent years have seen the Western world slowly swinging back towards its spiritual roots as its population feels more and more purposeless.

Since innovations in science began to replace Christianity as the explanation for why the sky is blue and where the rain comes from, our world has grown increasingly secular. Within the last century especially, the Earth has seen the biggest boom of technological advances and industrial growth in all of human history, and it isn't over yet. You can blame Darwin, but the outcome remains: people have learned that the Bible is not the answer to life's questions, and throwing the baby out with the bathwater has left us a mostly religious-less culture. We feel empty but Our Lady of Atoms lacks the means to tell us why.

Now, after decades of worshipping Science Itself, people are starting to feel their emptiness more acutely and have been actively searching to revive their starving souls. Take a look in your local bookstore – see the endless rows of New Age books on spirituality?

The market is reacting to a huge demand for life-affirming knowledge and, more importantly, methods of practice.

Rather than moving backwards – a term that makes Westerners cringe and cower – the new trend has not steered us towards traditional religions but rather towards Neopaganism. Even Hollywood's fascination with Buddhism and other Eastern practices has not been powerful enough to capture the attention of the general public – just compare the racks of books on Paganism to those on Eastern studies wherever books are sold. The verdict is in: people are hungry for something new, and Witchcraft is it.

Why Witchcraft instead of a friendlier, more "PC" branch of Neopaganism? Perhaps because, while we crave nourishment for our souls, we also have an ingrained Western value of active living. One of the strongest Wiccan beliefs centers on the concept of magick, which at its best is about taking responsibility for your own life and happiness. What is more active than working with the forces of the universe to achieve your heart's desire?

Moreover, Witchcraft is highly fashion-friendly. One can actually dress like a Witch, and what's more, there are numerous accessories! Instead of wax pentacles made to melt in the Medieval hearth fire when the local inquisitor comes knocking, elaborate brass plates are on display in store-front windows, right next to athames and grimoires

People are hungry for something new, and Witchcraft is it.

that weren't hand-copied from your great great grandmother. One can never own (or wear) enough pentacles and crystals, and incense and candles are extremely consumable and need to be replaced almost daily! Buddhism, on the other hand, can range from the usual Western style to Zen minimalism, a marketing nightmare.

Why else would Witchcraft be the spiritual path of choice for so many thinking citizens? I'd like to say it has something to do with intelligence level. Because of its lack of centralization, Witchcraft forces you to think independently, unlike majority religions that follow the sit-stand-kneel format and pray as

to meet Witches who are teachers in our public and private schools. Education is vital to the Old Religion, as Witches consider themselves the inheritors of all the world's mystical wisdom. Witches are adepts at shamanism, divination, ritual technique, spellcraft, herbal lore, crystal healing, and many other fields of metaphysical science. They consider life to be an eternal classroom with Experience as teacher and master, and they continue to learn new skills throughout their lives.

As randomly placed throughout the culture as we are, aspects of Witchcraft are even more pervasive than the Witches themselves. Just the other day, my boss referred to a five-

We are everywhere, and there are more of us than you think.

you follow along. Whether you work in a Coven (a small, close-knit group which worships together and serves as a support base for everything from movie night to deaths in the family) or are a solitaire (single people practicing on their own or with a few friends informally), no one is telling you what words to use or how to ask the deities for help.

In fact, there is no one holy text in Witchcraft, as followers choose from a canon as colorful as the rainbow and growing every day. With no one telling you what to do, living as a Witch can be very difficult and often confusing. But, Witches say, the results are also the most rewarding. For example, Witchcraft encourages the writing of new prayers and rituals, believing that words from the heart are most powerful. This befits creative-types, and such artistic personalities are often drawn to Paganism and the trappings of Witchcraft in particular.

Beyond the business world, Witchcraft has attracted followers from many other professions. It has become more and more common

pointed star as a "pentacle," and May Day festivals are on the rise. Movies such as *Practical Magic* and shows like *Sabrina the Teenage Witch* and *Charmed* bring back the old friendly nose-twitching neighbor image, like *Bewitched*, instead of evil old hags cackling their way through a baby stew.

The bottom line: we are everywhere, and there are more of us than you think.

fire-light and moon-shadows
a summary of wiccan lore
Morning Glory Zell-Ravenheart

Witchcraft is a very ancient system which has its roots in the Paleolithic arts of the Shaman and the worship of the Great Earth Mother. Mother Earth, and all the other gods and goddesses of Nature, are not mere metaphysical abstractions dwelling in some nebulous otherworld. They are as real as you and I, and possess tangible physical bodies. The body of Mother Earth is quite literally the living biosphere of the planet Earth, including all the various collective life forms that inhabit Her. Knowledge of the aspects and purposes of the various Nature deities and the ability to communicate with them are at the very core of any school of Pagan shamanism, whether it be the Mysteries of the African Orishas, the teachings of the Hawaiian Kahunas, or the way of the Wicca. This is what is meant by the word *Pantheism*. It is as ancient as the Hollow Hills and as modern as tomorrow's starship.

Magick is simply coincidence control ...

Definitions

Witchcraft can be defined as a survival or reconstruction of an order of fertility-based Pagan European Shamanism. Witches worship Nature and use their psychic talents as channels of power with which to work magick. Magick is simply coincidence control or, as Anodea Judith succinctly puts it, "probability enhancement" – the ability to shape Reality in accordance with Will by methods that cannot be explained theoretically by the modern scientific paradigm. A Shaman is a magickal practitioner who utilizes altered states of consciousness to control psychic phenomena.

Since the repeal of the Witchcraft Acts in England in 1954, many Covens have formed or gone public and a revival and reconstruction of the Craft has become a large and vocal part of the Pagan Movement as a whole. The word *Witch* does not mean "wise one" as it is popularly maintained. The Saxon word for "wise" is *wys*, and it is the root for Wizard. The word *Witch* can be traced back to the Anglo-Saxon verb *wik*, which means "to change, bend or shape." So etymologically, Witchcraft is related to wicker baskets! *Wicce* (feminine, and pronounced "*witch*" or "*witch-eh*") means "Changing woman." *Wikccancraeften* translates as "the craft, or art, of the changer or shaper" – and rightly so, because it is primarily concerned with understanding and controlling one's reality. The two main divisions of practical Witchcraft are Ceremonial and Operative.

Ceremonial Witchcraft

Ceremonial Witchcraft deals primarily with the worship of the Goddess and, in most traditions, the Horned God, and the celebration of lunar and seasonal rites. The worship of the Goddess takes two forms: there is the ritual where power is raised and released to the Goddess, and there is the ritual where power is *drawn down from* the Goddess.

The former utilizes the principles of immanent divinity in order to *charge* the deity (seen as a collective consciousness) with energy in order to make that deity stronger through the devotional act. Hence the emphasis many modern Covens place on the worship of the Goddess – Her circuits have been starved for centuries and the balance must be restored.

In the latter ritual form, energy is drawn down, making use of the transcendent divinity concept to charge the worshippers with energy from the collective conscious energy pool of the deity. Calling forth the deity *within* is called *evocation*, and calling upon deity *without* is called *invocation*.

Rites of worship

Specific ritual celebrations are held at different times, either to honor a specific deity or to celebrate the Seasonal Round, often called the Wheel of the Year. This latter constitutes the celebration of eight Sabbats which symbolize the Birth-Death-Rebirth cycle of the Divine Children from the womb of the Earth Mother. The Sabbats are based on ancient agricultural events (like the sowing and harvesting of crops) and astronomical events like solstices and equinoxes the exact dates of which vary slightly from year to year).

In the Northern Hemisphere the Sabbats are traditionally dated as: Ostara (Spring Equinox) – March 21; Beltane (May Day) – May 1; Litha (Summer Solstice) – June 21; Lughnasadh (or Lammas) (First Fruits) – August 1; Mabon (Fall Equinox) – September 21; Samhain (Hallowe'en) – October 31 (though some celebrate this Sabbat on November 1); Yule (Winter Solstice) – December 21; and Oimelc or Imbolg (another spelling is Imbolc) (Lady Day) – February 1.

In the Southern Hemisphere these Sabbats are essentially a mirror reflection of the above to take into account that it is the other side of the world and the seasons are opposite to when they are experienced in the North. The traditional Southern Hemisphere dates are: Ostara (Spring Equinox) – September 21; Beltane – October 31 (or November 1); Litha (Summer Solstice) – December 21; Lughnasadh (or Lammas) (First Fruits) – February 1; Mabon (Fall – called *Autumn* in the South - Equinox) – March 21; Samhain (Hallowe'en) – May 1; Yule (Winter Solstice) – June 21; and Oimelc or Imbolg/Imbolc (Lady Day) – August 1.

The other main worship rites of Witchcraft are called Esbats, and they are lunar celebrations, normally held at the full Moon. Though the Goddess is of course honored at these times, the Esbat ritual is usually more concerned with "Drawing Down the Moon" and using this lunar energy combined with energy the Coven raises in order to perform magickal workings. Energy can be raised by Witches, either solitarily or in a Coven, by a number of techniques: drumming, dancing, chanting, singing, hyperventilating and sex. The techniques used depend on the tradition and training of the Witches involved. This brings us to the next category of practical Witchcraft, which is Operative.

Operative Witchcraft

Operative Witchcraft, or as it is known in magickal terminology *thaumaturgy*, is sometimes referred to as "Low Magick." Ceremonial Witchcraft, or *theurgy*, is thus considered to be "High Magick." I dislike these terms as they stigmatize the use of energy as opposed to the gathering of it.

Operative Witchcraft is a complex and

The Magick Circle is the primary ingredient in most Craft-work involved study, making use of many diverse elements and procedures. There are numerous techniques for implementing those procedures. Some techniques that Witches use to alter reality through Operative Witchcraft are: the use of Magick Circle and Names of Power; the consecration and use of Magickal Tools and Ornaments; the creation of Amulets and Talismans; the making of Philtres and Potions; Wortcunning; the working of Spells; the reading and controlling of the Aura; Divination; and the creation and use of Familiars and Fetches.

The Magick Circle

The Magick Circle is the primary ingredient in most Craft-work. The Circle is traditionally drawn/cast *deosil* or clockwise in the Northern Hemisphere, essentially "with the sun" and opened/released *widdershins* or counterclockwise for negative work. In the Southern Hemisphere the Circle is cast "anticlockwise" as that is the direction the sun appears to move across the sky as it veers north in its east/west arc. Hence the Circle is opened in clockwise direction in the South. (To put this all in context, if clocks had been invented in the Southern hemisphere the hands would move anticlockwise.)

The Circle is traditionally nine feet in diameter and, since in many systems the number nine is connected with the Moon, it is sometimes visualized as the circular shadow of the Moon cast upon the Earth. It is a door between the

Names of words of power rely on the principle that there is actual power in the very vibrations of the spoken word. Some, like the Hindu *Om* chant or the names of certain deities, have power because they have collected energy through continuous repetition by countless people over many centuries. Some, like the words ARARITA and ABRAHADABRA, are powerful because of their symbolism, their supposed secrecy and the tonal vibrations with which they resonate when properly intoned. Others, such as one's Witch, magickal or Coven name, and also the names of certain deities, are powerful because they are a secret known only to a select few and are only used in ritual, so their power is never dissipated by casual use.

Tools of Magick

Magickal tools are created and used by the Witch as an aid to increase and direct one's powers. Some of these tools are: the Athame, the Thurible, the Wand, the Pentacle and the Chalice. There are many others, and all have specific uses which vary somewhat from tradition to tradition.

All tools, ornaments and magickal implements are made within a Circle, and Witches chant a rhyming charm or mantra while they work to clear their minds and to weave the power into the object. The details vary with the tools and the tradition, but the important thing is that each instrument is first purified, then consecrated, and finally charged with

The Circle ... is a door between the worlds — a way of freezing a portion of space and setting it outside the flow of time.

worlds – a way of freezing a portion of space and setting it outside the flow of time. Circles are used by both solitary Witches and Covens. They are used as a focus of power for both Ceremonial and Operative rituals.

power to do a certain task – and is never used for any other purpose. Tools are always kept on the Altar, which may be as simple as a consecrated lamp table covered with cloth or as elaborate as a specially engraved marble slab mounted on an antique cabinet.

Adornments

Adornments or ornaments are worn by the Witch for purposes of identification, esoteric symbolism, or as charged objects for use as an auxiliary power supply. Like the Tools, Adornments are purified and charged before being worn. Some common pieces of Witch Jewelry are: Ring, Pendant, Necklace, Bracelet and Garter. All but the Garter may be worn publicly.

The Ring, Pendant and Bracelet are usually made of some metal that has symbolic attributions: Gold = Sun, Silver = Moon, Iron = Mars, Bronze/Brass = Mercury, Tin = Jupiter, Copper = Venus, Lead = Saturn. They are sometimes set with some gemstone that the Witch identifies with, such as an astrological birthstone. Sometimes a bracelet will have inscribed upon it the Witch's name and degree, or personal sigil, so she can be identified by other Witches.

The Necklace is worn within the Circle, especially by women, and symbolizes the Circle of Rebirth sacred to the Goddess. It is traditionally made by hand and utilizes natural objects such as shells, wooden beads, seeds, amber and small holy stones.

The Garter is sewn with the Witch's name and sigil and is worn above the left knee. It is never worn outside the Circle.

Ritual garments and skyclad workings

There are three main forms of dress for Witchcraft: robes or other ceremonial costumes (some traditions prefer these to match, while others encourage individual expression); street clothes; or skyclad.

Skyclad is the term used to describe the naked Witch – meaning "pure and in a sacred state – clad by the sky." Some traditions never work skyclad; others always or very regularly work just as nature made them (or almost – jewelry, cords and the like sometimes adorn the otherwise naked Witch).

A Witch should never allow him or herself to feel coerced to work skyclad in a group (it is much more sensible to find another group than to spend a ritual feeling awkward and uncomfortable), but by the same token, those who always work clothed should never denigrate individuals and groups who view naked as sacred. In practice, most Witches are adaptable enough to feel comfortable with any of these approaches, and dress (or don't!) to suit the ritual and circumstances.

Amulets and Talismans

Amulets and Talismans are kinds of portable auxiliary power units. Amulets are usually natural objects which need no consecration, such as holy stones (stones with natural holes completely through them), horseshoes, glass fishing floats (found on the beach), and lodestones. Talismans are usually created and consecrated, such as the Rowan Cross, the Mandragora, or the Pentacle of Protection. Both Amulets and Talismans are either worn or hung up in the room or other place one wishes to bless.

Philtres and Potions

The making of Philtres and Potions is a traditional occupation of the Witch. The Philtre is a blend of herbs, oils and other substances (like honey or blood). Usually it is edible and is used to bind a Spell by transferring one's powers to the object of the Spell. The most common example is the Love Philtre, which is compounded at the correct phase of the Moon, with the correct herbs and other ingredients, while chanting the correct rhyme. Then it is placed in the food or drink of the one who is to be enchanted.

Some Books of Shadows are quite old, containing laws, rituals and ceremonies that have been used and passed down by generations of Covens of the same tradition.

Potions, on the other hand, tend to be herbal brews that are used as auxiliary homeopathic remedies in conjunction with psychic healing. The most famous of these "Old Wives' Potions" was foxglove tea, long used for people with heart conditions. Foxglove was eventually discovered to contain digitalis.

Wortcunning

Closely linked to the brewing of herbal Philtres and Potions is the study of Wortcunning of Herbcraft. This is primarily dealt with in two ways: first is Woodcraft, which is concerned with the identification, classification and location of wild plants and herbs. Second is Garden Craft – the planting, growing and harvesting of one's own herbs. Both are deeply concerned with ritual times and ritual preparations designed to put one in touch with the cosmic cycles and aid in communication with the *Devas*, or plant spirits.

Herbs used for healing and positive magick are cut while the Moon is waxing, using a white-hilted knife or a Boline (a small crescent-bladed sickle). For banishing magick and blighting spells, herbs are cut with the black-hilted Athame during the waning Moon. Ritual preparation is observed, and certain of the same herbs used in several different kinds of Spells may be planted when the Moon is in different signs.

Spellweaving

Spellweaving is the single most important technique Witches use to work their Will. A Spell is a complex tapestry woven of herbs, incense, Moonlight, rhymes and energy. It seeks to use all the powers of suggestion and symbolism to charge the bioplasmic force and the morphogenetic field and direct them to influence the very fabric of Time and Space. A Spell is a recipe to titillate the tastebuds of Entropy. Witches use Spells to warp and shift the future into the shape they desire, for *Wikccancraeften* is truly the Craft of Changes.

Spells come in all forms and colors for all purposes. Commonly used Spells are for: protection, divination, romance, blasting, blessing, healing and weather working. The concept of "Black Magick" as evil and "White Magick" as good is just another example of applied racism. Black and White are merely color-coded energy wavelengths in the larger spectrum, as are Green, Yellow, Blue and Red. One of the most powerful and beloved Witches in North America uses Black Magick in the form of blighting to starve the growth of cancer cells!

Auras

The Aura is the bio-magnetic field which surrounds all living things and can be read, manipulated, and photographed by the Kirlian technique. The Aura radiates outward from the acupuncture points of the body and is capable of expanding outward, exerting a positively polarized force by pushing, and being used as a repulsor beam; or it can be extended and then negatively polarized to become a pulling force, like a tractor beam. This is the principle behind much weather work. Witches can use their Auras as Shields by stabilizing the field, which can be tuned for different purposes by varying the density and quality of the Auric emanations.

Divination

There are so many systems of Divination that I wouldn't begin to try and catalog them all here. Popular methods include: Astrology, Tarot, I Ching, Runes (sticks and stones), Pendulum and Scrying (crystal gazing). Some ancient traditional methods include True Dreaming, Turning the Sieve and Shears, Knuckle Bones and Augury.

Whatever system is used, you begin with a period of meditation in which you resonate with the flow of time and space. Then you read from the moving fingers of events the probable future, based on the set of current events and the medium's success in manipulating certain laws of Chaos physics, especially the Markov Process and the Heisenberg Uncertainty Principle. There is no absolutely foolproof method of divining, for you are dealing with the ever-shifting matrix of possibilities. One should try out several systems of Divination before settling on the one (or ones) that are most suitable and feel the best.

Familiars and Fetches

The final technique used by Witches to influ-

ence reality is through the use of Familiars and Fetches. A Familiar bond is established by entering into a symbiotic empathic bond with another creature (the Familiar). The Witch learns a great deal from this relationship, especially about the nature of the universe when seen through other and alien eyes. There is also the practical benefit of seeing what the Familiar sees wherever it goes. The Familiar is frequently a member of one's Totem. The Totem is the tutelary spirit, or collective consciousness, of a particular species under whose aegis a Shaman operates.

The Fetch is simply an astral projection. It can be a projection of a solitary Witch or the collective Fetch of the entire Coven, and it commonly takes the form of the individual's or Coven's Totem. The latter is a very complex and dangerous procedure because the collective Fetch or projection of up to thirteen people will acquire a certain amount of life and personality of its own. The chemistry of the Coven had better be compatible, or else the projection will either fail, or, worst of all, become a vampiric "Id Beast" as in the movie *Forbidden Planet*.

The Coven

These last sections will deal with the Coven. Since many people enjoy the company of like-minded folk, and since Magick is stronger (if more difficult to perform) when done by a group, Witches frequently form Covens. The Coven is composed of up to thirteen people, and is usually influenced and structured according to a particular tradition. These diverse Traditions form a framework of theology and custom within which the Coven works.

Initiation

One usually becomes a Witch by Initiation

and after a suitable time spent in training. The training period may take anywhere up to a year and a day. Often you hear of people being initiated after only a few weeks (or less) preparation, but the validity of a Witch's Initiation is ultimately dependent upon the time and effectiveness of the training received, for this is how one learns the Craft.

The Initiation is of two varieties: a Self-Initiation, done in the eyes of the Gods and Goddesses that are one's Patrons; or by cloning power from the High Priestess or High Priest of the Coven. In order to become part of a Coven, the latter is usually required, although a Witch who has been previously Initiated may be brought into a Coven by an Adoption ceremony rather than a second Initiation.

Similarly, there are a number of different degree systems which vary with traditions. The most common of these is the three degrees used by Gardnerians and Alexandrians. The system of degrees is falling into disrepute among some Covens who favor a more democratic approach. The pioneers in this department were the New Reformed Orthodox Order of the Golden Dawn (NROOGD) and Starhawk's orginal group, Reclaiming, which is more of a collective. There are some who say that the old Hereditary Traditions never used any degrees at all, and that the degree system was begun by Witches who were influenced by Occult Fraternities and Ceremonial Magick Lodges.

Book of Shadows

Many Covens have a Book of Shadows that is kept by the High Priestess and High Priest, but can be copied by any Coven member and can be added to by vote of the Council of Elders. Some Books of Shadows are quite old, containing laws, rituals and ceremonies that have been used and passed down by generations of Covens of the same tradition.

Other newer Covens have Books of Shadows that were collectively written and contain different rituals and ceremonies for each Sabbat. Still others make up entirely new rituals each time. The Book of Shadows is traditionally copied down in one's own handwriting to guarantee that the person learns what is written therein. This custom, however, is becoming less common due to the advent of copy machines and computers, and many modern "Techno-Pagan" Witches keep all their spells and lore in a Disk of Shadows!

The other book that comes into play in a Witch's life is the Grimoire or Spellbook. This is simply the personal workbook that the Witch uses to record successful Spells, Philtres, Potions and Charms.

In conclusion

This has been an attempt to summarize a religio-magickal system that is many generations old, has thousands of adherents and whose ranks are growing every day. It is a system that is not absolute, in that the specifics of technique may vary considerably from one tradition to another, and even from Coven to Coven. This diversity is not only acceptable, but welcomed within the overall framework of modern Witchcraft.

This is also a bare sketch of a path whose roots are religion and whose fruits are magick. It is a path I have walked since I was a teenager, and I have barely scratched the surface in that time.

a history of wicca in england
1939 to the present day
Julia Phillips

Introduction to the 2004 Revised Edition by Julia Phillips

This chapter is adapted from a talk I gave at the Australian Wiccan Conference in Canberra, 1991. It is mainly about the early days of Wicca in England – specifically what we now call Gardnerian and Alexandrian Traditions.

The notes from which the original talk was derived were compiled during the 1980s from a myriad of sources, and were intended only for private use within my own Coven. I did not gather the material alone – Paul Greenslade and Rufus Harrington were equally involved in the research, and it gives me great pleasure to have the opportunity to record their important contribution in this introduction.

When I immigrated to Australia at the end of 1988, I quickly discovered that very few Australian Wiccans had a very detailed concept of the origins of Wicca or of their own place within the Wiccan family. I therefore accepted an invitation to speak on the history of Wicca at the 1991 Australian Wiccan Conference, and consolidated the notes mentioned above into a lecture intended to clarify to Australian Wiccans how the path came to be and where they fitted in. It was for this reason that I included information and anecdotes about influential people within the Craft (though I initialized names where those people were not known publicly).

The lecture was subsequently published in the collected papers of the Conference in a limited numbered edition of 200 copies. From there, it was later posted to the internet and now exists on over 500 websites in a non-tarted up form. This, in case you were wondering, is its first appearance in the sort of format you can put in your bookshelf.

In September 2002, the owners of www.gardnerian.com contacted me to ask for permission to place the lecture on the site, and also to see whether I had any plans to revise the text. I hadn't ever thought about it, but on reflection it seemed a good idea as a great deal of material had become available since the 1980s, and it would give me the opportunity to correct some errors and provide some additional information.

In closing, I would like to record my thanks to Ronald Hutton and Philip Heselton for their outstanding research on the subject of Gerald Gardner and the origins and development of British Wicca. Their work goes way beyond the simple lecture that you see here, and I am indebted to both of them for material used in this revised copy. This 2004 version of the lecture has also been edited, tweaked and twiddled about with by Liam Cyfrin especially for this anthology. Any errors that remain in the text are, however, almost certainly the author's, and the erudite souls she mentioned above should not be blamed for any inaccuracies.

GBG 101

As Professor Ronald Hutton of the University of Bristol has observed (in his foreword to *Wiccan Roots* by Philip Heselton, Capall Bann, 2000), Wicca is "the only religion [as opposed to denomination] which England has ever given the world." From its humble beginnings it spread throughout Europe and North America, Australia, New Zealand, and

South Africa, and today there are also Wiccans in Malaysia, Singapore, Japan, Fiji, and probably a great many more places I know nothing about. The areas of biggest growth have been in North America and Australia, where the numbers of Wiccans/Witches – according to the latest census data – exceed that in its homeland.

There are, of course, numerous other forms of Witchcraft still thriving that have as much to do with Gerald Gardner as Tibetan Buddhism has to do with a certain stable in Bethlehem (and please try hard not to draw any loopy inferences from that comparison), but Hutton is, as ever, right on the money when it comes to tracing the primary source of the modern intermingling of Pagan revivalism and practical Witchcraft to a select number of English ladies and gentlemen who were, by divine intervention or otherwise, clearly in the right place at the right time. Would the Craft today as practiced in the US, Britain, Canada, Australia, New Zealand and so many other lands exist if it were not for these individuals? It's hard to determine, and fortunately academic. Gardner, Valiente and the other founders of contemporary Wicca were indeed around when they were needed, and their legacy continues to change lives on a daily basis.

To understand the Craft today, it is necessary to examine where it came from. To this end, there are three main strands of this I intend to examine in this chapter: first, Gerald Brosseau Gardner's claim of traditional initiation and its subsequent development; secondly, magical traditions to which Gardner would have had access; and thirdly, literary sources.

As we look at these three main threads, it is important to bear in mind that Gardner was 55 years old at the time of his claimed initiation, that he had spent many years in Malaysia, and had an enormous interest in magic, folklore and mythology. By the time he published *High Magic's Aid*, he was 65, and he was 75 when *The Meaning of Witchcraft* appeared. He died in 1964, at the age of 79.

Gardner was born in 1884, and spent a great deal of his childhood, and most of his working adult life, overseas. His adult years were spent mainly in Malaysia, with a period of three years in Borneo. Between 1900 and his retirement in 1936, Gardner made four visits to England, each for a period of several months.

Upon his permanent return to England in 1936, Gardner and his wife Donna took a flat in London, and joined a naturist club in Finchley, North London. Gardner found the winters in London hard though and, in 1936-37 and 1937-38, took long holidays to Cyprus where he found the inspiration for his novel, *A Goddess Arrives*.

The Gardners remained in London until the threatened outbreak of war in 1938 caused them to seek a home in the country. Probably through friends made at the naturist camp, Gardner was introduced to the New Forest area, and he purchased a house at Highcliffe, a small town between Poole and Lymington in Dorset. Very soon after moving there, Gardner came into contact with the Rosicrucian Order Crotona Fellowship and the Rosicrucian Theatre near Christchurch, and it is thought that he met his fellow Coven-members there.

I chose 1939 as my arbitrary starting point as that was the year that Gerald Gardner claimed that he was initiated into a Coven of

To understand the Craft today, it is necessary to examine where it came from.

the Old Religion who met in the New Forest area of Hampshire. In his own words:

"I realised that I had stumbled upon something interesting; but I was half-initiated before the word, 'Wica' which they used hit me like a thunderbolt, and I knew where I was, and that the Old Religion still existed. And so I found myself in the Circle, and there took the usual oath of secrecy, which bound me not to reveal certain things." (Gerald Gardner, *The Meaning of Witchcraft*, 1959.)

It is interesting that in this quote, Gardner spells Wicca with only one "c" – in the earlier *High Magic's Aid* (1949) and *Witchcraft Today* (1954) the word "*Wicca*" is not even used. His own derivation for the word, given in *The Meaning of Witchcraft*, is as follows:

"As [the Dane and Saxon invaders of England] had no witches of their own they had no special name for them; however, they made one up from '*wig*' an idol, and '*laer*', learning, '*wiglaer*' which they shortened into '*Wicca*'. It is a curious fact that when the witches became English-speaking they adopted their Saxon name, '*Wica*'."

In *An ABC of Witchcraft Past and Present* (Hale, 1973), Doreen Valiente did not have an entry for "Wicca" but, when discussing Witchcraft, mentioned a Saxon derivation from the word "*Wicca*" or "*Wicce*." In *The Rebirth Of Witchcraft* (Hale, 1989), however, she rejected this Saxon theory in favor of Professor Russell's derivation from the Indo-European root "*Weik*" which relates to things connected with magic and religion.

Doreen Valiente (1922-1999) strongly supported Gardner's claim of traditional initiation, and published the results of her successful attempt to prove the existence of Dorothy Clutterbuck, reputedly the High Priestess of the Coven into which Gardner was initiated, in an appendix to *The Witches' Way* by Janet

and Stewart Farrar (Hale, 1984). It is a marvelous piece of investigation, but proving that Old Dorothy existed does not, of course, prove that she was a Witch or that she initiated Gardner. More recent research suggests that there is another contender for Gardner's initiator, a woman known as "Dafo" but whose real name was Edith Woodford-Grimes, and in Philip Heselton's latest book – *Gerald Gardner and the Cauldron of Inspiration* (Capall Bann, 2003) – he makes a strong case for Rosamund Sabine, known as "Mother Sabine."

In his book, *Ritual Magic in England* (Neville Spearman, 1970), occultist Francis King offers some anecdotal evidence in support of Gardner's claims. It is only fair to point out, however, that in the same book he virtually accuses Moina Mathers of murder, based upon a misunderstanding of a story told by Dion Fortune. With that caveat, I'll recount the tale in full.

King relates that in 1953, he became acquainted with Louis Wilkinson, who wrote under the pen-name of Louis Marlow, and had contributed essays to Crowley's *Equinox*. Wilkinson later became one of Crowley's literary executors. King says that in conversation, Wilkinson told him that Crowley had claimed to have been offered initiation into a Witch Coven, but that he refused, as he didn't want to be bossed around by a bunch of women. (This story is well known and is frequently repeated, but it is almost impossible to track down the origin.)

Wilkinson then proceeded to tell King that he had become friendly with members of a Coven operating in the New Forest area, and he thought that while it was possible that they derived their existence from Margaret Murray's *The Witch Cult in Western Europe* (OUP, 1921), he felt that they were rather older. King draws the conclusion that these Witches were the very same as those who initiated Gardner. King claims that the conversation with Wilkinson took place in 1953, although *Ritual Magic in England* was not published – or presumably written – until 1970. However, on September 27, 1952, *Illustrated* magazine published a feature by Allen Andrews, which included details of a working by "the Southern Coven of British Witches" where seventeen men and women met in the New Forest to work magic intended to repel an invasion by Hitler.

Wilkinson had told King of this working during their conversation, which King believes to be proof that such a Coven existed. Despite some differences in the two stories, it is possible that they are reporting the same event, but as Wilkinson's conversation with King came after the magazine article, we shall never know.

Of one thing we can be certain though: whatever its origin, modern Wicca derives from Gardner. There may, of course, be other traditional, hereditary Witches, but even if they are genuine, then it is unlikely that they would have been able to "go public" had it not been for Gardner.

There have been many claims of "hereditary" origin, none of them able to be proven one way or the other. Roy Bowers, who used the pseudonym Robert Cochrane, was perhaps the best known of these controversialists. Doreen Valiente describes her association with him in *The Rebirth of Witchcraft*, and the Roebuck Tradition, which is still active in the USA today, derives directly from Cochrane via Joe Wilson. *Witchcraft: A Tradition Renewed* by Evan John Jones with Doreen Valiente (Hale, 1990) describes a tradition derived from Robert Cochrane. Alex Sanders, of course, is another who claimed hereditary lineage, and like Cochrane, deserves his own place in this history, and we'll get to both of them later.

Many people have been suspicious of

Gardner's claims, and have accused him of making the whole thing up. They suggest that the Wicca is no more than the fantasy of an old man colored by a romantic imagination. One particularly virulent attack upon Gardner came from Charles Cardell, writing under the pseudonym of Rex Nemorensis.

One of Gardner's initiates who is still active in the Wicca today [at the time of the original lecture] has an interesting tale to tell about Cardell, whom he knew:

"Cardell claimed to be a Witch, but from a different tradition to Gardner's … He managed to get a woman called Olive Green (Florannis) into Gardner's Coven, and told her to copy out the Book of Shadows so that Cardell could publish it, and destroy Gardner. He also contacted a London paper, and told them when and where the Coven meetings were held, and of course the paper got quite a scoop. Cardell led people in the Coven to believe that it was Doreen Valiente who had informed on them. Doreen had just left Gardner in a bit of a huff after a disagreement; another Coven member, Ned Grove, left with her. Anyway, the day the paper printed the exposure, Cardell sent Gardner a telegram saying, 'Remember Ameth tonight'." [Author's note: "Ameth" was Valiente's Craft name, and as it has already been published, I see no reason not to use it here.]

My informant also said that Olive Green was associated with Michael Houghton, owner of Atlantis Bookshop in Museum Street, London, and publisher of *High Magic's Aid*. Through this association, she encountered Kenneth Grant of the OTO, although their association was not friendly.

Cecil Williamson, the original owner of the Witchcraft Museum on the Isle of Man, and later owner of the Witchcraft Museum in Boscastle, has also published a number of articles in which he states quite categorically that Gardner was an utter fraud, but he offers only anecdotes to support these allegations.

Although Gardner claimed his initiation occurred in 1939, we don't really hear anything about him until 1949, when Houghton published *High Magic's Aid*. This novel has very strong Solomonic leanings but, like Gardner's own religious beliefs, it combined the more natural forms of magic with high ceremonial. In his introduction to the book, Gardner says that: "The Magical rituals are authentic, partly from *The Key of Solomon* (MacGregor Mathers' translation) and partly from magical MSS in my possession." Gardner did indeed have a large collection of such manuscripts, which passed with the rest of his goods to Ripley's in Toronto after his death.

Scire was the name Gardner took as a member of Crowley's branch of the Ordo Templi Orientis (my first edition copy of *High Magic's Aid* is credited to "Scire" on the dust jacket, but to "Scrire" on the frontispiece). Although it is generally agreed that his membership was purely nominal, he was certainly in contact with people like Kenneth Grant and Madeline Montalban (founder of the Order of the Morning Star). Gardner was given his OTO degree and Charter by Aleister Crowley, to whom he was introduced in 1946 by Arnold Crowther. As Crowley died in 1947, their association was not long-lived, but Crowther said that the two men enjoyed each other's company.

So, after that brief introduction we can have a look at the first of the strands I mentioned.

Gardner and the Golden Dawn

In 1888, the Hermetic Order of the Golden Dawn was born, beginning a renaissance of interest in the occult that has continued to the present day. It is impossible to overstate the importance of the Golden Dawn to modern occultists; not only through its rituals, but also through its personalities and, of course, the Order's making available a large body of occult lore that would otherwise have remained unknown or hidden in obscurity. I will be looking at this body of occult lore with other literary influences later, and will here concentrate on the Order's rituals and personalities that have influenced Wicca.

We cannot look at the Golden Dawn in isolation from its own origins. It is descended from a myriad of esoteric traditions including Rosicrucianism, Theosophy and Freemasonry – the latter in its own right, as well as via the Societas Rosicruciana in Anglia (SRIA), a scholarly and ceremonial association open to Master Masons only.

Whether the German Lodge or its obliging representative Frau Sprengel actually existed is a matter still under debate but, either in fact or in spirit, these were the source for the *Cipher Manuscripts* which were used to found the Isis-Urania Lodge in 1888.

Isis-Urania was founded by Dr. William Wynn Westcott, Dr. William Woodman, and Samuel Liddell ("MacGregor") Mathers. Not only were all three Master Masons, Westcott and Mathers were also members of the Theosophical Society. Most importantly though, the three were a ruling triumvirate that managed the affairs of the SRIA. This is significant, for the SRIA numbered among its members Hargrave Jennings, who is reputed to have been involved with a Pagan group at the end of the nineteenth century which drew its inspiration from Apuleius' *The Golden Ass*.

But back to the Golden Dawn. Whether the *Cipher Manuscripts* actually existed, or Westcott manufactured them is now largely irrelevant. Mathers was commissioned to edit the rituals into a workable shape, and thus the Golden Dawn was born. Members of the Isis-Urania Lodge at various times also included Allan Bennett, Moina Mathers, Aleister

Crowley, Florence Farr, Maud Gonne, Annie Horniman, Arthur Machen, William Sharp (aka novelist "Fiona Macleod"),

Arthur Waite and WB Yeats. Also associated were Lady Gregory, and GW Russell or "AE" whose *The Candle of Vision* was included in the bibliography of *The Meaning of Witchcraft*. The literary and Celtic influences within the Golden Dawn were immense.

From the Isis-Urania Lodge sprang all the others, including the so-called Dissident Orders derived through Crowley. It is this line that some commentators trace to modern Wicca, so it is upon this one that we will now concentrate.

Aleister Crowley was initiated into the Isis-Urania Lodge on November 18, 1898. He later quarrelled with Mathers, and in 1903 created his own Order, the Argenteum Astrum (Silver Star). In 1912, Crowley was initiated into the OTO, and in 1921, succeeded Theodor Reuss as its Chief.

of the lines by Crowley which are rather familiar to modern Wiccans:

"I give unimaginable joys on earth; certainty, not faith, while in life; upon death, peace unutterable, rest, ecstasy; nor do I demand aught in sacrifice." (*The Book of the Law*, (1904), ch 1, v 58.)

"I am Life, and the giver of Life, yet therefore is the knowledge of me the knowledge of death." (*ibid.*, ch 2, v 6.)

And of course, Crowley's Gnostic Mass has been immensely influential.

Not only poetry, but also magical practices in Wicca are often derived from Golden Dawn sources. For example:

The method of casting the circle – the visualization of the circle and the pentagrams at the quarters – is based upon the standard Golden Dawn Pentagram Ritual;

"Indeed, the influence of Crowley was very apparent throughout the [Wiccan] rituals."

According to Arnold Crowther's account, it was in 1946, a year before Crowley's death, that Crowley gave Gardner an OTO Charter. Ithell Colquhoun says only that it occurred in the 1940s, and further states that Gardner introduced material from the OTO – and, less directly, from the Golden Dawn – into "the lore of his Covens."

As Doreen Valiente also admits, "Indeed, the influence of Crowley was very apparent throughout the [Wiccan] rituals." This, Gardner explained to her, was because the rituals he received from his Coven were very fragmentary, and in order to make them workable, he had to supplement them with other material. To give an example of some

Both the concept of and word "Watchtowers" are from the Enochian system of Magic, passed to Wicca via the Golden Dawn (although I would like to make it very clear that their use within Wicca bears no relation to the use within Enochia – the only similarity is in the name);

The Elements and colors generally attributed to the Quarters are those of the Golden Dawn;

The weapons and their attributions are a combination of Golden Dawn, Crowley and *The Key of Solomon*.

In *Witchcraft Today*, Gardner says, "The people who certainly would have had the knowledge and ability to invent [the Wiccan rites]

were the people who formed the Order of the Golden Dawn about seventy years ago ..."

The Golden Dawn was not the only influence upon Gardner. Freemasonry has also had a tremendous impact upon the Wicca. Not only were the three founders of Isis-Urania Temple Masons, so too were Crowley and Arthur Waite. Gardner and at least one member of the first Coven, Edith Woodford-Grimes, were both Co-Masons.

Gardner was also a friend of JSM Ward, who had published a number of books about Masonry. Doreen Valiente describes Ward as a "leading Mason" but Francis King refers to him as "a bogus Bishop ... who had written some quite good but far-fetched books on masonry, and who ran a peculiar religious-cum-occult community called The Abbey of Christ the King ..." However far-fetched Ward's books may have been, we can assume that some of the many similarities between Wicca and Masonry are in some ways due to Ward's influence. Some of these concepts and phrases include:

- The three degrees
- "The Craft"
- "So Mote It Be"
- The Challenge
- "Properly Prepared"
- The first degree oath (in part)
- Presentation of the Working Tools at first degree.

It seems to me quite clear that even if Gardner received a traditional set of rituals from his Coven, they must have been exceptionally sparse, as the concepts that we know of as Wicca today certainly derive from ceremonial magic and Freemasonry to a very great extent. Indeed, Gardner always claimed that they were sparse.

It could be argued that all derive from a common source; that the appearance of a phrase or technique in one tradition does not automatically suggest that its appearance elsewhere means that the one was taken from the other. However, Gardner admits his sources in many cases, and Valiente confirms them in others, so I think it is safe to assume that the rituals and philosophy used by Wicca descended from the traditions of Freemasonry and ceremonial magic, rather than having been derived from a single common source. However, as D Hudson Frew points out in his commentary upon Aidan Kelly's *Crafting the Art of Magic* (Llewellyn, 1991), the phenomena of the techniques and practices of ceremonial magic influencing folk magic and traditions is widely recognized by anthropologists, and certainly does not indicate plagiarism. And of course there are many traditional Witchcraft aspects in Wicca.

Leaf and flower and fruit

Having looked at the development of the magical orders which resulted from the British occult revival of the nineteenth and 20th centuries, we can see where this ties in with Wicca and Gardner's claim of traditional initiation. We can now move on to consider the convoluted family trees of modern Witchcraft.

Turning first to possible roots of the Gardnerian tree, we encounter two candidates for the title of "hereditary" sources of Gardner's formulation of Wicca: the New Forest Coven and the Cumbrian Group, into which Eleanor Bone (1911-2001) claimed to have been initiated before meeting Gardner. (Eleanor Bone was one of Gardner's High Priestesses, and her "line" has been immensely important to the modern Wicca. She was featured in the magazine series, *Man, Myth and Magic*, and in her heyday she ran two Covens: one in Cumbria, and one in South London.)

Sybil Leek (1923-1983) refers in her later

books to the existence of the Horsa Coven in the New Forest area, and there is also sometimes mention of a St. Alban's group that pre-dates Gardner, but as far as I know, this is mistaken. The St. Albans group was Gardner's own group, which, as far as we have been able to ascertain to date, did not pre-date him.

While on the subject of pre-Gardnerian Witchcraft, I will mention George Pickingill – briefly, as I think it extremely dubious that he had any connection with Gardner, or any other modern Wiccan.

Pickingill died in 1909, whilst Gardner was still in Malaysia. Eric Maple is largely responsible for the beginnings of the Pickingill myth, which were expanded by Bill Liddell (Lugh) writing in two early and influential Craft magazines, *The Wiccan* and *The Cauldron*. The articles were initially published throughout the 1970s, but *The Cauldron* continued to publish Lugh's material for quite some time. I met Bill Liddell and his wife in Brisbane in 2001, and found them to be a charming couple and very hospitable. We spoke a little about George Pickingill, and Bill is aware that I am extremely sceptical of any relationship between Pickingill and Gardner, or indeed with any modern Wiccan tradition.

In the book, *The Dark World of Witches*, published in 1962, Maple tells of a number of village wise women and cunning men, one of whom was George Pickingill. There is a photograph included of an old man with a stick, holding a hat, who Maple identifies as Pickingill. This photograph has subsequently been re-used many times in books about Witchcraft and Wicca.

Issue number 31 of *Insight* magazine, dated July 1984, contains a very interesting letter from John Pope: "The photograph purporting to be Old George Pickingill is in fact a photo of Alf Cavill, a station porter at Ellstree, taken in the early 1960s. Alf is now dead, but he was no witch, and laughed over the photograph when he saw it." However, a very respected Craft authority has told me that he believes the photo, which is in his possession, to be of Pickingill, and I have no reason to disbelieve him.

Although most of the many claims made about Pickingill seem extremely far-fetched, some could, with a stretch of the imagination, be accepted. Still, notions like Pickingill, an illiterate farm laborer, co-ordinating and supervising nine Covens across the breadth of the UK are staggering. I lived in a small village in Cambridgeshire in the 1980s, and the locals considered a trip to London (maybe an hour or two away) to be the journey of a lifetime. Just going to Kings Lynn (less than 20 miles away) was considered to be a lengthy trip. The claim that Pickingill supervised Covens over several counties beggars belief, and to accept that he had the likes of Allan Bennett and Aleister Crowley as his pupils bends credulity even further.

When we return to the more credible side of the Wiccan family tree, we encounter numerous names that many readers will find familiar, such as Doreen Valiente, Jack Bracelin, Monique Wilson, Pat and Arnold Crowther, and Lois Bourne (Hemmings).

Jack Bracelin is best remembered as the author of Gardner's biography, *Gerald Gardner, Witch* (first published in 1960; republished in 2000 by IHO Books). There have been suggestions that this book was actually written by Idries Shah and simply published under Bracelin's name, but I doubt the truth of that will be known unless an authenticated manuscript is discovered.

I have a copy of Bracelin's Book of Shadows, which it is claimed dates from 1949, although in *The Rebirth Of Witchcraft*, Doreen Valiente states that Bracelin was a "relative newcomer" in the mid-1950s. I have also been told by two different sources that Bracelin helped Gardner write "The Laws" of Witchcraft. In *The Rebirth Of Witchcraft*, Valiente states that she did not see these Laws until the mid-1950s, when she and her partner, Ned Grove, accused Gardner of concocting them in order to re-assert control over the Coven. As Bracelin was in the Gardner camp during the break-up of the group, it seems reasonable that he did in fact help with their composition. Alex Sanders increased the number of The Laws much later – these appeared in June Johns's book, *The King of the Witches* (Davies, 1969).

Although Doreen claims that the reason for the Coven break-up was the fact that Gardner and Bracelin were publicity crazy, there was another reason, which was the instatement of a new lady into the Coven, effectively replacing Doreen as High Priestess. This is believed to be behind the creation of Gerald's Law which states that the High Priestess will "gracefully retire in favor of a younger woman, should the Coven so decide in council." Needless to say, Doreen was not impressed, and she and Ned left the Coven under very acrimonious circumstances. It was quite some time before Doreen had contact with Gardner again, and they never quite regained the degree of friendship that had previously existed.

Monique and Campbell "Scotty" Wilson are infamous, rather than famous, as Gardner's heirs who sold off his magical equipment and possessions after his death to Ripley's in the USA. Monique was the last of his Priestesses, and many Wiccans have not forgiven her for selling off all Gardner's possessions. Pat Crowther has been scathing about her in an interview, and although Doreen tells of the sale of Gardner's magical possessions to Ripley's in *The Rebirth Of Witchcraft*, she doesn't ever mention the Wilsons by name. In effect, the Craft closed ranks against them. (Fortunately, Richard and Tamarra James (of the Wiccan Church of Canada) managed to buy the bulk of Gardner's collection from Ripley's in 1987, and it is now back within the Craft and is available for initiates to consult and view.)

Eventually the Wilsons sold the Museum in Castletown and moved to Torremolinos, Spain, where they bought a café. Monique died nine years after selling the Museum. In the late 1990's I spoke to someone who knows the whereabouts of Campbell, and can confirm that he did move to the USA after Monique's death and that he still has connections to an operational Coven.

Monique Wilson was, of course, influential in a way that she could never have imagined, when in the early 1960s she initiated Raymond Buckland who, with his then wife Rosemary, was subsequently very influential in the development of the Wicca in the USA. (See Ray's chapter in this book for further details on his remarkable career.)

Another well-known and somewhat controversial individual in Craft history is Robert Cochrane. Cochrane's origins are obscure, but I have been told that he was initiated into the Gardnerian Tradition by someone I must refer to as CS (CS and partner, D, are fated to remain completely anonymous, and if it were not for the Cochrane connection are unlikely to have been remembered beyond their immediate circle). Cochrane met Doreen Valiente through a mutual acquaintance in 1964, and represented himself to her as an hereditary Witch, from a different tradition to Gardner's. Valiente states that he was contemptuous of what he called "Gardnerian" Witches – indeed, she believes he coined the adjective "Gardnerian." She also reports that she was completely taken in by Cochrane and, for a while, worked with him and "The Clan of Tubal Cain" as he described his tradition, which was also known as "The Royal Windsor Cuveen" or "1734."

The figures "1734" have an interesting history. In a letter to Joe Wilson dated "Twelfth Night 1966" Cochrane says:

"... the order of 1734 is not a date of an event but a grouping of numerals that mean something to a witch. One that becomes seven states of wisdom – the Goddess of the Cauldron. Three that are the Queens of the Elements – fire belonging alone to Man, and the Blacksmith God. Four that are Queens of the Wind Gods. The Jewish orthodoxy believe that whomever knows the Holy and Unspeakable name of God has absolute power over the world of form. Very briefly, the name of God spoken as Tetragrammaton ... breaks down in Hebrew to the letters YHVH, or the Adam Kadmon (The Heavenly Man). Adam Kadmon is a composite of all Archangels – in other words a poetic statement of the names of the Elements. So what the Jew and the Witch believe alike is that the man who discovers the secret of the Elements controls the physical world. 1734 is the witch way of saying YHVH." (Cochrane, 1966.)

Justine Glass (in *Witchcraft, The Sixth Sense – and Us*, Neville Spearman, 1965) and Doreen Valiente (in *The Rebirth of Witchcraft*) both mention a copper platter that bear the numerals "1724," a photo of which appears in Glass's book. Cochrane told Glass that the platter had been in his family for "several hundred years," only to admit to Valiente when challenged that this was not the case and to claim that it was the fault of

Cochrane, who had asked for her help in finding a platter suitable for the ritual meal of cakes and wine. I have not seen any explanation of the discrepancy between the "1734" of Cochrane's 1966 letter, and the "1724" that occurs in published sources.

Although Valiente says that Cochrane's group was small, it still proved to be remarkably influential. As well as Cochrane, his wife (who Doreen refers to as "Jean") and Doreen herself, there were others who are well-known today, and a man called Ronald White, who very much wanted to bring about a new age in England and was absorbed with the legends of King Arthur, the Once and Future King.

In *The Rebirth Of Witchcraft*, Doreen elaborates upon the circumstances surrounding the death of Cochrane: the bald facts are that he died at the Summer Solstice of 1966 of an overdose of prescribed sleeping pills and narcotic herbs. Craft tradition believes that he became in fact, and of his own choice, the male ritual sacrifice which is sometimes symbolically enacted at the height of Summer.

The Royal Windsor Cuveen disbanded after Cochrane died, only to be reborn from the ashes at Samhain that year under a new name – The Regency. All of its early members were from the Royal Windsor Cuveen, and they were under the leadership of Ronald White. Meetings were held in North London, at a place called Queens Wood. As well as White and Valiente, the group includ-

So what the Jew and the Witch believe alike is that the man who discovers the secret of the Elements controls the physical world.

the publishers who had muddled the captions of two photos. In fact, Doreen Valiente had bought that platter from a Brighton antique shop at the request of Robert

ed "John Math" (founder of the Witchcraft Research Association in 1964, and editor of *Pentagram* magazine) and the founder of the Pagan Movement, Tony Kelly.

At The Regency's height, there were frequently more than 40 in attendance at rites, which tended to be of the dramatic, Pagan kind rather than the ceremonial associated with high ritual magic. The group operated fairly consistently for over twelve years, finally disbanding in 1978. It proved to be of great importance to the development of the Wicca, although its existence was kept a fairly close secret, and even today, there are relatively few people who have heard of it.

Returning to Eleanor Bone's line, we encounter a number of influential people whose initiatory lineage can traced to her and her initiates, Madge and Arthur. (It should be remembered, incidentally, that although Bone was initiated by Gardner, she also claimed hereditary status in her own right.) Madge and Arthur's initiates include John and Jean Score. John Score was the business partner of Michael Houghton and the founder of the Pagan Federation, which remains very active today.

Houghton died under curious circumstances, which are briefly mentioned in *The Sword of Wisdom* by Ithell Colquhoun (Neville Spearman, 1975). My Craft source told me that this was actually a ritual that went badly wrong, and Houghton ended up on the wrong end of some fairly potent energies. There is an interesting anecdote about Houghton in *The Rebirth Of Witchcraft*, which is taken from *Nightside of Eden* by Kenneth Grant (Frederick Muller, 1973; recently reprinted by Mandrake Press), and agrees in some respect to the similar story that I was told some years earlier.

Apparently one evening in 1949, Kenneth Grant and his wife, Gardner, Dolores North (Madeline Montalban), and an unnamed Witch (probably Olive Green) met to perform a ritual together, supposedly to contact an extraterrestrial being. The material basis for the rite was a drawing by AO Spare. Soon after the rite commenced, a nearby bookseller (presumably Michael Houghton) turned up and interrupted proceedings. On hearing that Kenneth Grant was within, he declined to enter and wandered off. The rite was disrupted, and everyone gave up and went home.

Grant claims that as a result of disturbing this working, Houghton's marriage broke up, and that Houghton subsequently died in mysterious circumstances. (The Houghton divorce was a *cause célèbre*, in fact, with his wife suing him for cruelty because he boasted of being a Sagittarian while sneering at her because she was only a dingy old Capricorn!)

The interrupted ritual could well have taken place. Madeline Montalban had a flat near to Houghton's Atlantis Bookshop and would certainly have known both Grant and Houghton. She was also acquainted with Gardner, although her opinion of both him and the Wicca was rather poor. One of Montalban's students told me that she thought Gardner rather a fraud and ritually inept. She also had a very low opinion of Wiccans and refused to allow her own students to participate in Wiccan rites. The reason for this may lie in an anecdote which Doreen Valiente doesn't relate: the story goes that Montalban agreed to participate in a rite with Gerald, which turned out to involve her being tied up and tickled with a feather duster! The great lady was not amused.

Two more individuals with an important position in the post-Gardnerian family tree are Pat and Arnold Crowther, as it is from their line that the infamous Alex Sanders derives. It is no secret anymore that Alex – far from being initiated by his grandmother when he was seven, as he liked to tell people – was in fact turned down for initiation by Pat Crowther in 1961.

There are numerous rumors about how Alex obtained access to a Book of Shadows, but I believe that Ronald Hutton has cleared away many of the smoke screens by revealing the existence of two letters, written nine days apart in August and September 1963, addressed to Gerald Gardner. The first letter was from Alex; the second from a lady known as Pat Kopanski, who was a member of Pat and Arnold Crowther's Coven. The letters both confirm that Alex was initiated to first degree by a High Priestess called Medea in March 1963, and that Pat Kopanski was initiated to second degree on the following day. This allowed Sanders and Kopanski to set up a Coven together.

Pat Crowther continues to dispute the legitimacy of the initiations, pointing to the fact that there is no mention of a High Priest officiating at the rites. In my experience, it is not uncommon for initiations to refer to the High Priestess alone (I can't recall mention of Eleanor Bone's High Priest, and yet no one, as far as I am aware, has ever questioned the legitimacy of initiations performed by her), so I would not dispute the claim on those grounds.

In *The Rebirth of Witchcraft,* Valiente also states that Sanders was initiated by an ex-member of Pat Crowther's Coven, but adds that he later visited Gardner and was allowed to copy from his Book of Shadows. Craft tradition has always said that the main differences between the Alexandrian and Gardnerian Books of Shadows occur where Alex misheard, or miscopied something!

Alex needed a High Priestess and chose Maxine Morris for the role. Maxine was, and remains, a striking Priestess, and made a very good visual focus for Sanders' Alexandrian line and the Wiccan movement in general, both of which grew in leaps and bounds. In the late 1960s, Alex and Maxine were prolific initiators, and a number of their initiates have become well known. Their most famous initiates are almost certainly Janet and Stewart Farrar, who left them in

1971 to form their own Coven, first in England, and subsequently in Ireland. Through their many books, they have had enormous influence over the direction that the modern Craft has taken. Certainly in Australia, the publication of Stewart's *What Witches Do* in 1971 was an absolute watershed. Stewart died in 2000 but Janet, in collaboration with Gavin Bone, maintains a consistent output of literature that makes their progressive form of Wicca more likely to become the "standard" than any other type.

Another notable Alexandrian initiate is Seldiy Bate who was originally magically trained by Madeline Montalban, and later then took initiation from Maxine and Alex. Her husband, Nigel, was also initiated by Maxine and Alex, and they have been "public" Witches for a number of years now, often appearing on television and radio, and in the press. Their background in ritual magic is expressed in the type of Coven that they run – a combination of Wicca and Ceremonial Magic.

In 1971, Alex and Maxine went their separate ways. For a number of years Maxine practiced the Liberal Catholic faith with her working partner, David Goddard, a Liberal Catholic Priest. In 1984, Maxine gathered together a group again, and started practicing a combination of Wicca, Qabalah and Liberal Catholicism. She and David separated in 1987, and since then her Coven has been exclusively Wiccan. In 1989, she married one of her initiates, Vincent, and they now live in North Wales.

Alex's history after the split was a little more sordid, with one girl he married, Jill, filling the gutter press with stories about Alex being homosexual and defrauding her of all her money to spend on his boyfriends. Alex weathered those storms as he had all others, however, and when he died in 1987 his funeral drew a large number of Witches to pay their respects.

The shadows of books

I'd now like to focus upon the last of the strands which I believe has been influential upon the birth and development of Wicca – that of the literary traditions and sources to which Gardner would have had access. To a certain extent these are contiguous with the magical traditions described earlier, as nowhere is it suggested that Gardner ever worked in a magical Lodge, and so we must assume that his knowledge came from the written form of the rites, rather than the practice of them.

From reading Gardner's books, it is quite apparent that Margaret Murray had a tremendous impact upon him. Her book *The God of the Witches* was published in 1931, and ten years previously, *The Witch Cult in Western Europe* had appeared. *The God of the Witches* has been extremely influential on a number of people, and certainly inspired Gardner. In fact, *Witchcraft Today*, first published in 1954, contained a foreword by Murray. At this time, Murray's academic work on Witchcraft was still taken seriously, and she remained the contributor on the subject of Witchcraft for the *Encyclopædia Britannica* for a number of years. Her work has subsequently been largely discredited, although she remains a source of inspiration, if not historical accuracy.

In Gardner's day, the idea of a continuing worship of the old Pagan Gods must have been a staggering concept, and in the second article in my series about Murray (published in *The Cauldron*), I made the point that Murray may have had to pretend scientific veracity in order to get her work published in such times. Don't forget that Dion Fortune had to publish her work privately, as did Gardner with *High Magic's Aid*. Carlo Ginzburg's excellent book, *Ecstasies* (Pantheon, 1991), also supports Murray's basic premise, although he regrets her historical deceptions.

There were numerous sources other than Murray, however. In 1899, Charles Godfrey Leland's *Aradia: Gospel of the Witches* was published. Most of Crowley's work was available in published form during the pre- and post-war years, as were the texts written and translated by MacGregor Mathers and Waite. Also readily available were works such as *The Magus* by Francis Barrett and, of course, the many classics from which Gardner drew much inspiration.

Of particular importance would have been *The White Goddess* by Robert Graves, which is still a standard reference book on any British Wiccan's bookshelf. This was published in 1952, three years after *High Magic's Aid* appeared, and two years before Gardner's first non-fictional book about Witchcraft. I would like to observe at this point that Graves has taken some very unfair criticism in respect of this book. *The White Goddess* was written as a work of poetry, not history, and to criticize it for being historically inaccurate is to miss the point. Unfortunately, I agree that some writers have referred to it as an "authority," thereby leading their readers up the garden path. This is not Graves's fault, however, nor do I believe it was his intention.

Another book that has had a profound influence on many Wiccans, and would undoubtedly have been well known by Gardner is *The Golden Bough* by Sir JG Frazer. Although the entire book was written based upon purely secondary research, it is an extensive examination of many Pagan practices from the Ancient World, and the emphasis of the Sacrificed God could certainly have been taken from here equally as well as from Murray. It is likely that some of the Gardnerian ritual practices were derived from *The Golden Bough*, or from Frazer's own sources listed in its bibliography.

In *Witchcraft Today* Gardner mentions a number of authors when speculating where the Wiccan rites came from. He says that,

"The only man I can think of who could have invented the rites was the late Aleister Crowley." He continues, "The only other man I can think of who could have done it is Kipling." He also mentions that, "Hargrave Jennings might have had a hand in them ..." and then allows that "Barrat [sic] of The Magus, circa 1800, would have had the ability to invent or resurrect the cult."

It's possible that these references are something of a damage control operation by Gardner, who, according to Doreen Valiente, was not too impressed when she kept telling him that she recognized passages in the Witch rites! Witchcraft Today was published the year after Valiente's initiation, and perhaps by seeming to be genuinely interested in where the Rites came from, Gardner felt he might give the appearance of innocence of their construction.

As mentioned previously, Gardner also had a large collection of unpublished esoteric manuscripts that he used extensively, and one has only to read his books to realize that he was a very well-read man with wide-ranging interests. Exactly the sort of man who would be able to draw together a set of rituals if required.

The extensive bibliography to The Meaning of Witchcraft published in 1959 demonstrates this rather well. Gardner includes: Magick in Theory and Practice and The Equinox of the Gods by Crowley; The Mystical Qabalah by Dion Fortune; The Goetia; The White Goddess (Graves); Lady Charlotte Guest's translation of The Mabinogion; English Folklore by Christina Hole; The Kabbalah Unveiled and The Abramelin by Mathers; both Margaret Murray's books on Witchcraft; and Godfrey Leland's Gypsy Sorcery – as well as a myriad of classic texts, from Plato to Bede.

Although this bibliography postdates the creation of Gardnerian Wicca, it certainly suggests the sources of Gardner's inspiration.

There are also several books listed which are either directly or indirectly concerned with sex magic, Priapic Cults or Tantra. Hargrave Jennings wrote a book called The Rosicrucians, Their Rites and Mysteries, which Francis King describes as being "concerned almost exclusively with phallicism and phallic images – Jennings saw the penis everywhere." As mentioned earlier, Hargrave Jennings, a member of the SRIA, also belonged to a group described as a Coven, which met in the Cambridge area in the 1870s, and performed rituals based upon the classical traditions – specifically, from The Golden Ass. There is, however, no evidence to support this, except that there are often found references to a "Cambridge Coven" linked to Jennings' name.

Many of the rituals we are familiar with today were later additions by Doreen Valiente, and these have been well documented by both her and the Farrars. Doreen admits that she deliberately cut much of the poetry by Aleister Crowley because she felt it to be unsuitable, and substituted either her own work, or poems from other sources such as the Carmina Gadelica.

Of course we can never really know the truth about the origins of the Wicca. Gardner may have been an utter fraud; he may have actually received a "Traditional" initiation; or, as a number of people have suggested, he may have created the Wicca as a result of a genuine religious experience, drawing upon his extensive literary and magical knowledge to create, or help create, the rites and philosophy.

What I think we can be fairly certain about is that he was sincere in his belief. If there had been no more to the whole thing than an old man's fantasy, then the Wicca would not have grown to be the force that it is today, and the talk on which this chapter is based would never have been given on a long-ago Saturday morning in Canberra!

wicca and satanism
a case of confused identity
Nevill Drury

In the popular imagination – and especially among fundamentalist Christians – Wicca and Satanism have come to mean much the same thing. Both are seen as forms of "Devil worship" … deviant forays into the realm of the Black Arts.

Of course, Wiccans know that this is way off the mark and most Satanists object to the label as well. For a start, contemporary Satanism rejects the idea of any form of worship at all, especially when that worship involves what Temple of Set leader Dr. Michael Aquino has called "protective transcendental deities." For the self-respecting Satanist, Gods and Goddesses in any shape or guise are equally anathema. As leading American Satanist Don Webb has put it, the central task of Satanists today is self-deifica-

tic kind of religious practice that celebrates the earth and its journey around the sun. Now, we got a bad rap from the Christians about this. We have been told that we worship Satan, the Devil. Well, the Devil is a Christian God. We have never heard of the Devil. Many of us got burned [in the Middle Ages] because we didn't know who they were talking about ... so many died. Many were going to their death still wondering who the Devil was ..." (Personal communication to the author.)

If we are to distinguish between Satanism and Wicca we need look no further than Anton LaVey's notorious Church of Satan and compare with it with Wicca and Goddess worship as practiced today. The differences couldn't be more stark.

> For the self-respecting Satanist, Gods and Goddesses in any shape or guise are equally anathema.

tion, which means, essentially, that Satanists worship themselves. And if you worship your infinite potential, no other deities are required. Satanists may be accused of practicing black magic but for most contemporary practitioners the color black represents unmanifest human potential rather than "evil" as most of us would understand it.

Several prominent Neopagans have been outspoken on the issue of the confused identity of Wicca and Satanism, none more expressively than California-based Goddess worshipper Z Budapest. As Z has put it, in her characteristically colorful style:

"Witchcraft is a universal, joy-oriented, artis-

Anton LaVey and the Church of Satan

From the very beginning the Church of Satan was conceived as a religion of self-indulgence. Its founder, Anton LaVey (1930-1997), was himself a carnival performer and musician, and his new religion was intended to shock conservative mainstream America out of its complacency and moral double standards. LaVey would become known to his followers as the "Black Pope" and was fond of parading as an intentionally sinister figure sporting a pointed goatee beard and wearing a black cloak and inverted pentagram. An intimate of celebrities like Marilyn Monroe and Jayne Mansfield, and a close friend of Sammy Davis Jr., Anton LaVey had no peer as an orchestrator of occult extravaganzas.

Born in Chicago on April 11, 1930, Anton Szandor LaVey was of French, Alsatian, German, Russian and Romanian descent and claimed Gypsy blood as well. According to LaVey's biographer, Blanche Barton, LaVey left his home in Oakland at the age of sixteen and joined the Clyde Beatty Circus as a cage boy, later becoming an assistant lion tamer. He then worked in the Pike Amusement Park in Long Beach, California,

gruesome side of urban life – "people shot by nuts, knifed by friends, kids splattered in the gutter by hit-and-run drivers. It was disgusting and depressing ..." (Arthur Lyons, *The Second Coming: Satanism in America*, Dodd Mead, New York, 1970, p. 173). These grim events had a strong impact on LaVey's spiritual perspectives. He concluded that violence was a part of the divine and inscrutable plan of God, and he turned away from God altogether as a source of inspiration and benevolence.

We have been told that we worship Satan, the Devil. Well, the Devil is a Christian God. We have never heard of the Devil.

playing a steam calliope, a Wurlitzer band organ or a Hammond organ in a variety of carnival settings. It was here that he got his first taste of what he regarded as Christian hypocrisy:

"On Saturday night I would see men lusting after half-naked girls dancing at the carnival, and on Sunday morning when I was playing the organ for tent-show evangelists at the other end of the carnival lot, I would see these same men sitting in the pews with their wives and children, asking God to forgive them and purge them of their carnal desires. And the next Saturday night they'd be back at the carnival or some other place of indulgence. I knew then that the Christian Church thrives on hypocrisy, and that man's carnal nature will out!" (Quoted by Blanche Barton, *The Secret Life of a Satanist: the authorized biography of Anton LaVey*, Feral House, Los Angeles, 1990, pp. 39-40.)

Although it looked likely that Anton LaVey would make his career as an entertainer, he was inspired by his first wife to study criminology at San Francisco City College and then, for a brief period, became a photographer with the San Francisco Police Department. It was here that he observed the

After leaving his position as a police photographer, LaVey continued to play the organ for his livelihood, immersing himself still further in his study of the occult and parapsychology. Soon he was holding weekly classes on various esoteric topics, and these were attended by a diverse range of people, including novelist Stephen Schneck and avant-garde film producer Kenneth Anger. The so-called Magic Circle meetings were held in his tightly shuttered house at 6114 California Street, San Francisco, and included lectures on vampires, werewolves, haunted houses, extra-sensory perception and zombies – and other related subjects intended to stir the imagination. LaVey also lampooned the Catholic Church with a "Black Mass" which involved desecrating the Host, using an inverted cross and black candles, and reciting prayers backwards.

LaVey was fascinated by the concept of Sir Francis Dashwood's eighteenth century Hellfire Club – where establishment figures would meet for an evening of reveling and debauchery – and it occurred to him that the Magic Circle could provide the basis for a modern-day equivalent. Finally, in a typical act of bravado, LaVey shaved his head and announced the formation of the Church of

Satan on the most demonic night of the year, Walpurgisnacht, traditionally associated with the ascendancy of the Powers of Darkness. LaVey declared 1966 to be Year One, *Anno Satanas*, the first year of the reign of Satan. The Age of Fire had begun ...

LaVey also made a pronouncement about his new Church: "Satanism is the only religion in which a person can 'turn on' to the pleasures around him without 'dropping out' of society." This was an emphatic rephrasing of the hippie dictum "Turn on, tune in and drop out" then being advocated by counter-culture guru Timothy Leary. LaVey was opposed to any notion of drug-based escapism: instead he emphasized sensual indulgence and personal empowerment. LaVey believed, essentially, that Man is God and God is Man. The ceremonies of the Church of Satan would become a means for channeling magical

While Witches certainly know how to have a good time and many would consider themselves sexually liberated, the whole idea of a female "sexual altar" as a focus of carnal indulgence would be totally repugnant to most practicing Wiccans. The concept of worshipping the self stands out in marked contrast as well. Wicca is essentially a Nature-based religion with the Great Goddess at the very heart of contemporary belief and practice.

As the Great Mother or Mother Nature, the Goddess finds expression in world mythologies as deities like Artemis, Astarte, Athene, Demeter, Diana, Aphrodite, Hathor and Isis, among many others. In contemporary Witchcraft, the High Priestess incarnates the spirit of the Goddess in a ceremonial context when the High Priest "draws down the Moon" into her body. The High Priestess is regarded

Wicca is essentially a Nature-based religion with the Great Goddess at the very heart of contemporary belief and practice.

power into a full expression of human carnal desire. At 6114 California Street the ritual altar room was completely black with an inverted pentagram mounted on the wall above the fireplace. Services began and ended with Satanic hymns and a ritual invocation to Satan, and a naked woman – a symbol of lust and self-indulgence – was used as a ceremonial "altar."

This was modern Satanism as practiced in the Church of Satan in the 1960s and early 1970s. How, then, does it compare with Wicca, the way of the Goddess?

The Way of the Goddess

Most forms of modern Witchcraft have a very different focus from the sexual self-indulgence practiced in the Church of Satan.

as the receptacle of wisdom and intuition and is symbolized by the cup, whereas her consort is represented by a short sword or dagger known as the athame. Many Witchcraft rituals feature the act of uniting athame and cup as a symbol of sexual union, and there is also a comparable relationship in Celtic mythology between the sacred oak tree and Mother Earth. Accordingly the High Priest, or consort, is sometimes known as the Oak King, a reference to the Oak of the Celts, and at other times as Cernunnos, "The Horned One." In Witchcraft the Horned God personifies fertility, and in ancient Greece the Great God Pan, the goat-footed God, was a symbol of Nature and the universal life-force. There is no connection between the Horned God of Witchcraft and the Christian horned Devil, although since the time of the Witchcraft persecutions of the Middle Ages, this has been a common error.

Responding to the Goddess

Beliefs and ritual practices inevitably reflect individual perceptions and there are numerous ways of honoring the Goddess, whose sacred presence defines the very heart of the Wiccan perspective. Many Wiccans relate to the Goddess of the Moon as a Triple Goddess. As the waxing moon she is seen as the Maiden; as the full moon she is the Mother; and as the waning moon she is the Crone.

This symbolic personification of the three phases of womanhood are represented, for example, by the Celtic triad Brigid, Dana and Morrigan, the Greek Goddess in her three aspects Persephone, Demeter and Hecate, or by the three Furies Alecto (Goddess of beginnings), Tisiphone (Goddess of continuation) and Megaera (Goddess of death and rebirth). These threefold aspects are particularly emphasized by feminist Wicca groups in their development of "women's mysteries." As American Neopagan Z Budapest writes in her *Holy Book of Women's Mysteries*: "Images of the Mother Goddess, female principle of the universe and source of all life, abound ...[for she is] the Goddess of ten thousand names."

For most Wiccans this threefold Mother Goddess is also very much a deity of the *here and now*. As Starhawk has put it: "The Goddess is around us and within us. She is immanent and transcendent ... the Goddess represents the divine embodied in Nature, in human beings, in the flesh."

For Starhawk, encountering the Goddess should also be based on personal *experience*, and not on religious belief:

"In the Craft, we do not *believe* in the Goddess – we connect with Her; through the moon, the stars, the ocean, the earth, through trees, animals, through other human beings, through ourselves. She is here. She is within us all. She is the full circle: earth, air, fire, water and essence – body, mind, spirit, emotions, change.

The Goddess is first of all earth, the dark, nurturing mother who brings forth all life. She is the power of fertility and generation; the womb, and also the receptive tomb, the power of death. All proceeds from Her, all returns to Her ..." (Starhawk, "The Goddess" in Roger S Gottlieb (ed.), *A New Creation: America's Contemporary Spiritual Voices*, Crossroad, New York, 1990, pp. 213-214.)

A final summation

In Wicca, as in other contemporary forms of Neopagan practice, magic is usually classified as "black" or "white" and this has very much to do with intent. Black magic is pursued in order to cause harm or another person – through injury, illness or misfortune – and it also aims to enhance the personal power of the magician in bringing about this result. White magic, on the other hand, seeks a beneficial outcome

Wicca and Satanism are very different from each other

and is often associated with rites of healing, with eliminating evil or disease, and with the expansion of spiritual awareness. Most forms of contemporary Wicca are distinctly *white* and promote a holistic bond between the individual and the cosmos.

It should be clear from this comparison that Wicca and Satanism are very different from each other, in terms of both their essential outlooks on life and the values and orientation promoted by their respective devotees and practitioners. While contemporary Satanism as practiced in the Temple of Set has now moved away from the LaVey model of total sexual indulgence towards the more specific pursuit of self-deification, Wicca's focus is clearly very different. Wicca re-sacralizes Nature and honors the Goddess as the embodiment of Life. The sort of Satanic practice promoted in Anton LaVey's Church of Satan, on the other hand, had nothing to do with a universal life-principle and focused instead on responding blatantly to Christian morality and perceived notions of sexual repression.

So what do Wicca and Satanism share in common?

In my view, nothing at all. Wicca and Satanism belong in two different worlds. It's as simple as that.

If you spend much time footling about on the internet, you've doubtless noticed a lot of websites go in for lists of *Frequently Asked Questions*. Some even give answers to these questions. This, arguably, takes a little of the mystery out of life, and often when reading these answers, you may occasionally feel as if they'd have been much more entertaining if the website owner's imagination hadn't been stymied by his or her desire to pander to reality.

With that in mind, my first idea for this section of the book was to compile a long list of terribly abstract questions (with entirely erroneous, if mentally stimulating, answers) to be placed in a chapter called "Frequently Unintelligible Questions." However, upon determining that the acronym of that title was less than decorous, I plumped instead for a list of the sort of questions I've spent many years wriggling out of.

Wicca … is really Witchcraft plus Pagan spirituality.

I hope this will prove useful (and stranger things happen at sea, by all accounts).

Is Witchcraft/Wicca a religion?

That depends not only upon whom you ask, but upon why you're asking. For some people Witchcraft has a religious function; for others, that's the last thing they'd want it to be lumbered with.

As with many metaphysical questions, it helps if we think in terms of polarities – in this case, the poles are the social roles of *priest*

and *shaman*. Priest and priestess type people of most religions tend to fit comfortably into their society where they act as intermediaries between deity and the populace. They are typically respectable (at least within the parameters of their community's expectations), are custodians of communal beliefs, and may, when not noticeably divinely inspired, perform a function not dissimilar to that of spiritual civil servants. They are, ideally, what psychologists would call "other centered" and speak with the authority of established tradition and teachings.

Shamans, in their purest state, aren't. They're more inclined to be a trifle mad, bad and dangerous to know. They are likely to ride roughshod over prevailing concepts of morality and social behavior, are no great respecters of tradition for its own sake and, these days, are more frequently associated with the arts than with religion. They speak entirely on their own authority and work on William Blake's principle of "I must Create a System or be enslav'd by another Man's."

What's been happening over the last couple of decades is this: since Wicca in the Gardnerian and post-Gardnerian sense is really Witchcraft plus Pagan spirituality, thousands of its more or less priest(ess)ly practitioners have been out and about trying to establish their path as a faith as legitimate and worthy of respect as any other religion on the spiritual smorgasbord.

Many battles have been successfully fought

by Wiccans and other Pagans regarding anti-defamation and civil rights issues, and a few Wiccan organizations have achieved the same legal recognition as other religious societies regarding issues such as tax concessions, being able to perform legal-binding handfastings, and the religious rights of military personnel and prisoners (curious how those two categories seem to go together). It's a shame that such battles against discrimination are necessary, but that's human history for you. People of assorted races, genders, ages, religions, sexual preferences and political persuasions are perpetually having to fiddle about with the scales of justice to achieve anything like a true balance, so there's nothing much new there.

Unsurprisingly, other Witches (including some Wiccans) of the madly shamanic disposition have had certain problems with all of this. For many, one of Wicca's main attractions is that it breaks the established patterns of what spirituality is. While there are widely shared values, theology and approaches to ritual form in modern Witchcraft, a lot of branches retain a *Do It Yourself* sort of set up in which the individual is expected to think, create, explore and generally get on with the business of having a magical life with a degree of independence utterly foreign to most widely recognized religions.

Consequently, a lot of Wiccans out there tend to see several shades of vermilion at the first mention of a "Wiccan spokesperson" or a "Council of Elders." Some even go a bit quiet and grumpy around a phrase like "High Priestess." If pressed as to whether Witchcraft is a religion, these more shamanically inclined Witches will most likely tell you: (a) that each Wiccan creates her or his own religion which will have a maximum membership of one; or

(b) that Witchcraft isn't a religion at all but simply a collection of techniques, more akin, say, to yoga than to Hinduism.

So, basically there's no categorical answer here. The jury may be out for a century or two yet.

What is your personal stance on this issue?

I try to keep my head up and knees slightly bent in case of sudden impact.

No, really.

When Wicca is classed as a religion it's usually for two major reasons: first, in order to achieve the aforementioned civil rights and legal protection for its adherents (since the law still has trouble coming to terms with spirituality that doesn't follow the formal, hierarchical pattern of, for instance, Catholicism); and secondly, because for most Wiccans their Craft fulfills the same need that in a Jew, a Hindu or a Moslem is satisfied by his or her faith.

All the same, Groucho Marx said that he'd never want to join a club that would accept him as a member and, similarly, we should all occasionally have a small ponder about whether it's desirable to belong to any religion that accepts members at all. Those who profess to belong to one particular religion often seem to feel excluded from enjoying bits and bobs of all the others. In a musical analogy, some people exist quite happily listening solely to jazz, classical, Macedonian goat-herding tunes or even (speak it softly) Billy Joel, ignoring all the other odd and amusing musical

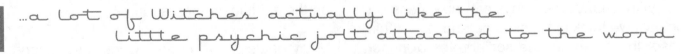
...a lot of Witches actually like the little psychic jolt attached to the word

noises people make. Personally, it'd drive me up the wall. Variety, spice of life, all that.

Isn't using a word as loaded as *Witchcraft* to describe a movement sort of asking for trouble?

It would indeed make a lot of Witchy people's lives easier if they dropped the *W* word. While they're at it, they could drop the magickal stuff, the polytheism, the animism, the feminism and the reverence for nature. By the same token, gay people would have an easier time of life if they'd get married to someone of the opposite sex and stop all that boy-boy/girl-girl nonsense. And what is it with left-handed people? Just who are *they* trying to impress?

The truth is, of course, that a lot of Witches actually like the little psychic jolt attached to the word, much as other people like to identify themselves with such traditionally abrasive terms as punks, dykes or Republicans.

Many Witches seem to be heavily into dressing up in funny costumes – what's the point?

Oh come on now, why does the Pope wear a frock?

Most religions use just as much dressing up in funny costumes and waving about exotic (and often rather expensive) props as your average Witchy clan. Even those exhausting televangelists that haunt your TV set during the grim, pre-dawn hours seem to go in for some extraordinarily peculiar shirts and hairstyles. Theater, religion and magic are like flour, eggs and sugar – all very well and good in themselves but mix them up together and you've got … well, whatever, you get when you mix them up. Some sort of cake possibly (note to self: people who need a recipe book to make toast oughtn't to attempt culinary analogies).

Admittedly, a lot of Witches like dressing up for its own sake. A section of the subculture seems to comprise the spiritual equivalent of the Society of Creative Anachronism, for instance. No Wiccan gathering is quite complete without a few of these ardent medievalists wafting through the proceedings like models in search for the last surviving Pre-Raphaelite artist to slap them down on canvas. Then there are the Goths, the *any-color-you-like-as-long-as-it's-black* contingent inspired more profoundly by Siouxsie Sioux than by Loreena McKennitt, with complexions that make Liquid Paper look healthily tanned and more body piercings than Saint Sebastian. And, of course, there's the hippie Pagans too – a little flashback to the Summer of Love, even at Yule.

It's really all about belonging. The costumes, like all clothing and personal ornamentation, are intended to advertise aspects of the individual's personality and attract kindred spirits.

Other Witches seem to be heavily into dressing up in nothing at all – what's the point?

The celebrated Wiccan fondness for sporting little more than a smile in their rituals has endeared the Craft to journalists and photographers for decades but has done little for the attempts to present the Craft to the community at large as just another religion. This may be why many American books and websites on Wicca present the tradition as being a declining and thoroughly modern innovation, despite the disobliging fact that artistic depictions of the marriage of proto-naturism and Witchery, Paganism and Faerie stretch back to prehistory. British, European and Australian Wiccan writers, among others, are generally less coy about the issue, possibly because they've less to worry about from the disapproval of the Religious Right (who are seldom terribly religious and hardly ever right).

Is there a point to all this wild Pagan naked flesh? Well, some authorities claim that there are psychic benefits in allowing energy to flow equally from every pore of the body whilst working magic. If this were the sole reason, presumably Witches could get by doing rituals in smallish swimsuits (somehow, though, the notion of *Donning the Sacred Speedos* lacks esoteric resonance, don't you think?). The reason why they don't – besides not being keen to look like a candlelit re-enactment of *Beach Blanket Bingo* – has to do with the message that would be broadcasting; namely, that some bits of the body are respectable and some are rather rude and embarrassing and are best kept hidden out of harm's way.

To the Wiccan, this is clearly bollocks (for want of a better word). Wicca is on its most genuinely traditional Pagan ground when it embraces issues such as the integration of the body, mind and spirit, the acknowledgement of sexuality as a sacrament, and the recognition of the sacredness of the physical world. An outbreak of little fluorescent nylon garments to censor the naughty bits just wouldn't fit in.

…if their fellow Witches find them aesthetically disappointing, it's time to get a new, less juvenile bunch of friends to work with.

The skyclad Witch is the Witch as the world made him or her, and to feel ashamed or embarrassed of that is hardly a powerful position from which to work magic. It's not the nakedness that empowers the Witch so much as the implicit statement through this cheerfully radical fashion statement that they have a perfect right to exist and to be accepted exactly as nature and life have fashioned them.

One writer on the Craft has expressed her belief that the skyclad tradition was fine for the young and pretty but not so good for those like herself who were "fat and forty." It would be harder to miss the point so completely if the point were transported to the far side of the world and locked in a suitcase with a label on it saying: "No points in here." If the physically less taunt'n'terrific feel it undignified to be bare, it's probably time to do a little self-image magick; if their fellow Witches find them aesthetically disappointing, it's time to get a new, less juvenile bunch of friends to work with. The sort of dignity that you take off whenever you have a shower isn't worth a whole lot anyway.

William Blake had another damned fine line about the body being that portion of the soul which is discernible by the five senses. Having a reasonably good relationship with as much of the soul as possible isn't a bad strategy for living.

Are Witches into illicit drugs and/or incredibly bizarre sexual practices?

Are Moslems good at juggling? Are Buddhists heavily into Willie Nelson albums? Are Baptists fond of strawberry-flavored custard? The answer in each case is some might well be but the two factors aren't what you'd call inherently connected.

Does *Magic happen*?

My treasured spouse is quite fond of the *Magic Happens* slogan. On the other hand, an old friend recently sent me a *Magic Doesn't Happen* bumper sticker. I think I'd like the franchise on one reading *Magic Doesn't **Just** Happen*. The miraculous does flash down like lightning from a blue sky once in a while but not often enough to set your watch by it.

Magic *does* happen (just as well or you'd be wanting a refund on this book round about now) but it seems to kick in more readily when you apply it to something already in motion than when it's your sole strategy. It's better at locating lines of least resistance than actually moving mountains a foot or two to the left. It's the sort of thing to use to enhance your efforts, not to be a substitute for them.

If magic works, why aren't all Witches millionaires?

If money works, why aren't all rich people happy?

It's all to do with how much you really want something. It's been said that it's not hard to become obscenely wealthy if all you want to do with your life is become obscenely wealthy.

Is there really a God/Goddess/Meaning of Life/Point to it all?

Books aren't especially reliable places to try to find out. Instead, find a nice patch of ground and a cloudless night sky well away from a polluted city. Lie down. Look up. Have a bit of a think. (If any UFOs show up, just try to ignore them. They only do it to distract you from more productive lines of contemplation.)

Are Gods and Goddesses and similar beings like real people?

They're older, slightly taller and a few get royalties on the day of the week named after them.

Oh, stop it.

All right. It's sensible to treat them as if they were real, independent people because they appear to respond better if you do. However, psychiatrists get good results out of treating patients' invisible friends and/or multiple personalities that way too, so I'm not convinced that that proves anything. Quite probably, it all makes far less difference than we might suppose.

Want to elaborate?

We're all familiar with people who crop up in dreams and tell us things that we're pretty sure we didn't know. We're also aware that people in dreams (which, according to conventional wisdom, are our own inventions) often behave in ways that can astonish, bewilder or terrify their supposed creators. So what's going on?

Well, a nice metaphor for the mind goes along these lines: imagine that your consciousness is a nice little sunny field out in the wilderness somewhere. Nearby is a cave in a very imposing mountainside. If you pop your head in, you can see a little detail in there but not too much. That's the subconscious.

Now amble in a little deeper. If you can pick your way far enough in without tripping over something and fracturing anything important, you'll soon start feeling little draughts of air as if connecting passageways were opening out into your little piece of darkness. You might get to wondering what would happen were you to go through one of those connecting tunnels. Could it be that you'd find your way into someone else's piece of darkness? And if so, and you were to follow that cave back to the light, would you be in a different part of the country, out in the sunshine in a different field? That is to say, would you have crept through someone else's subconscious mind and into their consciousness?

Instead of taking the connecting tunnels, just keep on moving deeper and deeper into your own cave. After a while you sense that the walls are now much further apart. Your impression is that a large number of caves have merged and, having an inquiring mind that needs to know, you wonder what that means. Continuing on, you perceive a glimmer of light ahead. As you approach it, you realize that the cave (which is now dozens of times broader than the small cavern you first entered) is opening out to daylight again. You've come right out the other side of the mountain into a new country.

Looking along the mountain, you see that your cave is only one of thousands opening out into this different world and that other people are emerging from other caves. At the same time, a large group of people is moving about in the fields in front of you. This isn't consciousness or subconsciousness anymore – this is a different place altogether and you can be fairly sure it's not Kansas.

What you're not sure about is who all these people are, where they came from and whether any of them have ever made their way through the cave system and out into your own private little sunny field on the far side of the mountain. Some look a little familiar now you think about it.

One thing you're very sure of, though, is it's best to treat them all as real, independent people.

What happens after you die?

You don't.

chant the spell and be it done

a sprinkling of practical magick

There is a lot more to Witchcraft than casting spells, but weaving magick and potential into your life using the evocative and tantalizing Craft of spellcasting is lots of fun and very rewarding on every level – spiritually, mentally, emotionally and physically. I encourage every Witch to research, collate and, most importantly, *create* the rituals and spells that will form your practice – it is your comprehension of your spellcasting and the intent with which you fuel it which makes it truly magickal … and truly effective.

There are many books out there that focus on spells and rituals (including all my previous books which feature various charms and enchantments in addition to overall information on the Craft). I have recommended some of my favorite spells in the second half of this article and I encourage you to compile a personal selection from these and all the others that are out there in the Witchy world that inspire and excite you and that you feel intuitively drawn to.

processes that I think have created the often utterly extraordinary results I have obtained – that is, spells cast to help others. Interestingly, spells cast for myself don't often have the same effect. I do a lot of rituals which make me feel good generally, but I don't request specific results from them. Why this is so I will cover shortly. People need to find the key that unlocks their individual belief that something extraordinary is possible. For some it is Witchcraft; for others not. Not everyone who goes to an Anthony Robbins seminar becomes a millionaire, but many do. In the same way, not every spell works, but many do.

Science acknowledges that part of the world's manifesting the way it does is because of the way we perceive it. We need to believe something extraordinary is possible in order to switch on the potential for what we want to manifest. That's why spells can work – because often the concept of them and the process of them stimulate something deep inside us. It triggers hope, and awak-

> Spellcraft … awakens the child within who once lived in a world full of enchantment and magic and infinite possibilities.

If you feel so inclined please check out my enormous spell-book at www.fionahorne.com. The spells there were created from my two-year gig hosting a radio show in Australia where I "prescribed" spells for call-in listeners and their various dilemmas!

Following are some personal musings on how, after seventeen years of practice, I think spells work. This is something I have spent a lot of time thinking about. I am not an irrational or illogical person, and I have analyzed the

ens the child within who once lived in a world full of enchantment and magic and infinite possibilities.

Why do my spells work on others but not for me?

Well, most likely because I so rarely do them for myself! I do a lot more rituals for myself than spells and there is a difference. A ritual is like building a home, and spells are the furniture you put in it. In my Craft I concentrate on building a strong home in which people can visit safely and with maximum enjoyment, if they choose. Maybe this has to do with my long years of practicing – perhaps it is appropriate now that I spend more time in service to others. But to do this the best I can I have to be spiritually strong and that's where the rituals and regular observances (like my morning Coven dedication ritual) help.

Spellcasting is a powerful activity for all the reasons I mention above. But there is something more to it. There *is* power in the symbols, words, herbs, crystals, colors, numbers, and phases of the Moon. That power manifests when we recognize it to. If we look to it, it makes itself visible. For example, if I relate to an herb as a benign food source, then it will be just that. To work magick with it, though, I see it as a vibrating mass of energy particles, evolved of a planet that created me as well, sharing my life force, sharing the very same chemical molecules that I have making up my body, my reality and my consciousness. I can then align myself and interact with its power, harnessing it to assist me in manifesting my Will.

Evolution of the species takes millions of years – with magick we can speed things up a bit, which is part of the magickal revolution. Look how talent develops in the human species when it is acknowledged and encouraged. Our athletes are fitter, stronger and more capable than ever. And it's not just improved nutrition and training methods or illegal steroids – it is the mindset that is encouraged – the sense that we can be more extraordinary, that we can continually better the heights we reach.

As the Western world awakens to the subtle energies of existence, psychic powers, kinetic powers, and all those other "super" natural qualities that we have, so they will awaken and evolve within us, becoming more present,

more relevant and more powerful. As a species we must continue to evolve: death, destruction, pain and suffering are all necessary in the cycles of life. But when these dark experiences are tempered with acceptance, honor and respect, they cease to rule us and become our trials of strength that we must face and embrace bravely, for they hold us together and give us a point of reference to encourage us to keep moving forward. Then we can know that love, goodness and compassion manifesting as growth and enlightenment are the foundations upon which we build our lives and are the most powerful expressions of our existence in this extraordinary universe.

I was at the gym a while back pedaling away on the stationary bike, reading my book and listening to Interpol (a very cool band I still love) when the TV screens above my head caught my eye. I rarely watch TV but the sight of a news reporter with her lollipop pink suit and neatly coiffed brown helmet of hair giggling as she inexpertly handled an enormous Uzi machine gun horrified me and stopped me in my tracks. Without a soundtrack, the vision, unjustified by words, was inexplicably macabre and sad. No doubt it was sensationalist reporting on the "terror threat." It was utterly surreal but highlighted to me that there really is no inherent power in a gun until a human decides to pick it up and fire it – even if it has been designed to kill and the vision of it inspires awe and fear.

It reminded me of a scene that a good girlfriend of mine, Briane, a reporter for CNN in the Afghanistan war, shared with me. Upon her arrival in Kabul she entered the foyer of a hotel and spotted a large rifle casually leant in the doorway. In its barrel was a single red rose.

From this anecdote, it is obvious to me that our *perception* of the power of an object will be its power – and this applies very much to the magickal tools of Witchcraft. It is your *knowledge* and *comprehension* of potential power and the way that you use it that determines the effect it can have. Your world will be as magickal as you let it be; as soon as you start doubting what you are doing and feeling that it is silly or rubbish, then it will be.

A very simple analogy I like to use to explain this is: imagine that you are at a dinner party, sitting at a table with twelve other people and everyone is speaking Italian. You don't speak Italian (and if you really do, then stretch the imagination a little harder and forget the fact). You listen to the babble around you and watch the wild gestures and expressive movements of the people passionately talking and it all seems charming though completely incomprehensible! You have barely any idea of what is going on. However, if you learn the language of Italian suddenly a fascinating world reveals itself, full of interesting stories, passion and excitement and, most importantly, understanding. It is the same for awakening your Witchiness. Learn the language of magick and the world becomes a magickal place! That seemingly elusive, ethereal otherworld of real magick can be a lot closer than you think – it is inside you, in your desires, hopes, fears and dreams. Open the door to that world inside you and watch the world around you shift and change and shape itself to please you and be everything you dreamed it could be.

Tips from the top

Here's a selection of general tips and ideas that can equip you to see obstacles as opportunities and trials as transformation.

Stick with it

The beauty of practicing the Craft, both as a solitary and as part of a Coven, is that the experience becomes more textured, complex and deeper, yet easier as you go along. Persevere through the teething stages. What was once an effort to remember and organize shifts to become intuitive. You "trust your gut" thus conjuring satisfying spiritual and magickal experiences effortlessly. It's as if you awaken an age-old sense of what it is to be human, the purest expression of the extraordinary life-force of this universe. Know that not even the smallest magickal act is wasted; they all contribute to the divine tapestry of life that we design for ourselves.

I did it my way

Don't feel you have to abide by someone else's way of doing things as if they're standing over your shoulder judging you. This is a hang-up left over (for most of us) from growing up in a patriarchal religion with the wrathful and vengeful Father God sitting in the sky judging us. You will never feel and experience real, tangible magick if you seek it solely outside yourself.

Just chill

The more complicated and elaborate a ritual is doesn't necessarily mean it is more powerful. Be relaxed, confident and deeply connected emotionally, spiritually and physically with your intent. Then it will be more powerful and effective to simply light a red candle and make a wish for love than spend a whole day concocting an elaborate ritual only to perform it feeling un-centered and distracted from worrying about getting it right.

Also, don't expect that the "tingle of magick" feeling has to go on for hours for it to be a

Your world will be as magickal as you let it be

sign that your spell has worked and that magick is indeed real. Magickal transformation occurs outside the physical construct of linear time and you can indeed trust that you are experiencing infinite potential the moment a shiver goes up your spine, or you feel different as the spell is cast or the ritual evoked.

I've said it before and I'll say it again

The only thing you need to believe in is yourself – trust your inner voice, trust your methods, trust your choices. You are a Witch, and that is enough.

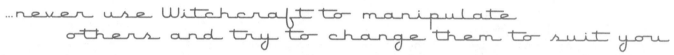
...never use Witchcraft to manipulate others and try to change them to suit you

And remember...

There are three laws in Witchcraft:

1. Do what you will but hurt none
2. Do what you will but do not interfere with another's free will
3. As you send out so returns three fold.

Pretty simple hey? Well perhaps on face value but dig a little deeper and there is important wisdom expressed here across the three laws. Always remember that you are responsible for your actions – magickal and practical. Know that it is a far greater expression of powerful Witchcraft to help and heal than it is to harm and bother. A good way to understand this is to consider, how hard is it to fire a gun? How hard is it to have the skill and knowledge to heal the person hit by the bullet? Clearly it is a greater show of power to heal. Also you must respect that everyone is on their own journey in life – even if it is one that you do not agree with or would not follow yourself – never use Witchcraft to manipulate others and try to change them to suit you – for good or otherwise.

A few of my favorite spells ...

The following spells are a selection of those I created for the listeners of my radio show and includes both the original queries and my replies, as well as some general magickal advice I gave out over the air and some spells I have created for various people in private consultation.

I'm always broke but I desperately want to buy a car next year. Can you give me a spell for bringing money my way?

The first thing you need to do is stop saying, "I'm always broke," and start saying, "I always have the money I need to do what I want to do." Every morning anoint a green candle with some almond oil, light it, focus on the flame and repeat this affirmation three times. Snuff the flame – don't blow the magick away! Start believing in every fiber of your being that prosperity is your rightful state – magick works with your powerful will.

Seeds represent prosperity and can be used to charm your money situation. Wrap some alfalfa seeds in green cloth and carry them in your pocket for a week. Every time you place your hand in your pocket say, "money comes, money grows." At the end of the week, plant and nurture the seeds, continuing to say, "money comes, money grows." As the plants prosper, so will your fortune. When the plants are fully grown, make a lovely salad of alfalfa, parsley, lush red tomatoes and balsamic vinegar – eat it slowly, savoring every mouthful and taking the power of your spell within. You will soon have more money than you need. Make sure you give some to charity to honor the bounty of the Universe!

Here is another spell for banishing poverty. Perform this spell on a Wednesday.

You will need:
- A black candle and a green candle, with holders;
- Dried mint;
- Salt;
- A knife or something similar for carving into the wax;
- Nag champa or sandalwood incense for purity.

Cut into the bottom of the black candle to expose the wick. Carve into the candle the words, "poverty" and "fear." Carve into the green candle the words, "wealth" and "joy."

Sprinkle a circle of salt, placing the black candle in the holder upside down and the green candle upright. Sprinkle the mint around the base of the green candle. Light both candles, being aware that the inverted black candle is draining away and banishing poverty and the green candle is attracting wealth.

Say the following charm:

> "The Power of sacred fire is great;"
> "Bound to the flame I control my fate."

Then focus on seeing yourself wealthy and successful, and say three times:

> "I banish fear and poverty;"
> "I welcome growth and money."

Seal the spell by saying: "So Mote it be." Leave the candles to burn – if you have to go out, snuff them and relight until both are completely burned down. The spell is complete.

other and the good energy in the house. Anyway, she broke up with him (thank god) and now we're repairing the damage. We'd like a spell that the three of us can do together to cleanse the house of his negative energy and strengthen our relationship.

The power of three is great! You can clear the air and start afresh by sprinkling a circle of salt large enough for you all to sit within. Burn purifying incense of white sage or sandalwood. Each of you hold a white candle. In the center, have a lit black candle representing the murky energy. Say as one:

> "By the power of three, we release negativity. By the power of fire we realize out desire. In the name of all good, things be now as they should"

Together light your white candles from the black and snuff its flame. Holding the candles, speak openly about what you like and treasure about each other. Know that you are healing the past for a bright future and happy home together.

After the ritual, vacuum up the salt and make a little altar on the kitchen table (the heart of the home) with the white candles (throw out the black one), three eggs (for new beginnings) and fresh flowers (new energies). Keep this altar in place for one week and then bury the eggs – they will have absorbed any final lingering "nasties." Burn basil essential oil in an oil burner to ensure a harmonious home and fill the rooms with fresh flowers and growing plants for happiness.

Burn basil essential oil in an oil burner to ensure a harmonious home

I live with two other women, one of my roommates recently had a boyfriend who turned all our lives upside-down and seriously strained the relationship we have with each

I once lived in a house and had a lot of experience with ghosts – not always unpleasant, mind you! Still some of the spirits just passing through weren't the nice ones! I have moved recently and wondering if there is anything that I can do to protect my new home from spirits cruising on by?

Place a white candle anointed with jasmine oil (if the flowers are blooming, make a blessing wreath of them around each candle) in each room of the house and burn for at least an hour a day. This not only gives psychic protection, but looks and smells divine!

If you think your house already has some unwanted spirits and ghosts you can "loosen" their grip on your home by striking a gong or bell which has a clear resonating sound, three times at the stroke of midnight for seven nights. As the tone of each ring fades away to silence, clearly say: "Farewell to the past that dwells here – be gone spirits of the dead – may you find rest in another space. This home is now one of peace and grace." If you like you can change these words to your own – it's important that you feel emotionally connected to this statement of release for it to be fuelled with magickal intent.

Remember spirits are generally not malicious or harmful, just perhaps confused and lost. Often they need your interaction to exist, so the best way to make them go away is just to ignore them!

I am hoping you can help me. I would like to request a spell to help me feel happier about my appearance – especially my height. Please don't think that I am being vain or anything – it's just that I am really below average and it is proving a bit of a handicap in my everyday life and my confidence.

To be honest I can't suggest a spell that is guaranteed to help you grow taller. I don't think you're being vain. I think your desire to be taller is perfectly valid but you need to make peace with this straight away. Don't be hard on yourself – it will only make you feel more mis-

erable! I presume you have talked to doctors about possible ways for you to grow taller, especially nutritional ideas – you don't mention your age, but if you are in your teens, there is a good chance you'll hit a late growth spurt.

I can, though, give you a terrific spell that will help you feel better about yourself inside and out, regardless of whether your are ten or three feet tall! Really powerful transformational magick is more about changing consciousness rather than actually directly manipulating the physical realm. But although "magick is the art of changing consciousness at will," its results do flow onto the physical plane and affect it. This spell will work for anyone who is feeling that their outward appearance does not adequately represent the divine person within!

The "I Feel Unreal!" Spell

You will need:
• a large white feather (the element of air);
• your favorite perfume in an atomizer bottle (if you don't have one, choose a scent that that is fruity, floral and uplifting – the company Jurlique makes beautiful organic non-chemical perfumes);
• a silver candle (the element of fire);
• a pin.

With the pin, carve your name into the candle, lick your thumb and trace over your carving with your spit to seal your personal energy into the candle and make it your own.

Light the candle and stare at the flame for a few moments, taking some deep breaths and focusing on feeling calm and centered. When you are ready, pick up the feather and spray it with one blast of the perfume and then hold it towards the flame as you say:

> "Feather of air transform me;
> "Free me from cares that hold me
> "Back from that which I can be."

Stroke your body from feet to head with the feather – enjoy the beautiful scent of the perfume and be aware that the feather is a symbol of transformation and freedom from obstacles and limiting ways of thinking.

When you have finished place the feather in front of the candle and spray one short burst of perfume through the flame – being ultra careful that the alcohol doesn't ignite in a blast! As you do this say:

> "By fire I am pure;
> "By air I am transformed;
> "Inside my heart I now am tall."

Snuff the flame (don't blow it out – you blow away the magick) and leave the perfume, feather and candle standing together. Perform this spell every morning upon waking, and once you've done it don't think about it again. Just know that inside you are tall and you will project a different presence – bewitching people (and yourself) so that no one will think of you as short again and you won't feel inconvenienced anymore.

I keep dreaming of a man – every night he appears in my dreams and we always end up dancing and kissing. Sometimes when I've woken up I feel like I've met him in reality. I've dubbed him "Dream Boy" since in my dreams he never seems to have a name. I was hoping you might know a spell that will get him to come to me if he really does exist?

If you are dreaming of him regularly, he is probably on his way to you already! To speed up the process, create the following amulet and keep it on you at all times to help him find you during waking hours as well as during sleep.

You will need:
- a handful of dried mugwort (herb aligned with the energy of dreams);

- a piece of smoky quartz crystal (for male energy);
- a piece of rose quartz crystal (for female energy);
- a red pouch of natural fabric (cotton, silk, etc.);
- a white candle.

Place the herb and crystals into the pouch and seal it closed. Each night before sleep, light the white candle, and holding the pouch in both hands gaze at the flame as you say three times:

> "By the light of the Moon, come to me;
> "By the light of the Sun, know me."

Snuff the candle flame and place the amulet under your pillow. Upon waking, keep it with you at all times to help him find you beyond the land of dreams.

I am lonely and need to attract the attention of a companion – a boyfriend or better yet a husband! Can you help me?

A morning ritual affirming your attractiveness with some Witchy ammunition in the way of herbs and oils will definitely assist. Bathe every morning, washing yourself with a soft cloth in the following bath salts and meditating as you do on your unique personal beauty, and men will start falling at your feet!

Love Attracting Bath Salts

You will need:
- a quarter pound of Epsom salts (from the drugstore);
- three drops of rose oil;
- two drops of geranium oil;
- four drops (or more) of green vegetable food coloring (to tint the salts the pure color of your heart chakra).

Concentrate on what is not working for you in your career and write down the problems on the black paper.

Note: if you don't have a bath, disperse the salts in a basin and have a sponge bath.

In a glass bowl, stir the above with a metal spoon in a sunwise (clockwise direction in the Northern Hemisphere; anticlockwise south of the Equator) as you repeat this charm over and over until all the ingredients are thoroughly blended:

> "I weave a spell of Witchery
> "So all men are bewitched by me."

Store the salts in a glass jar and use a cup in the bath or half a cup in the basin.

I am feeling very frustrated in my career and need to do a spell to feel motivated and to help me advance.

This spell will help to keep your career on track!

You will need:
- a piece of black paper;
- a piece of green paper;
- a lead pencil;
- an eraser;
- a healthy pot plant.

Imagine a sphere of white light around you to help you focus your energies. Concentrate on what is not working for you in your career and write down the problems on the black paper. Now take the rubber and slowly erase the list as you say:

> "I release my frustrations;
> "I welcome new situations"

Fold the paper with the rubber shavings inside and throw away.

Now on the green paper write what *is* working and what you would like to see develop. Fold this paper and stand it in the pot plant as you say:

> "Magick grows both fast and well;
> "Child of Earth, bless my spell."

Nourish the plant, watering it and tending to it carefully. As the plant grows and flourishes, so shall your career.

I feel tired and listless. I am not ill – I just feel like the joy has gone out of my life for no particular reason. I think I am just bored and need to experience something new.

Here's something a bit different for you! Try this Bohemian Health Charm.

You will need:
- Flax seeds (buy them from a health food store);
- four white candles.

Early Witches in Northern Europe would send their children to dance in fields of flax to encourage good health and happiness. As the full moon rises, place the candles at the four directions of the compass (north, south, east and west). Sprinkle a large circle of flax seed within. Light the candles and put on your favorite music and dance! For maximum magickal potential, do this ritual skyclad in the light of the full moon and let your skin and spirit absorb its magickal luminescence. You will soon start to feel more enthusiastic about life – and if nothing else, performing the above ritual will definitely put a smile on your face!

My friends think I'm lucky but I don't know

what to do! I am in love with two guys and they love me, but I have to choose between them! I have been juggling them but it is just too crazy. I love them both but for different reasons. How do I choose?

You can use flowers to help decide matters of love (or choose between anything really!) as they are a sacred and natural expression of the beauty of the Goddess and their advice can be trusted.

Roses would be best but any flower that is in bud can be used. Tie a small white ribbon around the stem of one bud and a small blue one around the other. Then make yourself known to the plant by saying:

> "I respectfully ask, oh flower divine,
> "To reveal a solution for this dilemma of mine."

Pour an offering of spring water on its roots and name one bud after your first lover (or your first choice) and the second bud after the other.

Whichever flower blooms fully first shall be the man (or best choice) for you.

You need to do this spell using only one species of plant as some bloom faster than others, but rather than tying ribbons you could choose two plants of the same species whose flowers are different colors. Decide which color will represent which person or choice.

Lately I have been really sick with the flu and I can't seem to shake off the bug. Can you recommend a spell for good health?

Here's a good health ritual that can be done regularly to avoid getting sick in the first place and to clear up a lingering illness. I hope you have been to the doctor and had a complete check up – you may have a condi-tion that requires medical treatment.

You will need:
- A blue candle (for healing);
- A piece of turquoise (for protection and good health);
- Lavender oil;
- A pin.

With the pin carve your name into one side of the candle and the words "health and happi-ness" into the other side. Lick your thumb and trace over your name and the words with your spit to seal your energy into the candle.

Now anoint the candle with some lavender oil and light it. Hold the turquoise and gaze at the flame as you say this charm:

> "I cast out ill and take my fill
> "Of health and harmony,
> "Strength and skill;
> "The blessings of fire I call to me
> "To charge and empower my energy."

Snuff the flame and keep the turquoise next to the candle. Repeat this ritual as often as you like by resealing the carvings with your spit and lavender oil, lighting the candle and saying the charm again.

Here is another charm that can help get you back on your way to good health.

You will need:
- Eucalyptus or tea tree oil;
- A blue cord long enough to go around your wrist or ankle three times.

Tie a knot in the cord, dab it with some oil and say, "Illness be gone, body be strong!"

Tie another knot further along the cord, dab with oil and say again, "Illness be gone, body be strong!"

Do this three more times and then tie the

cord around your wrist or ankle as you say the Witches' binding charm: "So Mote It Be!"

Wear the cord, reapplying the oil every morning and repeating the charm. Your symptoms will soon abate. And please see your doctor. Magick works but you have to take practical action too for the best results!

Do you know any magic to help someone get through a whole heap of dental work?

Coca (from which cocaine is made) is considered a sacred funeral herb in South America. Some tribes will bury parcels of coca with their loved dead ones. They believe this will please the spirits and make entry to the next world easier

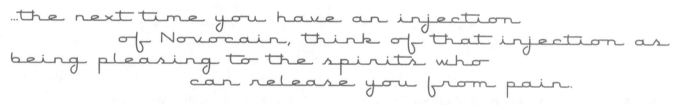

...the next time you have an injection of Novocain, think of that injection as being pleasing to the spirits who can release you from pain.

In modern times, seeing as it's unlikely anyone would bury coca in the western world, they'd probably snort it (unfortunately, since it's not only illegal – it's lousy for you). So if you want to ask for blessings of the Gods whilst having dental work, the next time you have an injection of Novocain, think of that injection as being pleasing to the spirits who can release you from pain – and they will stop it from returning.

A Witchy Dental gargle you can make to clean the mouth and numb it is as follows:

- Two drops of clove oil in half a cup of warm spring water;
- Stir in half a teaspoon of salt.

Gargle well, swishing around mouth – the salt will clean and the cloves will numb. And ask for the pain relieving blessings of the Coca Gods whilst you're at it!

What's a good Witchy solution to the sort of dweeb at your office who harasses you and distracts you from your work for no reason other than to amuse themselves?

If there is someone bothering you, you can rub them out. And never do a day in jail! As they walk towards you, imagine a giant eraser deleting them – or maybe see them disappearing under a flood of liquid paper. When they are gone say: "For the good of all with harm to none."

Visualization is the key to a lot of magick, so hold your vision and focus. Be aware that you're working with the power of your will to remove those things from your life that no longer serve you or that irritate you. You will find that gradually the person will stop bothering you and approaching you – and also that you will feel less irritated if you have to be around them for any reason.

You can double up this spell by doing the "big freeze." Write the aforesaid dweeb's name on a piece of paper, put it in an ice tray, pour water over it and freeze in the freezer.

If you have to associate with the person and it's maybe just one aspect of their behavior that bugs you, next to their name write that aspect and freeze that to be more specific.

Life's getting way too stressful lately! How can I deal with frustrations like getting caught in traffic or missing my deadlines, preferably without exploding?

Here's a spell to help calm down and allow your perspective of time to shift so that there is always plenty for everything you need to do.

You will need:
- A wind up clock (symbolizing time);
- A yellow candle (symbolizing intellect and rationality);
- Lavender incense (symbolizing calmness).

By the light of the yellow candle inhale the incense and sit quietly. Slowly wind the clock hands backwards as you intone:

> "There is time for everything to be
> "In its place and orderly;
> "I free my space in good grace;
> "Everything has its time and place."

Repeat this over and over as you keep winding the clock back.

Leave the candle and the clock by the bed and repeat this ritual every night for a week.

Okay, a tricky one: how do I give up smoking?

Thankfully countless people are now realizing that this disgusting habit is out of style and are giving up Earth-destroying cancer sticks. This spell will help you stop for good. It's best performed during the waning moon (i.e., the fourteen days after the full Moon).

has electromagnetic properties that will magnify the intent of your spell.

Carve the bottom of the candle to expose the wick and place it upside down in the stand. Every night before you go to bed, light the candle and by its light slowly push one of the cigarettes into the dirt until it is covered. As you do this say:

> "I banish you from my life;
> "My will is strong, free from strife;
> "My resolve is firm, my courage great;
> ."No longer do you rule my fate."

Then snuff the candle flame. Do this every night until the pack of cigarettes is empty, and then throw the whole lot in the trash and walk away without looking back.

Be aware that the objects you are using are like magnets to draw your intent to you, and the incantation is a power tool to make your subconscious shift into a new thought process – that is, no more smoking.

Is seeing a rainbow really likely to bring good luck?

Absolutely! Rainbows carry every color in the spectrum and are charged with visible heal-

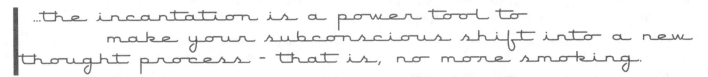
...the incantation is a power tool to make your subconscious shift into a new thought process - that is, no more smoking.

You will need:
- Your half-finished packet of cigarettes (at least thirteen left);
- A pot of dirt;
- three clear quartz crystals;
- a black candle and a stand;
- a candle snuffer (unless you want to risk burning your fingers).

Stud the earth with the quartz crystals – it

ing and transformative powers. They are the fusion of two of the most transformative elements, water and fire, and are visually awe-inspiring also.

Albertus Magnus in his *Book of Secrets* (as reported in Paul Beyerl's *Herbal Magick*) reveals this magickal formula for conjuring rainbows – and thunder storms for that matter! Mix the ashes of a cremated snake with dried sage and throw into the air as you call on a rainbow and one should appear. (Maybe a Rainbow Serpent of Australian Aboriginal spiritual lore will grace your presence!)

If you see a rainbow in its full arc, make a wish and it will surely be granted. If it fades to a partial arc as you do this, however, your wish will be shown to be misguided or misplaced.

Rainbow blessings can enter your life by surrounding yourself with the seven colors of the light spectrum: red, orange, yellow, green, blue, indigo and violet. So go wild decorating your bedroom or your school or office space and let rainbow colors work their magick in your life!

How do I go about doing a spell for personal protection?

So many people out there need help – they may be refugees or victims of crime or friends who have hit hard times. Here is a simple ritual of love and protection for them.

Make an altar that features a picture of the person or people needing protection.

Anoint a purple or white candle for protection and energy assistance with one of the following herbal oils: Clary sage, frankincense, juniper, rue, rosemary, thyme and vervain. If you don't have the extracted herbal oils, infuse some of the fresh herb in olive oil for at least a week in a dark place, strain and use.

Light the candle, gaze at the photo and ask the Goddess to help and bless the people you feel need assistance and protection.

There was recently a Smart Sex Week, a government initiative to encourage safe sex amongst young people, which seemed a pretty smart idea. How would a Witch go

about adding to that energy?

Here's a ritual that does precisely that, and I can just about bet anyone doing it will enjoy it.

You will need:
- Pink, strawberry-flavored condoms for love and fun;
- Massage oil with ylang ylang and rose geranium essential oils – pure aphrodisiacs;
- Musk and patchouli incense for lust;
- Red and pink candles for love and passion;
- Pink tiger lily flowers or other opulent, pink, sweetly scented blooms;
- Vanilla bean ice-cream for happiness;
- White soft feathers.

Set up your space with candles and incense burning. Place the flowers in vases and scatter the feathers around so the area looks opulent and inviting.

Honor the God/Goddess within your lover by indulging them in sensual pleasures (all acts of love and pleasure are sacred to the Goddess) – tickle them with feathers, eat ice-cream off their skin, massage the warm oil into their body, maybe even drip some of the candle wax on them for extra excitement – and have fun using the condoms! The whole time focus on being aware that you are worshipping your lover and celebrating everything that is pure and holy about humanity – our divine sexuality!

I know this sounds a bit borderline ethically but is there any way to use magic to get someone to fall in love with you?

A bit borderline!?! Even if it weren't for the ethical issues, I'd still always say don't interfere with another's free will or your love spell is bound to backfire. Well, if you don't care, in the interests of "freedom of information" here's the sort of thing you have in mind. Be aware, though, this is not a karma-free spell by any stretch of the imagination.

First you need to scoop some soil from the footprint of your desired one. Sprinkle this around the base of a red candle anointed with your spit and some patchouli oil. Light the candle and focus on your desired one being with you. See the two of you and in each other's arms and beds.

When the vision is strong intone as many times as you like:

"Come to me – my will is great;
"Your new fate you can't escape."

Do this every night until the next full moon. S/he will be yours – but it probably won't be the blissful experience that you hope for! Spells like this can work, but usually make the person casting them wish they'd failed! You're way better off just trying to attract a suitable lover.

Here are a few smarter alternative spells concerned with inviting and maintaining real love.

Witches know that herbs are very powerful magical tools and fantastic aids to help sort out your love life.

Spells like this can work, but usually make the person casting them wish they'd failed!

- Pop a sprig of lavender into your bra to attract a lover.

- Dip a sprig of rosemary into your lover's wine and have him do the same to yours and your love will always flourish.

- Three pinches of cinnamon in your lover's morning coffee will ensure he performs well in bed that night!

- To ensure a lover is faithful, break a bay leaf in two, giving one half to him and keeping the other yourself.

- To ward off arguments in the home, grow a pot of basil in the kitchen.

Still more magickal lore

Magick in the kitchen

These items are found easily in most kitchens and used everyday but are very magickal too.

Camphor: We put it in cupboards and drawers to keep away moths, but it is very magickal too. It is a wonderful cleansing herb to rid spaces of negative energies and unwanted, unhappy energies.

Burn some camphor on a charcoal block in each room with the windows closed. When it has burned, allow the smoke to escape by opening the windows, taking the negativity with it.

You can also burn camphor when you're doing Tarot reading or other forms of divination, and it can help in achieving prophetic dreams. Put a few drops of the oil on a hankie and place next to your pillow.

Cedar: again good for keeping clothes and objects fresh whilst in storage. It can be burned as an incense in a house where a newborn baby sleeps to bless it and bestow on it good fortune. You can also purposefully breathe in the smoke to create a profound and prophetic inner state or consciousness.

And you can keep a small piece of cedar in

your wallet to "keep the moths away" and attract money.

Potato: It is a pretty everyday vegetable – but so much more! For example, a potato can be stored for a long time, yet when it is cut into pieces is capable of regenerating a new plant. In the days when people lived closer to the land, the person who dug up the final potato during the last harvest, was called "Old Potato Woman" and was considered lucky. In Peru, the goddess of the potato is "The Potato Mother" known as "Axo-mama." So next time you are cutting up a potato give thanks to Axo-mama and ask for her blessings of sustenance for another year.

Rice: If you want rice to grow well, do as the women in Sumatra do and let your hair hang loose down your back as you plant it, and it will grow thick and well! Most of you won't be growing rice, but honor the custom by eating rice with your hair hanging loose and offering a portion to the Goddess. If you are working with a group such as a Coven, share rice together to affirm your magickal bond.

Rice represents fruitfulness, fertility and prosperity – hence showering newlyweds with it.

Gay and lesbian magick

Gays and lesbians have special magickal totems.

One of the most sacred flowers for homosexual men is the hyacinth. The God Apollo – also sacred to gay men – loved young boys and fell in love with a young Spartan prince named Hyacinthus. One day they were both throwing discus in the gymnasium, when the discus hit a stone, rebounded and struck Hyacinthus' head, killing him. Apollo was distraught and turned Hyacinthus' body into a flower to make him immortal. The oil of the flower anointed to the skin or the petals dried and carried on the person will affirm the masculinity of gay men and give them the special protection of Apollo.

Cypress is also sacred to gay men – another of Apollo's lovers, Cyparissus, was playing with his stag and accidentally killed it with a spear. Broken-hearted he asked Apollo to kill him so he could be with his stag. Apollo was touched but couldn't bear to lose him forever and so turned him into a cypress tree. Cypress represents love transcending difficulty, torment and death. It can be burned as incense, planted at the door of a house to bless its inhabitants, and its oil can be worn on the person.

The sacred flower for lesbians is the rose. It is sacred to Aphrodite, Goddess of love and beauty. Sappho, the legendary lesbian poet of ancient Greece called the rose "Queen of the Flowers." Lesbians making a commitment to a partnership can exchange emerald rings anointed with rose oil to ensure that their union is blessed by love and beauty. Another ritual can be pricking each other's thumbs with a rose thorn, mixing a drop of each person's blood in wine and drinking to declare their love for each other in the eyes of the Goddess. Roses of all colors are sacred to lesbians – red for lust, pink for love, white for fidelity and health, yellow for wisdom.

Full Moon ritual

During the full Moon the Earth is poised between the Moon and the Sun and is bathed in psychic energy. It is a very sacred and potent

The sacred flower for lesbians is the rose. It is sacred to Aphrodite, Goddess of love and beauty.

time for Witches to recharge their powers.

Here is a form of full Moon meditation. Light a silver candle and using an oil burner, infuse a few drops of chamomile oil (or geranium, or jasmine). Dress in something magickal and white or work skyclad. Using your fingers or a feather, douse your meditation area in "moon water" (to make this, soak some mandrake root in spring water and leave it under the light of the waxing moon for the three nights leading up to the full, never allowing the sun's direct rays to fall upon it).

Lie down and place cucumber peel upon your eyelids (for psychic vision). Call on the Moon Goddess:

> "Selene, Selene, show me in dreams
> What your eyes see, Selene, Selene."

Selene, maiden Goddess of the Moon will appear and take you on a journey – make note of all you see and learn in your Book of Shadows. Stay out in the night as long as you like "moon baking."

Herbs, flowers and vegetables sacred to the Moon

The following are aligned to the moon and can nurture your intuition by eating them, wearing their scent or carrying them in an amulet bag.

- Herbs: Clary sage, star anise, coriander, ginger.
- Flowers: Poppy, white rose, gardenia, jasmine, geranium, iris.
- Foods: cabbage, cucumber, pumpkin.

Blessing for newborns and young children

Decorate the cot or bed with daisies. The night before the ritual, sprinkle a circle of flax seed around the baby's sleeping area to protect and begin the blessing.

Bathe the baby in a warm bath that has a piece of elderwood in it (or place a handful of elderflower blossoms in a muslin bag and float in the water). Burn incense that is made of one part cedar, one part lavender, and half a part rosemary. Grind this with a mortar and pestle and burn on a charcoal disc or just throw handfuls of the mixture on an open fire.

Set up a small altar with a crystal or glass bowl of spring water in which a piece of rose quartz crystal has been placed. Also place on the altar a white candle in which the name of your baby has been carved and traced over with some lavender oil.

Hold the baby in your arms and say: "[Name], you are held in the embrace of the Lady and Lord. May your life be a divine work of art, and all the blessings of the Universe bestowed upon you."

Sprinkle a little of the spring water on her head as you say: "Blessed is [Name] by sacred Water and Earth."

COLORS
- Red: passion, love, willpower
- Pink: friendship, beauty, peace and harmony
- Blue: healing, communication and truth
- Yellow: clarity of thought and brain power
- Orange: creativity, legal matters and pride
- Green: prosperity, fertility, employment and good luck
- Purple: spiritual insight, inspiration, power and success
- Black: to prevent harm or to get rid of something
- White: cleansing, protection and can also take the place of any color except black.

Fan a little of the incense smoke over her as you say: "Blessed is [Name] by sacred Fire and Air."

Seal the blessing with the Witches' sacred words: "So Mote It Be."

Now have a celebratory party to honor your child's blessing.

Plant a patch of Iris on the day of your baby blessing ceremony. It can be done as a part of the rite and as the flowers grow so will your child's well-being and happiness. Feel free to elaborate on the above and include words and actions that are particularly meaningful to you. As a part of the ceremony you might like to write a letter to your child expressing your love, hopes and dreams for her. Seal it with wax and place it in a safe chamber until the child's sixteenth birthday, upon which can you have another "Rites of Maturing" blessing ceremony, when the child can break the seal, open the letter and read.

More tips for happy babies

- Hang a mulberry leaf above your baby's cot to protect it.
- Adding half a cup of chamomile tea to a baby's milk, with a little honey to sweeten it, will soothe the baby. (Check with your doctor first.)
- The juice of the milkweed herb (extracted by pressing the leaves and stem) can be anointed on the baby's third eye (in the center of the forehead) upon waking, to enhance imagination and creativity.
- Add parsley to the baby's bathwater for protection.

An un-hexing spell

You will need:
- A Handful of Dirt from your back yard;
- A Handful of Dirt from the mountains;
- A Handful of sand from the ocean (all three being natural places of great power);
- A cup of seawater (for purification);
- Sixteen small stones (to absorb negativity);
- Big piece of red cloth (for protection);
- Cigar;
- Rum (both the cigar and rum are sacred to the Orishas, the Voodoo Gods on whom you are calling to assist you);
- White candle in large glass jar (purity).

Place the sixteen stones in a large bowl. Take a mouthful of rum and spray it over the stones three times. Light the cigar and blow smoke over the stones three times (you have now invoked the power of the Orishas). Pour the seawater over the stones. Light a white candle and leave burning over night.

In the morning drain the fluid from the bowl onto the earth. Place the stones on the red cloth with the backyard dirt, mountain dirt and sand and a lock of your hair. Tie up the bundle and bury it under your front step with a teaspoon of honey. You will now be protected from hexes and any current ones are banished.

Just to be on the very safe side, also bathe in a warm bath with three handfuls of fresh basil leaves and three handfuls of fresh rose petals floating on the water – these will further purify and protect you.

Crystals

Witches believe nature to be sacred and that all things of the natural world have a magickal power that can be directly experienced by us because we are also born of this world. Crystals are packed with "Earth power" – they are born of the Earth and most actually grow within it until they are disturbed or moved by a collector. Witches believe various crystals are aligned to certain qualities and actions and these abilities can be called upon according to the Witch's will. So we wear them in ceremonial jewelry, use them for healings by placing them on the body and we store them with our herbs and other objects we use for ritual and spellcasting.

In spellcasting a Witch can charge her crystals with her intent to bless the spell and make it more effective.

Top five crystals for the Witch

5. Turquoise (protection and healing)
Native Americans believe that turquoise protects against snakebite and gives the ability to stand amongst wild animals without being harmed. It is a very powerful healing stone, either carried in an amulet bag, worn as jewelry or placed on the chakra points to clear negative energy.

4. Moonstone (especially good for women)
Moonstone strengthens the will, calms the mind, brings a sense of inner security and encourages happiness – great for those PMT blues! Priestesses wear moonstone as their sacred stone, and as it becomes attuned to the wearer's energy it changes tint.

3. Bloodstone (strength and bravery)
Wearing bloodstone encourages fame and recognition for your efforts. It also supports a long life. Bloodstone has been used as a talisman for soldiers and warriors. Expectant mothers can also wear bloodstone on their left arms until labor to prevent miscarriage, and then swap to their right arms for an easy delivery.

2. Clear Quartz (multi-purpose)
Clear quartz can take the place of any crystal if you charge it (hold in your hand and project your energy into it) and imprint your intent into it. It has piezoelectric qualities, which means it can convert physical energy into electrical energy and vice versa. Keep your quartz out of direct sunlight when using it magickally. Smoky quartz is aligned to men, much as moonstone if aligned to women. The best crystal balls are made of clear quartz.

1. Amethyst (psychic power)
A member of the quartz family, amethyst is the ultimate psychic stimulator – I always keep some on my altar. It brings peace of mind and can increase beauty and keep love alive. Place over the third eye when meditating as it assists to connect you with the Universal soul.

The all-purpose candle spell

An adept Witch will be a wiz at candle magick. It is very effective as it works with the element of fire, which brings swift action. All you need is a candle in an appropriate color for your desire, some essential oil that corresponds with your goal, a sharp pin or knife, and a lighter or matches.

OILS:
- Basil: harmony and communication
- Bergamot: prosperity
- Cinnamon: better sex
- Ginger: courage and strength
- Lavender: Healing, love, anti-depression
- Lemon: purification
- Mandarin: happiness
- Peppermint: luck and success
- Patchouli: love (especially good for attracting lovers)
- Sandalwood: spirituality and protection
- Ylang Ylang: aphrodisiac and beauty

Choose your candle and oil. For example, if you have trouble remembering your boyfriend's birthday, you may want to do a spell for a better memory, which means you'd choose a yellow candle and rosemary oil. Now take a few deep breaths focusing on your desire.

When you are ready imagine a sphere of white light around you giving you a pure and powerful space to work magick within. With the knife or pin, carve your name into one side of the candle and your goal into the other. In this case your goal would be "Better Memory." Now lick your thumb and trace it over your name to make the candle your own. Take a couple of drops of the oil and rub it well into your goal, concentrating on achieving your desired outcome. Next light the candle and gaze on the flame as you picture success. Spend at least five minutes doing this. When you are finished, snuff the flame. Relight the candle every day for at least seven days to really pack a magickal punch. Each time rub a little more oil into the candle to keep charging it up! You will have results within seven days.

Street Magick is urban magick. It can be used anywhere, by anyone with the will and determination to make it their own. Based on the techniques of Wicca, Ceremonial Magick and the Western Mystery Traditions, Street Magick also borrows cheerfully from martial arts, chi kung, healing disciplines and whole body movement methods. It is, however, free from the need to join a group, club, magickal order or Coven, though you may, of course, do those things if it gives you pleasure to do so.

My partner, Raven, and I have been teaching classes in Street Magicks for ten years now. Sometimes accompanied by other teachers, but more often nowadays as a teaching team of two, we lead intensive workshops in Seattle on the various attitudes, stances and disciplines of this hybrid system. Nowadays, we're engaged in working on a website which will have sound and video clips, in order to make it more widely available. Details about that will be announced at www.shadow-playzine.com soon.

We came to this place with the understanding that the study of magick is often made too obscure and secret, and for no good reason. We've studied a bunch of different traditions along the way and each one has one or two really cool tricks in their training materials. It seemed a good idea, without breaking any oaths, to share those tricks for people who

street, in a park, or off in the woods. While there's a lot of great mythology and some really fine stories about the origins of magickal traditions, we wanted to see what was useful for basic training of the innate skills and abilities of a range of people. It also struck us as a fun idea to concentrate on the things we do every day to stretch our psychic senses.

Our classes move through the following areas. These are the basis of things we do every day.

Energy of the body
Visualization
Sound Magick
Movement
Magickal Tools
Spells, Charms and Magickal Arts
Ritual Construction

In working with the energy body, we focus on identifying what works best for each individual. Do you feel energy, sense it, hear it, smell it, taste it? Where are the boundaries of your senses and how do you know where you end and the world begins. Raven says that there are two sources of energy: energy from within and energy from without. The first, energy from within, is the place we start, especially with "centering" your physical, emotional, intellectual and psychic senses to a single point.

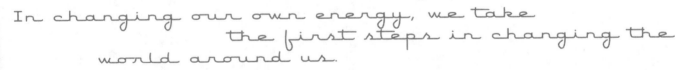

In changing our own energy, we take the first steps in changing the world around us.

like that kind of thing. Practical information and tools for living a magickal life every day, in every place we walk, whether that's on the

So why start with energy of the body? We all have a body. Because we believe that we are spirit, a large amount of this energy is manifest in a physical form. If you want to think that each of us is an incredible machine that generates energy on its own, that's all good too. Our experience tells us that beginning to sense and manipulate the energy of our body is the easiest and most fundamental of energy work. In changing our own energy, we take the first steps in changing the world around us.

Centering

First you need to focus your attention and awareness, to center your energy to a single point within the body. Think of the body as a circle with the one-point as the center of that circle, just below your navel, at the top of your hip girdle. This is the center of gravity, the center of hara, prana, or chi, to use terms from the East.

All movement expands and contracts in a balanced way around this center. Likewise, our energy expands and contracts around this point.

Breathe into the one-point, your center, and feel how breathing energizes your center. Dancers, martial artists, skateboard riders, surfers and athletes all work with the way their bodies move around this center.

Finding your center

Place your hands in a triangle facing downwards, with your thumbs resting on your navel. Within this triangle is your physical reference point for your center, though you need to imagine the triangle goes inwards like a pyramid, rather than just existing on the surface of your skin. Think of your center as three fingers down from your navel and three fingers inside the body. Breathe and concentrate on this place.

Once you have found this spot, stand with your feet shoulder-width apart, knees slightly bent, and head upright (you might want to look in a mirror to check your stance and that's okay for the first few times).

Breathe deeply and evenly into your center.

You should feel your hands move a little as you breathe.

Let your thoughts slow to stillness as you feel the energy deep within.

Move your feelings to your center, feeling wholeness deep within.

Be aware of how it is to be centered in mind, spirit and emotions.

Take three deep breaths to feel the energy of your center. And relax.

Journal

Write your impressions of magickal exercises, thoughts and feelings in your journal. Did you feel a tingling in any part of your body when you were centered? An inner sound? A sensation that let you know you were centered? Record those thoughts now.

It's fun to keep a journal and see how much progress you've made. In doing Street Magick, journal entries remind us later of times when we needed to center. We do it at concerts, at work, when we're walking down the street and at night, when we come home from a day in the world. It's a way of connecting with our innermost thoughts.

Anchoring

We exist in relation to the rest of the universe. While every man and every woman is a star, as Crowley put it, we are not isolated lights. To use the metaphor of balancing and centering, it's occasionally necessary to make a connection to a larger collection of energy to give you something to brace yourself against. Creating dynamic equilibrium between our center and another thing helps us to be relatively stable.

If we imagine being in a boat that has an anchor, we can use an anchor to keep the boat relatively stable. However, you need to tie the anchor to the boat, to have a connection. Making an anchor to your center is like that; you center first and then connect the anchor (via energy) to your center.

How to anchor

Center to the one-point. Make a connection with an object that is bigger than you and in your direct vision. Make sure it is something with more energetic complexity or more mass or stability than you. Examples are a mailbox bolted to the concrete, a light pole, a safe, a car, a big desk or maybe a refrigerator. Later, you'll connect and anchor to energized talismans and other complex magickal

runes, sigils, talismans and tools. Anchoring is where you reach out from your center and make a connection to stabilize your center. This keeps you from being distracted or knocked off balance emotionally.

Making an earth connection

Making a connection to the earth is useful if you want to balance too much air energy (earth and air are elements with opposite qualities).

Please be careful about using the earth as a place to dump your toxic waste energy on the assumption that the earth will take care of it all and transform it into good stuff. If you have negative energy, work on transforming it before disposing of it.

If you have excess nervous energy, or leftover energy from some creative, magickal or sexual energy work, you can store it in a talisman and it will be available to you later.

Making an earth connection is a way of making a relationship with Gaia, the spirit of earth, so it's good to remember that relationships involve a positive exchange of energies.

Balancing energies

When you are on the street, at work or socializing, or even at home, it's sometimes hard to keep your energies in balance. This makes it more difficult to stay focused and centered, or to keep your emotions stable. Fortunately, there are some easy ways to work with the elements to even things out and keep your energy field strong and flexible.

When you are on the street, at work or socializing, or even at home, it's sometimes hard to keep your energies in balance.

Balancing earth: If you have an excess of earth energy, you might feel weighed down, depressed, easily stuck in one way of thinking, or your home and finances might be stubbornly not working for you. A good way to balance this is to work with the opposite element – air.

Get outside into the air, go for a walk to get your body moving, light some incense in your house, get your bills paid and checkbook balanced, or lighten up with laughter, a good movie, socializing with friends. If you are doing a magickal working, calling on the winds or the element of air, breathing exercises and singing will balance too much earth.

Balancing air: If you have an excess of air energy, you might feel scattered, nervous, fidgety, easily startled, hypersensitive or unable to concentrate. If any of these sound like what is happening, you might try working with the opposite element – earth.

Physical exercise is good, as is gardening, organizing your work-spaces, vigorously cleaning your house, making things with your hands, craftwork, walking on the grass or going out into the woods. If you are doing a magickal working, making an earth connection and working with earth elementals is a good way to balance too much air.

Balancing fire: If you have an excess of fire energy, you might be easily angered, prone to arguments, too sexually charged and frustrated, or feel a need to constantly pace and move or be very restless. You can balance too much fire by concentrating on the element of water.

Take a long shower or bath, treat yourself to a spa or a massage, sooth your nerves by breathing, stretching, doing some tai chi or yoga to burn off the fire. Or you can turn on relaxing music to listen and rest. Concentrate on divination, making scented oils, relaxing with friends at home and letting the stresses (whatever they are) wash away for a while. Be gentle with your emotions and, if it is a waxing or full moon, concentrate on making a connection with the moon. Alternatively, take a trip to a nearby stream, waterfall or beach to hear, see and sense the power of water to soothe and balance you.

Balancing water: If you have an excess of water energy, you might be lost in dreams or fears of what might be, be feeling overly emotional and find it hard to find the courage to make decisions. You might be over-whelmed by feelings and find it difficult to be aware of your personal boundaries. A way to balance too much water is to work with fire.

Turn off the electric lights and light your house with candles. Sex magick workings, either solo work or with a friend or lover, can help balance too much water. It can help to dress up and go out to dance to loud music at a club or at home, to do belly dancing, martial arts or some kind of expressive creative work. You will want to generate energy, to move your body and muscles and distract yourself from being too inwardly focused. Think of something fun and exciting to do that is outwardly focused. If you are doing a magickal working, try making a connection with the sun, early in the morning or at midday.

Working with Street Magicks

These are places to start with Street Magicks. You then move on from these to concentrate on shielding, warding and protecting yourself from the random energies of strangers or the unwanted energies of co-workers and social acquaintances. There are lots of techniques for shielding, so I will not go into that here. In our classes, we then move on to the other senses – to visualization, sound and movement work and then to working with tools and ritual construction.

However, these are the basics, in working with our body, our breath, centering and being aware of balancing our energies so we can be stronger and more powerful in the world, on the street, and in our lives.

birds, bugs and spiritual growth
totem animals and the witch
Scaerie Faerie

"As the creeper that girdles the tree-trunk the Law runneth forward and back –
For the strength of the Pack is the Wolf, and the strength of the Wolf is the Pack ..."
~ The Jungle Book, Rudyard Kipling

The concept of totem animals is one rooted in Native American culture. Their Shamans, who see animals as symbols of the Great Spirit, hold the belief that an individual's life, temperament, soul, and purpose in this life may be reflected in totem animals, and their symbolism meanings to our species. In many Native tribes it is still common for youths on the threshold of maturity to make a solitary pilgrimage to areas far from human contact and observe the wildlife there in search of their totem.

own animal nature, and the Godlike status of nature itself. Think of the millions of phrases we use to describe human temperaments using the traits of animals, and of the astrology systems used across the world which classify people using animal symbols to tell us something about the people born under that sign. Call it what you will, the idea of totem animals is everywhere.

To the modern Witch, totem animals are astral companions for ritual and magic as well as self-understanding. You may wish to invoke the essence of a totem animal during a ritual or spellcasting if their nature is pertinent to the working. Some people have more than one totem (and with human nature and experience being as diverse as it is, this is likely to amount to a lot of people!) and find

> to the modern Witch, totem animals are astral companions for ritual and magic as well as self-understanding.

Now, although many of you reading this may not be of Native American descent (and I, for one, am about as Native American as a poodle), the use of totem animals still has a lot to offer to the busy, nine-to-five working, Westernized Witch. Throughout history and across the globe, people have turned to animals for inspiration, symbolism, and self-definition. Think of Richard the Lionheart using the symbol of the King of the Jungle to portray an image of power, strength and courage. Think of Robert the Bruce watching a tiny spider refusing to give up on constructing its web, and seeing a reflection of his own battle for the freedom of Scotland. Think of the animal-headed, human-bodied deities of Ancient Egypt, rife with symbolism of our

that they can associate each totem with an Elemental direction, may wish to use their totems to invoke the elements while casting a circle in place of other symbolic figures, such as Deities. I personally do have a totem for each Element – although I have to confess that I didn't recognize that for quite a while!

Given the association of many Deities with animals, you may wish to look at your totems in conjunction with Patron Deities or, in the case of people like myself who don't have Patron Deities, instead of them. You may use a totem as a symbol of a trait you would like to cultivate or accentuate in yourself, such as the aforementioned lion for confidence, or the monkey for ease in social situations –

although perhaps not formal ones! Among students and those who live to learn, the owl may prove a useful guide.

Don't think, though, that your totems must all be grand, impressive creatures. I have done a substantial amount of exploration, both in books and online, and it does seem that new-comers to the subject could be forgiven for thinking that their totem has to be something along the lines of the wolf, eagle, or bear. While these totems are common among Native Americans (after all, they used to be surrounded by them!), remember that we do have a whole world of animals out there, and they're not all mammals and birds, for that matter. There is no reason why the wood-louse couldn't be a totem – after all, they are resilient, stoical, and excellent team members. For someone with a love of languages and communication, perhaps the parrot is a more appropriate bird than the hawk, given that it can even learn to speak the language of another species. The humble goldfish actually has sharper vision than we do, and can see in the dark via thermal imaging. A good symbol for the clairvoyant, perhaps –especially if they're also a Piscean!

In this way, a totem animal may reflect one or more traits of the individual, although they may very well also do quite the opposite. I am an avowed vegetarian, and at the time of writing this have been for thirteen years, yet all five of my totems are obligate carnivores, some of them being pretty savage killers. Nature likes nothing better than to remind us of the need for balance!

So don't resist the more "mundane" (a very subjective word anyway) creatures should they present themselves to you as totems; they have just as much to offer. But how do you find your totem? Are there any animals which you have been surrounded by, and/or felt a kinship with for much or all of your life? Have you ever had a strange experience involving animals, such as being landed on by a flock of birds? Actually, I was once landed on by a flock of pigeons, but that may have had more to do with the birdseed I was carrying! These kind of things are the markers which can initiate some research into your totems – reading up on the animal's characteristics, physical traits and behavior can often unearth some eerily accurate correspondences.

So, what are my totems? I wanted to talk about them a little as they have given me a tremendous amount of support and inspiration, and they are also pretty good examples of how proficient totem animal energies are at selecting the right people! As I said previously, I've only recently come to recognize Elemental qualities in my totems, so I'll explain these, too.

the cat:

Probably my oldest totem; I was born into a house with a cat, and I still live surrounded by them. My closest friend and companion – my soulmate, even – is my cat Rosie, with whom I have had the privilege of sharing my life with since I was ten and she was a tiny kitten. Cats are generally loners by nature, but are certainly very loving and loyal to those who have proven themselves worthy. (If you're a dog person, go and ask a cat person for clarification on that one!) They seem to approach life with the idea of sharing the space of others, but not of begging for approval or playing the role of the servant; they can live quite happily if not everyone is in agreement with them. They are very intense, passionate creatures, as anyone who has seen the bliss on the face of a puss purring by the fire, or the fury and hatred in the eyes of a hissing, battling feline can testify. For this reason, I associate them with the raw, unpredictable Element of Fire.

the owl:

As I mentioned previously, this is a totem I

hold dear due to my lifelong love of learning and knowledge. We've all seen the image of the owl wearing a mortarboard (such as those seen on graduation cards), and there is certainly something wise about this silent, nocturnal creature who can seemingly stare right through us with its huge golden eyes. The owl is silent practically all the time (except when calling for a mate), preferring to sit and watch what is unfolding on the earth below from their vantage point among the branches. They can even glide soundlessly through the air as they descend on their prey. To me they epitomize the process of learning – sitting, watching, listening, waiting as your understanding develops before you apply your new knowledge. This, and their power of flight, puts me in mind of the intellectual and rational Element of Air.

the weasel/ferret:

One of my more enigmatic totems, I was fascinated by these tough little mammals for many years, frequently dreaming of being in an elongated body on tiny legs, snuffling through the undergrowth in search of something interesting. I wanted a pet ferret for a long time, and now share my life with two of these adorable sock puppets of the animal kingdom, who continue to teach me new things about the nature of the mustelid family (which also includes mink, otters, stoats and the like). Their lives are one long cruise for something enjoyable, be it a tasty morsel to eat, a companion to chase and flip around with, or, in the case of my two little horrors, a tummy rub. They are, however, sturdy little beasts who can adjust to pretty much any situation if needs be, and in the wild will find a way to survive in fairly harsh climates. This union of the hedonist with the survivor is what makes me associate this animal with the corporeal, solid Element of Earth.

the frog/toad:

Although there are many varieties of frogs and toads indigenous to the area in which I live, they are such secretive creatures that it is still a thrill to happen upon one in the wild. They are the perfect example of the dual nature of the amphibian family and their ability to survive both in water and on land; in fact, they thrive off both – going about their business of feeding, breeding and seeking shelter between the two "worlds." Although they may be a substantial threat to insects, their diminutive stature and minimal physical defences leave them vulnerable, and so they have mastered the art of avoiding any exposure to that which could harm them. This flair for the dramatically polarized, as well as their vulnerability and semi-aquatic nature, is what led me to associate them with the sensitive, changeable Element of Water.

the spider:

While most little girls run screaming from these creepy-crawlies, I was always utterly captivated by the tiny creature who could achieve so much while living in such a small fragile body. I actually had a spider "friend" who lived behind the dresser in my bedroom when I was about six or seven, and I was most distressed when we had to move house (my parents ended up assuring me that they'd seen him going into one of the drawers, ready for the move). The spider is such a dichotomy – to one creature, they are venomous killers, while to another they are easily stepped on. The human population's reactions to them range from phobias and disgust to fascination and appreciation for their insect-controlling skills. They are not particularly well understood by many; they are not "insects" as they are frequently labelled, but arachnids. They are determined creators that can spin the entire structure of their delicate,

I was always utterly captivated by the tiny creature who could achieve so much while living in such a small fragile body.

detailed webs in one night, while remaining prepared to destroy the whole thing and start again if it suits their purpose. Their silk has enormous tensile strength and memory for its size, and can withstand a downpour of rain. They alternate between boundless attentiveness and detached predation in their dealings with their own kind. For so many contradictions in one tiny, seemingly innocuous powerhouse of a creature, I associate these animals with the all-encompassing, mysterious Element of Spirit.

Hopefully my potted interpretations of my own totems will help you to get into your own "flow" when meditating on your personal animal guides. It really is as simple as thinking about the creature, the ways that it is commonly viewed, and the reality of how it goes about its everyday life (this is where research, reading and wildlife documentaries are invaluable). If you have met this animal in the flesh, how did it appear to you? The following examples may help you practice the art and skill of interpreting totems further:

the dog:

One of humanity's oldest animal allies, the dog represents a loyalty and love that puts them on a level with the most devoted parent, or truest friend. This animal enjoys making their human happy, and is a steadfast and formidable protector of their home and family. For what or whom do you feel such devotion and unconditional love?

the crocodile:

Often misunderstood and feared as a monster, this ancient creature is so brilliantly equipped for its environment that it has not needed to adapt itself since prehistory – how many other species can say the same? The colossal mouth which drags its prey underwater also tenderly gathers the crocodile's tiny newborn offspring together for protection when danger threatens. These creatures exists in an aquatic world of their own, away from the high-speed, high-tech atmosphere of today. How strong are your connections to your wild and ancient roots?

the dolphin:

It is now possible in several areas across the globe to swim with wild dolphins, and (when they are not trapped in pools and forced to commune with us) once their echolocation senses another being in the water, they will come to investigate and play just because they want to. The dolphin shows us the importance of playing and enjoying life. How much time and energy do you put into enjoying yourself and others?

the bee:

In many ways, the bee can be seen to represent magical effort – a tiny creature which can achieve more than its size suggests. You may have heard of the axiom that, according to the laws of physics, the bee's relative body and wing sizes mean that it cannot fly. It seems nobody told the bees! Bees are also nature's alchemists, creating honey to feed their young from pollen. They are tireless workers within their communities and peerless proponents of teamwork ethics. How much can you achieve with the resources available to you?

the shark:

This skilled hunter is usually the victim of propaganda which labels them evil killers, with one particularly famous film being ingrained deep on humanity's collective consciousness. But how is the shark a more dangerous animal than the human? Sharks kill to survive, not for monopoly, profit or entertainment. They remain in the briny depths that are their natural environments, away from the snap judgments of hypocrites. How desperate are you to silence your critics, or are you just happy to go on being yourself?

the hamster:

This tiny, busy little animal succeeds despite its size. The cute, comic little entertainer that dwells in so many Western homes is naturally a loner, meeting up only to breed, co-existing with its offspring just long enough to wean them and prepare them for the world. Nobody is watching the wild hamster's back for them from the time they leave the nest onwards, yet they are adept at providing for themselves (they can carry a third of their bodyweight in the food pouches in their cheeks) and skilled burrowers. They are also not bad at self-defense when they need to be – ask anyone who's ever been bitten by one! How well can you take care of your own needs?

the crow:

Legends abound featuring this bird as a messenger between this world and the Underworld or afterlife (these were later popularized as the story which became actor Brandon Lee's last film, *The Crow*, and its sequels). These associations may have arisen from the crow's natural position as a clearer of carrion; they feed on the bodies of the dead, cleaning the environment and continuing the life and death cycle. There is no masking of the darker, messier side of life in a crow's world. Are you accepting of the cycles of life and death, or are you resisting an inevitable part of nature?

the horse:

Horses are nomadic animals, rarely staying in the same place for long. They are able to join their herd's journey only a few hours after birth, by which time they can stand, walk and run with their family. The horse has been a powerful symbol of the free spirit for centuries, with images such as the centaur expressing a wish for equine strength and freedom in humanity. Are you happy to move on and go where life takes you?

For those of you doing research for the purpose of interpreting your own totem animals, one source I ferreted (!) out which covers a wider range of creatures and their possible interpretations in brief detail can be found at www.crystalinks.com/animals.html

Creating magic with your child, by sharing your magical beliefs and helping the little one grow and develop spiritually and emotionally, is one of the most rewarding aspects of parenting. By helping a child to find the magic in their everyday lives, you can open new levels of communication between yourself and your child. The child will develop an increased awareness of the rhythms of life, while you enrich your own magical life through relearning the inherent and very straightforward magic understood by children and frequently forgotten by adults.

There is nothing like the scrutiny of a child to help us tighten up our own practices!

Not only does spellcraft help the child to strengthen their intuition and self-esteem, and to assimilate the basic precepts of the Craft, it also helps the parent to understand themselves better and their interaction with their child. By devising spells for your child (and eventually getting him or her to create their own spells), you help them to discover the infinite potential of the world you have brought them into. To so many children,

> By devising spells for your child ... you help them to discover the infinite potential of the world you have brought them into.

Allowing your child to become part of your magical rituals through helping in festival circles and moon rituals is an excellent way for them to observe you practicing your religion. Whether your path involves the full gamut of living a public, community-serving life as a Witch or choosing to celebrate only certain aspects of the magic of the "Old Ones" in combination with another faith, your child's ability to link into your belief system depends on this sense of inclusion. A child's spiritual path will not always be that of his or her parents, but we owe it to our children to see that they make their decisions from a position of knowledge and insight.

After some time of sharing simple seasonal and lunar celebrations, however, you may notice that your child wants something more. If so, spellcraft is one of the most satisfying areas of the Craft to share with a child. And once again, the benefits flow both ways.

growing older is a journey of disenchantment. Adults who have either resisted this darkening of the world or rediscovered its magic in later life should do all they can to help their children keep their own sense of wonder flourishing.

Spellcraft is deep magic, which can help heal rifts and hurts, and if used with perception and understanding can lead to a deep bonding between the child and the parent. If a child does not want to share their feelings or seems emotionally cut off, spellcraft can help them reconnect with their world, especially if spells can be devised to help them feel safe, protected and valued.

Like all aspects of child rearing, however, developing spellcraft with your child may have its challenges. Regular spellcraft sessions will sometimes highlight what you may feel are shortcomings in your parenting or in your magical work. These thoughts may feel overwhelming at times, but shouldn't be allowed to undermine or interfere with what you are doing with your child. Use a journal to record these emotions and allow yourself time to work on these issues in your private circle space.

Just as your regular magical work is best performed with an uncluttered mind, so you should put your own preoccupations to one side when developing spells for your child. If you are to help them tailor spells for their own growth, you must take the time to learn what makes them tick. If you have been working several jobs to make ends meet, this may seem challenging. Although it is common knowledge that most behavioral problems arise from a child not getting the attention they need, modern life often contrives to make this difficult. A parent is dragged in many directions, needing to work, maintain a home, and attempt to sustain often complex adult relationships.

However, you will find that by having regular spellcraft sessions a dramatic reduction in these behavioral problems may occur. You will garner a deeper understanding about why these problems are surfacing, and also become more deeply in tune with some of the changes in their personalities that might otherwise have gone unnoticed. Finding out what a child would ask for if given three wishes, for instance, will often give a very precise image of where their thoughts are currently focused. Your spellcraft sessions do not have to be long but, by their nature, the quality of inter-

vidual sessions with each child, using the discussion of magic to clarify their individual needs. At the same time, it may also be rewarding on a weekly basis to have the whole group together as a family bonding exercise to cast a spell, possibly focusing on a bigger issue, such as world healing or helping a sick family member or friend.

As a starting point in your shared spellcraft sessions, you may find it useful to consult, in books or on the internet, sources of spells written specifically for children. These don't need to be followed slavishly but can be a useful resource to help give you and your child ideas. We have written several books on magic for children – some for girls and some for boys. The publisher specifically commissioned these books in this format, and at first we were slightly alarmed at having to devise "girl" and "boy" spells. Teaching sexual stereotypes along with magic didn't seem an especially attractive prospect!

However, as we observed the various children we knew, we were soon convinced that, despite some concerted efforts by their parents, many girls do tend to like "girl-type" things and just as many boys favor "boy-type" things. One politically correct but harassed mother had tried unsuccessfully to get her growing boy of three to play with dolls and experiment with toys outside his preferred choice of toy trucks, cars, fire engines, trains and tools. Another mother found that she could not interest her five-year-old daughter in anything that wasn't pink and glittery! We obviously can't teach our children to

We obviously can't teach our children to think independently by forcing our choices on them.

action between you and your child they encourage will make up for a lot of what you may perceive as lost time. If you have more than one child, it may be an idea to have indi-

think independently by forcing our choices on them, so an alternative strategy was needed. Unsurprisingly, it emerged through the very nature of the Craft.

Magically speaking, this dichotomy of taste can be used positively to underpin teachings about "male" and "female" energy and make the point that it is when both these energies are combined in balance that *Magic Happens*. This might prove useful when you are trying to convince your daughter that her brother is not just a mere annoyance or a waste of space! You can easily transcend male and female stereotypes by stripping away the social trappings and explaining the core energies behind this form of duality and the associated dynamics between day and night, summer and winter, and solar and lunar magic. This will also help them begin to understand the difference between a magical upbringing – particularly one that worships both the God and the Goddess – and the imbalances of the mundane world and a still predominantly patriarchal society.

It is important when exploring how to teach your child or children about magic that the unique individuality of your child is honored. During their childhood years, their potential is limitless and their ability to absorb the world and its lessons will never be more powerful. It is not a time for molding personalities but for encouraging their true natures to flourish.

When helping develop your child's abilities to create their own form of magic, the theory of the Craft should be incorporated in action and activities. This is why spellcraft can be one of the most appealing ways for a child to develop their magical skills. Simple spells can help you present a goldmine of information about the Craft. The balance to cultivate is that between a child's intuition and the techniques a parent has learned from their own practice and research. It is important that the child knows the basics of your Craft so that they can understand what you are doing and why you are doing it. This passed-on knowledge will enhance their own magic as they develop their own individualized version.

Where a parent prepares a spell for a child, it is important to ensure that the child really taps into the spell ingredients. For example, magical lore recommends the use of rose quartz in certain love spells. Such a spell could be devised for a child who has difficulty in feeling love, particularly if they are undergoing some trauma in their life such as the separation of their parents. However, if your child rejects rose quartz as a stone for feeling love, it is important to take this on board and work together to discover an alternative.

Your first step will be to make sure that the child is truly connecting with the stone and that there is no particular prejudice informing their decision. For instance, if this spell is for a boy, he may feel that pink is way too "girly" to be bothering about. If you suspect that your boy may feel like this, consider giving him the stone in a bag so that the color will not immediately put him off. If he holds it for a while and feels that the stone is good for a spell about feeling loved, then you can gently reveal that even pink stones have power! However, it is important that once the stone is revealed he does not feel tricked or conned – simply informed.

If your child is definitely not connecting with the stone, this is an ideal opportunity to hone their intuition. If you feel that a stone or crystal is needed in a spell – and they are particularly useful if a child is going through a tantrums phase and needs some grounding (literally) – show your child your own collection of stones or teach them a simple way of finding their own stones for a spell. If you are seeking a store-bought stone or crystal, ask the child to think of the spell you are both concocting while you visit a New Age or crystal shop with a wide selection. Keep your own mind clear and shelve any preconceived notions of what stone would be best. When in front of the stone display, ask your child to concentrate on the spell and let them choose the stone they need, possibly with their eyes shut.

If your child does not feel drawn to any of these stones, consider an excursion to find an "ordinary" stone or shell at the child's favorite place. This could be a park or a beach where the child has experienced a sense of happiness and freedom. The positive associations of the place will then infuse the spell. Ask your child to find the stone for the type of spell you are both developing. If they don't seem inspired, check whether you are in the right place.

Safety and health issues must always be considered in choosing spell ingredients and implements. If you are using herbs, make sure that they are digestible. It may be wise to stick to culinary herbs that are friendly to small stomachs (perhaps avoiding overly spicy, pungent or hot herbs, such as hot peppers and garlic). There is always a very good chance that the child, despite many admonitions not to, will be quite happy to put the herb in his or her mouth. Remember, this is a time of great exploration and adventure for a child when the urge to explore new scents, tastes and textures can be overwhelming.

Be warned that these spellcraft sessions may also throw up tricky behavioral issues such as greed and the manipulation of others' wills. The earlier it can be emphasized that spellcraft should be used only for the child's higher benefit or that of others, instead of simply trying to attract whatever they happen to currently desire, the happier will be your child's progress through life. This provides scope for a parent to set out some very simple ground-rules for the ethics of spellcraft, and to help a child understand their specific higher path and learn what spells will facilitate these goals.

Once this is established, the child will develop a sense of being part of the natural flow of energy (which is, of course, what magic is all about). Selfish spellcraft, in children as in adults, is usually symptomatic of a sense of powerlessness to achieve change through any other method. This is the opposite of the self-esteem that results from aligning ourselves with the natural source of magic to strengthen others and ourselves emotionally and spiritually.

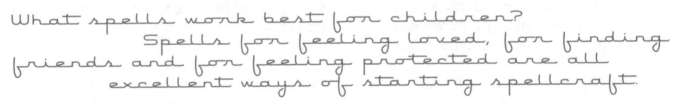

What spells work best for children? Spells for feeling loved, for finding friends and for feeling protected are all excellent ways of starting spellcraft.

Keep smaller ingredients out of the hands of your three- to six-year-olds. To avoid choking hazards, stay away from small pebble shaped crystals or stones. If you are seeking a stone for a spell, it may be wise to find a good-sized stone from a park or riverbed or a large shell from the beach. Also assess whether your child can yet be trusted with sharp objects, such as knives and scissors, and around fire, perhaps delaying their introduction to candle magic for an appropriate period of time (although you can get them to assist in preparing an unlighted candle for later use in your own ritual).

What spells work best for children? Spells for feeling loved, for finding friends and for feeling protected are all excellent ways of starting spellcraft. They can also be invaluable in overcoming fears and uncontrollable emotions, such as anger and frustration. For example, a spell for releasing anger could be called "Releasing the Tiger" and ideally should be done outside, preferably on the grass, to keep the energy grounded.

Let's look at an example of how this type of spell may be structured. To prepare, gather a heavy, makeshift walking stick (preferably made from a branch that has fallen from a tree rather than being cut), a bowl of salty water, a roll each of orange and black party streamers (or a long length of orange paper or cloth and a similar length of black) with one end pinned to the top of the walking stick, a stone large enough to have a satisfying heaviness to the child (hematite, obsidian and ironstone are all good) and a sweet sounding bell.

The spell should be kept very simple and involve a great deal of action. You can officiate in the spell by first having your child place the walking stick, the bowl of salty water and the stone in the middle of the circle. Next, ask them to walk clockwise sprinkling the salty water to create a circle of protection (which can be as big as your outdoor space allows). You may wish to stay outside the circle but still within hearing distance with them. Then have the child pretend to be a tiger prowling along the perimeter of the circle, growling and snapping and keeping imaginary intruders away. The circle is to be the child's territory, into which no one can enter uninvited.

Once you have a very believable little tiger stalking round the circle, ask your child to imagine that the tiger feels as angry as they'd felt when they last had a tantrum (this would be an excellent spell to do soon after a particularly bad tantrum). Let them access that anger again. This time they are in a protected space and the spell will include a release and a grounding to counterbalance the expression of anger. Try to be objective about their anger. Do not judge or fear their emotion.

Before your child tires, ask them to take up the walking stick and run anti-clockwise (widdershins) within the perimeter of the circle, the orange and black streamers fluttering behind them. Tell them that in doing that, they are releasing all the anger and frustration. You could encourage them to sing a specific chant as they run, and perhaps visu-

alize the energy being released as they circle round. The energy will soon peak and you will sense that your child is tiring.

At this point, ask your child to thump the stick into the ground as they slow down to a walk (still in a widdershins direction). They can imagine that they are now a medicine person or shaman/shamanka (if they are familiar with the words) who is protected by the spirit of the tiger. Next, ask them to rest in the middle of the circle, pushing the stone into the ground. As they perform this important grounding exercise, you walk widdershins outside the perimeter of the circle ringing the bell, dispersing the negative energy of their anger. At the same time, you may yourself catch insights into how to manage or dissipate your child's propensity towards anger. Consider incorporating these insights into your everyday life together.

Depending on your own magical practice, you may have the child set up the circle space by inviting the four elements and an appropriate Goddess, God or combination. If so, of course, remind the child to thank them for their support and nurture at the end of the spell. Asking your child to open the circle by making a doorway through which they can step can close the spell. This will subtly help to enforce the concept that the circle is a magic space in which the child is protected.

One way of tailoring spells to your child is to assess which element will help them rebalance their current disposition. If they are angry (Fire), use a grounding (Earth) spell to help them deal with the emotion. If they are too emotional (Water), use a spell where they can be like owls perching upon a branch seeing everything around them or a flying eagle seeing all the problems as only minuscule fragments of the landscape (Air).

Another way of teaching a child about the elements of Earth, Air, Fire and Water is to create a special indoor space for the child to do magic. Help them set up their altar in a space where it is both convenient from your point of view and magically potent from theirs. They may also like to have another altar in the garden – this one could be made from natural items, such as large, flattened stones, with a ceramic bowl filled with water to attract the birds. Floating candles may be lit in the evening to help create a magical atmosphere around your child's sacred altar.

You may consider getting your child to go to their outside altar during the late spring, summer and early autumn months when they wake or after breakfast when they can place an offering there. The offering could be anything from a bit of their breakfast toast to a sprig of herb or their favorite flower. During the winter months, the child may do something similar with their indoor altar.

Children are in themselves magical.

Naturally, these spellcraft sessions must never ever be used to manipulate or trick your child or to interfere with their sense of privacy – things no responsible Craft parents would consider. The child must at all times feel safe, strong and supported in their magic. The sessions must have an element of play but the need for discipline and following some instruction must also be instilled. A balance must be maintained, although it is sometimes a fine line with particularly unruly children. However, no matter what, every child responds to the strongest magic of all: love. If they can sense the love, nurture and integrity in these sessions, the true beauty of your relationship together will grow and grow.

To some extent our children are mirrors of ourselves and of our relationships and they have an uncanny habit of highlighting the flaws and foibles of our lives. No matter how annoying this might be, try to take notice of this, as your child may be offering you a gift:

a further chance to address issues in your own life that need attention, as much as children need attention themselves. Children are in themselves magical. Love and nurture them always, and do your best to keep their eyes open to the undying enchantment of the world they have entered.

In *Chaos International # 25*, Peter Carroll notes that:

"With Divination (trying to detect which of the manifold superpositions of the present which actually manifest in the future), things become gruesomely more complicated as the very act of 'looking' seems to act as an enchantment ..." (2002, p. 29.)

Carroll also explains what enchantment is:

"Consider first enchantment, increasing the probability of a desired event by will or intent or whatever. The moment of the present consists of a superposition of all possible pasts that could have lead to the present. Some of those superposed states will contribute to the probability of the desired outcome and some will not ..." (2002, p. 29.)

What intrigues me about all of this is Carroll's two positions on divination. First the stereotypical consideration of divination as an act of seeing into the future, and secondly his acknowledgement that divination seems to act as enchantment. I will go one step further and suggest that, while many writers and practitioners of magick take the stance of divination being a means of telling the future, others do realize that divination is actually a powerful, if subtle, form of enchantment.

In order to work with the concepts of space/time magick, most people will start out with a system of divination that on the surface represents a linear model of space and time. Eventually some people will feel they have advanced beyond the need for such divination systems, while others will continue to use them for the rest of their lives. Neither approach is wrong, but both have their pros and cons. I hope to show that, depending on how one approaches a system of divination such as Tarot, it can be both extremely useful and extremely problematic in working space/time magick.

However, before I do that I want to consider the ways one can approach divination as medium of space/time magick. My focus is on the Tarot (mainly because I have not worked with other systems of divination), but I imagine that a similar conceptual approach to other systems of divination would yield similar results. Gareth Knight writes in *The Magical World of the Tarot: Fourfold Mirror of the Universe*:

"the intriguing system of interlocking images ... can reveal the inner workings of the mind and the world about us. This system requires no special clairvoyant gifts or other rare abilities, simply a knack for using the creative imagination ... By these means the Tarot becomes a symbolic language by which we can communicate with a level of consciousness that is different from the everyday mode ..." (Knight, 1996, p. 2.)

How does this relate to space/time magick? In order to work with time/space magick we are working in part with layers of consciousness that we don't utilize in our everyday

Divination is actually a powerful, if subtle, form of enchantment.

activities. The awareness of space/time must be cultivated and divination is a useful tool for that cultivation. But the practitioner of magick should not become over-reliant on a system of divination. There are several ways to avoid this. One method is to be very creative in various approaches one uses systems of divination for. Another is to use the system for a period of time and then abandon it in favor of delving more deeply into the more conceptual realms of space/time magick. Both of these approaches will enable the reader to explore the layers of consciousness as they relate to space/time.

Let's consider the former approach first. More often than not people will try and memorize the traditional meanings of the Tarot cards. Rarely, however, will people try to define the Tarot cards for themselves. But Knight observes:

"it is not sufficient simply to learn the 'meanings' of the cards from a fortune telling book or instruction booklet that is sold with each pack of cards. We have to meet each face of the Tarot and make it a part of our own experience, just like cultivating a host of friends …" (Knight, 1996, p. 38.)

In "meeting" the Tarot – the personalities inherent in the cards – we open ourselves to meanings that we can understand from a basis of personal experience. Such personalized meanings are very useful in terms of working the Tarot for probability magick.

Elaborating on this, Mary K Greer points out that:

"Through a symbol system such as the Tarot, practitioners may discover an inner as well as outer meaning to the words, images and events we experience in our lives. Carl Jung used the term 'synchronicity' to indicate the simultaneous occurrence of meaningfully but not causally connected events. The key … is the word 'meaningfully.' If there is meaning to the seemingly haphazard events of our lives, then this meaning can be discovered by asking what the events symbolize to us. Another way of looking at this is to imagine everything connected with everything else, a living network or giant web, in which the movement of any part is experienced in all parts simultaneously." (Greer, 1988, p. 2.)

Meaning is interconnected with events, and it is our investiture of meaning on an event that creates the probabilities that spread from that event. The Tarot is not only a method of seeing the reality we create, but the means of creating the possibilities we seek. "The Tarot reflects our reality back to us! Through it we see what we are creating in our environment consisting not only of the past and present, but the forking probabilities from which we choose our future." (Greer, 1988, pp. 2-3.)

As a personal example of this, once a year on New Year's Eve I would do a reading to receive a forecast of the major influence of each month. I used a twelve-card spread, each card representing a month. Every year I did this I would note the card and meaning for each month and then wait to see if the influence manifested for that month. Invariably it did so. (Admittedly the influence of any month never manifested the way I expected it to, but the reading was very general and leaving room for variable possibilities in the manner of its appearance.) What didn't occur to me for some time was the possibility that my imbuing each influence with meaning affected the probability of its manifesting in the relevant month. For this reason I gave up this technique on New Year's Eve 2002 in case I was limiting the potential of each month through my own projection. Sometimes it is better not to know what might occur in order to increase the probabilities of anything occurring.

Greer likens Tarot to a mirror: "Each card represents a mirror of ourselves at the moment we draw it from the deck. The deck itself represents all our probable selves existing simultaneously, but in a sense, not elected in the moment" (Greer, 1988, p. 3). This view of the Tarot, in which the cards are seen as extensions of our selves rather than images of a fixed future, acknowledges that divination is not a linear system but one that takes into account permutations of possibilities. The popular view of Tarot as a means of reading the future creates the danger of believing in a specific, predetermined future. This particular future may then be brought into existence by the individual's belief in it, to the exclusion of all other possible realities. The alternative to this is to remain open to chance and to a non-linear consideration of divination and consequently space/time. This non-linear perspective of space/time leads us out of the traditional perception of reality as existing only on the level we currently inhabit. It opens us up to a multi-dimensional perspective of reality.

how I wanted it resolved, what I would do, and factors that could modify the way in which this resolution was achieved. I highly recommend Greer's book as a means of exploring space/time probabilities through Tarot.

As mentioned above, belief can open us to possibilities or exclude them. As with any other form of magick, belief is the key to the temple. Belief in what we do is integral to making the magick work, but sometimes it can hinder more than it helps. In the case of the Tarot, where the concept of being able to *read* the future is so pervasive, belief is much more of a hindrance than a help unless we are willing to change our preconceptions about the supposed reality of a situation. What we must remember is that beliefs can be changed and the more malleable we are with our beliefs, the better we will be at working magick effectively. Occasionally it can be useful to believe that the Tarot has predicted a specific future, but the reading has to be exceedingly specific to iron out the random factors that can negatively affect the out-

Belief in what we do is integral to making the magick work.

Greer suggests a number of exercises that I would recommend to readers in exploring the Tarot as gateways of multi-dimensional realities. One such exercise is the "moving meditations," in which the reader becomes each aspect of the Major Arcana via movement. This meditation helps to open us up to the probabilities the Tarot card represents. Another exercise is one where the emotions and intuition guide the reading of the card. In this summer of 2003 I was feeling a lot of bitterness about my financial matters, and this emotional/intuitive exercise not only allowed me to come to grips with the emotions, but also presented me opportunities I'd blinded myself to in my resentment. What I did was to pick out cards that represented my situation,

come. Greer points out that:

"A belief is any idea that you accept as truth, whether it is limiting or spontaneous. Core beliefs are ideas about your own existence that attract supporting beliefs to them. They form the basis of your experience of the world and your way of organizing data. Beliefs function like particles of light in quantum physics: they are true and not true simultaneously. They are true in that you can accept them as truth, and they are not true in that you can change them and their reality. Beliefs are often experienced as fate. By choosing to change those beliefs that limit your experience in undesirable ways, you make your own reality; this is the true secret of creativity and ultimate responsibility of freedom." (Greer, 1988, p. 123.)

In other words when we cling to our beliefs too tightly, they can dictate our reality. The true power of a magickian is knowing how to change reality to suit our needs. Accordingly we must be cautious of stereotypes that reinforce preconceptions about a tool of magick. Even with the recognition that the Tarot can represent more than one or two futures we must still be wary of mistaking the tool for the actual practice. The Tarot serves as a tool, as an expression of the magickian, but precisely because it can confine the scope of our possibilities by predicting a limited number of probabilities, we have to be willing to explore alternative avenues of space/time magick.

Works Cited

Peter Carroll, "Cutting Edge Theory" in *Chaos International* #25, Edited by Ian Read (London, 2002).

Mary K Greer, *Tarot Mirrors: Reflections of Personal Meaning* (North Hollywood, New Castle Publishing Co, Inc, 1988).

Gareth Knight, *The Magical World of Tarot: Fourfold Mirror of the Universe* (York Beach: Samuel Weiser, Inc, 1996).

the oracle tarot
clearing the karma of this sacred witches' tool
Lucy Cavendish

The Tarot is an ancient and fascinating Witches' tool. Its mystic symbols contain traces of the world's most powerful magical traditions and archetypes, from those of Egypt to European alchemical traditions, up to and including the great magical work done by late nineteenth and early 20th century Theosophists.

Official Tarot history starts in fifteenth century Italy. Many wealthy Italian families actually had their own "family" decks made. Faces of the family members were used as the models for cards such as the Hierophant, or the Empress or Justice – completely depending on the family's self image. The hand-painted Visconti deck illustrates this tendency perfectly with one female Visconti lending her face and form for the High Priestess.

When the intellectual and pioneering magicians and the Spiritualist movement flourished in the nineteenth and 20th centuries, many magical groups used the Tarot for study, divination and meditation. Groups like the Hermetic Order of the Golden Dawn believed to have found links between the Alchemical Path and the Qabala (the Tree of Life can be seen as a metaphor for the Fool's journey through the Major Arcana). As the tombs of the pharaohs had been discovered, Egyptology was all the rage. A fabulous theory – that the cards were in fact the 78 pages of the lost book of Egyptian wisdom, known as the *Book of Thoth* – captured many imaginations. This influence can still be seen in many decks today – there is even a Thoth deck (the design of which was overseen by Aleister Crowley). Many believe that these secrets of Egypt were carried into medieval Europe and into the cards by the gypsy tribes, like the Romanies.

My own love affair with the Tarot

When I purchased my first deck, I felt like I'd just entered a club. No, that wasn't the word. An order. A history. An enchanted realm.

I spent the little money I earned on works like *A Feminist Tarot,* old hardbacks on rare decks with handwritten notes in them, and discovered Dion Fortune and the Order of the Golden Dawn in the esoteric section at Waterstone's booksellers.

Deep into the night, I worked with the cards. I would light a candle and an incense stick in the tiny, freezing, shabby one-bedroom room which served as my home, and gaze upon the images, committing their meanings to my memory with far more enthusiasm than I'd ever applied myself to mathematics tables, though the cards were infinitely more subtle and complex. I kept a journal where I outlined my thoughts and my readings, and slowly my life began to take shape. It was as if the Tarot was helping me find the meaning I knew had been there, but which I'd lost along the way.

I progressed to a complete deck, and began to read for friends and the neo-family that grew slowly around me. I hand-stitched a black silk wrap for them, which I still use to this day. I did not go a single day without them. I read for myself and I read for strangers and I read for friends.

The beautiful images of every Tarot deck I

saw became my home, my fantasy, my country, and my self.

As much as I love the traditional decks, I was eventually guided to recreate the myth and mystery of the Tarot for a new generation, many of whom expressed fear and guilt at using traditional cards, such as the Rider Waite deck. Many had heard tales of demonic magicians and had been influenced by the media's generally freakish treatment of the Craft and those who practice it. Since fear and guilt hold us back from our destiny, I decided to reclaim and rework the deck to enhance the cards' inner meanings, to make them relevant for today, and to create a new universal symbolic language. That way they can be used with confidence, love and hope – and healing and power can take place hand in hand.

The beautiful images of every Tarot deck I saw became my home, my fantasy, my country, and my self.

I meditated every day to seek guidance when developing the *Oracle Tarot*. I'd head out to a nearby grove of very old, very wise Moreton Bay Figs, my very own sacred magical space. I received some very powerful guidance during my meditations. I was definitely being guided to make changes to this ancient art of divination – to bring it into a new era, just as it had been done with Pamela Coleman Smith in 1904. She made the Tarot easier for people to read – instead of, for example, the Ten of Swords literally being an image of ten interlinked swords, she painted a man, fallen, with ten swords thrust into his back. She painted these visual allegories for every single card.

Re-naming cards became an important part of the recreation that is the *Oracle Tarot*. The Death card's name was altered to Change. The Hierophant (or Pope) became Tradition. The Devil became Bondage. Numbers were re-ordered to reflect my goal: clarity and purpose and direction. Key words were chosen to enhance the meaning of the image, in order to prompt the reader to find a key to open the door to each card's myriad meanings. The more I asked for guidance, the clearer the voice of the Goddess became for me.

In revising the names of the cards, the *Oracle Tarot* has brought this mystical tradition firmly into the 21st century. I truly believe that the name of a thing holds its inner meaning. It is said that your first name holds within its letters and sound every single one of your soul's secrets. A name links to the Akashic Records, the energetic record that holds all information about every being incarnated on this planet – and others (stay with me here!). So, names are powerful and carry karmic loads. Names that were traditionally used for Tarot cards reflected the cultures in which they were created, and they are, therefore, mirrors of their times – and in some cases they are frightening, when the meanings of the cards are *NOT*. I wanted to give people access to the secrets using images, words and names that would be clearly understood and go directly to the meaning of the card. These images and words are the key, but the cards themselves and their names hold deeper secrets, which anyone can have access to if they are willing to study and learn and develop their psychic and magical powers.

Overall, the *Oracle Tarot* can bring you closer to your own spiritual insights, as well as guiding you along life's rocky roads. These cards are ultimately all about listening to your Higher Self, connecting to the universe, and trusting in your own wisdom. The *Oracle Tarot* can also help you make better choices and deal wisely with difficult situations. Best of all, they will re-introduce you to a sense of the sacred in your everyday life, which will raise your self-esteem and make every day just that little bit more magical. Used regularly, they could help guide you into a greater understanding of both your internal world (your spirit and your psyche), and the material world around you (your health, wealth, work and love life). The *Oracle Tarot* is of great benefit in relationships, too. Its symbology can help you unlock the key to the true issue within a loving relationship, point to the issue within a career path dilemma or even suggest a clever way to get on top of your bills.

The *Oracle Tarot* is truly practical magic, safe, positive and a genuine helping hand for those souls wishing to lead a more enchanted, more meaningful life. May you have many inspiring, enlightening readings.

Following are some of the most common questions that I have been asked over the years about reading the cards, whether my Oracle Cards or any Tarot deck.

Who should work with the cards?

Anyone, really. The only rule (which isn't really a rule anyway) is that working with your cards should be kept simple, especially when you are first getting to know your deck. Okay, maybe there are two rules. The second is that working with them is not about becoming some kind of guru – they're not supposed to be used to impress people or to give you the illusion that you're all-powerful.

You may find that many people are curious, and ask you for readings. How many times should you read for others? Put it this way. It's best if friends get their own deck if they're seriously pestering you or ringing you up at three in the morning for a relationship action

update. As for people who want to test your "powers" – give them a reading if you feel it's the right thing to do, but never read for people to make a point or prove something.

Can I read the cards for myself?

There is an old myth that does the spiritual rounds about Tarot decks which states that you should never read the Tarot for yourself. Actually, I come from the opposite school of thought – I believe (because I've seen it work time and time again) that it's definitely best to learn by reading for yourself. Apart from anything else, you will never have a harder reading! As you do this, over time, your psychic level will rise. You do not have to be extreme when developing this bond either – simply respectfully handle your cards each day, looking at cards, reading about them, gazing at the images on each of them, and developing familiarity and trust.

Should I use ritual?

Before reading your Tarot at night, give yourself a quiet minute or two to shake off the day's influences and call back your psychic self. It can help to breathe in white light or to visualize yourself safely within a circle of sacred white light energy before working with your cards. This will help contain your psychic potential, and will give you the highest, most accurate reading possible.

You may not like the cards you get, but remember, that's not the point. The cards are messengers – they're not negative and fixed. The cards will always indicate the most likely outcome of events if you continue on your present course. If you don't like what they're

The cards will always indicate the most likely outcome of events if you continue on your present course.

saying, sorry, the lesson will keep coming up for you anyway, so make some changes where it counts – in the present.

What should I do when I first purchase or am given my own Tarot cards?

The first thing you need to do once you bring your new Tarot deck home is to simply get used to the feel of the cards under your fingers. Bonding with your cards will bring you much more accurate and intuitive readings.

Another simple way to increase the power of your readings is to set aside a small part of your home where you conduct a morning card meditation. This area is preferably one where you will have some privacy, can decorate as you wish, and feel safe and positive in.

Why are there no court cards in the Oracle Tarot deck?

When I began work on this deck, I communicated with Goddesses and angels on an etheric level, all of whom requested that the court cards be left out of this deck. I was quite startled at this request, as obviously they are a standard part of most Tarot decks. But they do have their difficulties. Traditionally there are three male cards to only one female card. There are no cards that represent children in the courts.

And they reflect the make-up of a very patriarchal, medieval culture. In a more equitable and less gender-stereotyped world, you do not have the same need for these cards. It is quite simple to recognize "types" of people within the cards, the energy of each can be affiliated with certain personality types beyond gender. The layout of your readings can also indicate personalities who are coming in to play. So omitting the court cards worked well with my desire to create a fresh

and modern Tarot deck.

Can I accept money for readings?

Of course you can read for money. Money is an energy and you *MUST* exchange energy when you read for someone. Even if they simply clean your house or give you some apples or herbs grown from their garden, you must have your energy investment reciprocated. People value what they must give something up for. You must, however, be *asked* to read for someone. We don't go about telling people they need a Tarot reading, like Witchy busybodies. It's intrusive to deliberately scan people for their weaknesses and needs, and then exploit them – intrusive and unethical. You can put the offer out there (for example, if you advertize your readings) but you do not do readings for people without their permission.

Do I have to wait to be given a deck?

No. You may purchase your own deck – whichever you are guided to choose. It's a good idea to look at an opened deck first to compare the images, key words and underlying philosophy of the creator, and see whether it's a good match for your own magical values and personal energy.

If another person touches your deck, will it be infected with their energy?

You can cleanse and re-consecrate your cards several times a day if you wish. Some readers believe that the cards must be touched by the querent in order for their energy to intermingle with that of the cards, and for them to take responsibility regarding the guidance they are given. There can be no denial when they have shuffled the cards or handled the cards.

Are the cards, or some of the cards, evil?

The cards are not evil. They are beautiful sacred tools. Intention is the only quality that can be positive or negative. Work with high intentions and you will reap the rewards karmically, according to the law of the three-fold return. The Tarot can also help you connect to your guides, and help you unlock your own psychic powers.

Does getting the Death card in a reading mean you will die?

No, it does not. This assumption that so many people quite understandably make is the very reason I renamed some of the cards carrying negative energy, and reworked their images to accurately reflect their meaning. (By the way, the name that I created for this

The tougher our challenges, the more potential for growth and enlightenment there is.

card when I reinterpreted it for my *Oracle Cards*, and the true meaning, of the Death card in other decks is Change.) Please do not reject the card because of these sorts of superstitions. It and the other "darker" cards of any Tarot deck truly have so much magical help to offer you. The tougher our challenges, the more potential for growth and enlightenment there is.

the holistic witch

integrating the magick of body and soul

the everyday life of
a modern witch
Carmela Leone

My spirituality

I consider my life as a Witch and a Pagan to be a spiritual life. My spirituality is nature-centered, derived from my relationship to Mother Earth, Father Sky and all living things, and from the deep love I have for nature.

Awake to the rhythms and patterns of my natural environment, I recognize that my everyday life resonates with the greater cycles of Life. I am conscious of the recurring cycle of life, death and rebirth in my life in each growth experience, in each transition, and in each day from sunrise to sunset to sunrise. I am acutely aware of the deep

I believe and know to be true for myself: that I am a child of nature, ever-changing and ever-growing with the natural cycles, and a part of Gaia (described by James Lovelock as the "single living entity that comprises of all living things and the environment"). As a Witch and a Pagan, I follow a life-affirming, nature-celebrating tradition that provides me with the opportunity to re-enchant my life, and to live it with soul and spirit.

I respect the balance I witness in nature and in my own life, and I honor both a God and a Goddess. I experience God/dess through my reverence for the Earth beneath me, for the sky above and for all living things. Nature's constant evolution inspires me to practice

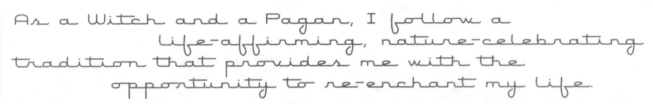

As a Witch and a Pagan, I follow a life-affirming, nature-celebrating tradition that provides me with the opportunity to re-enchant my life.

changes in myself that accompany the changing seasons of the year, and of how my own nature quietens as thoughts and feelings turn inward in fall and winter, only to blossom out again in spring and summer. I intuitively sense that I am living in a constant ebb and flow that mirrors the waxing and waning of the Moon. This expresses itself not only in my body through menstruation, but in my heart and mind, through the fluctuation of emotions and thoughts. I call living in this connected and deeply conscious way, a soulful existence.

My Witchcraft is not simply a matter of what I do, say, think and feel – it is a reflection of who I am. My everyday life is guided by what

self-development and nurture self-understanding. I attempt to live with passion and humility underlying all I think and do, and I express this in my life through intention and mindfulness, respect and reverence, and observance and ritual.

Intention and mindfulness

I attempt to live each day with intention. By this I mean that whatever it is that I am doing, I try to be guided by a clear sense of purpose. To apply the mind towards a purpose gives meaning to what we do. Whether I am thinking or acting, I attempt to keep my mind directed towards my deepest intentions as a

Witch: to serve the highest good of all, including myself; to live in a way that honors the Earth; and to remain true to myself, in the light and the love of the God/dess.

Each day when I wake up, I try to think about my specific intentions for the day. This is not just a matter of thinking about the day's agenda but of considering how I intend to do the things that need doing. With what attitude will I approach life today? How will I receive the challenges of the day ahead? In what frame of mind and heart will I engage with others? I often offer a prayer to the God/dess as my day begins, to ask for guidance and strength in being true to my intentions for the day ahead.

Living with intention is something that has gained greater importance for me since my best friend left this life two years ago. To see the significance of living every day, every moment if we can, with clear intention is a gift that came to me through the observation of death. I realized that one day my life would also end. I saw that I needed to live each day with the intention of being completely honest and faithful to myself, and that in all matters, I should follow my heart.

Intention goes hand in hand with mindfulness. To live in a mindful way is to be attentive to whatever is going on, both inside and outside ourselves, and taking care with whatever we do. It helps us to fully experience the here and now, to be aware of our connection to all living things and to live our lives consciously, being fully awake and not just breathing!

Part of this approach to life involves being open, honest and considerate to ourselves and to others. When I speak, I try to speak from my heart and with love, since careless words can hurt others or create harm. Likewise, when I act, I try to do so out of love and respect for myself and for others. If we are mindful of what we are saying and doing, we are given the opportunity to grow spiritually and to support others in their spiritual growth. Taking time to find the right words to express ourselves and giving thought to whatever it is we are doing means that we remain open to the love and the inspiration of the God/dess.

In this state, everyday activities can become meditative episodes and opportunities to find peace in our day. The sensation of being one with what we are doing, the feeling of losing ourselves in a task, the transcendence of time and space when we feel that we just *are* – these are experiences that can come from living with intention and mindfulness.

As an example of intention in action, when I cook, I take time and care with what I do. My intention is to provide my family with delicious food that is healthy and nutritious, and by focusing on this intention I am able to cook with love. My kitchen tools are beautiful, sensual and of good quality; the ingredients I use are organic (where available); and I try to cook with locally grown, seasonal produce. While shopping, I support organic farmers, who honor and respect the Earth by growing food in a sustainable and environmentally responsible way. I try to buy locally grown, seasonal produce, since buying food that has been transported long distances is costly to the Earth. Food that has been grown far away from where we live is not in harmony with our bodies.

I also enjoy hand sewing as it offers me the opportunity to reflect and contemplate whilst slowly and attentively creating beautiful things. Often while sewing, I am reminded of the care and attention paid to such tasks as embroidery and spinning by the women in the book *The Mists of Avalon* by Marion Zimmer Bradley. In the story, Morgan le Fay uses the meditative act of spinning wool to put her into a trance-like state, in which she is able to see the future or events taking place elsewhere (the Sight). Last year, I hand sewed a double-bed-sized patchwork quilt for my beloved. It took me two weeks to complete, day after day, sewing the patches whilst thinking of my love, from whom I was separated at the time. As I took the time and care to create a beautiful quilt, I thought of my love sleeping under the quilt. I wanted him to dream of me while he slept under it, and as I sewed the patches together, I imagined us making love beneath the mosaic of color. It was a love spell of sorts.

Weaving our magic into our ordinary activities can make for very powerful spellcraft. I have a friend, a Witch, from whom I recently asked assistance during a particularly difficult time for me. I was to be away from my home for two months, facing challenges that at the time scared me, and so I asked for her support during that period. A Water sign, my friend chose to think of me as she washed her dishes! Each day for two months, after her evening meal, she dedicated her washing up to me, using that time to think of me and send me love and support.

I wanted him to dream of me while he slept under it.

Intention is by far the most important thing in spellcasting. Of course, this may be strengthened by our choice of ritual and tools, but even if we are without an athame or wand, Witches can cast powerful spells with intention alone. For this reason, it is vitally important to be very sure of our intentions. As some of my own spells have backfired when my intentions were clouded, I've learned how vital this mental and spiritual clarity can be.

The nature of our intention can be either positive or negative – we can either help or harm – but we need to be aware that the things we send out come back to us threefold. For this reason, before spellcasting I always consider whether my intentions and actions could possibly harm others. It is not just in magic and ritual that the nature of our intention requires consideration. Whenever we speak or act out of anger or fear, we create more of these emotions. Although it can often be challenging to wait until our intention is clear before acting or speaking, when we take time to think through what it is we want to achieve, our communication becomes clearer and we have more chance of achieving our desired outcome.

Living mindfully provides me with a feeling of being centered and grounded, and gives my life meaning. There is a strength that comes through remaining focused on my thoughts, my emotions and my actions. As a Witch and a Pagan, I find it impossible to separate who I am, what I believe and feel, from what I do.

Respect and reverence

As William Blake decreed: "Everything that lives is holy." To walk on the Earth with respect for Her, means living with an awareness of how our lives impact on Her. The God/dess is to be found in all living things. I believe in the interconnectedness of all things, and that all we do affects something and, therefore, everything. To honor and respect nature requires me to consider these effects and to make choices on that basis.

When we extend our respect to all living things, we affirm the value and sacredness of life. Mother Earth and Father Sky, all people (including ourselves), animals and plants are worthy of honor and respect. The Wiccan Rede – "And it harm none, do as you will" – reminds us always to consider the effects of our actions.

In order for us to live, we take life. Whether we eat animals or plants, something dies so that we may be nourished. It is respectful to take only what we need to live, and it is appropriate to offer thanks for the life that has been taken. To sustain our lifestyles, we make choices that have far-reaching effects on the lives of others and on the Earth. Among the actions I take in my attempt to live with respect for the Earth and for other people are reducing consumption, supporting sustainable practices for the production of food, clothing and consumer items, choosing to live a low-impact lifestyle, and supporting Fair Trade organizations.

Likewise, since we are all children of the Earth and worthy of respect, I try to live with love and compassion towards myself and towards others. We share the same needs for physical survival, the same desire to be happy and to be loved, the same fears and the same faults. In honoring all people, I try to be tolerant of people with opinions that differ from my own, I attempt to be compassionate towards those who attack and hurt others out

crystals on the mantelpiece in the living room; and in the kitchen there is a "nature table" on which there are sticks, stones, shells, seedpods, feathers and flowers from our walks in the woods and trips to the beach.

I have objects from nature in the house, not just because I find them find beautiful, but because in bringing them into my living space, Mother Earth is brought inside, and I feel more at home, more connected to the natural environment. Similarly, my connection to nature is enhanced by walks in the woods or along the beach, going for paddles in the river or in the ocean, visiting natural sacred sites, and working in the garden where I can feel Mother Earth beneath my feet and Father Sky above my head.

Reverence is part of my spiritual experience, and I could not imagine living without the feeling of transcendence and peace that comes to me through the contemplation of greater things. For me, living with this reverence for nature creates a feeling of connectedness and wholeness.

I could not imagine living without the feeling of transcendence and peace that comes to me through the contemplation of greater things.

of their own pain and fear, and I try to accept people as they are and acknowledge that they are on their own journey in life. I want to live in a world where there is Peace, and feel this is only possible when we promote tolerance and understanding amongst people.

The fullness of our love, awe and respect for our world finds expression in reverence. I have an altar in my bedroom, on which the four elements are represented. On my dresser, I have an image to represent the God/dess. Nature is displayed in various special places in the house: in the bathroom, there are shells on a wooden shelf; there are feathers and

Natural sacred places provide us with the most inspired settings for contemplation and magic. Sitting in the presence of a majestic old tree, walking in the area of a ley line, sitting beneath a waterfall or on top of a mountain all allow us to feel the awe and wonder that underlies reverence. To visit such places is like visiting a chapel or a temple for me, and a garden tended with love and allowed to express its wildness can be one of the greatest of sacred spaces.

To venerate the Earth is like a silent worship for me. It is an expression of the deep love I have for Mother Earth and requires no effort.

In practice, respect and reverence can become observance and ritual.

Observance and ritual

In following the tradition of Wicca, I observe the eight Sabbats of the Wheel of the Year. For me, observance of these days punctuates life and helps to celebrate it. Observance of the Sabbats reinforces our awareness of the relationship of the Earth to the Sun, Moon and stars, and of our own relationship to nature.

As most of us lead lives that are no longer intimately connected to the land, these festival days offer us opportunities to acknowledge and experience our links to Mother Earth and Father Sky. Celebration of the Sabbats provides us with the experience of the recurring cycles, patterns and rhythms in our lives. All life is circular – in every turn of the Wheel of the Year, as in every day's dawn, sunset and subsequent sunrise and each cycle of the Moon's phases, we witness the cycle of life, death and rebirth.

I lived for a time in a shack in a native forest in Australia, with no television, radio or phone. Living a simple, uncomplicated life increased my feeling for the circular rhythms of nature. With this realization came a deeper trust in the workings of nature, and a strong sense of security regarding my place in it. Every day provides me with a new beginning, and that every ending is but a new beginning.

In conjunction with the seasons, I celebrate the cycles of my soul. Like many people, I respond to winter by withdrawing and turning inwards, both physically and emotionally. It is like a time of death that needs to take place before the rebirth of spring. I "fall clean" the house to prepare for the winter and the days to be spent inside, and I "spring clean" the house to clear out the stagnant energy after the cold months indoors.

I also respect the cycles of my body. My initiation into womanhood was not a positive experience for me, and later in life I felt the need to establish some kind of custom to honor my menstruation. I decided to wear red when I am bleeding, not for anyone else but for myself, to celebrate my womanhood. I have come to appreciate my menstruation and especially its significance for me at this later stage in life, where it reminds me of the creative power that is still available to me. When I was pregnant with my son, and afterwards for almost a year, I missed bleeding. It had become a rhythm in my life, a natural occurrence that reminded me that my body was fertile and functioning normally.

The important transitions of life known as Rites of Passage – the coming of a soul into this life, the journey of a young person into manhood or womanhood, the union of two people, and the passing of a soul from this life to the next – all call for observance and celebration. Observance and celebration of such important occasions brings a sacredness and holiness into our lives.

It may also feel appropriate to acknowledge other types of transitions or important events with simple rituals or customs. For instance, I bought my child a new backpack for preschool to mark his transition from home into the world of school. I was recently separated from my beloved for two months, during which time we both felt that we had moved to a new phase in our relationship. We felt that our relationship had been reborn, and to mark the new beginning, after being reunited at the airport and arriving at our home together, we paused before entering our house, looking at each other, we held hands and we walked through the doorway of our house together.

Although these types of observance can be personal, informal gestures, it is often appropriate at times of celebration to perform some kind of formal ceremony or ritual. Rituals offer us the opportunity to re-enchant our lives and to express and understand the sacredness of what we are celebrating. I personally like creating rituals, as well as performing them. The process behind creating a ritual can be especially rewarding when we are able to trust that the God/dess will send inspiration for the right thoughts, words and actions for the ceremony.

I have, over the years, created my own rituals to celebrate personal events. The birth of my child was not only a Rite of Passage for him, but an important time of transition for me, as I became a mother. The months of my pregnancy, the birth itself, and the weeks after my child was born were filled with ritual and celebration for me, my baby and those around me. First, whilst I was pregnant, I traveled to see my Nonna, my maternal grandmother, to speak with her about childbirth and her experience of giving birth to five children at home, in a rustic peasant village. Then I made a necklace from beads I had received from each of my close female friends, so that I might have something of them present with me during the birth. While in labor, I created a sacred space for myself and for those who were to be present, invoking the God/dess and the four elements into my house.

After the birth, the father of my child and I chose not to cut the umbilical cord in keeping with our minimal-intervention approach to the birth, and out of respect for the natural flow and timing of all things. After my child was born, I did not venture out of the house with him for close to 40 days, to allow a gentle transition from the womb to the world. When the 40 days were over, we had a welcoming party with all our friends and family who came to offer our child a blessing.

Other less dramatic events can also benefit from ritual. For example, shared meals are sacred times for me and my family. The sharing of food with loved ones is a ritual in itself, and we acknowledge this with a blessing. When cooking, I pour oil into the pan as if drawing a pentagram. It requires a steady hand not to pour too much oil, but I have practiced this gesture for some time now! I also serve the meal onto the plates at the table, following the direction of the Sun. My family and I bless our meal, each evening: "*Dear Earth, Dear Sky, by whom we live, Our grateful thanks to you we give. Blessings on our meal.*"

I do not always formally observe Full Moons and Dark Moons with a ritual, but I sometimes offer a prayer to the God/dess at these times, "draw down the Moon" or pull out a Rune or Tarot card for meditation. On or near the Full Moon, I sometimes meet with friends, or bake Full Moon cookies. Circumstances do not always allow for ritual, and I find that observance and intention can be just as effective when time and energy for ritual are unavailable.

Even simple rituals like lighting a candle with intention, taking space and time for meditation, or taking care in the way we dress or look after ourselves are small, but not insignificant, ways in which we can incorporate ritual into our lives. Any time we observe something in our lives, with intention and mindfulness, respect and reverence, it can become ritual.

Every day of my life

My life as a Witch is not something I deliber-

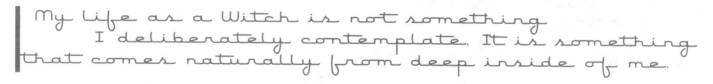

My life as a Witch is not something I deliberately contemplate. It is something that comes naturally from deep inside of me.

ately contemplate. It is something that comes naturally from deep inside of me. As a child, I spent most of my time in the garden, climbing the fruit trees, and sitting amongst the flowers and the vegetables. I felt at home there, and I remember sensing the presence of spirit or something "other-worldly" and magical in our garden. I believe that as children we know and feel that we are connected to nature, and we feel "at home" on the Earth.

For most of my childhood and teenage years, I attended church each Sunday. My feeling of being connected to nature remained with me, and as I grew older, I gradually came to believe in God, in my own way. As a teenager, I longed for a spirituality that merged my belief in God with my love of nature, and I proclaimed that I was a Pantheist, recognizing God in all things. I was later to call myself a Pagan.

When I discovered the appropriateness of naming myself a Pagan, I also found that I felt a strong affinity with the Wiccan tradition, and so named myself a Witch. I know people who are reluctant to label themselves but, for me, defining myself more clearly has given me a sense of belonging to a group and a community.

The way in which I choose to live affords me a soulful and meaningful existence. I don't believe that, as a Witch, my life has any more or less challenges than anyone else's life. I do believe, however, that having a spirituality that is based in the wisdom of nature enables me to accept those challenges, and learn from them through a strong sense of connection to all living things and security in knowing my place in the world.

As in nature, there is balance in my life. My life has both positive and negative experiences. It contains dark and light moments. I know love and I know fear. My soul knows night and day, and my heart has known great joy and deep sorrow. In keeping with the cycle of life, death and rebirth, I know that my own death will be but another transition. I am not afraid of death, and I am not afraid to live. As a Witch and a Pagan, I know this life of mine is sacred, so I honor it, by living as meaningfully as I can, every day.

who what wear
dress with intent
Francesca Gentille

Her brow was furrowed as she pushed through the racks of Hallowe'en Costumes for the year. Her choices never seemed to be quite right. The maid outfit was too slutty. The lion outfit too baggy. The astronaut was fun but perhaps too distancing with its helmet.

She slowed down inside, deepened her breathing and tried to tune into what her gut instinct might tell her. The loud store music, the laughter of the children faded away. Suddenly she knew. It was the belly dancer "look" that would fit her perfectly. Something about it delighted her. The shiny coin spangles, the shimmering fabric, the sense of mystery of the face veil. The seductive hide-and-seek of the cloth.

She rummaged through the disheveled racks and found the last one in her size. She left the store with a feeling of success. It would be a great Hallowe'en.

Costumes? Roles? How do we choose? How do we choose for Hallowe'en? For a meet-the-parents evening? For a business interview? For a first date? For a church social? Or a Pagan ritual?

So often we look into our closets and barely think of the clothing or costuming we have chosen for our every day lives. We are habituated to the way we dress, the way we think and the roles we have chosen to play.

Some of us play roles of rebellion, ensuring that we're not like our parents, the establish-ment, or some grouping of THEM. Others of us play roles of conformity or belonging, so we're clearly like our family, our religion, our social strata, our business or some grouping of US. Some of us somehow manage to both feel like rebels and to conform to our group.

Some of us have lost a sense of "me-ness." We wear whatever is typical, popular or called for in our environment. We may feel dis-ease. We ignore it and move on.

Each group, each role we choose or identify with has "a look," a style, a type of clothing, a range of colors. How easy it is to identify someone as hippie, neo-hippie, retro-hippie, techno, artsie, gangsta, preppie, yuppie, upscale, downtempo, slutty, studly, sloppy, uptight, goth, and so on.

Sometimes we have moments in our life where our world breaks open and we realize we have the power to choose a new role and a new set of costumes. Some of us never realize it. Most of us forget again after re-choosing.

How often we say or hear: "This is just me." "It feels comfortable." "I like it." "I like being elegant." "I like freaking the mundanes." "I don't put value into clothing."

And yet each statement leads to a series of choices of clothing and choices of behavior that become our intransigent role and costume. The sitcom or soap opera of our lives that is never canceled nor rewritten.

> We are habituated to the way we dress, the way we think and the roles we have chosen to play.

If we are lucky, at Hallowe'en or the Renaissance Faire or a Costume Party or a Role Playing Game, we step out of one persona and into another. For a while, a moment, or perhaps an hour or two.

Even then very few of us think that that choice might reflect a deep part of our psyche longing for integrated expression into our daily lives. Our habits fight the realization. "Who me, a devil?" "A suit?" "A monster?" "A vampire or a vampire's victim?" "A boring drone?"

Very few of us would know, or choose to dialogue with, our choices, to find out why we chose them, or explore what they might reveal of a lost ally or a forgotten power that now only lives in our shadow. Even fewer might find the patience and courage to compassionately get to know these misplaced pieces and integrate them into life.

Why might this be?

Debbie Ford, author of *The Dark Side of the Light Chasers*, suggests that:

"We believe that if we look closely enough at what lies deep within us, we will find something horrible. We fear ourselves. Many of us are so disconnected from this fear we can only see it by reflection. We project it onto the world, onto our families and friends, and onto strangers. We become so good at this we actually forget that we are wearing masks to hide our authentic selves. We believe we are the persons we see in the mirror."

In *Owning Your Own Shadow*, Robert A. Johnson writes:

"When we consciously approach the shadow, we examine a very powerful aspect of our personality that is almost universally shunned and avoided. And in this way, we enter the realm of paradox. All the great myths give instructions on this subject and remind us that the treasure will be found in one of the least likely or popular places. Contradiction (this or that, win or lose, bad or good, darkness or light) is barren and destructive, yet paradox is creative (this and that, win and lose, bad and good, darkness and light). It is a powerful embracing of reality."

So today as I talk to my son about what he might like "to be" at Hallowe'en, I think of my own inner characters, the clothes in my closet, my projections onto others, and the people in my dreams. I wonder where I am missing some aspect of my drama. What parts of me are directors in denial? Where I am a victim of life?

In honor of the season of Hallowe'en, and costumes, and roles, and shadows, would you be willing to go in and out of your closet with me (perhaps for the 1,000th time)?

Take a peak at what you say, who you think you are, the way you dress. What if it was all only a habit? What if you and I were a complete universe of possibilities that contained – EVERYTHING? I especially invite you to take a gander at the "looks" you despise, the people you denigrate and the groups you complain about. What if they were all you?

What will you wear this Hallowe'en? This Saturday night? Or to work?

What are your roles? What are your costumes? Would you choose them again if you had all the choices in the world?

What is your fear? Can you face it? Can you be it? Could you love it?

i feel good
healing self-esteem issues with witchcraft
(oh, and saving the planet!)
Lucy Cavendish

If you're attracted to Witchcraft, you've probably been through a bit of a struggle. Was that an understatement? Then you're definitely on the right path now. That's the way it is for us sensitive magical types. We *feel* things. We're *supposed* to. That's our *job*. I've often described the experience of being magical as akin to being born lacking an entire layer of skin. (I am speaking metaphorically here!) Now, this thin-skinned quality means you are a very powerful intuitive being; and it also means you are sensitive to the hurts and slights of just being alive in this world. It's rough out there, and being different can deal blows to your self-esteem. You can feel the pain of people you see suffering, burn with anger at the injustice you see being played out, weep for animals in trouble and wish you could do more to protect the planet. It's hard work being a sensitive new age Witch.

But the answer is not, as mainstream culture would have us think, to desensitize ourselves, conform and feel powerless. You sensitive Witchy types need to stay in the zone – that place where you are different and living your truth as a Witch. I mean, just how

chological armory. Once you work on these issues, you'll discover a network of fellow magical sensitives who will naturally be attracted to you, and begin to offer you their support. And you're going to be able to help them too. Then, when you work on yourself, practice magic, and make Witchcraft a life choice, you can get on with doing what you are meant to be doing in this world – being a teacher and making a difference.

But why am I sooo sensitive?

One of the constants I've noticed, from the emails and letters and conversations I've had with wise ones, is that each and every one of us practicing the Craft feels raw in the world. I've already said the world is harsh. But that's not the only reason we often wonder whether we are strong enough to make it in this world. Let me introduce you to a theory that really makes sense to me – and bear with me, because this is when you may start to think I'm pretty kooky. Just stay open-minded and see if this resonates with you. The line of thought I'm talking about goes like this: Witches who

> It's hard work being a sensitive new age Witch. But the answer is not ... to desensitize ourselves.

much more insensitivity can the earth handle? No! Stay sensitive. But by using magic to raise your self-esteem, overcome your addictions, work on your body issues, and protect and ground yourself, your natural sensitivity will become an incredible, powerful asset, rather than the problem child of your personality or the weak spot in your psy-

are being called up to the path at this time have actually been given a mission to save the planet – and to heal their karma. That's because, if you give any credence to the theory of past lives, most of us attracted to healing arts, crystals, mythology (which, of course, isn't *just* mythology), Tarot, Sabbats, spell work, star-craft and the moon have already suffered for our beliefs in previous lives. This is why I call it "standing in the fire" this lifetime. The fire of our beliefs can purify us, but taking the rejections it brings can be painful. But stand in the fire anyway. The reason it can be so terrifying is because we have already been tortured or burned at the stake in a past life as a Witch/healer/clairvoyant.

Now, if this resonates with you, as well as your self-esteem issues, you may also be feeling a great deal of anger. People may see pain in your eyes. You may feel very frightened to come out about your beliefs. You may also have taken a vow in a past life of secrecy, which is why coming out seems wrong to so many of us. You may have been rightly frightened by the distortions of what it means to be a Witch that permeate popular entertainment. Though many books, movies and television programs are beginning to acknowledge Witchcraft's basis as an Earth and nature based belief system, you still get the good old stereotypes coming through. But it *is* changing, so please don't overload yourself with negative notions of the Craft which are constantly being fed to you by (sigh – because it's a cliché – but truer now than ever before) the media. You know the sort I mean. Have any of you seen that so-corny-it's-almost-great soap, *Passions*? There's a Witch called Tabitha in that. And is

ent moment and on discovering more information about the nature of your life's mission. The more information you have, the more confident you will feel in embracing your path and, thus, fulfilling your mission.

Why am I a Witch?

Witchcraft is a beautiful path that encapsulates environmentalism, meditation, using organic produce, recycling, planting trees, working for animals and their welfare, acknowledging natural cycles of power, being unafraid and guilt-free regarding the (metaphorical) dark, supporting the diversity in the Earth's belief system, working with planetary cycles, celebrating the Sabbats, and being a living example to your friends and family – if you choose to be.

It is hard to work in isolation. As a person who worked as a solitaire for a long, long time, I know it can take courage and a good sense of judgment and timing to link up with other like-minded souls. I often felt that I was stuck in the Hermit card stage of the Tarot for a lot longer than was strictly necessary. In my *Oracle Tarot* deck, the card I most relate to now is Change, which is what I've re-named the old Death card (Editor's Note: See Lucy's chapter on the Tarot in this book.)

... spellcraft and magic needs to be for the good of the planet

she interested in healing the planet? Helping people? Just telling the truth? Nope, she's just a mischievous evil creature. (Why don't they put politicians in these roles? It would make far more sense!)

If these doubts and concerns seem to cluster around your Witchcraft and lifestyle patterns, you may need to work on clearing karmic residue. To do this, you'll need to work on raising your energetic frequency in the pres-

I also noticed there were people in Witchcraft who traded on their group as a power base. It seemed to be a manifestation of people just wanting to be right – and way too similar to traditional church and religious systems, with dominant personalities ruling groups. The issues I'd always had with organized religions still seem to manifest themselves in magical groups if the individuals involved were not working on themselves. I still believe that most spellcraft and magic needs to be for the good of the planet, and for your healing as an individual. It is not that you need to be free from all negative personal issues – there is no such being walking the planet (in human form, anyway). It's about working on your issues. Judgmental and egocentric individuals who professed to be highly trained Witches still alarmed me with their assumptions of superiority and desire to dominate. I felt they would not teach me, but take from me. And I was right. But that doesn't mean you must hide from others.

Find your path

So – to raise your self-esteem as a Witch, work on your issues in a magical way. Find, if you can, like-minded individuals who support your individual path, remembering that what resonates and works for one person may not work for another. Your skills may be in healing, or astrology, or working with herbs, or children, or animals. You may have natural endowments of clairsentience, powerful dreams, or the ability to trance, grow things, or to talk to and counsel people. Get in touch with *yourself* and really trust what comes through for you. Once you have an idea of what you are naturally inclined to work with, explore that with passion. I began with the Tarot – and it truly chose me. I just couldn't resist it. But my magical awareness began much earlier than that, with visitations from entities as a child, spontaneous astral travel and hearing voices. However, Tarot was the first concrete study I embarked upon. It gave me the key to open the door to a room where the riches of knowledge were housed. It gave me the disciplined framework to study and the courage to begin to explore myself as a psychic Witch.

What is your key? Take the time to discover what it is. Just stay open and you will be given the clues – you will inevitably be attracted to one discipline more than another. Use this as an opportunity to discover your true life calling. It could be art, music, fashion design, or rescuing native animals. You may invent something entirely new that I can't even begin to write about here. The bottom line is that you be of service in some way, no matter how humble it may seem to you to be. Diffusing tension through humor is magical. Being sweet and patient – that's magical too. Such talents are as powerful and important as spellcasting, especially at this time on the planet when diffusing tension and warlike tendencies is practically angelic work. Don't underrate your work. Witches tend to be a little bit shy about realizing just how much they have to offer other people and the planet. We shouldn't be. Boy, are we needed! Just look at the world.

Raise your power

Witches need to vote. Witches need to be in mainstream jobs so we can help change the world for the better – or even help save the world. We need to be working in the media, in the legal arena, in government and in hospital systems. At the same time you will occasionally have magical undercover assignments (just ask me about them!) and they are exhausting. But once you've undertaken a difficult mission and fulfilled it, you will be able to work more in alignment with your true purpose. Incidentally these undercover missions typically take a multiple of three to reach completion – three months, three years, sometimes three days or weeks. And some Witches have signed up for a very hard-working thirty years!

Once you align your soul purpose with your personality and your desires, you are really in the zone. You became very powerful and virtually unstoppable. This is the place where magic happens – jobs come up, you meet the right people, offers come through, and your voice is heard. Your life has momentum without the kind of effort that seems to go nowhere. You may currently be one of those people who try REALLY REALLY hard, but something that you are doing energetically is getting in the way of progress. If so, learn to let go a little more. Do work, meditate on the right results happening, and follow through – then let the Goddess handle it. She really does want to help you out you know. When a Witch finds his or her power, positive changes for the good of everybody out there can be easily accomplished. And the bonus side effect? You are healing your self-esteem issues.

Heal your body image and self-esteem issues

Maybe it's time for a little more detail on those issues. A lot of people who are attracted to Witchcraft have issues with sexuality and body image. These individuals are always beautiful. But they rarely think so.

(as we all are) will have body issues. Sometimes, in order to buffer themselves from the world, female Witches will really pile on the pounds, keeping their core self literally at a distance from those around them. It's a real "don't look at me" syndrome. If you work on shifting and healing your energetic patterns, you will find that your body naturally adjusts to a healthy weight. Notice that I said, "a healthy weight." I have no desire to add to the thousands of impressions each of us get every day advocating a typical ideal body type. But loading your body down with weight to keep you feeling safe and grounded may negatively affect your energy levels and lifespan. There is every reason to stay a big beautiful woman – but staying healthy physically will always have a flow-on effect with how to feel about yourself and thus how effective you can be in the world. It is how you feel and how you move that tells the world how to treat you.

… work on shifting and healing your energetic patterns, you will find that your body naturally adjusts to a healthy weight.

This is because the residual suffering they've experienced has been based in fear– others have rejected them for being so beautiful and so sexual. It is your right to shine as a gorgeous creation and to embrace your sexuality. This is one reason why I believe the mermaids are helping us at the moment. Mermaids are magical beings that help us heal our sexuality. If you feel you are dealing with sexual issues, keep a statue or images of mermaids around you. Work with their energy by taking sea-salt baths or visiting the ocean or waterways. Meditate on them and their gifts. Get involved in cleaning up the Earth's oceans. The by-product of this kind of activism is a healed personal life – the mermaids will send you blessings.

Women and men who are sensitive Witches

Please take great care of your health. We need you to be as strong and vital as you can be. This includes people with mental illnesses or disabilities and those who have suffered in accidents. There is always a higher point you can aspire to. You are not a victim. You can improve your health, and when doing so by using Earth-safe and ethical methods, you are also healing the planet. When we are obese, unconfident, scared and unable to move easily, when we focus on pain, we cannot be a spiritual activist – which is what the world needs now, and that, I suspect, is your calling.

Overcome your addictions

Many Witches have, or have had, drug and

alcohol issues. Again, this may be the result of trying to blanket and shield themselves from the harsh world, or of an attempt to drown out their internal voices and their natural powers. You will be so much more aligned with your life mission (and thus your self-esteem will rise) if you allow this power to drive you instead of smothering your innate magical abilities with addictive behavior, whether this relates to drugs, food or destructive relationships. The discomfort of feeling unfulfilled will ultimately far outweigh the stresses of taking risks and extending yourself magically, of being committed to Witchcraft and helping the world.

... when we all raise our candles together, what a force for light we shall be.

Alcohol and drug addictions can also have their roots in past lives. If so, by working through these, you can release yourself from any vows or traumas you may have had that have led you to be attempting to smother your feelings or life purpose. You will not be burned at the stake this time round, I promise you. We won't make fun of you, or call you names, or tell each other we think you're weird behind your back. Reach out and trust us. We can help.

Light a candle in the dark – we'll see your light. And when we all raise our candles together, what a force for light we shall be.

Once upon a time, in ancient Greece, women sat around sharing bowls of plump olives, drinking wine and telling stories. One of their favorite characters was a wonderful old crone called Hecate. There were lots of stories about her, and she kept on cropping up in other people's stories whenever there was a need for the particular perspective she brought.

She had sparkling eyes, wrinkled skin, a tender heart and an endearing lack of pretentiousness. She was loved by many, feared by some and unquestioningly universally respected. She had something in common with other old women of storybook fame, like Baba Yaga and Cerridwen. She was a bit of a fairy godmother and a bit of the old woman who lived under the hill.

How do we know this about her? We know because about 2800 years ago a man called Hesiod wrote down many of the stories that were told in ancient Greece. In a huge work called *Theogony* he described the world of the Gods, the relationships between them and the time-honored stories about them. Hesiod was followed by others, such as Homer, Herodotus and the playwrights, who collectively cryogenically froze the Greek myths, so we can see them today as a beautifully preserved fossil of an ancient worldview.

These days Greek myths are seen in three ways. First, they may be filed away as children's stories or explained as the naïve attempts of uncivilized people to explain the physical world. This view of the myths may be right, but there's something a bit arrogant about calling the people who invented grammar, arithmetic, architecture and democracy naïve or uncivilized!

The second view is that held by well-respected mythologist Robert Graves, who posited that the myths were coded accounts of political history, and that their plots are about invasions and cultural shifts.

The third currently popular view of mythology is the Jungian perspective that's been massaged and promoted by the likes of Robert Johnson, James Hillman, Patricia Berry, Clarissa Pinkola Estes and Joseph Campbell. These folks take the view that myths are psychological maps that say something about the patterns that exist within the human mind. In order for this perspective to work for you, you have to be able to accept that there is something universal about the way that people think and that this something is not so different today from how it was 3000 years ago. If you can take that step, then the Greek myths become a treasure trove of tools that can be used to make sense of life and to find ways out of emotionally challenging situations.

Explaining this phenomena, Jungian author and therapist Clarissa Pinkola Estes says:

"Stories [such as the Greek myths] set the inner life in motion, and this is particularly important where the inner life is frightened, wedged or cornered. Story greases the hoists and pulleys, it causes adrenaline to surge, shows us the way out, down or up, and for our trouble, cuts for us fine wide doors in previously blank walls, openings that lead to the dreamland, that lead to love and learning, that lead us back to our own real lives." (*Women Who Run With Wolves*, Random House, 1992, p. 20.)

So when it comes to feeling a bit down about getting older, instead of reaching for another bottle of anti-aging serum, try a bit of Hecate-style thinking. Here are three short lessons to get you going:

One: False Colors

There's a curious story that begins with Hecate as a young woman, living on Olympus with her mother and father. She steals a pot of rouge, and fearful of her mother's anger she flees to earth and hides in the bed of a birthing woman. This renders her impure and prompts the Cabeiri (benevolent spirits associated with the fiery realms below the Earth) to grab her and plunge her into one of the rivers of the Underworld to be washed clean. Once in the Underworld she makes herself at home and becomes "the Invincible Queen of the Dead" and the Goddess of enchantments and magic charms. (This story is taken from *The New Larousse Encylopedia of Mythology* (Hamlyn, 1982, p. 165.)

becomes aware of what it really means to be a woman. This prompts the benevolent spirits to come to her assistance. The spirits were the Cabeiri, thought to be the sons of Hephaestus, the volcanic blacksmith God. Their presence in this story may indicate that Hecate's initiation into understanding childbirth was a bit of a trial by fire, alchemically changing her nature.

While the idea of being stained by contact with childbirth seems a bit anti-feminist, if we remember that we are dealing with an immature young girl, we can perhaps appreciate that she may have been feeling shocked and appalled by the blood and the screaming. What she needed was an understanding that, as well as being physically painful, childbirth can be emotionally exhilarating. Perhaps she also needed to understand the whole cycle of birth and death.

In this light the appearance of the Cabieri makes more sense. They dunk her into a river (water being equated with the emotions) and leave her in the Underworld (a place of deep understanding). It is worth remembering that while the Greek Underworld was the place where the dead went, it doesn't have

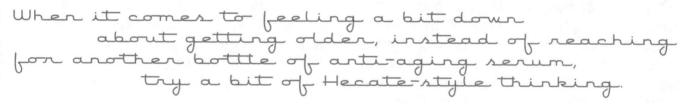

When it comes to feeling a bit down about getting older, instead of reaching for another bottle of anti-aging serum, try a bit of Hecate-style thinking.

Although this is a small story, it's packed with potent symbols such as the rouge, her mother's anger, the bed of a birthing woman, the stain, the Cabeiri and the river. What does it all mean? Well, for a woman-child to steal rouge is to pretend to be fully grown. But at this stage of the story, Hecate is no match for the power of her mother's presence. Rather than face a scolding from her mother, she runs away. In fleeing from her mother though, she encounters childbirth and

much in common with the Christian fire-and-brimstone Hell. In the Underworld Hecate learns to appreciate death as well as birth, and this understanding gives her the power to become not only the Queen of the realm, but the Invincible Queen with the power to charm and enchant people (which is what rouge is said to be good for). In the end Hecate has that power for real on the inside, rather than as something that isn't really hers and is only smeared on the surface.

So what can we learn from this story? It's so rich that you could probably spend a lifetime pondering it and going deeper and deeper into it. but here are just a few thoughts to get you started:

Don't pretend to be something you're not.

Consider what it means to be creative.

If something shocks and frightens you look at it more deeply. Try to understand it better.

Understand that, just as things need to begin, they also need to end.

Understand that real beauty comes from understanding and experience, and is more than skin deep.

Two: Keeping Silent

Hecate plays a small but important role in the famous story of Demeter, the Earth Mother, and her flower-maiden daughter, Persephone. In the Hellenic versions of the tale – and for a different take on this story, see Charlene Spretnak's pre-Hellenic version in *The Lost Goddesses of Early Greece* (Beacon Press, 1978) – Persephone is abducted by Hades, the God of the Underworld. It is Hecate who witnesses the abduction and who eventually tells Demeter what has happened. Note the word "eventually." Hecate waits until Demeter has wept and wailed and let the lush Earth go cold and barren before telling what she knows. Add to this the curious detail that Persephone, who eventually marries Hades and becomes Queen of the Underworld, remains good friends with Hecate for the rest of her life.

What can we pull out of this? Jungian writer Patricia Berry suggests (in her *Echo's Subtle Body* (Spring Publications, 1982)) that the characters in the myth are all different parts of ourselves, and that the wise old part of ourselves recognizes that the young naïve part's need for a brutal wake-up call every now and again. In this light Hecate keeps her mouth shut because she understands that the abduction is somehow necessary for overall growth.

Whether you share Patricia's view that we are each all of the characters or you take the view that we act out these dramas with the other people around us taking archetypal roles, it's a handy thing to bear in mind. It's about being a bit aloof, as Hecate is in this story, seeing what she sees from her home in the moon. It's also about letting other people have their dramas, being there for them, not judging them and not spinning into a crisis of your own that distracts from your ability to say the right thing at the right time. Again, it's a story about being in your power and understanding that sometimes things that seem like disasters can be blessings in the long run. The detail about Persephone's long-term friendship with Hecate shows that sometimes relationships are deepened by the act of letting go and allowing the other person to change, rather than clinging to them and stifling their growth.

Three: Choosing Directions

Archeologists have found places in ancient Greece that were once crossroads which have been marked with statues of Hecate or little pillars with three carved faces that they call triple Hecates. It is said that on the eve of

… a story about being in your power and understanding that sometimes things that seem like disasters can be blessings in the long run.

the full moon, offerings to the Goddess would be left before these stone images.

Given Hecate's strong association with crossroads, it is worth pondering what connection she may have had with them. Perhaps it's to do with the idea of choice and freedom. If you consider every moment of your life to be a crossroad, you end up living in what Eastern philosophers call "the Now." It goes deeper than just thinking about today's pleasures though. It's about choosing carefully which path you take because different paths go in different directions. The opportunities that tomorrow will offer depend on the steps you take today. Every day you are choosing one path rather than another, and while you are always free to turn in another direction, at the next crossroad, you cannot erase the steps you have taken.

In pondering the crossroads you are at, you can think about whether you are choosing to exercise, eat well, smoke, study, take risks or stay in a job or relationship you're not enjoying. People often stagnate in their homes, jobs and routines because they are waiting for a crossroad to appear, but Hecate's lesson is don't wait. You are always at a crossroad. You can always choose to do things differently. You can't magic yourself to a different destination but you can always choose to walk towards one.

Finally it is worth pointing out that while this kind of behavior may make you happier, and win you respect, it's not guaranteed to make you universally popular. Take note that while Hesiod, recording what were old folktales in his time (i.e., around 800 B.C.), described Hecate as the original Triple Goddess, supreme in Heaven, on Earth and in the Underworld, the glowing portrayal didn't last. As Robert Graves puts it, stories told later in the Hellenic period (776 BC – 323 BC), which followed a series of invasions of Greece, "emphasized her destructive powers at the expense of her creative ones until at last she was evoked only in clandestine rites of black magic, especially at places where three roads met …" (*The Greek Myths*, G. Braziller, 1955; The Folio Society, 2001, p. 123.)

Not that I think she minded. She's not the sort to kowtow to politicians, and if they wanted to call bunches of women getting together to laugh and dance and tell stories "Witches," fine, it wasn't going to discourage her from accepting invitations to attend. She was, and still is, the archetype of a woman with such deep understanding of the world that pettiness doesn't bother her. Rummage a bit and you'll find many stories about her that open easily to spill their treasures and offer practical advice if you sit with them for just a little while, or perhaps share them with some friends over a bottle of wine and bowl of plump olives.

When I was young, a girl at school told me I would go to hell because I didn't believe in God. Her God, a judgmental, masculine, western God. She lied, swore, stole, was sometimes mean to me and others. I told the truth, was nice to everyone, raised money for charity, helped anyone I could. So why would I burn in hell? It didn't make sense to me. What about the bad things she did? She smiled smugly. She was okay. It didn't matter what you did during the week, as long as you went to church on Sundays and confessed.

But it seemed to me that a God who couldn't see into our hearts wasn't much of a God. I knew deep within me that just because I didn't go to church it didn't make me a bad person. I believed in some kind of divinity, some higher power. I just couldn't reconcile the vengeful, unforgiving, narrow-minded God I heard about in religion class with my idea of the guiding force of the universe.

Somehow I knew that it wasn't about going to church, but about taking responsibility for my actions, treating everyone with respect and being the best person that I could be. I knew

ancient rocks as a teenager, and tried to find magic in the big city as I grew up and moved away to study, I could feel some kind of divine power moving through me. I met people, I went to university, I worked, I learned new ways to heal. I forged strong friendships and had my heart broken by those who betrayed me. I worked out my values, my desires, my beliefs. I began to understand the importance of free will, responsibility for my actions, being of service, unconditional love. I continued to formulate an idea of the divine force, of my concept of God.

And one morning I woke up and knew that all the things that made me me also made me a Witch. I felt the touch of the Goddess, Her hand guiding my life. In Her I saw the answers to all I had questioned about conventional religious views. She was gentle, understanding, all encompassing, strong, powerful. She was me and I was Her. She accepted women, rejoiced in the feminine. She expected a good and loving heart, not a roll call at church on Sunday. She saw into my soul and rejected the hypocrisy of people who were only going through the motions.

I reveled in the feminine, in the women I met who reflected the Goddess back at me.

that if I listened to my heart I would make the divine happy. So, was the divine within my heart? I believe it was and still is, and that the God/Goddess is within each person. It is that part of us that wants to be of service, to love and be loved, to be everything that we can be.

As I danced beneath the trees of our country property as a child, basked in the sunshine on

I met other Witches. I did ritual. I continued to learn. A kindred spirit gave me a Goddess statue that became the center of my altar. But there was no God. I figured that after 2000 years of patriarchal control, what was a bit of tipping the scales between friends? I reveled in the feminine, in the women I met who reflected the Goddess back at me, at the mystery that involved me and surrounded me and allowed me in.

How could I *not* believe in a religion or set of spiritual beliefs that embraced me? Quan Yin, eastern Goddess of compassion and mercy, comes to people in whatever form they need her to. A woman, a man, a pig, a bird. That makes sense. We create a God in our image. The Celtic Gods and Goddesses sprang from the forests and lakes of their homelands. Eastern deities likewise were a reflection of their life, their land and their situations.

And so my *God* was a woman of strength, compassion and wisdom – something to aspire to. Of course I wanted to see my face in *God*. As a woman, a healer and a feminist, how could I give over my power to someone other? Worship a white male image I couldn't relate to? So many Witches are women (and vice versa I suppose) because for so long we have been told we are worthless, second best; that we are here to serve men; that we have no power.

Christianity implies that. But I don't believe that Jesus ever said it or thought it. Men twisted His teachings to suit themselves, to try to control women and strip them of strength. Perhaps ancient Goddess religions did the same to men. Sadly it's human nature to want to take power and be in control.

For a long time I was a Goddess worshipping Witch who felt anger and hostility towards the male side, the patriarchal religious thing – and kind of rejected the Pagan God as well. I was going too far the other way to try to redress the balance. But now I know it's not about redressing past wrongs; it's about finding balance. It took me years to see this but how could it be any other way? The concept of God neglected the feminine side. Wasn't I equally denying the masculine? How was that any better?

It wasn't better for me, because I spent years denying and suppressing qualities I must have associated as male. I was strong, in my way, but I also put myself last and let myself be walked over and drained, because I refused to identify with a strength I saw as somehow male.

It was while I was sitting in the sunshine on Glastonbury Tor in England a few years ago that I first began to feel that I was missing the point in my rejection of the masculine. The mythical Isle of Avalon is a place of duality, where priestesses worked alongside druids to create magic. The masculine Tor rises above the more feminine Chalice Well, each complementing and drawing strength from the other. It was also a place where Paganism met Christianity and worked together, for a while at least.

I saw a healer in Glastonbury in a room of rose quartz crystals who asked me if I wanted him to channel Jesus. I shook my head, aghast at the notion. I've always believed Jesus existed, that He was a powerful healer and teacher (many Pagans agree if he was alive today he'd be labeled a Witch), but none of the other stuff associated with Him. I wondered what He could have to say to a little Goddess-worshipping Witch, and I didn't want to waste the session on religious messages and things I thought couldn't apply to me. The healer channeled Quan Yin instead, and it was beautiful. But now, years later, I wish I hadn't been so dismissive.

The lines started to blur then anyway. I walked from the healing room down to Gog and Magog, the two remaining trees of the avenue the druids used to walk for ceremony, and saw the polarities and balances of nature. Can anyone truly follow the cycles of the seasons without seeing the masculine as well as the feminine? I sat by the well of the priestesses, then under the thorn tree planted by Joseph of Arimathea in the abbey, and felt myself begin to open up. Truly alone in this magical place, I opened my mind to the universe. As I allowed feelings I had never acknowledged to pour out of me, I felt a huge shift within me. Initially it was my recognition that I was suppressing typically "male" emotions: anger, fearlessness, speaking my truth. Always empowered by the beauty of the Moon Goddess, I finally began to feel the strength of the Sun God too.

an instant, and people only need one to three sessions to reach that state. I tried it on a friend with a brain tumor, and he stunned his doctors because it has stopped growing and started dying from the inside. It has eased pain and straightened spines. Someone demanded "Heal my migraine" – and it did.

On an emotional level it has turned people's lives around as they somehow receive the guidance they need to take a new direction,

> *Truly alone in this magical place, I opened my mind to the universe.*

I opened my heart to the two.

I was gifted with an object for my altar that represented the God.

I invoked both with equal power when I cast circle.

I felt stronger, more powerful. Complete. I wondered how I could have been so one-sided for so long. I realized that in denying the God I had denied half of myself. And that's giving power away as completely as anyone who shuts out the Goddess.

That step was a beginning, but I continued on my merry Pagan way, seeing no similarities with any other religious beliefs. Certain Christians still told me I would burn in hell, and while I never argued with them (they're entitled to their opinion, despite none of them granting me that freedom), I saw no common ground. I saw only the damage their beliefs caused. War, division, guilt, fear, repression.

And then this year I started doing a new form of healing work that raises the vibrations of the person to a more healing level and alters the DNA of the body as well to bring about healing. It is powerful. I can feel it. It has initiated amazing physical healings and mind-blowing spiritual experiences. The healing happens in

cut something out of their life, and move forward without fear. A friend who is an amazing healer found the strength to begin fulfilling her purpose in life.

I know it doesn't come from me. It is from a greater power than me. It connects the 'patient' with the divine. I was told it came from God. I bristled at the connotation. My teacher said: "Get over it, it's just a word." That was his gift to me. He suggested "God/love/universe" and explained that it can go by whatever name you choose for the divine force, the All There Is.

Different cultures, races and sexes have their own idea and their own word, but it is all the same connection to a higher power. All cultures and religions have their own way of contacting and accessing this higher power too. Some sing hymns, others chant songs of praise or prayer, some whirl into ecstatic trance states through dance, ritual, or sacred medicine. Who are we to judge whether a Christian hymn is more or less effective at reaching the ears of the object of affection than a Goddess-loving song by Wendy Rule? Is a prayer to God more powerful than one whispered to the Moon Goddess? Peace and true healing will seem possible when people understand that the face of the divine is different for everyone, but no less valid.

And to me being a Witch is about healing, and this is an incredible way to do that. I can't stop because I don't like the label. It is just a word.

With each session, each surrendering of myself to the divine plan of healing, I feel closer to the source, by whatever name it is called. This brings me closer to God. And I no longer shrink in fear, or anger. People have had visions, some religious. During one of the first healings, the person on the table opened her eyes and stared at me, stunned. She said I had become Mary for a moment, blue clad and surrounded by light. Months later someone couldn't work out if Jesus was standing next to me, or within me, or if I was Him. Another was dragged back to the scene of the Crucifixion and painfully relived a lifetime that still had her riddled with guilt for not being able to stop it.

described the same two beings. I feel them with me, these angelic beings, my friends, the two I am helping to come through so they can do what needs to be done. And recently they showed themselves to me in the face of someone I was doing healing work on. They are ancient, wise and loving beyond anything I can describe. I am overwhelmed by the gentle, sweet and immense kindness flowing from them. I had felt them before, but seeing them gaze at me with so much love changed me. They are with me now, with me always, and I am overwhelmed by their lovingness. They open my heart and surround me with so much love. Powerful, immense and totally unconditional love.

And looking into the face of my friend – which was physically changing before my eyes, in size, shape and texture – I, a Goddess-loving

...whatever was happening was related to the Christ consciousness... and just as tangible as the Goddess energy I've always felt.

Others with more Eastern views have had metaphysical visions in keeping with their beliefs. It is personal, unique to them, and an opening of their heart to the All There Is. I am just the means to link them to their own concept of the divine. And I have learned to let go of the outcome or the way in which the healing will happen, because when working with the infinite intelligent mind of the divine source, things happen that I could never plan for or even begin to imagine. I defer to a greater wisdom that some call God and some call Goddess.

I've been told there are angels in the healing sessions. They hold people's hands, fix stomach problems, remove the pain of surgery, halt tumors, adjust pelvises, reveal the source of resentment and emotional blocks, and create forgiveness.

People of all different spiritual beliefs have

Witch, felt a shock of recognition that whatever was happening was related to the Christ consciousness. And I felt strongly that this power is just as real and just as tangible as the Goddess energy I've always felt.

Jesus came to earth to heal. He performed miracle healings. And I know that these beings of light that touch my heart and those I help to heal with so much love are from God. Not an angry judgmental Catholic God, but a God who is love. The frequencies that come through me (and many others, because anyone can do this) achieve miracle healings because they link us with the divine and our own inner selves.

When I first read angel lady Dr. Doreen Virtue's books and listened to her meditation compact discs, I baulked at her use of the word *God*. But when I interviewed her recently we realized that our beliefs – Witch and

closer to my divine craft 121

Christian Scientist – were closer than we imagined. She has worked with the Archangels and with God for years, but recently she's started to channel Goddesses too. It was a huge leap for her to accept the existence on some level of Quan Yin, Artemis, Isis, and Lakshmi, and to realize that Mary is Goddess energy. It was a similar leap for me to recognize that Archangel Michael has been in just as many of my healing sessions as the Goddess in all her forms.

I no longer see any irony or problem in embracing both Quan Yin and Jesus. I can call on Archangel Raphael as a healing energy, and Doreen has begun to work with Ishtar and other healing Goddesses. They are all faces of the divine, reflections of what we aspire to be. When I do healing work I feel them all around me, as she does. They are beyond religious labels, names and restrictions. They are pure light and love. Doreen says there are no holy wars on the other side between the deities of different religions, just here on Earth, because we are intolerant, judgmental and afraid. It would be a wonderful world if, instead of the monotheistic model of the major religions – which have inadvertently caused war, repression and a world of pain, as well as immense good – we could aim for henotheism, the worship of one deity while acknowledging that others also exist. In this approach to religion, our concept of God is just one side of the whole. We all show different sides of ourselves to different people depending on their worldviews and their perceptions of us. Why wouldn't God?

religions and spiritual belief systems aren't so different. The basis of all religions is love. We are all seeking some kind of connection with the divine, but it can be a dangerous journey if you refuse to accept the possibility that the reality is so much more immense than you will ever be able to imagine.

I don't suggest that everyone should think this way. Simply that this is a path that has led me to happiness, peace and immense healing for myself and others. Many Witches worship only the Goddess for many reasons, and that is good. The face of the divine that you see is the perfect one for you. If the forces of love, compassion and a greater power speak to you from the mouth of the Goddess, that is just as it should be. If they speak to you through a masculine God, through an ascended master, that is as it should be too.

I know there will be Christians who reject all this outright. I have a friend who is scared for me and freaked out that I can think there is any kind of healing that does not come from Jesus, the one true power (sadly she misses the point that this does). Many Witches will disagree with me too, and that's okay. I imagine there will be some of my Coven who will reject outright what I think. Some still cringe at the *God* word and glare if Jesus or the angels are mentioned. But why is excluding the masculine side any better? Why is it okay for a fellow Witch to tell me who to believe in or how to practice my religion? It's the same judgment and hierarchy I didn't like in the

Your God is a reflection of yourself, and you are a reflection of God. Whichever word you choose to use.

I am still wary of organized religions and their repression of women, but it is the clerics and ancient church leaders who have taken things out of context and twisted the true meaning. I think the actual teachings of all

church, and I don't like it any better when it comes from a woman professing to be better and more enlightened than a Christian.

The Goddess is not something to hide

behind while you persecute others for their beliefs. If we expect to have our religion respected, then we must do likewise to other faiths. It seems that to follow any religious dogma is to think you are right and others are wrong, and that your *God* is better than their *God*. That doesn't make sense to me either. It scares me when Witches succumb to this negative thinking that is really no better than what we have suffered for centuries. Two wrongs do not make a right, and an eye for an eye leaves everyone without sight.

Last week, fifteen years after we last spoke, my school friend called me. We live on different sides of the country now, but the universe has put us back in touch. She had been searching for someone to do this kind of healing on her, and she found me. She apologized for her lack of tolerance as a kid growing up in a traditional and strict Catholic family. But I thank her for it. She sent me on my quest somehow, and now here we are, in the same place. She's traveled with the God, I with the Goddess, but here we finally are in the presence of the divine. In seeking to understand ourselves and each other, we were led to our own truth.

I don't think it matters whether you worship God or Goddess, external or internal, a singular deity or a pantheon. It is all just faces of the divine – and it's your face, your heart, that is divine. It is all within you. Your *God* is a reflection of yourself, and you are a reflection of God. Whichever word you choose to use.

It starts with a phone call. It usually does. An anxious voice on the other end passes along the pertinent facts of the case. Within a few minutes, emails are sent, and calls are going out to those Coveners without web access. And in no time, the healing magic has begun.

From the earliest days of our religion, Witches have been healers. They were the wise women or men who lived on the edge of the community. They were the keepers of herb-lore and the art of healing magick. Those in need would be brought to the healer, and if it were within their power to do so, the afflicted person would be healed. So essential were they to the survival of the community they served, that the image of the "old woman or man down the road who could make things happen if you asked" not only survived the Burning Times, but also even survived into the last century in the remote sections of the United States.

Many things have changed since those ancient days. In many parts of the world, modern medicine now offers a wide variety of pills and elixirs to stave off, and in many cases eliminate the symptoms of most illnesses. Got a headache? Take a pill. Sinuses runny? We have a spray for that now too! Depressed? Take these twice a day, and you'll feel nothing! We've even got injectables for the most critical cases.

Now I'm not saying that modern medicine doesn't have its uses. Every form of healing has a part to play in the grand scheme of wellness, but there are many aspects to healing that no amount of chemical compounds will ever replace. Treating the symptoms is far from healing the whole. The body is only one aspect of the self, and while it manifests the most obvious signs of illness or injury, the whole self must be addressed in order to heal completely. Modern medicine will never be able to help a person heal their mind or mend their spirit. That is where Witches and other practitioners of the healing arts come in.

To a Witch, the concept of treating only the body is ludicrous and shortsighted. Illness, as opposed to physical injury, generally has a mental or spiritual component that is as important as the physical. If you only treat the physical form, the underlying causes for illness are left behind to re-manifest the physical symptoms at a later date. I'm not talking about what the modern medical community would consider "recurring psychosomatic symptoms" (although it could be argued that they are also a manifestation of underlying mental or spiritual issues), but rather things like cancer, cardiovascular illness and other symptoms that have quantifiable residue in the body. When we perform healing magick on a person, we look not only at their physical body, but also at the energies that surround them. These energies can tell us more about a person's condition than any CT scan or MRI. We see not only the manifestation of the illness, but also hints at the root cause of the illness in question. Once we have an idea what has brought about the illness, we work our magick on the body and the spirit. Afterward, we work with the person on what they need to do to eliminate the non-physical aspects of the illness.

Injuries, on the other hand, are very different.

With injuries, we don't usually see as many underlying issues. Such issues tend not to manifest themselves as snowboarding or car accidents and the like. When treating a patient with an injury, we examine the nature of the injury, and work toward healing the physical and spiritual bodies as quickly as possible. In critical cases, we focus additional energies toward supporting the body as it heals. In these types of cases, we are much closer to modern medical practitioners in our efforts, but we also focus on correcting any damage done to the non-manifest aspects of the patient. If those aspects are left untreated, they tend to leave the same kinds of residue that acupuncturists encounter when treating recurring pain. If corrected during the initial treatment of the injury, this residue can be eliminated and the injured person can recover fully with few, if any, lingering affects. If the cases of both illness and injury, the healing techniques of our kind still play a vital role in healing the complete self.

have gotten a reputation in the Craft community as a "healing tradition."

From the day a person dedicates into our tradition, they spend a minimum of at least a year and a day going through their basic Craft training. After learning the basics of magick (meditation, ritual procedure, etc.) and the essentials of anatomy and physiology (one of the perks of having all of those health care workers), the dedicant begins learning basic healing techniques. Beginning with simple "healing spheres" where names are projected towards a sphere of healing energy that is released to help those named heal themselves, the dedicants eventually work toward more advanced techniques such as absent healing.

Absent healing is a technique where the healer is given the name, age and location of a person, and then proceeds to "work" them. This is a technique that has changed little

Healing is perhaps the most manipulative form of magick. When we perform healing work on another person, we ... reorder their entire self.

Healing is a significant part of what Witches do, and in our tradition that is especially true. Among our members, we have an assortment of health care professionals. From doctors, to nurses, to EMTs and CNAs, we have most of the modern medical bases covered. On the other side of the coin, we also have a number of herbalists, Reiki practitioners, and other "alternative" healing practitioners. This combination of alternative healing techniques with modern medical knowledge has given our tradition a very strong foundation when it comes to caring for others. Add to this the number of absent (remote) and present magickal healing techniques that every dedicant to our tradition learns before they get their first degree, and it is no wonder we

since my wife learned it from Laurie Cabot many years ago. With sufficient practice, those three pieces of information are all that is required in order to begin a psychic diagnosis of the person being "worked." One person in the group acts as a control. They have detailed descriptions of the person as well as all of the relevant medical history for the issue in question. The others psychically "see" both the physical and spiritual aspects of the person. After diagnosing any health concerns that they might encounter, the group begins the healing work. This involves sending the appropriate magickal energies to aid the person in healing themselves.

One of the most important things that we

teach the members of our tradition is the great responsibility the goes along with being a healer. Many Witches say, "I don't do manipulative magick, I only do healings." All magick is by its very nature manipulative. We alter patterns, and reorder our universes, albeit in very subtle ways. Healing is perhaps the most manipulative form of magick. When we perform healing work on another person, we alter their patterns at the most basic level. We reorder their entire self. This has tremendous karmic ramifications for everyone involved in the healing. By altering a person's present, we alter a person's future. As an example: a person is suffering from cancer. A number of Covens work this person and the cancer disappears completely. This would appear to be a perfect happy ending, right? But, what if that person was supposed to go through chemotherapy, recover, and counsel others who have a similar type of cancer. Our intervention has just completely redirected that person's life. That is a tremendous karmic weight to bear.

Keeping that weight in mind, we teach our students that whenever possible it is better to aid the person in healing themselves rather than working directly on the person in question. We give them meditations, exercises and spells to aid in their healing. When we work our healing magick, we direct the energy toward them to reinforce their own workings. That puts the person in charge of his or her own future, for better or worse. That is not to say that we have never worked magick directly on a person, but those are rare cases where the person is so critically injured that they might not be able to work healing energy on themselves. On those rare occasions, every Witch who is involved in the healing fully accepts the karmic repercussions of their actions. Understanding and accepting the personal implications of healing others is the essence of the Healer's Path.

Walking the Healer's Path isn't always easy, but it is an essential part of being a Witch. We may be seers, priests and priestesses, or guides, but we reveal our truest natures when lending our hearts and magick to helping others. From the village wise woman or man, to the web-enabled Witch who communicates at the speed of electricity, the tradition of using our skills to ease the suffering of others continues to this day.

Magick is as natural as breathing. It is something we are born knowing, but many of us are trained out of that knowledge in the process of growing up and becoming socialized. All children come equipped with a sense of wonder, an ability to learn, and a desire for information. One of the first things we learn is to use our senses to explore the world. We learn that there are expected ways of interpreting the information from our senses, and that there are five senses that we categorize. When we are learning Magick, we revisit our senses, and learn to interpret the data we usually ignore. Our worldview shifts to one where Magick is taken for granted.

The sense of touch

Our kinesthetic sense is not limited to physical touch. It extends from the physical through to the extra-physical, and includes a sense of the touch and feeling of different energies. Just like a child, who knows what it feels like to walk into a room where an argument has taken place, we reactivate that awareness of residual energies. In a highly developed state, this can lead to an ability to psychometrize, to read the energies from physical objects we touch with our hands, or hold against our skin (forehead, inner arm, throat, or some other part of our body that is more sensitive to extra-physical energy).

Our kinesthetic sense also extends to the skill for finding things that are not physically present. We reach out with phantom limbs to touch things that are distant to us in time and space, to feel texture, heat and cold, judge weight and inertia. If we are also able to move objects that we are not physically in touch with, this is called telekinesis (_kinesis_ from the kinesthetic sense). There is thought that the act of perception makes a connection between an object and ourselves and that distance then becomes an illusion.

The sense of smell

Our sense of smell is little understood by researchers. We do know that it acts directly on the limbic part of the brain, the primal instincts, and may be how we recognize family. Certainly, it is a direct route to our emotions, and bypasses conscious thought in most cases. Smells summon memory, reminding us of times long gone, and alerting us to danger. A fear smell in a crowd instantly spreads, turning it into a mob. Coupled with our sense of hearing, it might be called a primal survival sense.

The Aromancy Guild (Australia and America) explores the deliberate use of aroma for ritual purposes. Incenses, essential oils, wood resins and pheromones are combined to heighten and change perception, enriching and enhancing experiences.

It is good to be conscious of the way smell affects you, and to identify the classes of aroma that make you feel most balanced and aware.

The sense of taste

We taste a variety of substances, among them salt, sweet, savory and bitter. Taste deteriorates over time, which is why older people tolerate spicy food better. Smoking also changes the sense of taste, as does any pervading smell. We can extend our sense of taste to energy, experiencing different kinds of energy like different kinds of food. While it is a rare skill, it is a useful one.

The sense of hearing

Sound vibrates our whole body. Chanting, pure ringing tones, the sounds of water, wind and life are all around us. We learn the skill of selective inattention as we mature, shutting down our awareness of the cacophony of unpleasant sounds that make up our environment. Very few places are actually quiet, so we need to work at it to balance the sounds, and mask them with sounds that are more pleasing to us.

When we are learning Magick, we revisit our senses, and learn to interpret the data we usually ignore.

Hearing needs to be relearned if you are to be a mage. You will need to be consciously aware of the sounds around you, and make a new conscious balance. By re-activating your sense of hearing, it is possible to have extrasensory hearing, up to and including distant hearing without a radio. Exquisite hearing is best practiced away from electronic "white noise" and out of the city.

The sense of sight

In the West, our sense of sight is the sense we use most often. We are so sure we know how it works that I've heard people tell me that they cannot "visualize" (a technique for holding an image in the mind). All sight is visualization. All we actually perceive are wavelengths of light that hit the back of the retina. We translate these patterns of light into recognizable pictures, all unconsciously. Trained artists are aware that each of them sees color differently. We mix colors from a limited palette, and then combine them to make 256 basic colors. Many discover that their range is limited to fewer colors, while some few find that they can identify all these hues plus their tints (adding white) and shades (adding black). In printing, we either use pre-mixed inks, or use a four-color process that uses CMYK (cyan, magenta, yellow and black) on white paper. For the Internet, we use RGB (red, green, blue), and that gives a different quality to the image.

Most people will feel comfortable interpreting colors as reddish, greenish or bluish, and some will add brownish. These are the colors of the earth, sea and sky, the colors of the forest and rivers, colors that reflect and refract.

The physical sense of sight can be easily extended. Often called "the sight" or second sight, this refers to deliberately seeing things that others around you are not aware of. It might be tracers of light, shadows, colors of an aura, or seeing into the realm of phantasm. This is called clairvoyance, though it might as easily be called far-vision.

Vision is also a phenomenon of conscious dreaming, and is shared by artists and visionaries, mages and dreamers alike.

Making connections

In various ways, we seek to use our enlarged and numerous senses, to become more connected with the world of spirit, as well as the world of form. Natural mages are joined to the world, creatively interacting with the enlarged world of perception, and celebrating the world of the senses.

We find connections in nature by watching the seasons unfold, seeing significance in the flight of clouds across the sky, the play of light and shadow, and the movement of the wind and stars. To the mage, all things are important, and none more so that knowing and recognizing their own place in the natural world. Begin your journey into Magick by exploring your senses, and by following the message of the Oracle of Delphi: "Know Yourself."

Know yourself: being real

Raven's rule of magick states that Magick comes from two sources: inside the body and outside the body. The corollary is that if you cannot work with the energy and the magick within your body, then you will not be able to tap into an outside source of magick or energy. In the words of the Charge of the Goddess: "If that which you seek you find not within you, you will never find it without you; for behold, I have been with you from the beginning, and I am that which is attained at the end of desire."

As you progress in your magical explorations and over time, your definitions of *Self* and *Other* may change. For the purposes of this chapter, we are referring to magicks of the Self as those energies generated within your own energy field. Our primary focus is on energy created through breathing, manipulating inner energies, harnessing sound, visualization and movement. Later, we extend that energy by using tools and making connections with outside forces and powers.

The first things we concentrate on are ways of working with the energy of your body, of knowing where the boundaries are between the Self and what is outside the Self.

In working with our bodies, first we take a really good look at ourselves. Who are we? What color is our hair, eyes, and skin? What is our ethnic background? How does that inform our ideas about who we are in the world? If you are a Caucasian person living in America, England, Europe or Australia, you will have certain assumptions about how your body should look. Society will have values related to whether you are male or female, what your body weight should be, how you ought to dress for your place/job in society, what kind of friendships and romantic and sexual relationships you should have, and what your leisure activities are allowed to be.

There will be a list of assumptions about what kind of chemicals it is all right to use — alkaloids such as coffee or chocolate, tea, sugar, salt, preservatives, flavor enhancers and colorings, alcohol, tobacco, prescribed drugs of various types, over-the-counter prescriptions like aspirin, cough and cold medicine, things to help you go to sleep and to stay awake, and so on. There will also be a whole list of things it is not all right to use, mostly herbs and their refined derivatives. The kind of work you do, where you live, the kind of house you live in, the car you drive and where your children (if any) go to school will also be part of your personal identification.

However, if you were a Caucasian living in Japan, China or the Middle East, those cultural markers would all be different from the people around you. Likewise if you are Chinese and living in America, Japanese and living in Africa, Martian and living in Afghanistan, all these are factors you must take into account. No one lives in a vacuum and in beginning any new endeavor, it is important to realize not only who you are, but also who other people think you are, or expect you to be.

Biases

Who do you think you are? Start by answering a few of these basic questions, and explore your biases and cultural assumptions.

1. What country are you from?

2. What is your ethnicity? Include parents and grandparents too.

3. What is your coloring?

4. How acute are your senses? Hearing? Touch? Taste? Smell? Vision?

5. How important is education to you? Why?

6. Do you notice your environment? Are the weather patterns around you the same as those where you grew up? What does the difference, or similarity, tell you about the world?

7. What is your personal ethical code? Is it okay to lie? Under what circumstances? Is it okay to kill? To maim? To defend yourself? To take revenge? Is it okay to run away? Is it important to keep your word? Is it important to do the things you say you will do? Do you make promises? If so, do you keep them? Are you a good friend? Are you good at relationships? How good are your communication skills? Can you debate? Can you think clearly? Are you passionate about things? Do you have a temper? If so, is it under your control? Do you love easily? Are you optimistic or pessimistic? Do you feel your actions have an impact on the world? Why? Will you stand up for yourself? Will you defend principles? Do you know what principles are? What are the personal things you are willing to live for? Are you a deist (belief in deity – one or many)?

8. Have you ever learned a meditation discipline? For how long?

9. Have you ever learned a martial art? Which one? What did it teach you about yourself?

10. Are you a dancer? What kind?

11. Have you done any kind of movement work? Any kind of bodywork that teaches you about balance, center, orienting yourself in space?

12. Are manners important to you?

13. Do you learn easily?

14. What is your learning mode? How do you learn? By listening? By writing things down? By reading about things and then trying them? By watching someone do something and learning from modeling their behavior? By having someone talk you through a skill? By reciting things out loud and hearing them? Do you learn from a combination of these things? Which combination best suits your learning patterns?

15. What are your goals for the next year of your life? What are your goals for the next five years?

16. What talents do you possess? Include everything, including all life skills – shopping, cleaning, cooking – plus creative talents. Can you draw? Can you dance? Can you balance a checkbook?

17. Do you consider yourself to be psychic? In what way? How does that work for you?

18. Have you ever had an "out of body" experience?

19. Have you ever known who was calling you on the phone before picking up the receiver?

20. Have you ever had a mind-altering experience? What was it?

21. Are you healthy? What physical or genetic health conditions do you have, or do you expect to develop? What are you doing to minimize the change of getting those? What is your family health background?

22. What are you allergic to?

23. What are your favorite foods?

24. What are your least favorite foods?

25. Do you like yourself? Do you enjoy your own company? Do you consider yourself to be a whole person?

26. What kind of emotional relationships are you drawn to?

27. Are you monogamous? Are you serially monogamous?

28. Are you polyamorous? Do you have more than one relationship at a time?

29. How important is honesty to you in a relationship?

30. Where on the Kinsey scale would you place yourself? The far left is heterosexual and the far right is homosexual – bisexual is in the middle. Are you right of center or left of center?

31. How do you feel about sexual expression?

32. Are you a romantic person? What does that mean to you?

33. Are you good at organizing? What lets you know that?

34. Are you generally a leader or a follower?

35. Do you have an adventurous spirit?

36. Do you prefer safety and comfortable known circumstances?

This is just a start of questions you might ask yourself. Know the answers to these questions and, from time to time, answer them again to learn how the answers change.

Live naked, pit against the wind
The soft skin power
Of a spirit freed;
No chill shall clothe the holy glow,
No eyes deflect the joy
Of boundless touch,
No lock upon my skin to guard
'Gainst censure or howling cold.
I dare
To walk exposed.
I will not fear to feel.

I love my feet. More accurately, I love being barefoot on the Good Earth (or even on Her not-quite-so-good cousins, Carpet, Asphalt and Linoleum). To me, the sensation of actually *feeling* the ground I walk upon is worth occasional inconveniences like frost, gravel and hot tarmac. (Don't ask me about broken glass or dog shit – my encounters with those came while shod – but more on that subject later.)

It wasn't always like this, though. As a child, I was self-repressed to the point of smothering. Although I lived for a time in Hawaii, a gorgeously sensual land where wearing shoes is the exception rather than the rule, I constantly wore shoes, socks, long pants, and occasionally even long sleeves while others looked askance at me.

Why?

I didn't get it from my family, nor was I raised in a repressive religious tradition. In hindsight, I realize now that I feared vulnerability. I feared feeling. And so, to justify my insecurity, I kidded myself that I was more "adult" than my peers – that short pants and bare feet were childish, and that I had moved beyond them.

Quite the opposite. As I later realized, that fear made me *less* mature, not more.

As puberty washed over me, I felt constrained by my own timidity, wrapped up in an identity no one had forced on me except myself. Rather than confront that identity head-on in public, I explored covert sensuality. Late at night, I'd slip out of my house at night clad only in ragged cutoffs, and then wander off into the woods near our home. Sometimes I even went out near-naked into snowstorms or driving rain, reveling in the sensations I had long denied myself.

I'd never felt so wonderful, so utterly at home.

In hindsight, I realize this was the birth of my Pagan heart.

Which brings me to my point.

"All rites of love and pleasure," says the Goddess, "are my rituals." Though often interpreted sexually, this charge also invites us to love the world in general, to draw pleasure from simple things that have little or nothing to do with sex. To Pagans, feeling is communion. Each act of conscious sensuality is an act of worship. To *feel* our world is to caress the God and Goddess both. While many other spiritual paths demand repression of the senses, our way exalts them.

And yet, so many of us hide behind heavy boots and thick cloaks (literal or otherwise) that deaden our sensations, that protect us from discomfort, yet interpose barriers between our selves and the sacred world around us. We accept the social dicta or creature comforts that cut us off from primal senses. And as much as we exalt sacred sensations, we rarely *feel* with true intensity. It's so much easier to just go numb.

It doesn't have to be this way.

As a living being, sensuality is your birthright; as a Pagan, it's your sacrament. You don't have to hide yourself from stimulation. Embrace it, and Creation embraces you in turn – not in an awkward "lurch hug," but with the passion of a happy bear.

Our path is a holy rebellion – a reclamation of experience that other faiths deny. Our commandment is to dance through life, naked to sensation. It's not always comfortable or safe but *it's not supposed to be!* Pain, too, is a

can see with skin as well as eyes. I notice hazards before I reach them, and skirt them unconsciously through instinct. Our senses, you see, are far keener than our minds admit. Unconstrained, our bodies' powers of perception grow.)

Going barefoot – both symbolically and literally – is a very Pagan thing to do. We see it in the art of Waterhouse or Mucha, in photos of Tori Amos or models from the Dragon and Roses catalogue. Nearly all my lovers have been barefoot women, and their sensual rebellion still fuels my own. Yes, we get a lot of flack from people disconcerted – even infuriated – by our abandon. And yes, we must be careful where we step. But isn't that the Pagan point? Experience with intention, conscientious freedom? To walk the paths of Gods unshod, you've got to be aware; in doing so, however, you reap the Gods' rewards: a vivid life, unbridled love, and integrated spirit.

> To Pagans, feeling is communion. Each act of conscious sensuality is an act of worship.

sacred part of life. The willingness to *dare* opens new roads of perception. Those roads are God-given and Goddess-sanctified, leading deeper into their realm.

Once I accepted sensuality as my road to the Divine, my perceptions opened to an incredible degree. Though sometimes painful, this awareness now helps me to appreciate life, sexuality and spirit more than I ever had before. True, I still step on occasional bits of broken glass (mostly symbolic; occasionally literal), but my freedom has been worth that risk. I feel far more alive.

(About that broken glass: I very rarely step on it at all. Without shoes, I'm far more intuitive about where and how I walk. It's like I

My bare feet reflect a greater sensitivity. By forsaking my childhood insecurities and embracing sensuality, I learned to appreciate Creation as a whole, Light and Dark, comfort and discomfort. It's been challenging – still is, at times – but I highly recommend it.

My lover calls it "living naked." I call it feeling free.

"There is nothing more powerful than an idea whose time has come."
— Victor Hugo

I have always had an inclination towards Paganism and Earth-centered spiritual paths. No other type of spirituality made sense to me as a child. I always felt that going with nature was the safest bet in life.

Luckily, I always doubted the things taught to me in school — to my parents' dismay! I felt intuitively that the best way to guide oneself through life's many decisions was to ask: "Is this natural?" If the answer was "yes," then I would usually do it. If the answer was "no," then I thought it was better to make another choice.

Another intuitive tool that was gifted to me as a child was the ability to understand that just because most (or even all) people believe something, does not mean it is right or true. It is possible that everyone could be wrong.

It was these two insights — an intuitive trust in nature and that a majority of people could be wrong — that eventually led me to the study of nutrition and eventually the discovery of raw-food diets.

The role of food

Different foods fuel different destinies. What you are eating now is leading you to a certain destination. Where are you headed with your current diet?

One of life's greatest goals is to design a proper diet for ourselves — one that makes us feel amazing in each moment, connects us *directly* with nature and nature spirits, benefits the environment, is compassionate, leads us to limitless beauty, and increases longevity.

These days, people are finally beginning to realize that chemical and artificial diets are failing. The upsurge in the popularity of organic food — the largest growing sector of the food market — is indicating that more and more people are fed up with junk food. And now comes a system as ancient as the ageless and as new as the future — an all-natural, organic living plant food regimen and lifestyle. Another fascinating and interesting choice is becoming available which has become known as: the raw-food diet.

The beginning

At some point in our history we must have eaten as every other creature on the planet eats — a raw diet — because there was nothing else. And most of our original raw diet was plant-based because it was the easiest to procure and most in alignment with our physiology. Our presumption as a civilization has been that cooking helped us evolve and mature as a species. This is simply an assumption. A growing body of archeological evidence is indicating that we have not evolved, but have been de-evolving as a species, becoming more de-mineralized, brutal, unconscious, materialistic, less spiritual, and fractured. (For an in-depth scientific treatise on this concept, see Michael Cremo's books *The Hidden History of the*

Human Race and *Human Devolution*.)

Is it possible that the food we have eaten all our lives has been inappropriate? Is it possible that the food our immediate ancestors ate all their lives was also unsuitable? Is it possible that the food we eat is not contributing to our highest potential? In the seminars I present I will often ask the audience: "What would happen if we fed a tribe of gorillas coffee and donuts for a week?" (At one lecture a woman blurted out: "They'd turn into cops!")

It is assumed since we have been eating animal food and cooked food for so long that we have become adapted to those substances. This may or may not be true. Just because we can chew something up, swallow it and live long enough to tell someone about it does not mean that this is an ideal spiritual or health food for us. We are always adapting to everything. I know that my body somehow adapted and survived eating Wonder Bread, Flintstone's Chewable Vitamins, Fruity Pebbles and Chicken McNuggets!

amount of energy expended to digest food increases dramatically. My experience was that I would have to sleep or nap for short periods after every large cooked meal – until I went raw. Now I never tire after eating; most of the time I have even more energy. (For more information on raw food and enzymes I recommend Dr. Edward Howell's seminal book *Food Enzymes For Health and Longevity* which contains hundreds of peer reviewed medical journal references on the subjects of enzymes, eating raw, effects of cooking, longevity, and much more.)

The field of raw nutrition is now zeroing in on a phenomenal health science strategy. We now know that raw plant foods – especially high-quality fats and oils – can restore elasticity to the tissues and chemistry to the brain. Green-leafy vegetables provide fiber and alkalinity to help keep us clean on the inside. The symmetry of fruit imparts its pattern upon us. Mineralized raw foods, and their juices or powders, can restore mineral density to the bones, hair and teeth.

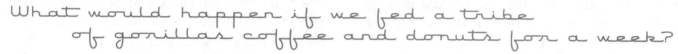

What would happen if we fed a tribe of gorillas coffee and donuts for a week?

Now I live on a diet of raw plant foods including: fruits, vegetables, nuts, seeds, sprouts, flowers, grasses, herbs, sea vegetables, and "superfoods" such as honey, bee pollen, spirulina, blue-green algae, cacao beans, wolfberries, etc. I have eaten this way 100% since 1994 – and, yes, I am still alive! A most remarkable metamorphosis has taken place in my soul indicating to me the true power of the cosmic law: "You are what you eat."

Scientifically the largest difference between raw food and cooked food is enzymes. Enzymes in our food are destroyed between 108 and 120 degrees Fahrenheit. When enzymes are missing and our food has lost its water content (through cooking), the

Benefits

We are a work of art in progress. Nature's paintbrush is always in motion. What we eat applies "food-mineral cosmetics" to the inner and outer painting which we call our tissues, which become visible externally in the warm, vivid, youthful freshness of the hair, nails and skin. Raw foods can be:

Cleansing – They help to move waste out of our digestive tract and colon.

Detoxifying – They assist in removing older debris that has accumulated deeper in our muscles, organs, bones and connective tissue.

Fun – What is more fun than eating a mango with your lover on the beach?

Juicy – We could all be juicier!

Tasty – I probably eat raw just for the taste. Imagine the taste sensation of a watermelon.

Sexy – Hmmmm … I could get into trouble here. No comment.

Rejuvenating – Feeling youthful all the days of one's life is the greatest feeling ever.

Simple – The fastest food on the planet.

Exciting – Anyone can get excited about dining at a raw-food restaurant.

I believe that mineral-rich, nutrient dense raw foods are nature's true fountain of youth. Raw antioxidant compounds in these foods help delay or slow free radical damage to cells and tissues, and help preserve the look and feel of youthful tissues and skin.

Nobody knows how long he or she will live, and when you feel great every day, you don't care, because you feel you are immortal. How we feel in the moment is everything. And my experience is that you will find eating raw brings you more into the moment and into the vibration of every day being the best day ever!

Myths

Conventionally grown food has enough minerals to keep us healthy.

False. Conventionally grown food is dangerously low in minerals such as zinc and selenium, and very low in organic sodium, and even major minerals such as calcium.

Organic food has a significantly higher mineral content than conventionally grown food, and even organic food may not be sufficiently rich in minerals. This is one of the reasons why I recommend raw superfoods such as grass powders, spirulina, blue-green algae, goji berries, wolfberries, hemp seed, maca, cacao beans, and other foods, such as herbs like nettles that have more than just normal nutrition. This is also one of the reasons why I recommend that each individual attend nutrition lectures or read books on the subject so that improved food choices become more consciously available.

Raw-food diets are the best diets for everybody.

False. I love that belief. However, it does not seem to be true. I'm glad it works for me. I believe it could work for anyone if they proceed cleverly, intuitively and with a smile. It is important not to be dogmatic. If the raw lifestyle happens for you naturally, perfect. If not, that is perfect too.

Eating 100% raw food is the best diet ever.

False. I feel that working towards an 80% raw-food diet is "safer" for beginners, more "real" in the "real" world, and probably easier to balance for vegetarian and vegan enthusiasts. I have been eating 100% raw since 1994, and I know it is the only way for me. I am deeply inspired by the magic of it. I like letting people know that eating 100% raw is an option. However, it is not the only option. I am a huge believer in freedom of choice. Let's put all the choices on the table and choose based on what is ecological, environmental, fun, enjoyable and empowering for us in the moment.

There is enough protein in a vegetarian, vegan or raw-food diet.

True. There can be, if the diet is considerably rich enough in high-quality amino acids. This brings us back to the superfoods. Superfoods contain an enormous array of amino acids. Most superfoods are actually complete proteins (see above list).

Some important oils are found only in fish.

False. Omega three fatty acids, found in oily fish, can also be found in flax or hemp seeds. Some of the more exotic oils found in fish, such as EPA and DHA (which are "long-chain" omega three fatty acids), can be found in spirulina, blue-green algae, golden algae (which can all be found in health-food stores) and purslane (an important wild herb for vegetarians).

You get all the nutrients you need on a vegetarian, vegan or raw-food diet.

True. One is likely to get more nutrients on a raw-based diet than a cooked diet simply due to degradation of most nutrients in the cooking process. I have extensively researched this concept of deriving all nutrients from the plant world. I recommend a very broad-based diet containing a wide-variety of plant foods – mineral-rich foods in particular – including vegetables (especially green vegetables), nuts, seeds, sea vegetables, sprouts, grasses (wheatgrass), herbs, flowers, superfoods and certain supplements for those needing them. I am also a strong advocate of MSM (a salt-like biological form of sulfur found naturally in rainwater, ocean water and trees which increases flexibility, healing time, rejuvenation, and more), whole-food vitamin C (vitamin C that comes from powdered fruits instead of synthetic laboratories), and a few other types of simple supplements.

Vitamin B12 must come from animal sources.

False. General estimates of the population of the United States indicate that as much as 39% of the general population are borderline deficient in Vitamin B12. Obviously, most of this group are meat eaters. This is indicating that even a meat diet may not meet B12 needs. Vitamin B12 is made by bacteria. The best source of vitamin B12 is, in fact, dirt. Remember the old phrase: "God made dirt, dirt don't hurt." (I do not believe in a bearded male deity in a bathrobe floating in outer space, but the saying could be switched to: "Nature made dirt, dirt don't hurt.") If we ate from the earth directly without washing, the way our ancestors ate, we would be getting appropriate nutrients (such as vitamin B12) and friendly bacteria for our intestines (our intestines are analogous to roots turned inside out).

There are other viable options to get Vitamin B12. The latest research on the powdered algae spirulina is that it contains "human active" vitamin B12 in significant quantities. My experience is that spirulina (three tablespoons per day) can reverse a vitamin B12 deficiency as long as it is not chronic and severe (which could require a brief period of vitamin B12 supplements or injections). Other plant-based Vitamin B12 sources include: sea vegetables (seaweeds), blue-green algae and fermented foods (sauerkraut). If one is uncertain or confused, plant-based Vitamin B12 supplements are available at any major health-food store.

Healing with nutrition and raw diets

"Doctors give drugs of which they know little,
Into bodies, of which they know less,
For diseases of which they know nothing
at all."
— Voltaire

I was raised by two medical doctors. That is why I am a raw foodist today. Luckily I got the picture early on that drugs and medicine were something other than the best substances ever and that good nutrition, exercise, sunshine, inner calm and fresh air made more sense.

From a child visiting my father's office through to experiences in the present day, I have come to realize that healing is a very personal journey. It seems that if someone shifts their diet too radically and too quickly, they can get quite out of balance. And balance is the most important key for long-term success and healing with vegetarian, vegan and raw-food diets.

No matter where we start, we can periodically undertake a cleansing program with raw foods, fresh juices, wheatgrass, superfoods and/or supplemental enzymes to keep ourselves pure. From there we find our way back into balance and continue moving forward.

Healing with nutrition

There is always a spiritual symbolic message contained within ill health to be discovered. Once one has unlocked the secrets of that message and "gotten the point" then healing is graceful. I have learned that the richer the diet is in minerals and raw food, the faster the healing that occurs.

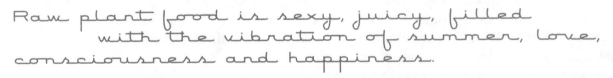

Raw plant food is sexy, juicy, filled with the vibration of summer, love, consciousness and happiness.

There are some fantastic raw-food healing centers available to you. You can go to these centers and fast or eat 100% raw, experience time away from the city in a vegan-friendly environment, get in touch with your spiritual side, and more! (For a list of raw-food detoxification and healing centers, see my website and click on links.)

Increasing popularity

I love Andrew Carnegie's famous phrase: "Anything worth having is worth working for." Unfortunately, or perhaps fortunately, nothing of real value ever comes easy in this world. Everything must be earned. The popularity of raw-food diets has been the result of an increasing number of raw-food enthusiasts, naturopaths, medical doctors, nutritionists, spiritual teachers, health-care practitioners, raw-food chefs, raw restaurateurs, raw-food educators, nutritional researchers, yoga teachers, and health-food store employees who have in a loosely combined effort slowly, yet surely, driven this movement into mainstream consciousness in America. I have been working tirelessly since 1994 at the heart of this movement and I feel like we are just starting to make progress. And I am not alone. There is a solid group of raw foodists in this movement who have been captured by the charm of the impossible: to bring this raw information into mainstream consciousness. But the real trick is that raw health makes the impossible probable.

I suspect that the main thing that draws people towards raw-food nutrition is simplicity and controllability. Plant foods are more controllable than animal foods. Their quality is more certain. Their purity is clearer. We, as a species, went so far to the extreme of trying to eat absolutely anything we could put in our mouths (shrubs, stones, bugs, small animals, large animals, sea animals, larvae, plastics, margarine, pesticides, antibiotics, and chemicals of every description) that the raw-food diet represents the karmic alternative to eating "anything." It is about discernment. It is about going from the worst food ever to the very best and noticing the difference.

Also, raw plant food is sexy, juicy, filled with the vibration of summer, love, consciousness and happiness. That is what is attracting celebrities, teenagers, and fun-loving individuals to the diet.

The future of raw-food nutrition

The philosopher Wittgenstein was asked if he was sure that what he was saying was true. He replied, "It's close enough." Wittgenstein's response is actually quite brilliant. There are patterns in nature. Through discerning those patterns and experimenting with them – even if our theories are not quite exact – they are close enough to allow automobiles to operate, to permit airplanes to fly, to launch satellites, to create computers, to communicate via email, and on and on.

This is what is happening in the field of nutrition – especially in vegetarian, vegan and raw-food nutrition. Due to the huge information resources that have been opened up in recent history by the internet, we have begun to see the patterns that can allow plant-based dietary systems to work for more and more people. We are now more capable of making it all work for larger and larger groups of people.

The culinary art of raw-food preparation has reached an extraordinary level of sophistication. Raw food tastes better than cooked food now. We have seen an enormous explosion in this field from people interested in raw cuisine – even people who are not vegetarian or raw-foodists. This is where we are seeing the biggest sector of growth in the raw-food field.

Conclusion

Raw-food nutrition reconnects us directly with nature. I believe it is an incredible addition to those on the path of Earth-based spirituality. The cleansing, healing and rejuvenation that raw food brings to our body and soul invites in a heightened sensory acuity that increases dormant powers. My experience, and the experiences that thousands of others on this path have shared, has proven to me that raw-food nutrition allows a more abundant array of dreams, magick, synchronicity, tribal wisdom, plant knowledge, psychic abilities and mystical experiences in nature to flow through you. This is what continuously inspires me, even after all these years.

Continue to educate yourself in the nutrition field. Please make informed and compassionate decisions. And most of all be sure to make every day the best day ever!

better it be when the moon is full

creating the magickal community

neophytes in the nest
starting out in witchcraft
Scaerie Faerie

If you decide to go for a wander down the path of the Witch, there are going to be a lot of people offering advice. Books, magazines, the web and personal contacts – everyone is likely to have an opinion on how you should proceed. Naturally, this can be more than a little daunting, since early on you're unlikely to be sure how much you should take to be carved in stone and how much is just individual opinion.

My advice (hell, what's one more opinion?) is to take most, if not all, of it as subjective. You came to explore this particular path because you feel you've something in common with its other people traveling along it, but take care to remember that some of them, however long they've practiced, will be no less confused about the Craft than you are. Make sure you don't allow their dogma to sneak up on you and sink its teeth in!

The usefulness of extensive reading is one of the few things nearly all Witches agree on. In the masses of books you'll be reading, not just as a neophyte Witch but for the rest of your life, you're bound to pick up countless tips to help you along your way. Treat them as just that, though – suggestions to get you started, not instructions for the rest of your life's practice. Take things slowly, and as you read, jot down any ideas and inspiration you find particularly helpful in a notebook. You can use or reject whatever is appropriate in this collection of ideas as you begin to find your feet magically. Experiment and gradually learn more about yourself as a Witch, Magical practitioner and spiritual individual.

The important thing is to read a wide variety of material. You wouldn't claim to be an authority on world customs if you'd never been outside your own country. Likewise, you can't expect to be an expert on magical traditions without studying as many up as you can. You won't agree with everything each writer says, but the most balanced view of reality is built from the bits and pieces you'll find in lots of different sources. Learn to recognize philosophy or practical suggestions which are right for you.

Similarly, don't feel you have to rush into obtaining all the traditional accoutrements of the Witch. Some beginner's manuals out there don't make it clear, as they offer advice on how to lay your hands on tools, Magical names and the like, that it is not necessary to have all these things from the word go. Some you may never find you need – I know Witches who've been practicing for years and still don't own an athame. I don't have patron deities, and doubt I ever will (more on that later). Don't let anyone poke you with broom-handles because you did things "wrong" (which usually means different from the way they'd do it) or to give you orders on how to conduct yourself on your own path.

If, for instance, you don't feel you need a permanent altar, hold back on putting one together until you do. For years I constructed a temporary one with whatever I had to hand for each spell and ritual. Allow your altar to change and evolve with you, rather than feel obliged to construct a textbook one just to feel Witchy. If you yet haven't found the perfect magical tools and elemental representatives for your altar, it's no big deal. In the end, the items you need will appear under your nose.

My seemingly endless search for a cauldron ended with an expenditure of seventy pence in a charity shop in Glasgow just this year!

In a similar vein, experiment with different methods of ritual and spellcraft until you find the ones that fit your personality. Nothing is going to diffuse the energy you whip up like feeling foolish while doing it. I have a favorite "recipe" for spell work that, with a few tweaks to colors and other correspondences, can fit any situation. It's these types of things that will probably serve you best.

…don't allow their dogma to sneak up on you and sink it's teeth in!

Probably the biggest mistake I made when I started out at around fourteen years old was to assume that my magical efforts would work first time round. Magic is the product of a focused mind and will – and you don't get that just by laying out ingredients and reciting some words. This is why accomplished Witches irritate so many neophytes by insisting that the best spells are ones you write yourself. That usually gets the response: "C'mon, don't be mean! Share one that works, huh?" Sorry, but it's true. When a spell or ritual comes out of your own time and effort, it's tailor-made to your purpose, styled to suit you personally and is much more likely to engender the necessary spark of magical energy. An athlete must train hard to be of Olympic standard and the most naturally gifted singers needs to exercise their vocals chords to achieve the most from their talent. In the same way, a student Witch needs to keep flexing their magical muscle sin order to produce spells and rituals he or she is happy with. So don't stress! The magic comes more naturally when you take the pressure off yourself.

Some "authorities" push the need to take a magical or Craft name (usually with words like "Silver," "Moon" and "Wolf" tucked in

there for some reason). If you have one or feel the need to acquire one, fine. Not having one won't make you less of a Witch, though, and you don't need one to self-initiate (although some Covens may insist you have one). I don't have a Craft name, just some pseudonyms I write under. I'm happy to approach the Circle under my given name, so again, if this feels right for you, don't feel obliged to develop a Magical alias.

As I mentioned earlier, I don't have a patron deity or deities either. This isn't because I haven't found mythological characters I identify strongly with – *au contraire*! It's because I personally don't believe that deities are independently sentient beings with personalities like our own. I'm with the Buddhists on the idea of the Creative Force as an all-encompassing neutral source, rather than something definable. If you feel the same, then there's no point allowing yourself to be pressured into devoting yourself to other people's belief systems.

An alternative for those of us who like to interact on the physical plane with our spiritual mentors is the honoring of totem animals, a concept derived largely from Native American spirituality (although we see vestiges of the idea in other cultures and in historical figures like Richard the Lionheart). If there are any animals you've been drawn to or surrounded by throughout your life, or if you feel that you share a lot of the character traits of the species, study them closer and learn. Sometimes they'll help you to develop potentials that you are finding it hard to cultivate within yourself. At other times they'll remind you of the need for balance in nature by displaying the complete opposite to a side of your personality and lifestyle.

Another topic that sometimes concerns new Witches is how "out" they're going to be about their Craft. Unless you've come up with a killer money spell (gimme gimme gimme!), it's pretty likely that you work for a living in some way. And unless you work in an occult book or supply shop, chances are that your beliefs would raise a couple of eyebrows among your workmates.

Witches and Pagans really are everywhere today. We work in the arts, sciences, law, manual labor, the caring professions, teaching, agriculture, arboriculture, retail – the list goes ever on. Many, however, keep their spirituality to themselves. It takes time for the world to change, and a lot of professions are often uncomfortable with being associated with any member of a more controversial spiritual path. Science and medicine, for example, tend to be pretty cagey about linking themselves with anything that cannot be proven by experimentation in laboratory conditions. This would probably even encompass more recognized religions such as Christianity, Judaism and Islam if it were not so difficult to take opposition to these paths publicly, but due to the major religions' political power, science has to accept that it plays host to Ph.D.s, M.Sc.s and B.Sc.s who believe that Jesus walked on water and rose from the dead. The more unusual spiritual paths, however, are easier to reject.

So, why would you even bring up the subject of your chosen path at work? Granted, society rarely changes of its own accord, and those brave souls who have stood up for their right to individual choice throughout the ages deserve our respect and gratitude, but that isn't to say that you should feel compelled to jump to the role of crusader (or possible martyr!) unless you are confident that this is what you want to do, and you have the practical and psychological resources to do it. Do you want to become a warrior for a cause, or do you just want to do your job well?

In Britain, where I live, Employment Discrimination laws protect differences in race, color, age, sex, sexual orientation and disability. If the law is applied to the letter, technically religion and spirituality are not protected. However, legally, an employer cannot ask you what your religion is. So why does the whole can of worms need to be opened at all?

I am an honest person. If somebody asks me a question, I will answer it truthfully, but I'm not going to run around starting conversations about spirituality just so I can tell everyone I'm a Witch. Wouldn't you find it a little nauseating if someone from any other path did that? Apart from anything else, I'd far rather be seen as me the person who is damn good at her job, than as me the Witch, especially when such a label is so open to misinterpretation. To define myself by any single aspect – sex, color, taste in clothing, anything – seems more than a little insulting, and a sad neglect of every other part of me. The only person I've ever discussed my path with at work was someone who recognized the meaning of my pendant, and then identified herself to me as a Witch, showing me her matching symbol.

The best way to be a Witch in the workplace is just to be a person in the workplace. If you don't act and speak as if you should be seen and treated differently, then it's highly unlikely that you will be. The best way Witches and Pagans can present themselves to society for attitudes to start changing is just to be normal people with the same interests as everyone else – music, films, books, TV programs and so on. Those topics make for more relaxing lunchtime talk, too!

I have this paralyzing fear that one day Witchcraft will be absorbed by the New Age Public Image Police ...

One final issue that the neophyte Witch will need to consider is the relationship between the Craft and the so-called darker aspects of life and magic. I have this paralyzing fear that one day Witchcraft will be absorbed by the New Age Public Image Police, and we'll all be told to run screaming from the darkness in life as if we were guilt-ridden trainee monks at Catholic camp. (As a Scorpio, I think I'd then be obliged to leap off a cliff or something.) My dictionary doesn't associate the word "dark" with evil, which is a subjective term in itself. It simply talks about "minimal or absent light" and "deep color or tint" – hardly grounds for an Inquisition!

We begin our existence in this life in the dark since very little light shone into our mothers' wombs. As a seed germinates underneath the soil, it is immersed in darkness. Our universe is an infinite mass of darkness peppered with planets and stars, tiny patches of exploding light amidst the enormous blackness. Darkness is the Alpha of existence as well as the unknown Omega which receives us at the end of what we usually view as our lives.

It's therefore worrying to find the association of darkness with evil in some of the newest waves of Paganism. For a belief system which prides itself in valuing balance, much of modern Witchcraft is now slipping into a fear of the dark and the use of phrases like "White Witch." There seems to me to be a lot of denial in such a statement. If someone is free from preconceptions about the nature of existence, it seems strange to be so quick to dissociate themselves from parts of it which are very evident.

A while ago, I was reading an introductory guide to Witchcraft, designed for the younger reader. My eyes nearly fell out of my head when the author advised their readers that to work a Circle widdershins (i.e., an anti-clockwise direction) was associated with quite nasty things and was best avoided. While I am not advocating teaching something as heavy as hexes (which is what I am assuming this writer was referring to) to beginners and the young, since when did this become the only purpose of this aspect of magic? Dark colors, the waning and dark moons, and the widdershins Circle are tools used to drive away and eliminate, such as a lingering illness (perhaps followed by a building of strength and health with the next waxing moon), excess weight, addictions or destructive behavioral patterns that are making the person unhealthy, or the negative influences of a domineering person? How is it a bad thing to wish to eliminate these things?

Myths and legends are full of the need to find equilibrium between darkness and light and consequently dark, but not inevitably evil, Gods and Goddesses are everywhere. Kali, the Hindu Goddess of creation and destruction, is a fierce warrior who cuts down the redundant to make room for the new. The Celtic Morrighan is a warrior Goddess and spirit of the phantoms of the psyche, fear, despair and fury. The Gorgons represented a similar concept of the darker side of our nature – Medusa's fury turned all those who looked upon her to stone. The Egyptian God Set is another example of the darker, more purpose-driven side of existence, while Hades, Greek God of the Underworld, and his bride Persephone relay a tale perfectly representative of the inevitable and unstoppable forces of puberty, the loss of innocence, and the passing from this life to the next.

Life is an ongoing cycle of creation and destruction, and those who worship nature have no reason to fear this. None of us are above the cycle, and the darker side of life will knock on our door from time to time. This needn't always be an unpleasant experience. Problems arise though when we close ourselves of to our personal darkness. It is when we don't recognize qualities such as our fear and anger that they tend to creep up on us unawares, working from the subconscious outward.

To banish or destroy is not "White Witchcraft" but neither is it evil. We all move through phases of discarding aspects of ourselves that are no longer useful. I certainly look, feel and carry myself very differently to the way I did when I was seven! Life keeps a pretty good balance, so honor the process. As in all aspects of your life as a Witch, see, listen, think, and then decide for yourself.

A profound sense of knowing

I remember the moment I knew there was a power in me that was ready to erupt. I felt a surge of knowing that I had never experienced before. It felt forbidden and I was confused and afraid. I knew I could not let this energy grow. It was much too strong for me. I had so many questions and no guidance. With fear of the unknown steering me, I buried the pulse deep within and never told a soul. I was thirteen years old …

Moment: it was Wednesday evening. I had just finished an amusing bath with Mr. Bubble. I was still giddy from the suds tickling my nose and I couldn't help but giggle while I slipped into my nightgown.

As I pranced down the hallway toward my bedroom, my mother approached me. "Your Grandmother is not feeling well today," she said. My feet came to an abrupt stop. Instantly, my mood shifted. A slow wave of energy crept through my feet and up to my heart. The beat of my heart began to accelerate. "Your Grandmother is not feeling well today." I know that is what my mother said to me.

But the echo in my ears said, "I am going to die."

My mother could see the look of panic in my eyes so she began to reassure me. "Don't worry, Grandma is going to be just fine," she said. But my heart knew a different truth that my mind could not decipher. In a split second, my awareness was transported to a parallel realm. Suddenly, I grew very cold and felt chills unfurl all over my body. I hugged my mother, said goodnight and decided to seek comfort under my lion and tiger print, ruffled bedspread. I knew my feline friends would protect me.

Out of complete stillness, I was jerked from a sound sleep. A force grabbed me by the shoulders and jolted me into a sitting position. In the same motion, my breath, my life's force, was sucked from my body. I clutched my throat. As I gasped for air, I could hear a whooshing sound soaring past my ears. Though I was in complete darkness, I could see the remnants of a tunnel, and I realized I was speeding through it. Confused, I tried desperately to calm my mind and relax my body. In an effort to gain my composure, I stopped struggling to breathe, and to my relief, the whooshing sound stopped as swiftly as it had begun. I was now floating in the tunnel. I felt as if I was suspended in time. There was tranquility all around me but the tunnel was so dark and I was incredibly frightened. What took only seconds felt like an eternity.

Again, my body jerked. This time air was propelled back into my lungs. My chest expanded rapidly. My life's force was returned to me. I could feel the energy massaging my heart as it did earlier in that evening. My pulse began to slow its hasty pace. Exhausted, I lay down to finish my sleep. As I rested my head on the pillow my eyes glanced at the time on the clock – 3:34 am.

I believe these two things to be true.

I felt my Grandmother take her last breath.

And it was she who had given me new life.

I was too young to know it then but this moment was a significant turning point in my life. This moment – so clear, so vivid and unmistakably fused with magick.

The power began to re-emerge in my late adolescent years. I decided not to suppress it any longer but to allow it to grow. I treated it as an exploration of the mind. I learned to follow my instincts and I learned to develop my senses. A thirst to broaden my skills was guiding me now. I was on a quest to cultivate my power, my spiritual self.

With each passing year I began to yearn so much for a spirituality that valued this magnificent Earth and cherished her many gifts. A creed that appreciated the nature of life and that nurtured life. My core was searching for a path and to my astonishment, my conductor was, of all things, a cherry wood bookcase called "The Piano."

Moment: late one evening I was assembling this gorgeous, cherry wood bookcase. As I inserted the shelves, I began to imagine the eclectic books that would fill the spaces. The shelf in the middle of the bookcase rested at an angle, similar to the top of a podium stand. As I stared at this featured shelf, the letters "B-O-S" popped into my mind. I paused for a moment to contemplate what the letters could represent. As I placed the bookcase in the bedroom I remember thinking, "This podium style shelf must have some amazingly fabulous book to rest upon it. I'll create something with an artistically antique guise – a book with a look that says: 'I've been around for centuries.'" I went to bed and pondered why this particular shelf was so hypnotic.

The next morning I rose, made my coffee and turned on the television to catch a glimpse of the news. The first image that appeared on the screen was a stunningly beautiful woman dressed in all white speaking about a book she wrote. Her name was Phyllis Curott and the name of her book was *Book of Shadows*.

B-O-S. I froze for a second and recalled the previous night's events. I then promptly got dressed and went on a quest for this book. Undoubtedly, I was meant to have it.

Book of Shadows was my oxygen. I consumed it. I related to the feelings, emotions and thoughts conveyed in the book so deeply. I felt as if Phyllis was reading my mind. It was the first time I realize that someone else experienced the same sensations that I did. Someone else had this sense of knowing. *Book of Shadows* was such a great comfort to me and reading it was one the most enriching experiences of my life. It helped me to open my mind, my heart and my soul to the core of me. And from the moment our energy converged, I knew – I was a Witch. It is something I will cherish eternally: the book, the experience and the moment.

As I delved deeper into the book, it became unmistakably clear that *Book of Shadows* was the conduit meant to broaden the world of Witchcraft to me. Upon reading it, phenomena that happened to Phyllis would happen to me. The magick was making itself more and more visible in my life. I was euphoric. My senses were thriving and I wanted to share my elation with the world and publicly proclaim: "I'm a Witch!"

But I didn't. I decided to take time to hone my skills. My desire was to be true to myself and true to the Craft. I sought to clarify the sanctity of Witchcraft. So, I declared myself a Solitary Witch.

The craft of being

Solitary power is intoxicating. I discovered so much about the true nature of my being, my core self. It led me down the path, through the forest and to the temple that housed the vital power I was on a quest to acquire. Here, in this exceptional place, is where I met the Goddess within. She obliged me to descend deeper and surrender to the power. For it was essential that I obtained power over *me*. This was no easy task. There were many tests involved. Tests in will, strength and courage; tests in believing in one's choices. It was an adventurous path through all intricacies of the self and a journey of acceptance.

Aligning with the elements and the universe allowed me to increase my power. I was able to explore deeper meditations and experience the purity of the Craft. Putting together all of the essential aspects to create a ritual or a spell gave me a sense of honor and pride. The magick provided specific guidance to ensure great success. My intent was pure, and with every ritual I became more and more powerful. My senses were heightened – notably, my inner vision.

> It takes time and endurance to understand the workings of communing with the Goddess within. It takes persistence to create the magick.

In visualization I experienced the most magnificent images of the Goddess. The colors were so rich and so true. The texture was velvety; the shapes, seamless. Her beauty was surreal. In visualization, my essence became elevated, and my mind and spirit soared to all dimensions. They were free to experience all without judgment or limits. Boundless was their journey to other realms.

Development of the mind holds much power. And on this solitary path, honing my visualization skills was significant to aid the release of the mysteries.

Traveling the path of a Solitary Witch taught me patience. It takes time and endurance to understand the workings of communing with

the Goddess within. It takes persistence to create the magick. I meditated and conducted countless rituals before I was able to experience the magickal conclusion I yearned for. The more I put my true intent and energies into my rituals, the more the magick came into fruition. I gained confidence in my ability and learned to appreciate the sacredness in everything. The spirit of the dark and the fortitude of the light enriched me. And the magick began to emerge in my life.

I kept my belief in the Craft hidden. I sought to contain the power of my secret self. I wanted to build this extraordinary part of me and make it strong and resilient. I desired to protect it before I permit the world to have its view. To know, to will, to dare, to be silent …

Kismet

I practiced numerous years as a solitary Witch and I found the venture to be of great reward. But as my power grew, I began to crave something more. I felt the need to commune with other Witches and to be a part of a sisterhood. An urge to mingle with other powerful women became a requirement in order to broaden my realm of knowledge. I pondered the idea of joining a Coven, but felt I needed to do some research first. So I went to my favorite bookstore to obtain inspiration.

The first book that popped into my view had a bright orange cover and was called *Witch Crafting*. Upon closer inspection and to my delight, I realized the book was written by Phyllis Curott. My mentor had written a new book. The magick was still charming my life! I thanked the Goddess, grabbed the book and read it from cover to cover. Since the book was new, I wondered if Phyllis would have a book tour. So, I checked the *Witch Crafting* website. The website was full of information and I was thrilled to see that Phyllis was coming to my town for a book tour and lecture. I explored the website for a short while and clicked on the links button. Intuitively, I was guided to a website for Fiona Horne. I read Fiona's biography and saw photos of her posing with a magnificent snake wrapped around her. I also noticed she had the most exceptional tattoo on her upper arm. I admired her style immediately and the photographs left me intrigued.

The day arrived for the lecture and book signing. I was very excited to meet Phyllis Curott in person and to hear her speak about her experiences in Witchcraft. She had the most valuable instruction and initiation into the Craft and I was curious to know how the guidance she received had enhanced her life. I listened carefully and savored every word. She was just as gracious and lovely in person as I had imagined her to be. I was so honored to speak with her and have her sign my book. The lecture had run longer than expected so she didn't have a lot of time to talk to each person for an extended amount of time, but I was grateful for the few moments I was able to personally seek her wisdom.

Witch Crafting covered many topics and the one I was most interested in at that moment was ways in which to start a Coven. I went to the lecture prepared with mission cards to give out to those who were interested in starting a Coven. I surveyed the room and recognized a familiar face – Fiona Horne. I remember thinking, had I not gone to her website days before, I would not have recognized her. Furthermore, she lived in Australia. I never expected to see her in my neighborhood!

Three months later, I was having coffee with Fiona Horne. She had just moved to Los Angeles. I didn't know it then, but Fiona and I would form a Coven together.

Windfall

I was ecstatic at the way the magick was weaving its way through my life. The movement of the energy was immanent and I went with the flow of it. I stayed focused and my mind mirrored timing and patience.

Seven months later Fiona and I formed our Coven. We had our first Coven meeting at the beach. We communed with the Goddess and discussed the structure and the bonding elements of our Coven. As I sat there, on the sand, I remember thinking how surreal this moment was. It was a beautiful summer day; we were two powerful Witches sitting on the sand, taking in the sun and constructing a potent core. My heart's desire was materializing. It took a few months, but at last, it did happen and it was well worth the wait.

As a founding member of a Coven I feel a grand sense of achievement. I didn't know what to expect. I just trusted my intuition and I am proud to say that being at the power center of a Coven is a momentous affair in my spiritual reality.

And then there were three: Fiona, Lupita and Tri

Fiona and I sought to have a third member of our Coven so that the rhythms and energies we crafted could circulate. I immediately thought about my good friend Lupita. She and I have always connected spiritually. I sensed she had just the right energy to merge with Fiona and me. The only thing was Lupita did not know I was a Witch! So before I could invite her, I had a lot of explaining to do. I thought of this as my next step in moving beyond my Solitary Witch status. Just as I had expected, Lupita was not surprised that I was a Witch. Not only did she celebrate my choices, she embraced me for my beliefs.

The moment the three of us came together there was an intense energy surrounding us. We were an inevitability. We had our core Coven. I remember seeing a circle of energy in motion above our heads. It was a lilac and white ring of light moving in a clockwise direction.

We were two powerful Witches sitting on the sand ...it was well worth the wait.

Our Coven initiation was astonishing. We commenced on the rooftop of an elegant house in the Hollywood Hills. It was late at night and the city lights seemed never ending. The moon was robust. The stars, the trees and the hills surrounded us. It was a picture perfect evening, and the image is forever embossed in my mind's eye. I could not have imagined a more tremendous initiation. Our movements flowed together as one harmonized wave. One power.

The most valuable aspect of being in the Coven for me is the bond the three of us share in and out of our rituals. The bond of sisterhood is the greatest of gifts to me in my life. It is supportive, understanding and non-judgmental. I will treasure this bond and my Coven sisters always.

Our rituals are so potent that my senses reel with passion. My visualization ability is so exceptional during our circles. They harvest immeasurable, vivid, feathery images that grow with each gathering. The rewards from Coven Crafting are boundless and the essence of the Coven is everlasting.

Destined to be

Magick was introduced into my life in the most transformational, mystical manner. I am eternally grateful. I didn't go searching for it. It sought me out, settled in my being and enlightened my existence. It was patient and waited until I was ready to receive the wisdom of my inner power. The wealth of knowledge I gained over the years has enriched my life beyond imagination and I feel as though I am in charge of my own destiny.

This journey into magick has been an exceptional one. It is forever ingrained in my every breath of life. For that is how it was bestowed upon me – through the breath of life.

It has often been said that organizing any group of people is like herding cats. When dealing with Pagans, with all of their various paths, insights, egos and spiritual understandings, this description is even more apt. Let me point out at the start that I am violently allergic to cats, so herding them is not a preferred pastime for me. If you, like myself, would rather see those metaphorical felines dancing in perfect spirals whilst attaining a spiritual epiphany, read on.

There are many ways of dealing with the feline phenomenon when it comes to writing and organizing group ritual, but it takes a willingness to understand both the big picture of ritual outcomes and the intricate details of staging and performance that allow a ritual to flow. Just because those involved in a ritual are of the same generic path does not mean that they will be able to work together, or share an understanding, well enough to make a ritual a success.

Most Witches and Wiccans are solitary creatures. We have our own intimate communication with deity and our spiritual selves. That said, we also tend to work in groups rather a lot, coming together to worship, to celebrate, to learn and to create magic. However, even in a group ritual with an almost perfect group mind, we also tend to keep that core of our own solitary natures at the forefront of any ritual practice. This, of course, adds a unique flavor to our rituals, but it can make organizing one something of a nightmare.

So how do you deal with this? How do you create a ritual that can be enjoyed by many, that has a strong energy base and can be experienced and understood by all those attending? Well, it is probably impossible, but you can get it to be a near thing. You just have to be aware that nothing is ever going to be perfect – this is not a stage show, it's a ritual – but if you take all of the various aspects of practical ritual writing into consideration, you should end up with a result that pleases the majority of participants.

So first off, before you even start thinking about things like form, structure, props, participants, venue, writing, casting, staging and presentation, you need to work out why are you running this ritual in the first place. Is it for a celebration, an act of worship, a means of teaching or understanding a mystery, a rite of passage, spellcraft, or even an ego massage? All of these rituals will have a different form that naturally lends itself to a creative starting point. Defining this purpose will help you to work out everything else.

In solitary work, we really don't need to worry about the final outcome of a ritual unless it involves spell work, as we have the ability to shape our ritual as it happens, to go with the flow and see where we end up. We only have to take responsibility for ourselves and, for the most part, we are in touch with what is going on in our own heads. We don't really have that luxury when we work with other people.

Establishing the main idea or central theme gives you a place to work from. You may wish to have the ritual begin with an outline of the main theme, then, during the ritual, explore the many facets of this theme. You may also have the main theme as the end result of the working, and the ritual built to enhance the idea. For example, a ritual that is intended as a celebration may begin with a story or background as to why participants are celebrating it in the first place. The participants may then begin to build up energy through various means and release it together, forming a rush of celebratory energy, wishes and magic.

A ritual to understand a mystery, on the other hand, may take on the form of a journey. Sometimes these rituals can be broken down into sections of individual journey and group journey, each designed to deepen understanding. A period of meditation or visualization can be thrown in to enhance the effect. Mystery rituals may also have some kind of barrier, whether physical, spiritual or mental, that needs to be broken through to gain the understanding.

al space? Does the theme lend itself to an outdoor or indoor setting, and how does this affect the number of people who can join in.

Like the Wheel of the Year, ritual writing has a flow and a cycle – no one aspect stands alone and each issue impacts on the overall outcome of the working itself. You can think of it as a mind-map with a central idea and veins or branches radiating out, linking with each other in multiple combinations.

From the overall form we move into structure itself. There are two ways to go from here. You may write all of the words that convey your theme and build a structure around them, or you can come up with a structure first and write words to fit it. Both of these systems work well, but for the purposes of this chapter, we will start with structure first. Since

Like the Wheel of the Year, ritual writing has a flow and a cycle – no one aspect stands alone and each issue impacts on the overall outcome of the working itself.

The central theme may have a particular flavor to it – it might be light and happy or dark and mysterious. You may even wish to embrace the darker aspect of a light-hearted theme. This tone is also important to understand when creating ritual, as it can be manipulated to achieve the desired outcome and effect.

Sometimes we might gain inspiration from a song, a story or our environment, and we will use this as our starting point and work from there. Always try to avoid ritual for ritual's sake. Even a low-key teaching ritual has a purpose.

When we know what the ritual's purpose, we can begin to work on the practicalities. How many people will be attending the ritual? Does this determine things like venue or ritu-

this is a ritual (usually religious in nature, and not a stage play), you may wish to begin it with the formation of sacred space by whichever methods you use. You can either have the space already prepared and lead people into it or have everyone assemble in the ritual space and form it around them. Whether you have just specific individuals creating the space or have all participants involved will be determined by your tradition, if you have one, and by the level and understanding of the participants themselves.

Sometimes it can give a good dramatic twist to start the ritual itself outside the sacred space or circle. An effective technique is to send people on individual journeys, having them meet guardians along the way, and then, once they have passed some kind of test or proof of understanding, entering the sacred space where the ritual continues in more structured, or an even wilder, form. In this way participants are able to feel the difference in the various areas or sections of the ritual.

The sacred space can be formed by your usual circle casting method or you may wish to create something unique that fits with the overall theme of the ritual, which may not require a full formal circle casting. Often this will be determined by the ritual's location – outside, you can use a more earthy or unstructured formation, although an urban environment may require a formal protection and consecration before working in it.

Another factor that can determine structure is the size of the space itself. If the ritual is self-contained within a small area, you really don't need to worry about moving the participants around – unless it is within the circle itself. For a large roaming outdoor ritual, you may need to mark pathways or have set gateways to give people visual cues as to where they need to go.

Alternatively you may wish to have guides assigned to the group. In very large roaming rituals we often break participants up into small groups and have the rituals structured as a form of round robin; that is, they move to different ritual sites but keep the same guides. We have even had 'sprites' keeping the groups moving and creating mini-rituals along the paths. The sprites may end up harassing the participants in an elemental way if that is required. For example, a summer elemental ritual of Water may have people dressed as water sprites that herd participants with water pistols to lighten the atmosphere and, if it is really hot, to keep people cool. This is practical and fun as well. In a night ritual, we have utilized fire sprites who carry flaming torches and lead participants on a merry dance through the bush.

Structure also includes things like giving the ritual a starting point, a middle point or body, and an end point. The ending can be very important as it can determine the final state-of-being of participants. Are they grounded or full of energy? What is needed and what is safe? Are they going to end up at a feast which will ground them, or will they be dancing and fire twirling into the night? Do you want them to be able to go to sleep and maybe dream answers for themselves? This is where the manipulation of energy levels becomes part of the ritual structure.

Not only do you have the structure of the ritual to consider, you also need to take into account the feelings of the participants as well. For example, in a ritual such as a hand-fasting, you have predetermined elements such as the binding of the couple and the jumping of the broom. How you incorporate these elements into your ritual is part of the skill of ritual writing. You also need to take into consideration the spiritual paths of the couple, as well as the presence of friends and family who may not be of the same path. These people may even be slightly hostile to the notions of a Pagan ceremony – so putting them at ease and making an enjoyable ritual for all is another consideration for the writer.

If you know beforehand who your participants are going to be, then you have the scope to incorporate their various skills into the ritual – they may be speaking lines, working with inspired utterance, leading group magic, leading a chant or playing music. If everyone is at a similar level or has an established group mind, you can use that to help build the structure of the ritual and keep the energy flowing in a desired way.

With public or open rituals, where there is no such group mind and many participants will be strangers to each other, some sort of bonding ceremony helps to make the ritual a little more cohesive. You may wish to have games before the ritual or some kind of offering made by each person, such as an offering of food to the communal cauldron or a stick to a sacred fire. Each person says their name and gives some information on their path and what they bring to the circle.

To establish a ritual link and understanding, it can be useful to also run some kind of pre-ritual workshop that will establish a level of understanding prior to the working itself. If this is done, there is more chance of participants joining in with high levels of energy and less selfishness. People are unlikely to allow themselves to be challenged if they are not within an environment in which they feel comfortable or sufficiently linked into the ritual. To ensure that this isn't a problem, you will need to find a balance between safety, common sense and the challenging elements of your ritual.

A public ritual usually has disparate energies and participants, which means that it can be hard to get people to let go of themselves and just *be* in the ritual. This is where particular methods of energy raising and working can be added to the structure to help participants get into the flow of the working. Methods such as vine dancing and spiral dancing can get a ritual moving, especially if you give people a simple chant to use or have drummers keeping a beat. This serves to energize and relax at the same time.

Another technique that can be built into the ritual structure to help people actively participate and get into the spirit of the thing is to have them make an object with a purpose in the ritual. If, for example, they are outdoors, have them find a stick or a leaf, a stone or a flower to use as an offering in the ritual. This ties the participants into the purpose of the working. Alternatively, if they are making something that they can take home with them, it gives participants a feeling of linking in to the ritual and fulfils that slight selfishness which can be a hallmark of public events.

Meditation and guided visualization are also used as tools within ritual structure, but the person who is leading these needs to radiate a level of trustworthiness and conduct themselves well in the ritual so that participants will relax into the visualization. Again, guardians who can watch specific sections of a group are a good idea as one person may have difficulty checking the state of a large group of people. In a large group, people will "come back" from the meditation at different times and having them awaken in a healthy state of mind is extremely important, as is keeping the ritual tight.

Once you have worked out the structure of the ritual and the nature of the participants, you can begin to move into the more specific realms of staging and props. Once more,

It can be hard to get people to let go of themselves and just be in ritual.

Appointing guardians whose only role is to observe the mind-set of the group and to let people in or out of the ritual space is also a good idea. These guardians and their roles are introduced in the ritual preparation, so that the participants do not feel trapped in an unfamiliar situation and can leave the area discreetly if they become uncomfortable. It also means that they will not disrupt the ritual for everyone else.

how you go about staging the ritual may be determined by the venue. Do you require a fire pit or will a brazier or cauldron of flame be appropriate? Is there a cleared space or will you wind in amongst the trees? Is the room bare or full of furniture that can be moved or incorporated into the ritual? The last thing you want are obstacles that could cause accidents or will disrupt your vision of the ritual outcomes. Be flexible and work with what you have. If you do not have access to a venue beforehand, then keep your ritual structure, and its staging, as flexible as possible and work in any contingencies that you can think of.

Decorations used to enhance the feeling and mood of the working can be very important as they give a sensory connection to the ritual. Outdoor rituals, however, may only require fresh flowers for the altar or maybe a circle marked out in flour. Circles of natural substances, such as barley, salt, feathers, shells, chilies, or hazelnuts, help to create a pleasing environment, as do lanterns or flaming torches at the quarter points. An indoor ritual may make use of wall hangings or banners, hides on the floor, multiple elemental altars, fresh greenery or seasonal decorations – basically whatever creates the mood and atmosphere you are looking to achieve. Preparing the ritual space with decorations makes people focus on the ritual and leave the mundane world behind. It gives a sense of "otherness" which can be very helpful in stimulating the senses in preparation for ritual.

The difference between decoration and props is that props have an actual physical use within the ritual. The props can include altar tools, a maypole, a wicker man, a scrying bowl or mirror, a flaming cauldron, a shroud, extra candles to be lit within ritual or a mortar and pestle for making incense. These props can be very important within large group ritual as they make visual cues available to all participants. Participants can then see what is actually happening.

The props should be within the ritual space before the working begins, unless the fetching or hunting out of the props is built into the ritual. If possible have someone assigned just to look after the props, making sure they are in the right place and everything is handy. Each person who will be using a prop should also double-check before they start to make

sure they also know where their particular prop is located. If you are using a prop in different parts or sections of the ritual, make sure that within the structure of the ritual there is some way to move that prop from one area to another. This plotting is very important and working it out beforehand can save a lot of messing about within the actual ritual. If someone is using a spear as a guardian before the working, and the same spear has a major function within the ritual itself, then either build that into the ritual with a scripted "handover" or make sure that the original carrier places it discreetly in the new location. This is where imagination comes to the fore. You may like to make a drawing or plan of the ritual's movement to help you to work out the plotting.

If you make up a props list to include with your ritual script, be sure to include items like matches, water for the chalice, charcoal for the censer and so on. It is all too easy to forget the little things when setting up the big picture.

If you chose to work on the structure of the ritual first, rather than the words, then now is the time to start the creative process of using language to bring the structure to life. You may have been making notes of poetry or invocations during the structuring process or maybe you are using the structure itself as the inspiration. Descriptive language that acts as verbal cues and explanations is a good place to start.

If you have a space within the ritual structure set aside for a blessing (say, of a particular element), you can tie the language of that blessing into the overall theme of the ritual. When structuring a formal ritual, the tone of the language should be consistent, so be sure to use formal language all the way through. Likewise, if the ritual is light in tone, make your words reflect this. You can also use the language to link ideas or bring in recurring themes – for example, you might have different participants speak the same phrase at various places in the ritual to highlight a point. If you are using poetic forms, again try to keep those forms consistent. If, for instance, you have four people representing the elements, then write a speech for each of them in which the poetic form is kept the same. This helps the listeners to tune in to what is being said, especially if you keep the last line of each poem the same. These final lines can be said with power and used to either invoke or release energy.

Alternatively you may have a story or long poem as your starting point. You can then use descriptive ideas within the piece to plot the physical structure of the ritual – remembering to break up the poem to suit the actions. The last thing participants want to hear in ritual is an overly long, boring speech. If you must have a long speech to convey the nature of the ritual, try to break it up between different voices. This will also make memorizing the speeches much easier, which is always desirable since reading from pieces of paper detracts from both the visual harmony and power that is sent behind the words. Question and answer styles of speech can also work well and make the participants actually think. However, it is a good idea to have a "plant" in this section as the ritual can come to a grinding halt if no one knows the answer! Just make sure that the plant waits an appropriate length of time before speaking.

er level of experience for all involved. On the other hand, there is nothing worse than someone shuffling to the center of the circle, mumbling some long bit of inane poetry read from a piece of paper. Not only will this bring the ritual crashing down, it also shows profound disrespect for whomever or whatever is being called. A good invocation with power behind it will generally echo off the walls even if the invoker is softly spoken, but a very quietly delivered (but still audible!) invocation or evocation can sometimes be extremely effective, creating a different atmosphere again.

This leads us into assembling our cast for the ritual. Not everyone is a performer, and in large public ritual, a strong performance is necessary. This does not necessarily involve great acting, but just an ability to understand and work with a part and not show reluctance or nervousness. I believe in giving everyone a chance but sometimes it is wise to give a first-time speaker in a large ritual a small part. This way they have the opportunity to show what they can do, but it will not cause too much grief if they stuff up. Part of the process of casting participants is to utilize the skills of those involved, as well as creating personal and group challenges. Again, finding the balance between these is important.

When you have a good first draft of your ritual, then it is time to start the process of visualizing the ritual itself. Check things like the

A good invocation will generally echo off the walls.

One of the only times that long poetic speeches works well in ritual is when used for an invocation or evocation. A stand-out piece of invocation can really enhance the tone and create the spiritual base for the ritual. If everyone can feel the energies building with each stanza, and the invoker has the voice for it, then the ritual can move to anoth-

flow of energies and the movements of the participants, and consider what sections can be moved around to enhance these. Check that you haven't made things overly complicated, and by all means have someone else read the ritual and give you some feedback. Often when we are too close to a subject, we don't convey what we really mean, as we write with an assumed level of understanding. I prefer writing rituals with at least one other person since they may have ideas on structure or language that I had not thought of. Try to allow for contingencies that might occur should something unforeseen happen. When you have your final draft, give copies of the ritual to the people who will be taking active roles. Also try to come up with some kind of ritual briefing that can be held before the ritual to let the rest of the participants know what to expect – well, within reason!

Generally it is wise to keep your ritual as simple as possible, taking form, structure, style, decorations, props and casting into consideration. If you enjoy working with other Pagans in a public or semi-public space, go for it. Just remember, if you are on an experiential path, to embrace the experiences that you encounter, both the good and the bad. Every aspect of cat-herding has something to teach us.

From a mother worried that her ex-husband will use her religious beliefs to challenge her custody of their children to a bank executive concerned that she will be fired if her superior discovers she's Wiccan or a High Priestess and Priest of a Coven who are fined by their municipal government for worshipping in their home, countless practitioners of the Old Religion remain hidden, justifiably afraid that going public will lead to discrimination and even danger.

As the Pagan religious movement grows, mainstream America is showing greater understanding and acceptance of it. Yet Pagans (I use the term "Pagan" here to refer to the Wiccan, Witchcraft, and overall Pagan communities) are also coming under increasing scrutiny and attack, not only by the extreme right, but by many who remain uninformed and fearful because of long-standing negative stereotypes and religious bigotry. Over the years, members of the Pagan community have battled for and won rights to religious freedom in a variety of important areas. Pagans must understand how the law protects them if they are to exercise their religious liberties. Whether you choose to be public, need to protect yourself, or wish to respond to injustices through social and political activism, being aware of your rights – and the past successes in securing those rights – can empower and liberate you.

The foundation for religious liberties

The United States Constitution, and specifically, the First Amendment, is the foundation for all religious liberties: "Congress shall make no law respecting an establishment of religion, or prohibiting the free exercise thereof; or abridging the freedom of speech, or of the press; or of the right of the people peaceably to assemble, and to petition the Government for a redress of grievances." Through the powers of the Fourteenth Amendment to the Constitution, the First Amendment is binding upon the states and most state constitutions provide similar protection. Although a violation of the First Amendment will usually also be a violation of the state constitution, most suits for protection of this right are generally brought in the federal courts, although state courts may also provide a forum for litigation.

The United States Supreme Court has not yet ruled on a case which recognizes Wicca, or Paganism, as a religion, although Wicca has been recognized as such by the Internal Revenue Service since 1974. However, the US Supreme Court has delineated standards for determining what constitutes a religion as set forth in *Thomas v. Review Board*, 450 US 707 (1981); *Welsh v. United States*, 398 US 333 (1970); *United States v. Seeger*, 380 US 163 (1965) (see Justice Douglas's concurring opinion wherein he mentions religions whose central figure is a Goddess); and *Torasco v. Watkins*, 367 US 488 (1961); and *United States v. Ballard*, 322 US 78 (1944).

Both federal and state courts have set forth guidelines regarding what constitutes a religion for the purposes of the First Amendment, including the notable case of the *International Society for Krishna Consciousness, Inc. v. Barber*, 650 F 2d 430 (2d Cir 1981). And most significantly, various Wiccan and Pagan spiritual traditions have been recognized by both federal and state courts as deserving of

Constitutional protection. The hallmark federal case is *Dettmer v. Landon*, 617 F Supp 592 (Dst Ct East Dst Va 1985) affirmed by the Fourth Circuit Court of Appeals at 799 F 2d 929 (4th Cir 1986). The state courts have taken a similar position: *Roberts v. Ravenwood Church of Wicca*, 249 Ga 348, 292 SE 2d 657 (Ga 1982). Subsequent cases, some discussed below, have conquered with these early these rulings.

It should be noted that in most cases to date, the terms Wicca and Witchcraft have been used synonymously by both federal and state courts.

Incorporation and clergy recognition

Wiccan and Pagan groups are increasingly organizing as legally recognized religious bodies in order to avail themselves of the numerous benefits of such status. These include the ability to conduct such religious services as legally binding marriages; provide pastoral counseling in hospitals, the military, and prisons; receive tax-deductible contributions; purchase land free of real estate taxes; obtain liability coverage for public events and group health insurance/insurance for clergy, and so forth.

We fought City Hall – and we won

Since 1975, increasing numbers of Wiccan congregations have successfully applied for and received tax-exempt status from the Internal Revenue Service as religious organizations, churches or temples. Careful attention must be paid to all legal requirements and correct wording in the drafting of all incorporation documents, by-laws, and submissions to states and the IRS, because not all state laws accommodate Pagan theological concepts and practices. This is particularly true with regard to the distinction made in Biblical religions between respective roles of the clergy

and laity in running an organization. This is often integrated into statutory language but doesn't apply to Pagan groups, which generally are not governed by a board of directors composed of laity. But with the assistance of attorneys and other Pagan groups who have successfully incorporated and received tax-exempt status, it is possible to vault any hurdles such language may present.

Once a group is properly incorporated, any discrimination against the group's clergy may constitute a violation of the First Amendment and/or Fourteenth Amendment and state statutes, and legal networks are available to provide assistance in such cases. For example, in 1985 I served as legal counsel, with the assistance of the New York Civil Liberties Union, to a group of Wiccans who were denied the right to register as clergy by the city of New York. Unless registered, they could not perform legally binding marriages within New York City. We fought City Hall – and we won. This was an important step in the process of obtaining recognition, both legally and publicly, as a legitimate and genuine religion, entitled to constitutional protection. It was also an important psychological step for our growing spiritual movement, inspiring the formation of more Wiccan temples, the registration of more Wiccan clergy, and the performance of legally binding Wiccan marriages in New York and around the nation.

Public worship

Generally, the use of any public facility, park or beach falls under constitutional protection. However, such use will require filing a permit application and adhering to the restrictions imposed, such as: bans against fires, limitation on sizes of groups (for large groups, payment of certain fees or additional restrictions may be justified by the attendant increase in support services, risk to public safety, etc.), hours of use, insurance, or public nudity. For example, if your group wishes to do a full-moon ritual at midnight, but the park closes for public use at 10 pm, your permit will be denied, and such denial will not be deemed unconstitutional.

If, however, your use conforms to all requirements and lawful restrictions, and the permit is denied, you have a basis for a constitutional challenge. For instance, in 1993 I was involved as an attorney and also president of the organization being discriminated against in a case involving the city of Chicago. As a Priestess, I was to lead a full-moon Goddess ritual in a public park for the Parliament of the World's Religions. The city of Chicago first denied our permit because the person filing it had requested use after the park was legally closed. The permit application was then corrected to conform to city regulations. The city, however, again denied the permit, even though other religious groups had previously been granted permits to use the park for worship. With the assistance of the local ACLU, the city was challenged, and a permit was finally granted. The ritual was attended by the media and more than 700 clergy and practitioners of the world's many faiths.

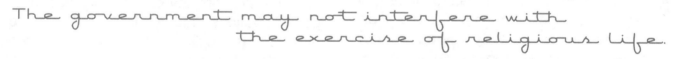

The government may not interfere with the exercise of religious life.

Home worship

As the Pagan community matures and expands, and its groups become involved in purchasing land, sponsoring festivals, and building spiritual retreats and centers, legal questions regarding zoning, religious institutions, and home worship become critical. The First Amendment protects the rights of individuals to worship in their homes, and the government may not interfere with the exercise of religious life except to protect safety or health.

A threat to the rights of any group is a threat to all

Zoning restrictions, however, may be used to inhibit the practice of religion in one's home. A recent example occurred in Palm Bay, Florida, where The Church of Iron Oak, a Wiccan congregation affiliated with the Aquarian Tabernacle Church, fought a lengthy and costly battle to protect the rights of its members to engage in "home worship." A Palm Bay ordinance required churches in residential areas to obtain a special zoning permit and restricted worship to no more than five people. The City of Palm Bay dropped its case against the church when it successfully argued that its legal offices were located elsewhere and that the home of the ministers, where Sabbat worship was held, did not meet the ordinance's legal definition of a church; that is, for a building to be a church, the practice of religion must be its primary use, whereas the home where the worship had occurred was used primarily as a residence. (Code Enforcement Board of the City of Palm Bay, Florida COMPLAINT #3292-94 City of Palm Bay, *Petitioner vs Respondent John R. Coleman, Jr. or*

Jacqueline Zaleski, Findings of Fact, Conclusions of Law, and Order 1994).

An important aspect in winning this case was the support from other religious organizations – including Jewish, Unitarian and Christian fundamentalist groups – whose First Amendment rights were also at risk. A positive relationship with the interfaith community can provide invaluable support in critical cases involving religious liberties, as even the most unlikely of religious allies understand that a threat to the rights of any group is a threat to all.

Child custody

There have been numerous instances where religion has been made an issue in child custody cases. Thus far, the US Supreme Court has chosen not to take any cases in this area, and state courts vary widely in their opinions and statutes. However, "the best interests of the child" is the main criterion in a majority of states for deciding which parent should be granted custody. However, it should be noted that to remove a child from a home or a parent based solely upon religion is unconstitutional: "Court have repeatedly held that custody cannot be awarded solely on the basis of the parents' religious affiliations and that to do so violates the First Amendment to the United States Constitution …" (*Pater v. Pater*, 63 Ohio St 3d, 588 NE 2d 794 (1992)).

nor will they discuss their beliefs for fear of being fired. While the Constitution does not protect employees of private (non-governmental) businesses, protection against religious discrimination is provided by Title VII of the 1964 *Civil Rights Act*, which requires an employer to accommodate an employee's religious practice so long as doing so would not cause any undue hardship to the employer. (The employer, however, need only make the most minimal accommodation, not the most favorable.) Title VII has been interpreted to include the right to take time off for religious holidays, and many states have enacted laws similar to and often more generous in the granting of rights and stricter in the enforcement of those rights than Title VII.

It is true, however, that individuals who "come out of the broom-closet" at work can find

A positive relationship with the interfaith community can provide invaluable support

Generally, most states consider religion in deciding custody only when specific religious beliefs or practices may impede a child's development in some definable way. Some states, such as New Hampshire, take the position that religion may never be addressed in a custody determination because it would improperly entangle the government, via the courts, in religious matters. Other states include religious beliefs as one among many considerations. Until the negative stereotypes about Witches and Pagans change, this area may present legal challenges, depending upon the state in which the parties reside. Domestic law attorneys and their clients can receive legal support through Pagan legal networks.

Discrimination in the workplace

Unfortunately, many Wiccans are afraid to wear a pentagram – the five-pointed star that is the symbol of the Pagan religion – at work

themselves facing subtle forms of discrimination, and termination justified on such grounds as poor performance or reduction in work-force size. But when an employee has had a stellar employment history and upon going public suddenly finds a pattern of harassment or criticism developing, the threat of a Title VII complaint could put an end to such behavior. And precedent has been established where Wiccans have successfully sued employers for Title VII discrimination. In the case of *Kosten v. Family Health Management, Inc.*, 955 F Supp 898 (19970, aff'd 124 F 3rd 373 (7th Cir 1998), the Northern District Court of Illinois specifically found Wicca to be a religion for purposes of Title VII. The most recent case is *Robert Hurston v. Henderson, Postmaster General, U.S. Postal Service*, 101 FEOR 3054 (EEOC, Jan 19, 2001). In addition to private legal representation, local governmental human rights agencies can assist someone who suffers religious discrimination in the workplace.

The military

Many Wiccans and Pagans serve their country in the military. Since 1980, the US Army has recognized Wicca as a legitimate religion, including it in what has been commonly referred to as the Army's Chaplain's Handbook, more precisely the *Dept of the Army (DA) Pamphlet 165-13-1, Religious Requirements and Practices of Certain Selected Groups: A Handbook for Chaplains* (April 1980), revising *A Pamphlet 165-13, Religious Requirements and Practices of Certain Selected Groups: A Handbook for Chaplains* (April 1978). In addition, the United States military courts have found Wicca to be a bona fide religion deserving of First Amendment protections and have upheld the rights of Wiccans to practice their religion: *United States v. Phillips*, 42 MJ 346 (1995); and 38 MJ 42. Judge Wiss, who wrote the concurring opinion stated: "First, Wicca is a socially recognized religion. It is acknowledged as such by the Army ... {specific reference to the Dept. of the Army Pamphlet 165-13-1, Handbook for Chaplains}."

suits or the threat of suits. Some of the most visible and recent cases have occurred in Lincoln Park, Michigan, Hammond, Indiana and Elmwood, Indiana. Most notable is the landmark case of *Crystal Seifferly v. Lincoln Park Public Schools*, Cause No. 90-DV-60070-DT, United States District Court, Eastern District of Michigan, Southern Division, where the defendant school board settled the lawsuit in which the right of Crystal Seifferly, an honor student, to wear her pentacle was upheld. That settlement included payment of over $14, 000 in legal fees to the ACLU, who represented Ms. Seifferly.

With the assistance of the ACLU and various Wiccan legal rights organization, students in various states have risked indefinite suspension, expulsion, loss of class credit, and other punishments in successfully defending their right to wear their pentagrams in school as a symbol of their religious belief. A notable example is the case of Brandi Lehman and Shauntee Chaffin, students at Elwood High School in Elwood, Indiana, who were forced to leave their posts as student teachers at

The wearing of the pentagram - termed a 'gang symbol' has been banned

Student rights

The right of students to wear a pentagram in school is an active area involving Pagan religious liberties. An increasing number of schools are instituting rules and policies forbidding students to belong to groups or engage in activities considered to be "inappropriate or unacceptable in the school setting." Some of these rules actually refer specifically to Pagans, Wiccans and/or Witches as forbidden groups, and the wearing of a pentagram – frequently termed a "gang symbol" – has been one of the banned activities.

Students – primarily teenage girls – have successfully fought these restrictions with law-

nearby Edgewood Elementary School after the school's principals instructed them to stop wearing their pentagrams in the third-grade classroom. In an interview with the Associated Press, Kenneth Lehman said of his daughter: "She did the best thing she could have done – she sought out a lawyer and took it to the courts ... The school taught her a lesson in one of her classes about individual rights, and she decided to take them up on what she was taught." With the help of the Indiana Civil Liberties Union, the students filed a lawsuit in US District Court. The federal court decision, issued by US District Judge S Hugh Dillin, said the school system had violated the students' First Amendment rights to wear the symbols of Wicca. The rul-

The First Amendment of the Constitution ensures that Wiccans and Pagans are entitled to the same right to practice their religion in peace and freedom as followers of any other religion in the United States.

ing imposed a preliminary injunction on the Elwood Community School Corporation to allow the students to wear their pentacles.

This issue has been successfully litigated and the rights of Wiccan students to wear a pentacle as a symbol of their religious faith are now well established.

Conclusion

The First Amendment of the Constitution ensures that Wiccans and Pagans are entitled to the same right to practice their religion in peace and freedom as followers of any other religion in the United States. An awareness of these rights and a vigorous commitment to their defense will transform the climate of negative stereotypes and religious bigotry that has long restrained their uninhibited enjoyment by all citizens. As with all cases of discrimination, it is wise to seek the representation of legal counsel in pursuing these and other remedies. Not only is that assistance often forthcoming from state chapters of the ACLU, but increasingly from Wiccan and Pagan attorneys.

intermission

a poetic interlude

Janet and Stewart Farrar

Introduction by Liam Cyfrin

Appropriately for two very major Wiccan authors, Londoner Janet Owen and Essex-born Stewart Farrar met in 1970 at a meeting of a Coven run by Alex and Maxine Sanders. Stewart, like Gerald Gardner, became involved in Wicca in his fifties, having encountered Sanders' Coven in his work as a journalist. Prior to this he had worked in the military, public relations and a wide range of professional writing engagements. The twenty-year-old Janet's career was no less colorful, including work as a model and an employee of The Beatles' Apple Corps. By the end of 1971 the pair were both initiates and had begun to run their own Coven. They were handfasted in 1974.

Stewart's first book on the Craft, *What Witches Do*, emerged in 1971. In the eighties, co-writing with Janet, he produced several follow-ups, the most significant of which were *Eight Sabbats for Witches* (Hale, 1981) and *The Witches' Way* (Hale, 1994), subsequently bundled together as *The Witches' Bible* (a singularly daft and misleading title that the authors had nothing to do with). The books were a huge leap forward in present-ing Gardnerian-derived material compiled in an honest and orderly fashion.

Stewart continued his exemplary Wiccan PR work, in conjunction with Janet and Gavin Bone, a registered nurse and expert in the healing aspects of the Craft, until his death in 2000. Janet and Gavin were subsequently handfasted in 2001 and continue to write and lecture internationally on the Craft. Their latest joint opus is *Progressive Witchcraft* (New Page, 2004). Janet and Gavin also regularly lecture and hold intensive experiential work-shops in the United States and Europe. Details of these and their latest published books can be found at www.wicca.utvinter-net.com. They live in southern Ireland.

Alongside his nonfiction, Stewart also pro-duced a number of works of supernatural fic-tion, most notably *The Twelve Maidens* (1974), *The Sword of Orley* (1977) and *Omega* (1980), and both he and Janet have produced a great deal of verse: sacred, dra-matic, erotic and plain old silly. We're very pleased to present this small anthology of (mostly) previously unpublished gems by two of contemporary Wicca's most respected authors.

little pagan priestess
Janet Farrar (circa 1990)

Little pagan priestess in the moonlight,
Fairy lady in your robes of gold –
Haven't they told you, didn't they warn you,
The poor Horned Lord is growing old?

Little fairy princess in the springtime,
Little lady in your robes of blue –
Haven't they said the Hornèd One is lonely?
He's searching in the empty woods for you.

Little fairy priestess in the summer,
Dancing all alone in woods of green –
Don't you know the Hornèd One must need you
To reign beside him as his Summer Queen?

Little pagan priestess in the autumn,
When the falling leaves are turning red –
Now summer's almost gone, and winter's coming on;
The Hornèd One hangs low his antlered head.

Little pagan priestess in the winter,
Can't you see you, too, are growing old?
The seasons all are lost, and the ground lies thick with frost;
The lonely antlered head is not so bold.

Little pagan priestess in the moonlight,
Dancing barefoot in a fairy ring –
Today you are a child, tomorrow woman wild;
Maybe next year you'll hear the Horned One sing.

O little girl who dances in the sunlight,
Is that your father's step upon the path?
Remember that I, too, was once a child like you.
Perhaps one day you'll make a good man laugh.

is anybody listening?
Stewart Farrar (circa 1991)

When Nile-born Isis spread her rainbow wings
From Nubia to York,
From Asia to the Pillars of Hercules,
Her silver voice rang clear: "There are no frontiers."

When the Nazarene drank at the Samaritan well,
When loin-clothed Ghandi stilled massacres with a word,
When Geldof swayed the spellbound stadium,
The word rang clear: "There are no frontiers."
... Was anybody listening?

In distant Chernobyl, one concrete room berserked;
And round the world the Geigers clicked: "There are no frontiers."
... Is anybody listening?

For God's sake –
Is anybody listening?

i know you

Janet Farrar (circa 1988)

I know you, Jonathan, Man in Black,
Betrayer of clan,
Traitor and knave.

We answered your summons to the forest meet,
Obeyed unquestioning the command you gave.
My mistress, our Queen, looked upon you well,
You found favor in her eyes.

I remember your mating,
You crowned with antlers proud.
I saw your embrace,
Saw the blood between her thighs;
And as the seasons turned
So your seed quickened within her womb.
My mistress,
Sunlight in her eyes, so full of joy,
Blossomed with the Moon.

Yes, Jonathan, I know you well,
Remember even now your treacherous deed.
While she slept
Your steps to strumpets strayed,
And filled with drink and greed for gold
You sold us to the Witchfinder,
Our lives lining your purse –
Blind Thomas, little Kate,
Matthew the Woodsman,
All of us,
Even our Queen,
And me, her nurse.

When he came for us,
From our homes,
Huddled like sheep we were herded to that field;
You rode beside him on a fine grey mare,
Our sword at your belt,
Cowardice your shield.

Our Queen regarded you with sorrowing eyes;
"I know you, Jonathan," quietly she said.
One look of fury crossed your face
And with our sword
You struck off her head.

By fire and rope we died;
Little Kate said not one word
But smiling through the flames
Became almost divine.
I did not leave this world so well,
But cursed you, Jonathan,
Swearing to hunt you throughout time.

Now I know I have found you again;
This time, too, you are the Man in Black,
We are all here, Kate, good Matthew,
Thomas no longer blind;
We are the monkey on your back.

I now reign as leader;
Revenge tasting sweet upon these lips
That long since, blackening, swore
To hurt, destroy you,
As you did us –
The clan, your Lady, our Queen,
Who gave you more
Than gold, or goods, or any earthly prize
Could bring;
She took you, low-born man,
Made you our King.

But even as we raise the power,
I think I hear, so far away,
Her voice:
It says to me
"Nay, stay your hand,
Seek not revenge;
Your Lady loves him even now –
Let him go free!"

But I do know you, Jonathan.

similes

Stewart Farrar (december 1995)

Similes are treacherous
And metaphors a menace;
I suffer tennis elbow
But I can't play tennis;
I'm certainly no housemaid
But I still get housemaid's knee -
And in spite of having athlete's foot,
The Olympics aren't for me.
Yet though I am a Pagan,
Madonna suits me fine;
I like her just the way she is –
No water in the wine!

the dominant gene

Stewart Farrar

(Originally published in *The Lancet*, Britain's leading medical journal March 1957)

The Dominant Gene, the Dominant Gene,
Is the happiest creature that ever was seen;
We mortals can only admire at a distance
The joys of a chromosomatic existence,
And marvel how Nature determines the sexes
By cunningly mixing the Y's and the X's
(For as Mendel has proved, it is only statistics
That settle our primary characteristics).

Imagine the life of ineffable bliss you
Could spend as a speck in the nuclear tissue,
Fraternally linked to a charming Recessive
(Your relationship tender, but firmly possessive),
Dictating the pigment, the shape of the nose,
Or whether your host should have suckers for toes.
You find immortality's promise seductive?
Make your home in a cell that is marked Reproductive.

A short life, but merry? You dread being static?
Your calling is plain – you are clearly Somatic;
For you cannot grow stale, with your every ambition
Fulfilled by perpetual cellular fission.
So banish your doubts, your neuroses, and revel
In life as it's lived at molecular level!

Princess! You'll discover the key to my riddle
By shuffling two chromosomes, split down the middle.

Victorian girls
Wore skirts of hooped whirls;
What did they do
In the loo?

———

Our cat is no tom's wife,
But she favors a full life;
She's shown markedly less respect to me
Since I hinted at hysterectomy.

———

I know a young lady of Ipswich
Who has very voluptuous lips, which
So disturb all her friends
Driving out at weekends
That they can't tell the clutch from the dipswitch.

———

There once was a girl who cried "Stop!
"If you squeeze me like that, I'll go pop.
"I'd look odd, you would find,
"With a balanced behind
"And a quite asymmetrical top."

———

Monsieur Fabergé
Once came to stay;
He confessed, when we'd got him well oiled,
That he really preferred eggs boiled.

———

A tailor who worked in Dún Laoghaire[1]
Cut his suits to the taste of the waoghaire;
Cash only – he said it
Was safer than credit,
And if view of inflation, much faoghaire.

1: Pronounced "Doon Lairuh"

———————

The Vikings they came to Ath Cliath[2]
With longboat, and helmet, and spear;
They might have gone back,

But they stayed for the craic[3]
The Molly Malones, and the beer.

2: Pronounced "Aw Cleeah" – Gaelic for Dublin
3: Pronounced "crack" – sociable fun, friendly chat

———————

Adam asked of Eve:
"What do you believe?"
– "Everything in *Genesis*
"But female androgenesis;
"Believing that is dumb,
"For Lilith was my Mum."

multimedia magic
magic
pop culture paganism

the mad mad house
(and what i did in it)
Fiona Horne

I completed filming *Mad Mad House* in late November 2003 before it premiered on the US SCI FI Channel in early March 2004. On the surface the show's premise may appear to many to be quite bizarre – a Witch, a Naturist, a Modern Primitive, a Vampyre and a Voudoun (a.k.a. Vodun, Vodoun, Voudou, Voodoo, Sevi Lwa) Priestess – collectively called "the Alts" – living together in a House and inviting ten "Joe Normal" guests to stay and compete together to win $100,000.

For quite some time I had been aware of SCI FI Channel's plan to create a show about what happens when people who live alternative lifestyles combine with (so-called) normal people. Over the last eighteen months I had regularly visited the SCI FI offices to pitch them my own show ideas. That's my real career – I am a writer, TV producer/presenter, not professional Witch! They had liked them but always passed, telling me they had a program in mind coming up which they thought I would be good for.

Now I understand why the Universe was pushing me so hard to do it.

When the casting call went out for *Mad Mad House* there was uproar in the Pagan/ Wiccan community – the initial outline of the show seemed very exploitative and shallow. Hence I turned it down. A month or so later the producers came back to me and I went in and took a meeting … and turned it down. They came back to me … I turned it down again.

By now it was early October, and after still more calls from the producers (and not wanting to burn any bridges in the industry within which I work), I decided to do the right thing and take a courtesy meeting to explain once and for all that I was flattered by their interest but did not want to do the show.

To cut a long story short, after that meeting my gut started telling me I should do the show. The producers and network executives were sincere when they described the other cast members (Alts) they had chosen – all older and respected leaders within their communities (not young "actor types" looking for their break). It was not a dating show or a survival show. The whole concept had been drastically revised from that original and it was clear that *Mad Mad House* was not intended to be a freak show, but a challenging sociological experiment, conducted within the framework of reality television but unlike anything ever attempted before. Where what you think is strange is actually very normal and what society accepts as normal is actually very strange!

I still hesitated though because, as someone very experienced in the television industry, I was also very aware of how life in front of the cameras 24/7 can be edited to appear in any way a "story editor" chooses. However, after some serious introspection I decided to take the path of least resistance and do the show.

And now I understand why the Universe was pushing me so hard to do it. *Mad Mad House* was easily one of the most profoundly rewarding things I have ever done. I have made friends for life and my personal practice of Witchcraft has gone through a very positive and empowered step as at all times I was treated with the utmost respect. I never felt that anyone was attempting to exploit me. No one told me what to do or suggested anything that was disrespectful. More often than not being in the house was like being in a spiritual retreat. I would awake in the morning and perform my Coven dedication rituals, and sometimes one of the guests would come into my room and we would discuss Witchcraft and do a ritual together. In this sense the show was a fantastic opportunity to "show by example" that Witches are not evil or Satan-worshippers, and to debunk many of the other damaging and ridiculous stereotypes that exist about us.

I did yoga everyday with Avocado (our Naturist) and went from a vegan diet to raw/vegan diet under his guidance which had extraordinary effects for not only my physical but also spiritual well-being. (Read the chapter by David Wolfe – aka "Avocado" – called "The Raw Food Revolution" for more on raw living.) I shared deep philosophical conversations about Goddess Worship and the African American spiritual tradition with Iya

Ta'Shia (our Voudoun Priestess, whose writing is also featured in *POP!* in the chapter entitled "Voodoo Queens and Goddesses"), discussed indigenous spiritual practices of the Mayans with Art, our Modern Primitive, and delved into Chaos Magick with Don, our Vampyre. Suffice it to say we "Alts" bonded in an incredibly profound way.

Our guests were amazing also – we challenged them mentally, emotionally, physically and *spiritually* and the results were extraordinary. There was so much serendipity within the House that it was truly the Divine hand of fate playing itself out in our lives. Together we created a magickal world within a world.

The winner ultimately took away something far more valuable than the prize money of $100,000. And so did everyone else in the household.

Of course there were hilarious, ridiculous, frustrating and even terrifying times – that's life! But the show became so much more than the producers or the network or even us Alts could have ever envisaged – and the positive effects of our time together will be felt around the world. The show promotes tolerance, acceptance and compassion for others' differences and the differences within ourselves. Every single person who entered the house left with a gift – a deeper, positive insight into themselves and the tools to share this wisdom with others.

When I went to live in the *Mad Mad House* I committed myself 500%, for better for worse. And so did the other "Alts" and our guests. We are all incredibly proud of what we achieved and the world we created and can share with you.

For more information, visit www.fionahorne.com and www.scifi.com/madmadhouse

I first began experimenting with popular culture as a viable method of practicing magick in 2000. One of the methods I devised was making a pop culture icon into a god-form. A pop culture icon is a person, cartoon character or the like, who is given a lot of attention by the media and by the public. For instance, Britney Spears was a pop culture icon for a couple of years. Her music was popular, as was her image. Her popularity didn't become part of mainstream culture, but was mainly restricted to teenage boys and preteen girls. In other words, she had a specific target audience and that audience made her famous and popular. That audience gave her energy in the form of the belief that she was a good singer (whether in reality she was or not).

Most of the occultists I have met in my life tend to sneer at the idea of blending pop culture and magick. However, I would argue that popular culture is an extremely effective medium that can be used magickally for any number of purposes. What it requires is creativity and a willingness to take an unconventional approach to magick.

A friend and I first experimented with this pop culture god-form method using the image of Miss Cleo. As her popularity and influence have since waned, and because any pop culture icon can be made into a god-form, I'll choose as an example in this chapter Buffy the Vampire Slayer. Buffy can be quite useful as a god-form of protection, equality, and magick.

Let's first consider this notion of Deity in popular culture. What is a god/goddess-form in popular culture? Popular culture has a lot of entities who pop up for a time and are extremely popular in some manner or form. I refer to such people as *entities* because we aren't dealing with the real person. We are dealing with the perception people have of the pop stars as well as the image that the pop star deliberately cultivates to continue getting energy. As such the entity of the celebrity, a being created by both the image fostered by the performer and the public, is what we wish to focus on in magickal workings.

Buffy is currently a well-known pop culture icon. Although her show has now ended, Buffy also appears in a series of books and comics and has a devout following of viewers who continue to watch old episodes of her show as repeats, DVDs and videos. Furthermore, the original program produced a successful and hopefully on-going spin-off, *Angel*. The media continues to pay attention to the Buffy character and she has entered the consciousness of tens of thousands of people who have never seen the show. Most of the media attention is positive but attention whether positive or negative fuels pop goddess icons like Buffy. This energy, for an accomplished mage or Witch, can be used to fuel his or her workings.

When I mention Buffy, I am not referring to Sarah Michelle Gellar, the actress who plays her, but Buffy Summers, the fictional character. The people who watch Buffy are more interested in the character than the actress. The character is the icon that lives in the minds of the viewers of Buffy and so it is the character we will focus on in a magickal context. One of the notable things about Buffy is how often she comes up in both the media and conversations. Since attention is energy here we have all this energy being directed to the character but no one has really thought to attempt to access all that energy heading her way.

The key to success with any kind of working like this is observation. You need to observe your target god or goddess very carefully, get an idea of his or her mannerisms and the kind of attributes you perceive he or she has. In the case of Buffy, I watched her show, read a few of the books about her, and took careful notes on her. I also weighed up the pros and cons of making her into a god-form for my magickal workings. This is useful to get you to think carefully about why you want to work with a pop culture god-form. As with any other kind of magick, this form of magick shouldn't be done casually.

When working with the Buffy god-form I used a collage of images from her show and fan sites and even book covers. The collage suited my needs as it showed several aspects about her that reinforced my list of attributes. Remember that visual reinforcement is useful in not only focusing your attention on the god-form but also getting other people to notice and therefore give energy to the god-form.

The night I did a ritual to Buffy to make her into a god-form that would function as a protector and affirmer of independence and strength, I had the collage on hand. I created an altar of Buffy with a couple of fantasy books, other images and even a videotape of Buffy episodes. I wrote my statement of intent on the back of the collage. It went something like this: "Buffy, through the medi-

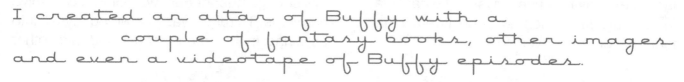

I created an altar of Buffy with a couple of fantasy books, other images and even a videotape of Buffy episodes.

I next came up with a list of attributes that I felt my Buffy god-form should have. I considered her to be compassionate, empathic, tough, strong, independent, determined, protective, and subversive to mainstream ideas while still looking mainstream. At no time did I consider Buffy in terms of money or anything negatively associated with her. The reason for that is simple. To consider Buffy as anything other that the attributes I'd assigned her god-form would be to diminish the magickal working I was doing with her. For instance, some people might become fixated by the amount of money Ms Gellar earned per episode or the fact that the show is unrealistic. I don't factor that hype into my Buffy god-form. My Buffy god-form, after all, is my perception of Buffy, specifically tailored so that her energy can help me. If I allow any negatives into that perception, I would weaken the god-form and so the potency of the magick I'm working.

um of this collage I create a link with you. I give of my self to you ..." (a personal sacrifice of some sort is always good, whether it's personal fluids or an object important to you) "... and in return ask that you act as my guardian when I call on you."

I next drew a sigil that represented both the character and my goals on the collage. I then went outside with a lighter, the personal sacrifice and the collage where I lit the paper on fire and chanted as it burned: "Through the power of Buffy I will focus myself on improving my independence and will." I chanted this until the paper had turned into ash. The chant might seem funny, but by chanting I was adding energy to the focus of the spell. By burning the image with the writing and something that was personal to me I was essentially making a sacrifice, an offering to Buffy. The medium of fire served as a medium of transformation. It signified how I would, with the help of the god-form, transform myself. I recommend that when you work with popular culture god/goddess-forms you make up a chant and have an image of what that god or goddess should appear to you as. The image and chant serve to focus your belief and energy toward the entity you are working with and create a link by which you can access whatever it is you need out of the god/goddess-form.

After I burned the paper and chanted, I went inside, lay down and tranced out, letting go of my conscious mind and following the energy I'd just released to the god-form of Buffy. While in the trance I felt the presence of Buffy. She and I spoke for a time about my situations and she explained how she'd keep me focused on improving the situations. She advised invoking her once a day to remind myself of what I was doing. This invocation was the chant I had done earlier in the evening.

ations by myself. Remember that any entity, pop culture or otherwise, should only be used for as long as you need it. Once the need is gone, it's time to move on. Otherwise the entity becomes a crutch and you are back where you started albeit now with an entity that can no longer help you.

One aspect of interest that I noted was the dynamic nature of the energy that I'd worked with. The energy of Buffy felt very powerful, very alive. I surmise several reasons for this. One was that she (or at least the medium she expresses herself through) is alive and in being alive in a physical sense has much more power and effect than a god or goddess-form from the past. Another was that because so many people give her energy through their attention, I was tapping into a form of belief in this strong, independent warrior that can solve problems. Thirdly, I was just willing myself into believing in her more than I had with other

Buffy felt very powerful, very alive... so many people give her energy through their attention.

Every day for several months I invoked Buffy in the morning. By doing so, even if I didn't watch an episode of her show or look at a book about Buffy, I still kept her presence in my life. I called on her every day and used her as an inspiration. The Buffy egregore for me was a general-purpose egregore that helped me through my Master's program, which had a lot of politics and nastiness for grad students. I was also dealing with a conservative Christian environment, with many would-be missionaries trying to convert me to their religion. Whenever a situation relevant to the attributes I associated with Buffy occurred, I simply invoked her.

I stopped invoking the Buffy entity only after the situations I felt I needed her help with had been resolved. By that point she'd served her purpose and I was ready to address the situ-

gods or goddesses that I occasionally work with. I could be wrong about this, but consequent workings with other popular culture icons have yielded similar results.

You might wonder why I stopped working with Buffy if this was the case. She is still popular in the media – more so, in fact, than when I'd initially worked with her. Nonetheless, she'd served her purpose. I didn't need to work with her any longer. I know that if and when I do need to work with her again I can simply invoke her as a god-form and then apply her toward the situation I need to address.

Belief is a very powerful energy for the mage or Witch to work with. Belief is especially easy to tap into with popular culture entities because in this age the different forms of media spread the pop culture icons everywhere. Simply put, the availability of pop culture icons is what makes them into gods. People choose to believe in the reality of Buffy the Vampire Slayer. If this weren't true the commercials and television shows that feature such icons wouldn't have the die-hard followings that they have. Even choosing to watch a show once gives the pop culture icon power over the viewer as the viewer has been imprinted with the character and what the character can do for him or her. Power is even gained when people complain about a disliked pop culture icon. Buffy worked so well for me precisely because I was willing to invest belief, and therefore energy, into the reality of her god-form and in turn I was able to access the energy that everyone else was putting into her.

Let me give a quick example. You may want to go on a diet, but know under ordinary circumstances you'd have trouble keeping to it. You can use the magick of working with a pop culture entity to help you. Who do you use? Were I to go on a diet I'd use the pop culture entity Jared, who represents the Subway franchise. You'll see him a lot on US television and each time he's showing the benefits of a successful diet. So what you do is create a god-form out of Jared. Observe the commercials, take notes on attributes you'd want your Jared god-form to have and then on the first night of the diet and each night after invoke the Jared god-form to help you keep to the diet. Now on a humorous aside you may find yourself having an inexplicable craving for Subway subs, but so be it. As long as you are dieting and reaching your target weight it doesn't matter. What does matter is that you invest Jared with your belief that he will keep you dieting. Use chants, images, and whatever else as needed.

Bear in mind you can do this with any pop culture entity. The one peril to this practice is

that you eventually may find yourself believing too much and that's always a risk. Speaking for myself, I worked with Buffy while she was useful to me and then I moved on to other pop culture god-forms such as Harry Potter. I didn't want to become too enmeshed or reliant in Buffy's reality because I knew that while it helped me in the short term, I'd ultimately need to address the situations myself. Buffy served as a useful beginning tool to inspire me to do just that.

the magickal purpose of horror
a feast of the powers of darkness stalking the dark archetype in mainstream media
Anatha Wolfkeepe

The unfailing mass appeal of the "dark and mysterious" is evident in the great popularity of TV series like *Buffy the Vampire Slayer* and *Charmed*, films like *Queen of the Damned*, and also sci-fi series such as *Stargate SG1*, *Sliders* and *The X-Files*. The mystery and fascination is invariably bound up with the Good-versus-Evil duality – the more fiendish the Evil, the more we enjoy the triumph of the Good.

The creative and destructive polarities of the ongoing Creation are real forces that operate in the Eternal Present. In dualistic thinking, these forces are interpreted as the moral opposites of Good and Evil in order to discriminate between the harmful and the beneficial in human terms. A daemon or demon (from the Greek *daimon*) was originally a god, angel or celestial power. Ultimately both angel and demon/devil are essentially the two polarities of the One Power of evolutionary creation. Both constructive and destructive forces are involved in the translation of Spirit into Matter, because creativity needs the lower-astral energies of materialization, and the energy of Shaping automatically involves the "negative" energy of Un-shaping. The only beings that could possibly be considered the personification of evil are those generated by the evil thoughts and passions of humankind, which hover in the lowest levels of the astral planes.

In the process of bringing our spiritual potential through into reality we naturally encounter pressure and restriction in working with the physical plane. This density has a resistance which has the evolutionary function of opposing our efforts, a "darkness" which has immense power and creative fertility. If you can stay conscious, these "dark spirits" of creation can be befriended and enlisted as allies. These natural forces and intelligences are neither intrinsically good nor evil, but have a tremendous potential for both. Because we are not separate from anything in the cosmos, "angel" and "demon" are aspects of our being on another frequency-level. Which polarity manifests at any given time depends on how aware and awake we are, and our ability to consciously choose positive or negative. This means that we get the energy-pattern and circumstance that we *need* for our evolutionary learning, but not necessarily the one a human ego would want.

In one episode of the television series *The Secret Life of Us*, a particularly wild party is described as a "feast of the powers of darkness" – a quirky combination of inebriation, sexual experimentation, accident, black humor and gate-crasher violence. Ancient mystery religions deliberately set aside sacred times for orgiastic celebration, so that such forces of chaos and disruption could be given the means to express themselves. In the more formal Apollonian mysteries of ancient Greece, the priesthood could direct the power released by the orgy into the needs of the community. In the Dionysian revels, however – much frowned upon by the state – the Maenads, crazed female followers of the shamanistic God, would tear apart and devour any animal or human in their path.

The gate of initiation is through the wrong side of the door, the dark side of the heart

Chaos and negativity are available to us at

any time we allow ourselves to slip into unconscious and low energy states, and whether we like it or not, sometimes these "blind side" states are necessary for transformation. These "dark energies" are necessary Gate-Guardians and allies for the transformational breakthrough and initiation into expanded consciousness. Like the process of cell regeneration in the body, they are the catabolic forces necessary for the continuation of life itself, breaking down old forms so that renewal is possible. It is through the crisis of darkness, madness or illness so often associated with creative genius, that the candidate for shamanic initiation descends into the inner or "under-world" and experiences dismemberment or fragmentation at the hands of the inner planes teaching-Spirits.

The shaman's subsequent "re-membering" or re-assembling into a more powerful form is a reflection of the process of physical death, when the elemental spirits of the body do their work of deconstruction, releasing and transmuting the energy and consciousness of the deceased. In both physical death and

consciously interpret these energies and communicate the deep unconscious urges and needs of the group, people will call you a genius. If, however, your identity is not strongly grounded, and you confuse your own personality with the archetypal stream instead of communicating it, you will lose touch with personal reality, and people will call you mad.

In astrology, it is the archetypal mythologies of the outer planets – Saturn, Uranus, Neptune and Pluto – that express the darker energies of both the personal and Collective Unconscious. In terms of the small, conscious human ego, these planets represent uncontrollable energies. Linked to the archetypal Godform of the Destroyer, they do not deal in petty physical destruction, but are the shakers and destroyers of limited ego boundaries. In their mythologies these deities are mostly invisible, mysterious, hidden and not easily approached. The outer-planet archetypal energies are strongly connected to both genius and madness, between which the line is indeed very thin.

> "Dark energies" are necessary Gate-Guardians and allies for the transformational breakthrough and initiation into expanded consciousness.

the metaphysical death of initiation, they will break down the habitual mental constructions of "normal" reality. The universal fear of "demons" is actually the fear of the disturbing natural anarchy that teems behind the outer stability of the universe, its flow and flux, the shape-shifting forces of transformation, which to the ego feels like annihilation.

There is always a fateful flaw in the structure of the ego-personality that breaches the protective auric shell, the "dark side of the door" that allows the energies of the Collective Unconscious to stream in. If you are able to

Divine Archetypes of creative chaos

The Godforms are "Divine Archetypes" and should not to be confused with the archetypes of Jungian psychology. While the true essences of the Gods are utterly formless and unknowable, their primordial creative fire remains as divine archetypal shapes and patterns in the human mind, both individual and collective, through which the Gods can manifest and communicate. So how then do we bring the blessing power of the Gods into manifestation? We give them material ritual offerings that express their archetypal imagery – incense, music, dance, flame, the wearing of masks or make-up, of symbolic robes and colors, and in ancient times, the animal sacrifice. The other way is through the Ritual Art of mediumship or possession – usually called "assumption of the Godform" – a conscious mediation where an individual's normal consciousness is suspended or expanded and their body is made available for the Being's expression by their free assent.

With his affectation of cartoonishly overdrawn lipstick and opaque, reflective contact lenses, the heavy metal artist Marilyn Manson is like a distorted male/bisexual Goth version of his fellow "archetype-priestess" Madonna, striving to push, morph and shape-shift himself into freakish extremes, inspired by such influences as Marilyn Monroe, Marlene Dietrich and the satire, parody and theatre of the grotesque that featured in the Cabaret of Weimar Berlin circa 1901. He creates multimedia art-forms in the tradition of the Dadaist and Surrealist art movements, based on subconscious, irrational processes, anarchy, rejection of socially

the archetypes – or "assumption of the Godform" – be conscious and controlled. In his case, it is as though a whole succession of mad monkeys are behind the wheel!

The loss of our Rites of Passage – a culture doomed to perpetual adolescence

Due to the loss of our cultural Rites of Passage, mainstream culture is mostly incapable of addressing the powerful physiological and metaphysical transition of adolescence. Most contemporary adults were never validated, guided or welcomed into the community as young adults themselves, so it's little wonder that adolescent children are a mirror too painful for their parents to look at or acknowledge. At puberty, new, raw faculties and feelings are being activated. According to Rudolf Steiner, the energy blueprint of our "soul purpose" comes into us at age fourteen. Whenever an inner psychic/spiritual process is denied and repressed into unconsciousness, it usually expresses itself negatively in the outer world.

Eminem is a priest of the random chaotic archetype.

conventional beauty: "I aim to revive the attitude of chaos and reckless regard for tomorrow, in order to make today's creations as genius as possible. No more rules to where the 'stage' ends and the audience begins." Like Eminem, he too is a priest of the random chaotic archetype, deliberately courting lower astral entities and thought-forms. His portrait paintings are full of eldritch, "goblin" people, a punk version of Brian Froud's nature-spirit and fairy illustrations.

In artistic terms, he may be "pushing the boundary," but from the magickal perspective, he is definitely not "driving the bus." Professionalism in the ritual arts of Priest/esshood requires that possession by

Deprived of the Rite of Passage that would give grounding and meaning to the sexual/spiritual quickening, our whole society is doomed to perpetual unresolved adolescence, obsessed with sex, money and power in their most addictive, ungrounded forms. One of the deeper causes of addiction is this society's suppression of the spiritual drive toward initiation. The orgasm of ecstasy, the shamanistic peak-experience that fuses love, sex and religion, has been driven underground, along with the ancient traditions that teach non-destructive ways of "getting high."

The adolescent need to rebel against any kind of authority will not respond to any "psychologizing" based on individual or family causes. This is an ancient, collective phenomenon that cuts across class, race and culture. The incoming "soul energy" that demands recognition and craves its own clan to belong to will often find it through rebel music, the alienated subcultures of rap and heavy metal. This raw, dumb and angry music with its driving, primitive, powerful rhythm appeases the unconscious desire for communal ritual. Sound is a Ritual Art capable of igniting deep primeval emotions hard to contain, a wonderful demonic rage that roars through the body-animal.

A torrent of ingeniously offensive and demented lyrics – randomly violent, misogynist, homophobic, and not without a certain crude black humor – has won a huge following for the hip-hop artist and hardcore rapper Eminem. With the brilliant but warped lyric talent of a "bent bard," he seems to be a frustrated shaman-priest, evoking the warrior archetype in its contemporary, darkened and wounded form.

This damaged male psyche (Animus) that dwells in both men and women is very repressed and unconscious in contemporary Western culture, and therefore restless and dangerous. The repressed masculine craving for power and aggressive expansion is perhaps best represented by the cultural denial and suppression of Wotan/Odin who is also related to Robin the Hooded Man, Kernunnos and the Green Man. Unlike the Graeco-Roman gods, who reincarnated in the saints, angels and divine attributes of Christianity and in the arts, alchemy and astrology of the Renaissance, Wotan was too wild and primitive to be integrated, erupting in his most negative form during the Nazi regime and in many urban guerrilla conflicts since.

Though the ancient Teutonic astrology is now mostly lost, some writers consider his closest affinity is with the planet Uranus, associated with magick, inspiration, sudden change, eccentricity, androgyny, invention, originality and rebellion. In the Greek mythology, Uranus is a son of Earth, and was also her lover, fertilizing her with rain, lakes, seas and life forms. After his castration by one of his sons (Saturn), Uranus separated from Earth, becoming a Sky-god, a wounded male creator, a castrated father, leaving Earth bereft and suffering without his fertilizing erotic power. For humankind, this represents a separation from our sexual Oneness and balance, which means that women need to marry their Inner Male (Animus) and men need to marry their Inner Female (Anima). While Wotan's outer aspect seems to involve power in the outer world of the ego's goals and aims, his essential shamanic nature as a "man of power" offers the potential ability to work with inner spiritual forces, changing consciousness and of shape-shifting "between the worlds" to gain wisdom.

There is a lot about an artist like Eminem that a disadvantaged member of our dysfunctional society could identify with – abandonment by his father; a psychologically unstable mother; switching schools every few months; getting beaten up on a regular basis; the loss to suicide of the uncle who introduced him to rap; his own suicide attempt when his first album, finances and marriage all failed. Deciding he had nothing to lose and everything to gain, he then regrouped, creating his performing character (his Magickal Personality!) "Slim Shady – a foul-mouth talkin', no remorse havin' prick" and recording his demos in character.

While cheerfully admitting that Black Sabbath's dark and "satanic" imagery was a marketing strategy promoted by their management, heavy-metal icon Ozzy Osbourne has nonetheless, fuelled by alcohol and drugs for much of his career, managed to do a pretty good imitation of a primitive, blood-sacrificing berserker-priest! A high school dropout and teenage jailbird who grew up in extreme poverty, his work experience included a stint at a mortuary, and his longest job before the band was in a slaughterhouse. Practicing opposite a cinema and noticing that people would "pay money to be scared," the band decided to "write scary music." Reportedly under contract to fling 25 pounds of calves' livers and pigs' intestines into the audience at one series of concerts, Ozzy soon started getting pelted with disgusting things in return, including, at one point, a live bat. Thinking it was a rubber toy, Osbourne bit into the animal only to find it was alive! Several rabies shots later, the media blew this bizarre incident out of all proportion, causing record sales to skyrocket, and his concerts to be hounded and boycotted by animal rights activists ever after.

Up to a point, the heavy-metal wild-man and the hardcore rap-artist could be seen as doing ritual battle with "dark spirits" in public, calling them out into the open. Whereas the indigenous shaman draws out the evil spirits, giving them to Mother Earth to "compost" and transform – the negative energies released through this kind of unconscious ritual performance are unfortunately just spewed back into the audience.

Without any pattern for transformation, no healing can occur, and the cathartic release of dark energies becomes a vicious cycle and addictive in itself. Because the arts in general have lost touch with their ancient origin as ritual skills, many talented performing artists are unnecessarily damaged or destroyed by their work. As an aspect of the Sacrificed God or the Scapegoat/Devil, the Anti-Hero is potentially a Healer-Shaman who feels the pulse of pain in our wounded society and carries the Collective Shadow in order to transform it. Why wouldn't the voiceless and disempowered, the alienated and the angry, love and worship the ones who make it to the public stage to howl, rant, twist in the wind and cathartically spew bad blood? The half-healing of validation, of finding some kind of clan-identity, must seem better than no healing at all.

It is usually the sensitives – the ones with artistic sensibilities, natural, raw mediumistic ability and a lot of unbalanced emotional psychic content – who are the weak link through which the unresolved "ghost" of family, community and society will play itself out. The burden of carrying the collective unconscious darkness gives them a self-destruct mentality, yet they also have a deep instinct that the dark forces contain a power that can help them.

This is a key to the adolescent appetite for intensity and dark energy. Tribal elders have always known that adolescence is the right time to hit them head-on with a frightening Rite of Passage that contains the patterns of transformation, the cosmic wisdom-traditions and initiatory Death-Mysteries of the tribe. Driven within themselves to confront their inner Fear-Guardian and take on their own power, they have little chance to "act out," or project power outwards onto perceived authority figures, because they are given a great deal of real and meaningful responsibility.

In its voluntary descent into the underworld of madness and chaos, there is a shamanistic parallel in the deeper aspects of the horror genre. Quoting Anne Rice (author of *Interview with the Vampire* and its many sequels):

"Vampires are who we are: our ruthlessness, our desperate quest for companionship, warmth, love and reassurance in a world full of gorgeous temptations and very real horrors … so much affluence and so much violence, injustice and poverty. Vampires are fallible beings with the power of Gods, exactly like us … Life is a horror story, but it is a horror story with great, great meaning."

The arts in general have lost touch with their ancient origin as ritual skills.

parallel paths
other kinds of magick

wicca and christians
some mutual challenges
Philip Johnson

Wicca and Christians

The historic relationship between Craft and Church has not been a very good one. Wiccans have many justifiable reasons for being upset with and wary of Christians. There are two primary reasons. One is the way Witches have been persecuted by the Church in Europe and North America. The other is that most Christian books about contemporary Witchcraft badly misrepresent and distort it.

What most Christians fail to realize is that Wicca has something serious to say and indeed offers some significant theological challenges to the Church. Instead of dismissing Wicca as being devilish or humbug, Christians ought to take a first-hand look at what Wiccans advocate. At a very basic level, Wicca is a mirror in which we can "see ourselves reflected for all the things we have neglected." Wicca has a role to play that parallels what some ancient theological movements did for the Church in other eras. Movements like Arianism and Gnosticism, which are known in Church history as "heresies," compelled the Church to take a serious look at what it really meant by its core teachings and to live by them consistently. Wicca is a goad to the Church to not merely assent to the person of Jesus, but to daily act on his teachings in every dimension of life and thought. Wiccans have perspectives on issues that resonate with today's seekers, and they flourish so well in the absence of any vital, articulated stance by Christians.

Sexuality and spirituality

The upsurge of women participating in Wicca surely says something to the Church in its mindset over the role and ministry of women. It is clear that Jesus set himself against the patriarchal attitudes of his day and upheld the equality of women in God's sight (e.g., *John* 4). He offered empowerment for them to live in a society that denigrated females. His kingdom teaching encompasses the dignity and worth of all humans irrespective of gender.

One of the overlooked yet striking features of the Gospels is that they give prominence to the testimony of women in connection with the death and resurrection of Jesus. It is perhaps not appreciated these days that back in Jesus' time the testimony of women was deemed worthless. What is so provocative about the Gospel accounts is that each one features without embarrassment the testimony of the women as providing an unbroken chain of witness to the crucifixion, burial and resurrection. The spiritual sensitivity of the women to Jesus is borne out in these narratives, whereas most of Jesus' male disciples go into hiding when he is arrested.

Elsewhere the New Testament affirms that every believer, male and female, is a priest before God (2 *Peter* 2: 4-10). The New Testament bears out that women exercised spiritual gifts, such as prophecy (*Acts* 2:17; 21:9). The Apostle Paul counted amongst his co-workers in ministry various women, such as those listed in his salutations in *Romans* 16. This same apostle likewise taught that there is

Jesus upheld the equality of women in God's sight.

neither male nor female in Christ (*Galatians* 3:28), for we are all one. Even in the patriarchal days of the Old Testament we find examples of women exercising spiritual gifts and leadership such as Deborah the judge of Israel (*Judges* 4:4ff.), and Huldah the prophetess (2 *Kings* 22:14; 2 *Chronicles* 34: 22).

The Church has become polarized around the issue of ordination, but has not thoroughly addressed the wider implications of women exercising a ministry beyond the pulpit. The Church must repent of the misogyny and wife abuse that occurs within its ranks. As long as Christians pretend these things don't happen, we need not be surprised that honest seekers

sensitivity to what menstruation entails for women. Whether it be the onset of period pain and the raw emotional tension women feel, or the potential social embarrassment caused by the discharge of bodily fluids and issues of personal hygiene, menstruation generally carries a stigma. Indeed menstruation has invariably been associated with notions of spiritual contamination and pollution.

Wiccans have found that patriarchal attitudes reinforce the denigration of women when menstruating, and has been used as a justification for isolation from spiritual rituals. Wiccans have inverted all this, and quite properly view menstruation as something to

The human body is God's handiwork and to be enjoyed not escaped as if it is some kind of prison

look elsewhere to find spiritual nourishment. On another level, many Wiccans relate sexuality to spirituality, as seen in their sex magic rites. At times the Church has been so terrified of sex it has espoused celibacy as a virtue and denigrated the human body. The repression of sex inevitably erupts into abuse or promiscuity. The Biblical texts clearly uphold sex as a gift from God to be enjoyed within the bounds of marriage. The human body is God's handiwork and is to be enjoyed, not escaped as if it were some sort of prison. To view the body as a prison for the spirit is to descend into Gnosticism. "The Song of Songs" in the Bible is entirely devoted to the celebration of sex.

The celebration of feminine empowerment through menstruation is another earthly instance of sexuality and spirituality being joined together. For too long menstruation has been seen an unmentionable subject or one where male jokes can be made at the expense of women. As males are biologically unable to experience the monthly cycle, they lack any

be affirmed, not denied. Thus various rites of passage associated with menstruation, menopause and post-menopause have been developed. Male Christians need to recall how Jesus treated the woman who suffered with a severe menstrual problem (*Matthew* 9: 20-22; *Mark* 5: 25-34; *Luke* 8: 43-48). In the Jewish context, a menstruating woman was classified as unclean and spiritually polluting. To have contact with a woman during menstruation was to share in that contamination. Two striking points emerge from this narrative with Jesus. First, is that the woman receives healing from Jesus and is commended for her faith. The second point is that the woman touched Jesus. She did not contaminate him, but rather Jesus transmitted healing and purity to her. Jesus was not constrained by the patriarchal attitude towards menstruating women and the taboo of physical contact with the woman concerned. Surely there is a lesson here for Christians. Wiccans feel strongly about celebrating their fertility. Why do Christians seem to have nothing positive to say on the subject?

Finally, there are neglected questions for Christians to address. What is it to be a female or male made in God's image? In other words, no matter what our marital status happens to be, we are inherently sexual beings. Our sexuality is not confined to the act of intercourse, but rather is an expression of who we are. The Church ought to be able to say some very meaningful things about this.

Human rights

With the defeat of Nazi Germany in 1945, a new movement in jurisprudence emerged concerned with the defense of human rights. The post-War reaction to Nazi atrocities stimulated the creation of both the United Nations (1945) and the European Convention on Human Rights (1950). Since then the expression "human rights" has entered into common usage.

It is interesting to note at the outset that several of the key architects for the *United Nations Universal Declaration of Human Rights* and the European Convention were firm believers in a personal creator God: Rene Cassin (Jewish believer), Charles Habib Malik (Lebanese Christian), and Arthur Henry Robertson (British Christian). Cassin, who won the Nobel Prize in 1969 and established the International Institute for Human Rights, maintained that the basis for the Universal Declaration derived from the Ten Commandments.

years ago. In our contemporary situation human rights questions about religious freedom, animal rights and environmental rights need to be tackled.

John Warwick Montgomery is a human rights specialist who served as Director of Studies at the International Institute of Human Rights, Strasbourg, from 1979-81. Montgomery has written extensively in the field tackling such subjects as the Marxist approach to human rights, the philosophical justification for human rights, and right-to-life issues. Montgomery was in Beijing at the time of the Tiananmen Square massacre, and has written about the problem of human rights in China. Montgomery has also written about Witch trial theory and legal practice. His scholarship on these many issues forms the basis of the following discussion.

A. Witch trials in retrospect

In retrospect one can always benefit from hindsight and hopefully learn from the lessons of history. The Witch trials are one of the many blights in the history of European jurisprudence. Judicial torture was a feature of ancient Roman law, but fell out of favor with the rise and spread of Christianity. Christians had been subjected to persecution and torture at the hands of the Roman Imperial legal system. In the fifth century, St. Augustine of Hippo wrote against the use of torture in obtaining confessions. Pope Gregory the

> Christians had been subjected to persecution and torture at the hands of the Roman Imperial legal system.

For Wiccans and Christians alike, the subject of human rights is important both retrospectively and in our contemporary circumstances. By retrospectively, I mean honestly dealing with the violation of human rights in the persecution of Witches hundreds of

Great echoed his stance in the sixth century and Pope Nicholas I did the same in the ninth century. In 928 A.D. "good King Wenceslas" of Bohemia destroyed instruments of torture. In the twelfth century Decretum of Gratian likewise repudiated torture.

The reintroduction of judicial torture into continental law occurred in the later Middle Ages and coincided with the efforts of monarchs to create centralized states over against the local autonomy of feudalism. At the same time the Roman Church was centralizing its administrative controls. Lamentably, ancient Roman Imperial law became the model for both civil and canon law. The sad irony is that the very faith that had once been the victim of persecution, now approved of the very methods once used against it to now tackle non-orthodox belief. These developments also coincided with the weakening and waning of the old social order in medieval Europe, and Witchcraft was not just a rival belief system but also represented a genuine movement of social protest and reform.

In England, and later on in the American colonies, the legal tradition developed along different lines to those on the continent. The common law tradition developed out of Biblical principles of law, such as the Ten Commandments, and Jesus' "Golden Rule" that you do to others as you would be done by them. The Magna Carta, which also reflected Biblical truths, originated from the work of Cardinal Stephen Langton, the Archbishop of Canterbury.

The common law tradition prohibited secret trials and the extraction of confessions by torture. Yet civil rights were curtailed at times whenever the monarch sought to reassert absolute power, as was the case with the Tudor and Stuart monarchs. The Star Chamber these monarchs created and perpetuated was struck down by Parliament in 1641 as contrary to the Magna Carta. Thus the use of torture and the denial of civil rights to Witches in England was not a product of the Biblically influenced common law, but rather arose when monarchs subverted it for their own gains. This, of course, does not excuse the Witch trials themselves.

However small comfort this may be, Wiccans nonetheless need to be aware that not all Christians approved of judicial torture. During the anti-Witch mania Protestants such as Johann Weyer and Reginald Scot sought to have reason rather than torture applied in the Witch trials. On the Catholic side, Alonso de Salazar y Frias as an Inquisitor was scrupulous about the civil rights of the accused being properly observed. Augustin Nicolas, a French Catholic jurist, wrote a treatise in 1682 opposing torture, branding it devilish and condemning it from the Bible. Samuel Sewall (1652-1730) was Chief Justice of the Massachusetts Supreme Court and he publicly recanted the part he played in the New England Witch trials.

The primary issue that needs to be faced is whether Witchcraft should have been considered a criminal offence in the first place. Montgomery notes that: "the proper function of human law is to regulate conduct so as to prevent injustice among men; it is not to regulate ideas or coerce opinions …" (*The Law Above the Law,* p. 77). Witchcraft entailed ideas and beliefs, more than it had to do with acts. If a Christian or a Wiccan commits murder, the offender should be prosecuted under the provisions of the law with due consideration for the evidence.

However, to prosecute a Wiccan simply by virtue of being a devotee of the Craft was and remains a colossal miscarriage of justice. Unless it can be demonstrated that the Craft itself involves criminal activity and is a threat to the body politic, then the prohibition, persecution and prosecution of Wiccans cannot be legally justified. The Craft does not involve the ritual sacrifice of humans or animals and thus poses no criminal threat to the body politic. The Witch trials were a violation of human rights and human dignity. Although the Christian prosecutors believed back then that they were opposing a genuine societal and theological evil, they assumed the role of

God to act as judge on the matter. They achieved far more evil themselves than the good that Jesus taught his followers to do.

B. Animal and environmental rights

In contemporary human rights both Wiccans and Christians have something to say about the rights of animals and the environment, and also on religious freedom. This is not the place to undertake a detailed discussion of these matters. However, I would like to highlight a few salient points.

In human rights law it has become commonplace to speak of there being three generations of rights: (a) civil and political; (b) economic, social and cultural; and (c) solidarity. The question of animal and environmental rights comes with the third category of solidarity rights, whilst religious freedom comes with the first category of civil and political rights. Although there is much admiration for the concept of human rights, our global community nonetheless embraces a smorgasbord of theories and groups concerning the definition and justification of human rights.

The expression human rights by definition refer to titles or entitlements given. The concept is relational because it presupposes a source for the entitlement given. In our human relationships we must ask who has the authority or power to confer a right or entitlement on us. If we considered this point at length, I believe it can be argued that in order to both define and justify rights, we must defer to the transcendent. The fundamental reason here is that the One who created us is the only One who can tell us what our intrinsic worth happens to be. Also being transcendent, the Creator is not limited by our fallible perspectives and prejudices.

From a Christian standpoint, God's perspective on human rights can be grounded in Biblical revelation. Both the theology of the creation and the incarnation of Christ provide the grounds for justifying rights. The rights are entitlements given to us by God. If we approach the question of animal and environmental rights, we find that both Wiccans and Christians have something to say. Wiccans affirm that the Earth is sacred and they seek to do no harm to others. A Christian understanding of the creation should be based on the awareness that the Earth belongs to the Lord and we have been appointed as stewards to care for it. With regards to animals, Christians need to reflect on their standing in the original creation, their inclusion in both the Noahic covenant and in the new Heaven and new Earth. Indeed, it is high time that Christians reflected more carefully on the fact that Jesus was born and placed in an animal's feeding trough in a stable, and that animals were also witnesses to his birth.

Andrew Linzey has discussed animal rights at length from a Christian standpoint. There will be points of overlap and difference on these matters between Wiccans and Christians primarily on the basis of who has revealed the essential values – the Goddess or the Biblical God.

As regards religious freedom both Wiccans and Christians have a keen desire to support this. The historical experience of the Witch trials looms large in the collective memory of Wiccans as a powerful incentive to oppose religious repression. For the Christian, the upholding of religious freedom is not alien to the proclamation of Jesus as the Savior of the world.

First, both Christians and Wiccans need to recall the positive role of Christians in championing a variety of causes. Here is a small list to contemplate: support and shelter for widows, orphans and the destitute; opposing infanticide in the Roman Empire; the framing of the Magna Carta; the building of hospitals and the emergence of the nursing profession; the abolition of child labor by William Wilberforce; the abolition of slavery; the establishment of the Red Cross by Henry Dunant; outlawing widow burnings in India; the African-American civil rights movement led by Martin Luther King; and Amnesty International, started by Catholic lawyer Peter Benenson – to name but a few.

Second, Montgomery addresses the misconception that the Christian Gospel is opposed to religious freedom. He states:

"the scriptural gospel cannot be forced on anyone: if it is not freely accepted, it is not accepted at all … Jesus never forces Himself on man, and the true Christian believer can hardly justify doing what his Master will not do. Thus, even viewed from the standpoint of the absolute truth of the gospel, repressing non-Christian beliefs is indefensible: in removing freedom of religious choice, one removes in principle the opportunity genuinely to choose Christ Himself …" (*Human Rights & Human Dignity,* pp. 171-172.)

In an open and free society Christians should be willing to defend the rights of others to adhere to the beliefs they have, whilst at the same time encouraging dialogue and sharing about the unique claims and teachings of Jesus to those who want to listen.

Community of Hope

The old catechism avers that our chief end is "to glorify God and enjoy him forever." I would hazard to say that a great many Christians have excelled on the glorification, but have lost all sense of how to enjoy God. This is in stark contrast to the enthusiasm, joy and sheer friendliness one finds among many Wiccans. It is high time Christians bore witness to Christ by their love, which is one of the distinguishing marks Jesus spoke of about his true followers. If Christians continue to subsist within the ghetto of the Church, then we need not be amazed that spiritual seekers find spiritual fraternity elsewhere. The time has arrived for Christians to truly become the community that is built on faith, hope and love.

Christ as the Fulfilment of Wicca?

Finally, are Christians convinced that Jesus Christ can transform lives and that his teachings work? Wiccans find fulfilment through Earth magic and devotion to the Goddess. Are Christians positive that the risen Christ empowers lives and gives the spiritual fulfilment that we long for? If we are sure that Christ's message is "good news," then we need to find that good news working in our lives before we invite others to share in its blessings. If we are sure that through the resurrection of Christ we are made whole again, then we have a very powerful message to offer.

The Apostle Paul was passionate in his efforts to share the power of the risen Christ. He shared with both Jew and Gentile the same message, but used a different method to reach the same goal. When he dialogued with his own Jewish people, he began with their sacred writings to disclose Christ was the fulfilment of their faith. When he approached Gentiles who had never read those books, he entered inside their culture and offered Christ as the fulfilment of their search for meaning.

Some Wiccans have had a background in the Church and sadly found it deficient. Other Wiccans have grown up outside the Church altogether. Wicca challenges Christianity to recover the heart and passion of its message. Fiona Horne has said that she is frustrated by her childhood experiences with the Church, yet she "digs Jesus." It seems to me that we have put obstacles in the way of people seeking faith. If Wiccans cannot see the living Christ in us, then it is no wonder they dismiss the Church as utterly irrelevant.

We have put obstacles in the way of people seeking faith.

When Jesus came to earth his purpose was to make people right again with God. Perhaps we have spent too much time telling people they are wrong, we have lost sight of Jesus' primary mission of enabling people to become right. Let us not bear false witness against our Wiccan neighbors by demonizing them or ridiculing them as being irrational. The basic game-plan of Jesus has always been about healing people and reconciling them with God. Instead of debunking or deconstructing Wicca, why not share the riches of Christ as the fulfilment of the quest? Wicca challenges us to have the love and integrity Jesus had. Are we listening to the voice of the Spirit who guides and comforts the Church?

There is a magic in the ancient rocks and red earth of Australia that still sings to me, although I have been back in my native lands, the British Isles, for some twelve years now. I never dreamed that I would be so captured when I married an Australian and traveled out there overland through Asia. I was then strict – I would only stay for three years. I wound up staying for 20. Today I still dream of that ancient land whose people so welcomed me. It did not take long to capture me.

In my second year in Australia an Aboriginal woman came to stay with us in our home, then a center of the anti-Vietnam war movement. Soon some 40 Aborigines had come to stay. Life was hectic. We ate and talked together and I soon found myself working with them in their fight to protect their lands and sacred places. I traveled throughout Australia with their elders, from the heart of the deserts to the monsoonal forests, and learned to understand how they saw their land. I had always been a fey child. I knew sacred places in England. Because I held my own land to be sacred, they shared more with me. They also taught me, I think, a little of how our ancestors must have once lived when they too were hunter/gatherers and honored the spirits of the animals and plants that fed them.

When I was with them, I wrote of the oppression they suffered and their struggle to retain their lands. I told of the dark side and of our culture's responsibility for wrecking much in their lives. I had books published and launched by elders. But I now wish to share a little of what I then learned that was beautiful, enchanting, that enriched me.

I want to sing of being taken by Aboriginal women to visit their sacred places around the great rock of Uluru in Central Australia, which Whites called Ayers Rock. I had not planned this. When I arrived, I had first walked into the local Aboriginal-owned store and bought a beautiful, carved wooden snake that had been lying dusty on a top shelf. Then the shopkeeper offered to introduce me to the community. He took me to where a group of senior men sat in a circle under a delicately branched desert tree. I approached but stopped and sat when I reached the distance from them that desert etiquette dictates. It is a rule of privacy. I estimate it as the length of a reasonably sized front garden. An Elder then called out and asked my business. I explained and he invited me to come closer. I moved in half way. He then said, to my surprise, that the women had been waiting for me. I looked around. A woman's voice was calling: "Sister, over here." She stood by a distant tree next to a group of sitting women.

They waved, made space and warmly welcomed me. We talked, eyes sparkling. Then one said, "We have something to show you." We climbed into the back of a truck parked with its engine idling expectantly, and then drove towards the red-grey-cliffed monolith that dominated their horizon like an enormous hunch-backed caterpillar.

They kept clear of a small fenced-off area at the base of the rock. This was reserved for Aboriginal men to use for sacred purposes. We walked single file towards a cave that was partially concealed behind trailing bushes. One woman started chanting to greet the spirits. Another turned to me to say with a grin: "See that cave? It looks just like a vagina, doesn't it?" And with laughter we sat down by its entrance. They then regaled me with the ancient stories of creation. It felt at first as if I was with the ancient tribe of Israel hearing its creation stories, but as I listened I found the stories were more like the early stories of Ireland. They were of the

ogists followed him and dismissed the women's spiritual work as just "magic." They thought women's "magic" was without power because it was theoretically unconnected to the Dreaming! Thus, when a vast deposit of diamonds was found on a women's Dreaming Place in the Kimberleys, the managing director of a mining company dragged out academ-

They regaled me with the ancient stories of creation.

Ancestors, the first races to inhabit this land. This cave was sacred to women and should not be knowingly approached by men. But I saw no fence protecting this sanctuary, and no warning like those that had protected the men's site. Tourists could freely enter and were doing so. I saw white men, cameras in hand, ignorantly exploring.

The women then told me how their men had secured government protection for their sacred place. Their sacred law allowed a man to tell a man where his sacred places were – so they could tell male government officials. But the women had lacked this opportunity. The government had not thought to appoint a woman officer whom they could tell. They did not see me as being bound by their restrictions. I could tell both men and women. Thus they wanted me to tell the world that the women of Uluru wanted their own treasured sacred places protected.

Until recently Western anthropology had served these women ill. AK Radcliffe-Brown, the first person to hold a Chair of Anthropology in Australia, did not know of the sacred women's business. He instead interpreted Aboriginal society according to the dualistic theories of Emile Durkheim. Not knowing of the secret ceremonies that celebrate a girl's menarche and only of the men's rituals, he saw initiated Aboriginal men as having a sacred realm but Aboriginal women as living in a non-initiated profane world. Many anthropol-

ic books to "prove" to me that the women were lying, that they had no sacred places.

The women then took me to two deep pools under the high cliffs of Uluru, now golden in the sinking sun. I learned that one of these was sacred to the Rainbow Serpent who slept within its depths. They showed me snake-like markings on the cliff, left to mark its movement into or out of the pool. Such permanent waterholes are very precious to a desert people, but even more so here where they are linked through the Serpent stories to the creation and renewal of the energies of water and earth.

There is an ancient story about one such sacred pool. It goes like this. One day two women came down to the pool to wash, not knowing that the Rainbow Serpent was sleeping below the water. The first woman who went into the water was menstruating. The Serpent smelt her blood and woke up. The second woman then went into the water and she too was menstruating. The smell of her blood woke the Serpent right up. It leapt up and swallowed both women alive. So far goes the story that is told to tourists – they are told not to pollute the waterholes. But this is not the true meaning, for in the old story the women only stay inside the great Rainbow Serpent while they are bleeding. When they stop, they step out of the mouth of the serpent, rich, strong and fertile.

There is also another story – this I know from

anthropologists rather than from the women because it pertains to male mysteries. It is that the pre-puberty boys are told just before they are circumcised, that by shedding their genital blood, they join with the magic of the women. But that day we did not talk of such male mysteries. The women took me into their birthing cave and showed me, with much laughter, how to sit astride a most precious thing, a large central sloping rock which served them as their birthing chair.

Pitjantjatjara. The traditions were both respected and enjoyed. Sex was clearly fun and seen to pervade the landscape. These were not a prudish people. Were our ancestors much the same? Did they laugh at the sexual implications of tall slim standing stones and fat squat diamond-shaped standing stones? I hope so. Certainly the British Pagans today note and much enjoy the implications of having slim and diamond-shaped standing stones facing each other in the many ancient Avebury stone

I learned … by simply being with them, traveling with them through thousands of miles of bush, forest and desert, eating together, sharing in their fight for their land.

They finally told me that I must write of all these things - for they were relying on me to make public that the women of Uluru had sacred places just as the men had. I felt extremely privileged. It had been a day of wonder for me. I had also learned how the women and men of the Central Australian tribes have two sacred codes of law, one for men and one for women. Both are of equal status and compatible. Both had their separate parliaments. Only when an elder had gray hair could she or he know secrets of the other gender's law. This was quite different from Aboriginal Law in southeastern Australia, a thousand miles away. There, from the Dreamtime, Aboriginal men and women had sat in the same circles.

A day after my visit to Uluru, an Aboriginal man took me in his utility truck past the smoothly eroded phallic-shaped rocks of the Olgas, a range of hills west of Uluru. As we passed, he directed me to avert my eyes. The other women with me also put up a hand to shield their eyes. These rocks are sacred to males. I had a sense that the sexual and sacred implications of caves and of tall slim rocks were a subject of much enjoyment and not a little fun among the local tribes of the Arunta and the

avenues. Here too I had been with an Aboriginal woman. I once had the privilege of taking an Elder to visit the great Avebury stone circles. She touched the stones, turned to me and, her face shining asked, "Why didn't anyone ever tell us that your people also had such places?" Today I sometimes work as a priestess in these stones – and when I do, I sometimes feel the gentle touch of the Aboriginal elders. This is just what they wanted me to do. They had told me I must go back to work with my own people.

The years I worked with Aborigines were a very special time for me. As my work with them extended over years, I became more and more immersed in the magic that lived in their land. I learned, not by being initiated by them, but by simply being with them, traveling with them through thousands of miles of bush, forest and desert, eating together, sharing in their fight for their land. This taught me to be sensitive to the energies within the vast ancient landscape of Australia. It was not my continent by birthright but it was part of the Earth that birthed me. I fell in love with Australia's vast wilderness as I got to know her better.

I sometimes wondered if Maria Gimbutas' theories that non-Patriarchical nations lived in greater harmony were true of non-Patriarchical societies. They did not construct fortifications, but their myths spoke of battles, much as did the earliest myths of the Irish. The women had pointed out to me where the spears had struck the surface of Uluru. Other elders told me of ancient hostility between Aboriginal nations.

Misunderstandings must have been common in a continent with over two hundred languages. But their fights seemed to have been over religious matters or marriage — never over land.

Aboriginal women are often expected to master the "fighting sticks" but their weapons historically seemed to have been magical and psychological rather than the spear and boomerang. Central Australian Aboriginal men still fear to hurt a woman since she can take ritual action to achieve justice or revenge. The spiritual power of an Aboriginal woman is said to be considerable and to entitle her to much respect. Her strength was said to come out of her enduring bond with her land. But she would undertake magical action only after much serious discussion with other women and weighing of consequences.

As for the word "Witchcraft," many Aborigines first heard of this word from missionaries who translated it into their language as "a worker of evil magic." Thus, those who held fast to the Old Ways, denied their spiritual work had anything to do with this "horrid" word. This was also true of other indigenous peoples. Thus many among the Sami, who traditionally herd reindeer in northern Scandinavia, honor their shamans while thinking "Witches" are evil.

The anthropologist Professor Robert Tomkinson, in a study of the Jigalong Aboriginal community of Western Australia entitled *The Jigalong Mob: Aboriginal victors of a desert campaign* (1974), told how Aboriginal people kept their religion intact despite the missionaries' efforts to suppress it. He reported, "the missionaries view the Aborigines as the children of the devil and the antithesis of Christian virtues." A 1901 Presbyterian Church mission report stated of their Mapoon Mission: "Where formerly Satan ruled supreme and kept his prisoners captive in sin, cruelty and superstition, the voice of prayer and song is being heard."

I found, however, in the 1970s that many Aborigines at Mapoon still prized what they sometimes called the "old ways." I found the same true in the 1980s in a remote Catholic mission run by Benedictine monks at Kalumburu in the far north of the Kimberleys. The Aborigines there assured me that they still initiated and honored the Dreaming Tracks — after the missionaries told me the opposite.

Mission staff worried about how hard it was to convert "witchdoctors." A Presbyterian missionary wrote about two witchdoctors living at Mapoon in the 1930s:

"Awari, or better known as old William, is a witch doctor and rainmaker. The other is Namatu ... Namatu's bearing is dignified ... he takes a leading part in the midnight councils and is held in esteem by all. Under these circumstances it seems strange that although he has been greatly influenced by the preaching of the Gospel ... he has never openly confessed Christ."

A brilliant anthropologist, Diane Bell reported that missionaries at Philip Creek in Central Australia in the 1970s labeled women doing traditional "love magic" or *yilpinji* as "Witches." Some men took advantage of this labeling to try to diminish the influence of the women while quietly continuing to do *yilpinji* themselves. Much the same may have happened in eighteenth century England when male

"Cunning Folk" found clients by suggesting they needed protection from female Witches. Likewise in Africa, male witchdoctors offered to protect clients against the evil magic of women. Yet, on closer inspection, the men and women believed in and shared similar magic.

Diane Bell has written extensively on Aboriginal women's magic. When we met in Alice Springs in the 1970s, she was in the midst of her research and enjoying life with her two children in an Aboriginal community north of Alice. She seemed to get on exceptionally well with Aboriginal people. She also did well academically. She was appointed around 1999 a professor of anthropology in Washington DC. She tells how Aboriginal women elders instructed her for years and took her, painted with ochre patterns from head to toe, with the "mothers" into many rituals including the initiations of boys – who cannot be initiated and made men without the help in ritual of the women. Before her work, Aboriginal women's magic was scarcely understood outside Aboriginal communities.

One of the most common forms of magic in Central Australia is "love magic." (One has to be careful to specify which people one is describing – there are over 200 Aboriginal nations in Australia and much variance in culture.) In the language of the Warrabri people in Central Australia love magic is called *yilpinji* and it is practiced by both genders. Bell wrote of the female practice:

"*Yilpinji* is achieved through a creative integration of myth, song, gesture and design against a background of country. The circle, the quintessential female symbol, finds expression in the body designs, the rolling hands gesture and patterns traced out by the dancing feet ... Ownership of myth and the rights to perform certain rituals provide the power base for the women's claims ... In *yilpinji* the women [describe their social world and] attempt to shape their world."

For example, if a woman wants rid of a husband because he is playing around, she may ask her group to perform *yilpinji* to help make him leave her. *Yilpinji* is invariably based in the empowering link with land possessed by everyone in Aboriginal culture.

Aboriginal women also work healing magic. This they might do by gifting the sick person with something that carries the healer's own energy. This could be a gift of blood, secretions from under the arms or tears from the eyes. I learned of the importance of "sweat from under the arm" from an Aboriginal elder in Mapoon in North Queensland (with whom I worked in the 1970s). He told me he was most upset by the police burning clothes containing his sweat "from under the arm" when they burned down his house. This loss affected him more than that of his house.

Senior healers had the ability to remove foreign bodies from the sick person's body. (Western medicine calls its foreign bodies germs or bacteria.) They used ritual and magical tools to draw the foreign element from the victim with a holistic approach that encouraged the sick person to take part in the healing. There was also magic used for revenge. In central Australia the victim of an assault might keep a sample of blood from the aggressor to use it later in a magical attack. Aboriginal people believe that they live in a world full of ancestral Dreamtime energy that could be used by the adept for good or hurtful purposes.

Diane Bell described the care and reverence with which women approached all their rituals. The senior women grease and then paint the naked bodies of the participating women with ochre patterns that show their link with their country. They do this while singing gently and harmoniously of the Dreamtime. During rituals the women might hold up the sacred boards and dance with them. These were marked with sacred signs denoting their links to their country. Beforehand energy was sung into the boards until the paint itself was said to "shine." Their bodies, their dances, their chants and their boards tell of their totem links to creatures such as the dingo, as well as to their much loved country. The red ochre they use represented the power of life and blood. Through their rites they reaffirm their bond with their sacred land and their responsibility for it.

Once the ritual is over, the energy of the Dreaming is sung back into the ground, the signs of dancing feet are erased and dirt is thrown on the ground where the sacred boards have lain to nullify and ground the energy. The boards are then rubbed on the women's bodies to remove the signs and re-absorb the energy. They see this grounding as extremely important. Men and women had separate sacred rituals as well as shared rites. The major themes and purposes of women's rituals are love, land and health.

jilimi. If any woman approached the ritual ground, she had to stop and wait until she was signed through.

In the *jilimi* the elder women taught the Dreaming to the younger women and arranged ritual events. Women might go out with their children to gather and hunt from here, as from the other camps. As they moved through the country, they would sing of the travels of the creating Ancestors and teach their children about the land and its Dreaming. All food gathered was first distributed among the women and children before any was given to the men.

Diane Bell noted that eminent male anthropologists, with no access to the senior women living in the *jilimi*, often had no understanding of the important place of women in rituals and of the vital role they played in the principal male celebration, that of the ritualized rebirth through circumcision of the

Offenders were put on trial and disputes resolved by ritual means.

Aboriginal women could, however, decide to live independently of men in a women's camp or *jilimi*. This was located out of sight of other camps. Aboriginal men would never walk in sight of it. The women built for their camp a long snake-like building. It had on its northern side a large clearing known as the "ring place" or "business ground." Here Aboriginal women conducted rituals, displayed their sacred boards telling the stories of their Dreaming, and sometimes slept – especially when ill or in trouble. The ring place was also traditionally the place where female offenders were put on trial and disputes resolved by ritual means. The storehouse for sacred objects backed onto its eastern side. On the far side of this, to the east, the structure opened onto a bough shelter where the women made or repaired ritual objects, or simply chatted and rested while monitoring all activity around the

young men. This ritual could not be performed without the women's participation. They could even bring it to a halt if they felt that the men were not performing it correctly.

Diane told how after many seasons of instruction she found herself "red ochred from top to toe and propelled into ritual action I had only previously observed from afar." She was present at twenty or so male initiations and, over time, she took "all the major female roles." In being painted with red ochre, Diane had become part of an extremely long tradition.

The whole of Australia is a cobweb of Dreaming Tracks woven in the shared mythology of the several hundred Aboriginal nations. These weave together many people of diverse languages, cultural customs and different skin and hair color. These tracks are rich in energy, for the Creating Ancestors, both male and female, once walked them while forming the land. Today the great creation sagas are re-enacted and renewed by the sacred boards that travel the same routes with their accompanying songs and dances, passed on from one community to another. The totemic animals, reptiles and birds also helped create these Dreaming Tracks. All these Tracks, all the Totems, all Aborigines have their songs, dances, painted sacred boards and chants.

These tracks are not seen as being confined to Australia. Some Aborigines said they sensed the dreaming tracks of North America when they first traveled there to meet the Native Americans. In Britain similar energy lines are sensed and called by some "ley lines." Could it be that they are sensing a natural worldwide pattern of creative energy?

One day I was walking with Aboriginal women along a path on a beautiful wild part of the coast of South-Eastern Australia when they told me to stop and wait until the men had gone on ahead. Then they quietly told me that we were in an ancient women's sacred place. I asked did they want it protected and fenced, as had the women at Uluru? They said no, too many whites around here. If it were fenced off with signs saying this place is sacred to women, it would be disgustingly vandalized and the place desecrated. I sadly agreed.

But in the center of Australia the women won their battle. As I had promised, I made public their need to get their sacred places protected. They had probably also involved other white women. Today at Uluru most of the women's sacred area is protected. For me, that day I spent with the women at Uluru was the most enormous of privileges, and a day that I will never forget. Uluru makes Australia very special, for how many nations have at its heart a women's sacred place enshrining the story of creation?

Bali. The island of the Gods, it is blessed with a magic which is at once tangible and potent. Poised on the edge of the vast continent of Asia and the merging point for two mighty oceans, the Pacific and Indian, Bali is charged with a volatile physical energy that bestows it with mighty volcanoes and raging tides. Yet it possesses a special calm, reflected in the lush green of the rice paddies and an ocean that sprawls out languidly round the island like cut blue glass.

It is this uncommon mix that endows Bali with its balmy mystique and provides a splendid backdrop to a culture that is just as rare. The Balinese people descend from a unique heritage of metaphysical kings and a royal court replete with artisans, aristocrats and priests, many of whom fled the spread of Islam across Indonesia in the fourteenth century. As a safe haven of Hindu tradition, the people clung tenaciously to their religious beliefs in an effort to preserve them. Woven into these was a fascinating mix of Buddhist discipline, animistic practices, a mystical world of cabbalistic symbols, and an intriguing undercurrent of tantric magic.

dressed in exquisite lace and sarongs. The essence is imparted to the deities, leaving the rest for the people. As resting places for the ancestors and Gods, the stone cavities of temples are left empty to invite an earthly visitation, while smoldering incense drifts to the heavens enticing their presence.

Reflecting the changing mood of the island, the Balinese believe strongly in the power of the yin and yang, black and white, and the forces of good and evil. Their belief is not one that advocates the vanquishing of evil but rather the *balancing* of the two energies, for both are valued and one is powerless without the other. The dark must be offered equal reverence as the light, so they can be kept in harmonious balance. Thus offerings to appease the demons are laid on the ground each day to placate the darker spirits, and ward off any evil.

Offerings to the Gods must be placed on high, close to the heavens. The highest point of heavenly energy in Bali is the sacred Mount Agung, which soars majestically into the clouds. Blessed with an ethereal energy,

> The dark must be offered equal reverence as the light, so they can be kept in harmonious balance.

The Balinese follow their religion with a true passion, and the island is studded with a myriad of temples. Not only is their faith all consuming, it is also breathtakingly beautiful. In order to attract the favor of their Gods, stunning pyramids of flowers and fruit are created as offerings then proudly carried to the temple on the heads of the women,

it commands devotion. As home to the Gods, it is the source of all that is good. To partake of its bounty, one must pray towards the mountain or look to the east to the power of the rising sun. To exorcise any negativity or dispel illness, one must turn away from the mountain and out to the west where the sun sets into the underworld, or towards the sea.

As mysterious as it is dangerous, the ocean is inhabited by its own powerful deities.

Acutely aware of the cycles of nature, the Balinese devised an elaborate array of ceremonies to tap into the earth's forces. Lavish offerings are made at the time of the full moon to attract abundance and wealth while the dark moon is reserved for introspection and meditation. Special days are set aside for the blessing of animals, trees and plants in homage for their perennial gift to man. There is also recognition of metals, which are duly honored for their unique properties. Kris daggers, often prized as family heirlooms, are believed to store the accumulated energy of the ancestors, and thus are repositories of great metaphysical power.

Of all the trees, the banyan is particularly revered for it is deemed to be holy and inhabited by spirit. Wrapped in a bolt of black and white checked cloth to represent the balance of the opposing forces, these trees are chosen as the site of temples and stacked full of offerings. Recently when a huge banyan tree had to be chopped down in a village, a band of men clad in ceremonial dress sang to the tree for hours to placate its spirit before it was finally cut down.

Man considered a mirror pattern of the cosmos follows the same intrinsic principles as nature. The head as the highest point on the body is the most hallowed. Thus it is not permissible to touch it – more so in the case of a child who is spiritually pure. Homes and villages are carefully laid out according to the divine plan, with orientation towards Mount Agung. All things holy, like the family temple, must be placed towards the mountain or in the eastern corner, while unclean areas, like the kitchen or animal pens, should lie to the west. To sleep, one must position one's bed so that the crown of the head lies facing one of the holy directions.

Energy and its flow are intrinsic concepts to the Balinese. Like the atmosphere, the human body is a storehouse of energy called *sakti,* which charges a person with great strength. This enables one to ward off attack whether it comes from a human or supernatural source, for the dark forces strive constantly to undermine the well being of the soul. Some people have a natural propensity to attract more *sakti* than others due to their heightened spiritual state, and so enlightened become priests or healers in order to use their special powers.

Further energy can be drawn from the presence of a person's spiritual brothers or sisters, who become one's inseparable companions from before birth until beyond death. Since an embryo must receive support from four aspects of the womb to survive, it is believed that they represent the four elder spirit siblings of the person. Their task is to accompany, protect and nourish the person throughout their life. As long as they are treated well they fulfill their roles dutifully. Otherwise they can transform into one's own demons and choose to wreak havoc.

As the person progresses through life, they undergo a series of rituals to mark their rites of passage. These include the actual birth, at 42 days to cleanse the baby's spirit from imperfections so that it can enter the temple and other holy places, and at 105 days to reinstate the soul to its body and give the child a name. This is the first time the baby is allowed to tread upon the earth for up till now it has been considered a divine being.

Puberty marks the transition to adulthood, and at this time a tooth filing ceremony is performed. In a symbolic act the front teeth are filed down to make them even and sever any connection with a demonic world of fanged monsters. It is hoped the six enemies that reside within the human soul – lust, greed, anger, drunkenness, arrogance and jealousy – will be eliminated. This ceremony must take place before marriage or any death rites can occur.

A major set of rituals embraces the cult of the dead, and the subsequent purification of the soul. These ceremonies are essential for deliverance from the torments of hell. Once they have been performed the path is clear for a heavenly existence, rebirth or the ultimate goal – transformation into a deity for those rare souls who have attained a state of enlightenment. These rites, performed by the children for their parents, are crucial for the liberation of the soul and to erase any existing debts before God, and so prepare for a successful reincarnation.

offend such a powerful entity. There were compelling omens prior to the blast to support this premise.

It was believed by many that the tragedy was the direct result of an incident that took place on a beach near the principal kingdom of Klungkung. Early in June 2002, fishermen there captured a giant turtle, measuring more than two metres in length and weighing over 500 kilograms. Instead of heeding the accepted custom of asking advice from a priest when faced with any strange occurrence, they went ahead and killed it. This was foolhardy, particularly when Balinese folklore proclaims that Bali was created on the back of a turtle and according to Hindu lore the turtle is sacred, an incarnation of the god Wisnu.

The tragic bombing had extreme metaphysical ramifications... Mother Nature is angered.

The tragic bombing that devastated Bali on October 12, 2002 not only caused a horrific loss of life but also had extreme metaphysical ramifications. In one terrible moment the dark seized control and the tenuous balance between good and evil was disrupted. Amazingly there were no calls for vengeance or random retributions, but rather the Balinese chose to look within for answers. After reflection came a passive realization that the Gods had been incited by a lapse in spiritual consciousness and that the onus was on the people to redress the balance.

According to Balinese belief every negative occurrence, including natural disasters like floods, fires, earthquakes and volcanic eruptions or man-made catastrophes such as the bombing, are omens that something is drastically wrong and that Mother Nature is angered. Even in the case of calamities inflicted by man, the Balinese relate these back to the displeasure of a God, and thus to the basic question of what has been done to

Even more ominous were the supernatural markings on the turtle, which provided clues to its elevated status. On the underbelly of the doomed turtle was a clear natural imprint of a swastika. The swastika is a holy Hindu symbol that signifies the Sun and the power of the light, and when reversed came historically to symbolize the power of darkness. Reports filtered through that those who ate of the flesh of the turtle became mysteriously ill, and that several fell into an eerie trance-like state. Wild stories circulated that spurts of blood shot up in fountains from the turtle's shallow grave and with each spurt came the ghostly sound of the *kul-kul* drum from a neighboring temple tower even though there was no one nearby to beat it.

Soothsayers divined that the turtle had been an incarnation of Nyai Loro Kidul, the powerful Goddess of the southern oceans and protector of their seaside village. Legend has it that the Goddess was once a beautiful princess of mortal blood whose stepsisters cast a horrible spell upon her in a jealous rage. Afflicted with leprosy, the distraught girl flung herself off the cliffs of southern Java, but as she plunged into the ocean's mighty grip, she was immediately transformed into the lustrous Goddess of the South Seas who was capable of bringing peace and calm into the world she governed or wreaking untold destruction. As mistress of both the ocean and fire, her power was untold and her mood unforgiving.

When offended the Goddess was quick to flaunt her anger. In a fit of pique she caused a tidal wave to flood one hotel in Java that ignored a prophecy to honor her. A huge fire destroyed another in Bali. In order to show her due respect, hotels on the ocean set aside a room for the exclusive use of the Goddess. With such seriousness is her presence taken, that offerings and meals are served to her daily. The furnishings of her room are lavish and to her taste, often decorated in bolts of sea-green satin, her favorite color, along with cosmetics and oils for her beautification, and a bathtub with fragrant blossoms floating for her pleasure.

Was it possible that the death of a turtle, her earthly manifestation, could cause such dire repercussions? Fearful of the consequences of eating the flesh of a God and anxious not to incur further rage, priests decreed that in order to protect the villagers the turtle was to be dug up, bathed and anointed with holy water in accordance with Hindu ritual and cremated with full rites, an honor traditionally reserved for the human soul as a final act of purification. It was the only time such a ceremony was conducted for an animal, albeit in the guise of a God.

Several days later in the Klungkung village of Tojan the ceremony took place to allow the soul of the turtle to find entry back into heaven. It was reported that 10,000 people and 500 spirits attended the rites, not only to honor the passing of the God but also repentant that they had not respected the basic Hindu tenet of *Tri Hita Kirana*, the balance between men, man and nature, and man and God, which had all been violated by the slaughter.

Stories circulated that the God had washed upon the shores of Bali in search of 200 devotees to take back to the underwater kingdom. This was close to the number of lives lost in the Kuta bombing. Prior to the bombing there were signs that something was seriously amiss, as nature vented its displeasure in a graphic display. The sea was raging along much of the island's coast, the waves battering its shoreline and cowering it into submission. A heavy black cloud hung over the island, dimming its light. On October 6th an ominous white ring circled the sun. Three days later a minor earthquake shook the island. Then came the terrible moment of the bombing that would rob the island of its innocence forever.

The spiritual innuendo was obvious for the small temple that stood guardian over the bombed club remained unscathed even though it had been at the center of impact and all else around it was annihilated. This was a remarkable parallel, for it echoed the tragedy of 1963 when the mighty Mount Agung erupted in a terrifying blast. An ominous cloud of ash shrouded the entire island in darkness and thousands of lives were lost. Streams of lava rolled down from the volcano demolishing everything in its path, yet incredibly Besakih, the mother temple of Bali, which stands on the mountain's side, was totally bypassed and all those praying inside spared.

Such is the power of the Gods in Bali. Aware that a serious breach had occurred, it was

The small temple that stood guardian over the club remained unscathed.

crucial that the balance be restored quickly. While the victims of the bombing were tended to on a physical level, those who had passed into spirit needed solace. Strange, unexplainable things were happening, and fear lingered all around. TV screens suddenly came alive in the dark of night in the burned-out homes of Kuta, even though the electricity was cut off. Locals told of seeing discarnate spirits roaming the streets, disheveled and dazed. Screams echoed through the night, the cries of the dispossessed. Taxi drivers reported foreigners getting into their cabs, but when they turned around to talk to them they simply disappeared.

Anxious that some souls of the dead may still be wandering around lost and confused, a ceremony was held within three days to contain any dispossessed spirits to the site. A 24-hour roster was drawn up and bands of men kept constant watch to protect the souls of the departed from any evil entities that may be lying in wait to whisk them away. The danger remained until the body could be cremated and the soul guided to heaven, so the guard stayed vigilant.

during one's lifetime it is first buried and then interred at the time of death. Thus the physical body can return whole in its next incarnation. With the devastating effects of the bomb, this was impossible and in some cases the person themselves was missing. In an uneasy solution, ashes from the remains along with the person's photo were cremated in their place.

Not only were purification rites necessary for the people but also for the area where the bombing occurred. Any person or place that has been defiled is considered unclean or *sebel.* Typically a person is vulnerable after an illness or severe stress, and psychically weakened may become the subject of attack. A place is tainted following any act of desecration or vandalism. In order to reverse the energy of such a heinous act of destruction as the bombing, it was decided by those in religious authority that a ceremony of immense magnitude was essential.

Before this could take place, a preparatory ritual was held to clear the way. Priests were sent to collect the holy water required for the

> The ceremony involved the ritual slaughter of 79 types of animals to be reborn into higher incarnation.

It is not uncommon in Bali to see men sit on a busy roadside, huddled around a woven basket placed at the site of an accident to protect spilt blood and so the vulnerable spirit. It is traditional practice that all members of a village group pay their respects at the home of someone who has passed away and take turns to sit throughout the day and night to protect the soul of the departed until the body can be buried or cremated and any risk has passed.

Particularly traumatic for the Balinese victims was the fact that when someone is to be cremated the body should be sent to its resting place intact. If a limb or other body part is lost

huge cleansing ceremony that was to follow. The Balinese religion is often referred to as the Religion of Holy Water, for it is believed that water obtained from a spiritually charged source has the capacity to cleanse, energize and heal.

Water was gathered from 30 sacred places and temples, including many of the holy mountains of Java, towering Mount Rinjana in Lombok and the most hallowed of all, Mount Agung in Bali. After prayer and purification rituals, bamboo containers holding the water were carried to the bombsite on the heads of women who formed a ceremonial line. During the preparation of the holy water, several men succumbing to the intense spiritual power fell into a trance state. Escorted by the traditional guards of Pecalang, these men led the procession to the site.

The *Pemarisudha Karipubhaya* ceremony is so sacrosanct that it can only take place when an area has suffered massive violent death, in the aftermath of war or enemy attack. *Pemarisudha* means to clean, *Karipubhaya* means disaster. According to a Brahmin priest this actual ceremony has never been held before in the history of Bali. On November 15th, on the day of Kajeng Kliwon, a day in the Balinese calendar reserved for the cleansing of any negativity or darkness, and on the auspicious full moon, the ceremony was centered at the site of the blast in order to restore balance to the Balinese cosmos, which had been severely shaken.

Young prepubescent girls performed the haunting *Dewa* dance, accompanied by the sound of chanting and gamelan, entreating the doors of heaven to open to allow entry for the departed souls. Thousands of people dressed in traditional costume joined together in prayer to plead for God's grace in allowing their spirits to find blessed release and so be guided on their celestial journey in a state of purity and peace. There was also a plea for divine forgiveness for any wrongdoing on the part of the Balinese people and to ask for atonement for their sins.

At the same time, villages all over the island held ceremonies to exorcise their ancestral land of the dreadful carnage that had been inflicted upon it. Ten high caste priests presided over the ceremony on Kuta beach, which involved the ritual slaughter of over 79 types of animals. Each once was carefully chosen then cleansed in preparation for its release. When killed in such a symbolic manner, it is believed that they will be reborn into a higher incarnation as beings. After the prayer had ended, the slow process of healing began.

As life resumes in Bali, a sense of calm has begun to prevail. Where recently there was overwhelming sadness and fear, now comes the pervading thread of hope – a hope that peace and harmony will return and that the balance between the elements be restored. While the laws of man ensure that justice is served, it falls to the Gods to preserve the spiritual integrity of the island. As the soft blue of the sky merges with the gentle drift of the sea on the shores of Bali, the Gods once more smile down upon the enchanted isle. A subtle light radiates from the lofty heights of Mount Agung, bestowing untold blessings on their sacred island.

voodoo queens and goddesses
feminine healers of the african diaspora
Iya Ta'Shia Asanti Karade

The legacy of Voodoo Queens in America

Voodoo is a word and practice that evokes immediate fear in non-believers. The authentic practice of Voodoo or Voudoun, as it is properly titled, has little to do with evoking fear or causing harm to anyone. Voodoo is about tapping into one's inner spirit and getting on a divine path of personal alignment with what one's ancestors have already placed in the universe to be claimed.

Voodoo worshippers honor spirits known as "Loa," which are deified spirits of an ancestral nature. The known "Queens" of Voodoo (recognized by public audiences and practitioners) are mostly all African-American women who grew up in what we know to have been slavery portals (places where slaves were taken to be sold) around the United States, such as in New Orleans, Alabama and South Carolina. Many of these women did not call themselves "Voodoo" practitioners or "Voodoo Queens." They were simply heirs, by birthright and intuitive ability, to traditions and practices that derived from traditional African religious rites and rituals that we know as Voodoo and other African based religious systems such as Ifa, Candomblé, Santeria and Lucumi.

Legacy of the African Goddess

The legacy of the African Goddess has been cast into the shadows of invisibility due to subtle racism and efforts to keep European history in the forefront of American and global culture. The faces and names of African Goddesses were literally changed and some eventually erased. Most Black adult women and young Black girls can't even name three African Goddesses by their original names.

For example, many are familiar with the name Isis, but few are aware that Isis's original name was Auset. Auset was a Kemetic Goddess of the African Diaspora. Auset's name, history and legacy were erased during the Christian destruction era in an effort to destroy all memory of the African lineage of the Egyptian/Kemetic African Goddess system.

Another example is that of Cleopatra, who was presented to the world as a White Greek Goddess, when in fact she was a beautiful, voluptuous, bronze-skinned African Goddess with a full nose and lips, and thick, kinky ebony braids. Some six years ago, a team of anthropologists and scientists confessed that the ancestral legacy of Cleopatra, known as the one of the most beautiful women in the world, was African. Ironically, once this admission was made, the scientists also said that the legacy of her beauty was a farce, that she was in fact a very ugly woman. I wonder why this startling fact was suddenly revealed?

Oshun, Yemoja and Oya are African Goddesses in the Yoruba pantheon called "Orisa." These Goddesses represent various earth energies including rivers, oceans and wind, and their legacies are rich in folklore, actual history and spiritual wisdom. The Goddess, Orisa Oshun, and Yemoja and Oya, all have villages in Nigeria dedicated to their memory, energy and *Ase* (see glossary below). *Ase* is an energy that represents the life-force in each human being that allows them to manifest as human life in all its incarnations.

Understanding Voodoo and Voodoo Queens

Historically, the practice of Voodoo been demonized both by Hollywood and the perpetrators of slavery. Voodoo traditionalists hid, and many continue to hide, behind the veil of Christian metaphysical practices. However, the roots of their spiritual and religious work are clearly based in Africa and African rites and rituals.

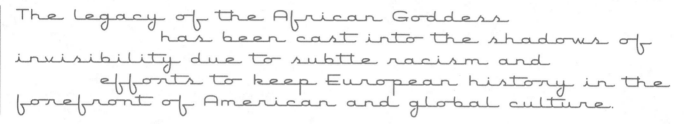

The legacy of the African Goddess has been cast into the shadows of invisibility due to subtle racism and efforts to keep European history in the forefront of American and global culture.

What makes one a Voodoo Queen or Voodoo Priestess? Most would say that undergoing rituals and initiations that historically and traditionally are connected to the Voodoo tradition makes one a priestess. But the institution of slavery, which forced African-Americans to abandon their religious ancestral legacy, changed the entire custom of connecting with and embracing African spiritual traditions. Today, many priestesses in the Voodoo tradition learned through independent study and later underwent initiations through various systems based in African spirituality. Whatever the system, an element of Voodoo is present in the practice. "Queenship" comes from earning respect of followers and students through dedicated service to traditional communities. Most priestesses use a combination of African religious practices, the degree of purity of practice varying from person to person. Because of slavery, and people from a myriad of tribes being thrown together on one plantation, a spiritual and religious jambalaya exists between traditional African religious leaders that will probably never be broken.

Embracing and affirming African Goddesses in modern times

As we study and learn about women leaders in other religious orders, it is imperative that the memories and legacies of African Goddesses and Voodoo Queens are not forgotten. Marie Laveau, who left her mark on New Orleans and made it the Voodoo capital of the world, should be celebrated for her healing work and efforts in keeping Voodoo practice alive during a very religiously oppressed era. And there are many others who have done amazing research and work in the various spiritual and religious traditions of the African Diaspora. If it were not for their unwavering faith and commitment to the legacy of the African ancestors, these traditions would have been lost forever. *Maferefun* to the African Queens and Goddesses! May their memories live on forever! *Ase*.

Glossary for this Chapter:

African Diaspora: Global African Countries and locations in the United States where African culture thrives.

Ase: A Yoruba word that means "So be it." *Ase* is "the life force within the manifests all things."

Maferefun: Yoruba word meaning "All praises to."

gender blending

love, sex, choice
and freedom

when a witch falls in love
with a guy who isn't
Lucy Cavendish

One of the greatest issues facing many women practicing natural magick is finding a partner who supports their magical life choices. And it's no Darren and Samantha situation. Women – they say – once wanted men who were attractive, solvent, had a good sense of humor and were loving. These days you can add a new set of criteria to the list – we want a man who is spiritually open, who isn't afraid of loving a Witch, and who may even be a Witch himself.

Loving someone who doesn't share their belief system affects the relationships of practicing Witches everywhere. Recently, during a powerful three-day workshop I contributed to on developing psychic ability, the same question kept coming up again and again from the wise women in the audience. Should I stay with my partner? The reason these wonderful sorceresses were asking themselves and each other this question was the vast sense of emptiness most felt when contemplating their relationship's spiritual capacity. (I want to point out that out of the 500 people attending this psychic conference, only 20 were men. Just to back up this point, on a recent yoga retreat, out of the 30 people attending, one was a man. And he was a Buddhist monk! So forgive me for focusing on women's needs in this story! Men, I'll get to you later – and the news is worth waiting for, believe me.)

I had always thought that other Witches must be wiser, more fortunate or perhaps more karmically advanced than myself. I imagined – mistakenly – that everyone else was having magical sex, celebrating Sabbats together, eating organically and trying to read each other's auras. I want to say right here that I love my partner very much, and we have many challenges that have nothing to do with Witchcraft, but there is a real gulf when we get down to spiritual issues. At one stage I wrestled with feelings of being misunderstood, rejected, patronized and, occasionally, good-humoredly indulged. Our most heated clashes in opinion were over mediumship, astrology and seasonal magick, though I always found it at least possible to discuss my belief in the seasonal powers inherent in nature. It's pretty hard to argue with the existence of a solstice or an equinox – though we profoundly differed in what we felt they symbolized.

One passionate debate was ignited when my husband launched a verbal attack on an astrologer, angrily accusing her of being a charlatan. I felt a flash-flood of anger surge through my body. The astrologer in question is a good person who works with the dying, is an environmentalist, and believes in what she does. So that word hurt, and I let him know what I thought of his judgmental attitude. And once he met her, and spent time with her, he realized she was a wonderful person and that his expectations had been incorrect. But the ugly word had made an impression on me: was that what he truly thought of my beliefs?

His anger at people who communicate with spirits was hard to take, but I understood that his motives were good. He felt it because he thought the people who were being read for were being robbed and offered false comfort. Both of us are passionate about what we believe in. And, after all, what did I expect? He had not suddenly changed or offered me false promises. When I met him, a mutual friend asked him what his star sign was. "Herpes," he answered flippantly. So the writing was on the wall from the very start of the relationship. I had no qualms telling him what I was into – I never hid anything. But I saw the raised eyebrows and I knew we were in for a challenge.

And he is an honest man. He would never pretend or be hypocritical. I would never have respected that. But I didn't like the feeling that my passion for the Craft was suffering due to my commitment to the relationship. As a clairsentient, this was no imagined dissipation of energy. Psychically I felt pulled in two different directions. This tug of war resulted in fatigue, depression and emotional burnout. It was extremely difficult to balance the two priorities in my life – but after six years, I guess I thought I had learned to live with it. But when I heard the other voices raised in pain, I felt a real fellowship with these women: fellowship and empathy and compassion.

I gave! Who read my stories with me. A soul partner. A magic man.

So, just days ago, I realized I was not, as I had falsely imagined, alone with this challenge. I saw strong women with tears streaming down their face, and realized this is a very big issue for any of us working in the Craft. Their question was, will my partner support me. Is he my soul mate? Can we stay together? How can I deal with the pain of him mocking me? How can I make him respect my Witchcraft? (And the answer is, of course, you cannot *make* anyone respect anything. You can just live your truth.)

One participant, Grace, said her husband had mocked her every evening when she got home after her Wicca classes. His fear seemed to be based around money. "He just thinks it's ridiculous. He doesn't see how I can make a living from my beliefs," she explained. She was passionate about the Tarot and healing, and wanted to be able to

...asked him what his starsign was. "Herpes" he answered flippantly.

I have often felt a gulf between the two of us when we struggle to communicate about spiritual matters. I find myself justifying my stance, my words. Explaining and trying to illustrate my beliefs in a context that will be meaningful for him. Yet he too admits my intuition astounds him – and that it frustrates him that he cannot find logical explanations for my abilities. I try to be tolerant too. I can see great value in his beliefs, though I find his attitude of powerlessness when faced with the dilemmas of the modern world dispiriting. And it has been hard work. And sometimes yes, I wonder what it would be like to have a soul companion. Imagine having a partner who shared my beliefs, who practiced with me, who encouraged me in my work and who attended workshops and talks

read for clients. As a group, we felt she would benefit when she brought home her first paycheck. That would solve *that* problem. But is being tolerated really enough?

Another woman's ex-husband believed her Witchcraft was "devilish and evil." She had taught her son how to clear the space in his room after he was alarmed by bad dreams and hearing voices.

Throughout the weekend, doing readings with Tarot, scanning auras and speaking to guides, the same issue came up over and over again. We had tapped a well of pain. The theme echoed through many women's stories – some partners didn't *actively* dislike their beliefs or *deliberately* seek to undermine these women's confidence – but their doubt and derision led to the same result. It was leading these women to question the appropriateness of their partner. It seemed that they were being forced to make choice: their partner or their Craft.

Living with and loving a man whose beliefs are a poor match for ours can be difficult and frustrating, and if you are not strong in your self, it can cause you to neglect or doubt your practice of Witchcraft – or any natural or unconventional path – just to avoid rocking the boat. The intimacy you crave with your partner may feel compromised by the fact that you find it difficult to discuss your spiritual beliefs with him. If he is tolerant, he may engage in conversation, but if he is blocked in his own spiritual growth, and has difficulty dealing with emotional issues, relationships can reach a crisis point. When you bring children into the mix, you can have a true dilemma in parenting, as well as a crisis in your relationship.

If you are experiencing ongoing frustration in your relationship because of spiritual incompatibility, I urge you to be gentle with yourself and, to the best of your ability, have patience with the relationship and your partner. It is in no one's best interest to pass judgment. Judgment implies *better than and worse than* – and your partner will sense this. Remember men, though they have become much better at disguising these feelings, are still vastly territorial and jealous. They often sense your involvement with another being or entity – especially if you are working with Gods and Goddesses – and they may feel threatened. Just as some men are threatened by their loved ones working, having strong friendships or achieving success, their sense of having an important place in your

life can easily be threatened when you have a passionate affair with your spiritual self going on. People practicing Witchcraft tend to be open-minded individuals who are sensitive, yet brave and courageous enough to "stand in the fire" – to take the pain that comes with being an outsider. Disrespect and discrimination can occur when we come out with our beliefs. When we go home, we want to be loved, we deserve to be safe and we do not want to be on the defensive. In an ideal magickal world, our partners would be our partners in beliefs. We not only wish to have someone to love and work magick with – we want to bring our children up with positive beliefs about the Earth, positive thinking and the law of attraction, and to be free to teach them herbalism, astrology, self-esteem and natural health. These disciplines are every bit as important as a strong traditional educational background.

Should I stay in the relationship?

Ask yourself whether you love your partner and whether you still feel attached or attracted to him. If you still feel attracted, there is definitely plenty to work with. Once attraction is no longer activated, it can be a sign that the relationship has run its course. If your partner is tolerant of your beliefs – in other words, if he does not actively interfere with your practice by destructive means – there is hope.

If, however, your partner:

• destroys your work;
• humiliates you in front of others or verbally abuses you;
• physically abuses you; or
• financially abuses you;

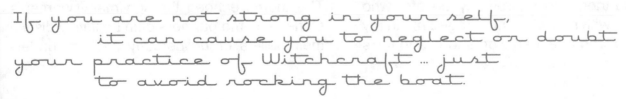

If you are not strong in your self,
      it can cause you to neglect or doubt
your practice of Witchcraft ... just
            to avoid rocking the boat.

you must take steps to shield yourself and seek professional help. Abusive partners seek weak spots in their lovers, and exploit those in order to feel powerful. If your partner is treating you in this way, the issue within the relationship could take many forms. It is not simply an issue of religious disharmony, but is a pattern of abuse this person needs to overcome with professional psychological help. If you are unsafe, please seek the appropriate professional or legal help in your state or country.

We want to bring our children up with positive beliefs about the Earth and the law of attraction.

Women who practice Witchcraft are sensitive – that is why you can work magick. This sensitivity is extremely undervalued in our culture, particularly by the masculine hierarchy. Being sensitive is why you feel hurt when you are mocked for your beliefs, but it is also one of the most precious qualities a person can have as we enter this new age.

Perhaps we choose partners who doubt or do not believe because we still have doubts. Somewhere in our psyches we may still feel a little embarrassed and shamed about our lifestyle. We are worried that we will be called silly, strange and weird. So we choose partners who mirror that internal fear, and then we project our anxieties on them. Examine yourself, and if this feels true for you, work on your right to be a self-fulfilling woman. Strengthen your confidence with spell work, ritual and empathetic comrades. It is natural to feel afraid from time to time. The greater the passion and purpose, the greater your fear. The stronger your beliefs become, the more powerful your own fear.

If you are a man reading this, wondering why I have ignored your needs, please take heart. Believe me, there are many, many women who have now got the words "magical soul mate" at the top of their list of requirements when it comes to men. You need to simply reach out. If you are hoping to bump into the right woman in a club or office, or actually bump into them down the street – well, you might get lucky. But if you attend classes, you will be surrounded by gorgeous, single, magical Witchy women who want nothing more than a magic man to share their lives with – and maybe even practice with. Come out of your broom closets, magickal men! I know you're out there and are fearful of being rejected. We need you to help us – (but a word of warning to some, don't make the mistake of thinking the Craft is just a pick-up scene! Witchy women have notoriously effective BS detectors!)

We want to have relationships with wise, spiritual, magickal men who will help us love the Earth, bring in the light, and spread the love.

We can't wait to meet you!

Ways to raise self-confidence

• Use the essential oil of rose.
• Carry rose quartz about you.
• Learn to shield yourself psychically.
• Build a strong support network of friends with whom you can discuss your beliefs.
• Call on the God and Goddess to help heal the patterns in your relationship.
• Be happy and peaceful – by being a serene, contented Witch you provide an incredible role model.
• Teach your partners how to treat you with love and respect.
• Ask the advice of like-minded people whose views you respect.
• Most of all, please continue with your mag-

ickal work – it will make you happy. Most men want their partners to be happy, so do what makes you happy. If they don't want you to be happy, you really have to question your reasons for staying in the relationship. Conforming to another person's worldview does not, will not, and can never make you a fulfilled being. And being that is your life's purpose and your responsibility. The rewards – spiritually and even materially – will come. Your relationship will naturally lose energy and dissipate in attraction when its time has come. If you wish to work on it, you can. Be open to positive change within the relationship.

calling the great god pan
the horned god in witchcraft today
Caroline Tully

"Hear me, Lord of the Stars,
For thee I have worshipped ever
With stains and sorrows and scars,
With joyful, joyful endeavor.
Hear me, O lilywhite goat
Crisp as a thicket of thorns,
With a collar of gold for thy throat,
A scarlet bow for thy horns."
—Aleister Crowley

"Our way is the way of the serpent in
the underbrush,
our knowledge is in the eyes of goats and
of women."
— Jack Parsons

citizens in the Craft, or the Horned God into a scapegoat.

I asked prominent Pagan Hawthorn if he thought the Craft was too girly? He replied:

"The relative lack of attention to the male aspect in some forms of modern Craft is unfortunate. When I got into the Craft, there were a lot more men than women involved in the groups I was aware of, particularly in positions of responsibility. That situation has changed considerably since then. There are now many more active women facilitators and I think that is a good thing. However, the apparent perception that the Craft is women's business is a worrying trend. The

> "The Craft has much to offer men and men have much to offer the Craft"

In the last decade or so Witchcraft's membership has swelled considerably, making it one of the fastest growing spiritual paths in the Western world. Many of the new recruits are female and this has led the media and other outside observers to adopt a skewed image of just who Witches are. Witchcraft is frequently portrayed as a women's religion; indeed, many people are actually surprised to learn that men can be Witches at all. Within the Craft itself there has also emerged a strong tendency to promote the Goddess over the God and to see the feminine as more worthy than the masculine. One of the reasons for this is to correct the imbalance incurred by thousands of years of women's oppression by patriarchal society, and this is admirable. However, we need to take care that we don't make men into second-class

Craft has much to offer men and men have much to offer the Craft."

One of the most attractive things about the Craft for women is undoubtedly the emphasis on a female deity, the Goddess. It is so empowering to discover *God* in our own image, a Goddess who actually understands us. Unlearning all the traditional taboos of femininity – submissiveness, silence, sin – and reclaiming menstruation and sexuality become spiritual journeys in themselves that Witchcraft actively encourages. It's therefore no wonder that women feel like we've "come home." Witchcraft can be a welcome respite from the "men's world" so prevalent in contemporary society, and a haven for many women who, quite often, have been so turned off the idea of any sort of male Gods that they see no need to include them in their practice. Witchy woman, Briar, says that:

"When I first came to realize my Path as a Witch, it was through discovering women's spirituality and Goddess worship. I come from a particularly negative Christian church experience, which also involved an abusive marriage, and I didn't want anything male in my sacred space ... It's only now, five years down the track, that I can even consider the thought of learning about and working with male Gods. I will always primarily work with Goddesses but I am in a place now where I am moving toward accepting God energy into my life."

Many men also welcome the chance to see deity as female. Regional Pagan Alliance coordinator, Kim Robertson, explains that:

"For the last year or so most of the magickal work I have done has been with Luna, the Moon Goddess in her raw and natural form, and also with Gaia, Mother Earth. Both of them are gentle. Luna is a wise teacher of those on the path to spiritual growth and is also a great deity to work with in ritual – she is like an older sister or young aunt. Gaia is more the one who is with me all the time, letting me know that I am loved as a person wherever I go, that I am a child of the Gods and will never be alone."

It can also be exhilarating for men to work in partnership with the Goddess's priestesses – strong, assertive, intelligent women. Indeed, according to Hawthorn: "being surrounded by lots of powerful, self-confident women is a big turn-on for many Pagan men, myself included."

Unlike many female Witches however, as much as Pagan men love and revere the Goddess, they are less likely to exclude her consort, the masculine aspect of deity known as the Horned God – and why would they?

One of humanity's most ancient deities, the Horned God of Witchcraft has a great deal to offer men, including a model of masculinity which rejects patriarchal "power-over." In her ground-breaking book *The Spiral Dance* Starhawk describes the Horned God as: "the power of feeling, and the image of what men could be if they were liberated from the constraints of patriarchal culture." Hawthorn explains that: "A lot of male Pagans are attracted to Paganism partly because the ideal of manliness doesn't buy into a lot of the aggressive male stereotypes that mainstream society does." Auld Hornie is strong but not violent, playful yet deep, sexual but not sleazy, loving without being possessive, and emotional without fearing disintegration. He is a God, a man, an animal, a plant, even a soil-bug, and is so connected to the Earth that if he lies down on the ground for too long he is likely to sprout leaves!

The Horned God also has a lot to give women. As a male paradigm which exists outside the cabal of the stern Father Gods and their sons, the Horned One offers a way for women to learn about, make peace with, and embrace masculinity if they choose to. Obviously no one should be coerced into acknowledging the traditional male aspects of the Witch Gods, and certainly within the Craft there are perfectly satisfying, exclusive women's mysteries honoring the Great Goddess. But that is only half the story. In Traditional Craft, alongside the Goddess there is an equal presence of a male deity: He of many names and faces, Lord of Life and Death. Like the Chinese symbol of Yin and Yang, the Goddess and God of Witchcraft are complementary and inseparable, two sides of the one coin.

Even if women choose to ignore male deities, and men in general, the masculine principle in nature is not simply going to disappear. Fathers, brothers, sons, the man in the local diner – men are unavoidable and the Horned God exists, whether we choose to acknowledge him or not. Maybe we are a bit scared of him? Pagan writer, Gavin Andrew, proposes that:

"... a lot of women (and men) exploring the Craft are dealing with a great deal of cultural imprinting as it relates to the Horned God/Devil paradigm. I'd suggest that the reason why the Goddess is more appealing is that the Fear Factor, learned at Sunday School or other places very early in life, isn't there. I think that men as well as women should look into the God of Witchcraft more, if only to help identify and alter this cultural imprinting within themselves."

The Goddess image provides a divine personage for women who extol the special attributes of being female. Yet I feel that it is important to balance the feminine force with the masculine, as night is complemented by day and the moon by the sun. According to a Jungian interpretation of the Craft, for an individual to attain inner unity, unrealized aspects of our inner self must be acknowledged and embraced – for women the animus or inner male, and for men the anima or inner female. So, for women, invoking the God is actually psychologically healthy, just as it is for men to invoke the Goddess. Meeting the divine opposite becomes a personal alchemical marriage. In Kim's experience:

"As a man and an active eclectic magickal practitioner, I have evoked and invoked Gods and Goddesses and played all parts in ritual. I find that playing either gender role in ritual is a journey where you learn, either about your own gender nature, or that of the opposite."

Restricting the deities we work with to a sin-

gle gender decreases the number of magickal experiences available to us by half. Why limit ourselves in this way? If we refuse to let biological gender determine the other aspects of our lives, why would we allow it in Witchcraft? Through familiarity with an energy which is dissimilar to our own, we grow and become wiser, our sphere of consciousness becomes broader – and connecting with the Horned God doesn't have to mean abandoning the Goddess! Katherine, a Witch who is very much involved in women's blood mysteries, says:

"I relate to the Horned God as lover mostly, the face of the primal, sexual masculine, erect, virile, powerful ... he's a big part of my pantheon. Him, the Green Man, Pan and Odin are the faces of the Gods that I relate to the most at present. [T]he Gods don't tend to have much to do with Menstrual Magick, although Odin has his own relationship with it, sly bugger."

The Horned God can be approached in many ways and it might be more useful to meet up with him in trance, before going all out and invoking him. Environmental activist and Witch, Indigo, describes a vision she had in which she encountered a Hunter figure:

"He stands to face the growing light of sunrise, and from behind I see that what I took to be a

Restricting the deities we work with to a single gender decreases the number of magickal experiences available to us by half.

headdress is the mass of his own tangled hair with a small set of horns protruding from his skull. As I watch, the horns change from one form to another. They are the horns of a goat, the antlers of the elk, the curved horns of the ibex, the heavy burden of the buffalo. They are the weapons of the bull, the curled protection of the ram, the tines of the stag, and the pointed scimitars of the oryx. In this half-light, he is all these things, the hunter, the hunted, prey and predator, poised to both flee and fight, the wild and free, and the beast of burden."

deity in antiquity, Pan survived in medieval Europe as the goat-footed God of the Witches. The Christian church turned him into the Devil and the cloven hoof, once the sign

It is important to balance the feminine force with the masculine, as night is complemented by day and the moon by the sun.

Or he may come to you of his own volition. I love this description of an epiphany which Hawthorn had:

"I've always felt a strong relationship with the God. The last time I was in England I went to see the Cerne Abbas Giant. Whilst wandering around the site I saw an amazing beech tree that was bent so that the upper trunk was at 90 degrees to the lower trunk and parallel with the ground. The top branches of the tree were brushing the top of a small earthen mound. I don't know if the mound was natural or man made, ancient or modern – it could have been a midden for all I know – but the tree drew me to it. I sat on the mound and closed my eyes. Within a short time the area around me was filled with the sounds of footsteps and rustling vegetation, but there was no wind. I heard and felt footsteps walk up behind me and felt an overwhelming presence. I opened my eyes, but did not look behind me. I looked down and noticed my shadow – jutting out from my head were the shadow outlines of a pair of horns. The feeling was uncanny, I did not look around, but stayed there in a sort of trance for an indeterminable time."

One of my own favorite manifestations of the Horned God is Pan who reminds me that we are all animals – smart ones, but animals nevertheless. The ancient Greeks represented Pan as having the legs and horns of a goat but his appearance can actually range from that of a real goat standing upright, through to a man with a goatish face, human torso and goat legs, to a wholly human form sporting curved horns upon his head. A very popular

of fertility and abundance, was regarded as evil. Anyone who has had much to do with real goats will know why they have a reputation as consorts of Witches. A buck goat looks like a man with a beard and wants to hump anything – including human females! Female readers, you might try going up to the fence next time you spy a billy goat and see if he doesn't curl his lip in an epicurean fashion whilst inhaling your woman scent! It can be quite confronting for a city-dweller, but that's Nature in all her incomprehensible glory.

A Ritual to Pan

This is a ritual that I have used to connect with the energy of Pan. It is written for the Solitary but can be adapted for group use. The rite is best performed outside in a natural setting and there is no need to cast a circle as the whole idea is to commune with the forces of Nature.

Make a small turf altar by piling up a mound of earth.

Place upon it a chalice of red wine, a plate of cakes and a censer in which is a burning charcoal block.

Stamp your left foot three times on the ground to signal the beginning of the ritual and then heap a small pile of Pan incense onto the charcoal block.

Recite or read the "Homeric Hymn to Pan" which begins:

"Sing to me O Muse, of Hermes' dear child,
The goat-footed, two-horned, din-loving one,
who roams
Over wooded glades with the dance-loving
nymphs:
They tread on the peaks of sheer cliffs,
Calling upon Pan, the splendid-haired and
unkempt
God of shepherds, to whose domain all the
snowy hills
And mountain peaks and rocky paths fall ..."

(Alternatively, Aleister Crowley's "Hymn to Pan" is very evocative.)

Begin free-form chanting: "Io Evohe, Io Pan, Evohe Pan. Io Evohe, Io Pan, Evohe Pan ..." [pronounced "ee-o, eve-oh-ay"]. Include whatever movements you feel are appropriate, such as clapping, dancing, whirling about, circling the altar or playing a musical instrument – especially pan pipes – for as long as it takes for you to feel that the deity has manifested.

Praise Him as your inspiration directs you, for example: "O thou Piper from the hills of Arcady. I adore thee Evohe. I adore thee IAO." [pronounced "eee-aaah-ooo"] "O cloven-hoofed, wildcrafting Greenman. I adore thee Evohe. I adore thee IAO. O Lord of plants and animals. I adore thee Evohe. I adore thee IAO ..." Continue to invent more titles to honor Him if you find yourself inspired, or else repeat the ones written here.

Sex magick is entirely appropriate here so feel free to indulge in some autoeroticism, becoming as wild and uninhibited as you please. When you exhaust yourself, relax, have a rest and then raise your cup and toast the Horned God of Nature. Offer Him wine and cakes and have some yourself. When ready, thank Pan for His presence and bid Him depart.

Lie down on the ground and allow your impressions of the ritual to gather. Allow yourself to "ground" by becoming super-aware of the Earth beneath you. Eventually, stand up and acknowledge formally that the ritual has concluded by stamping your right foot on the ground three times.

Erica Jong's Pan Incense

This incense is excellent to use when invoking Pan:

Grind the following dried ingredients to powder with a mortar and pestle:
• patchouli leaves;
• bay leaves;
• pine needles;
• wormwood;
• vervain.

Then mix in:
• four drops of clove oil;
• a pinch of honey;
• three drops of blood;
• three drops of urine;
• a dash of cayenne pepper;
• a pinch of powdered ginger.

Further reading

• Aleister Crowley, *Magick in Theory and Practice*, Dover, 1976.
• Vivianne Crowley, "Wicca as Modern Day Mystery Religion" in *Pagan Pathways* (eds. Graham Harvey and Charlotte Hardman), Thorsons, 1995.
• *The Homeric Hymn to Pan* (translated by Apostolos Athanassakis), Johns Hopkins University Press, 1976.
• Ronald Hutton, *Triumph of the Moon,* (especially "Chapter 3: Finding a God"), Oxford University Press, 1999.
• Margaret Murray, *The God of the Witches*, Oxford University Press, 1970.
• Peter O'Connor, *Understanding Jung*, Mandarin, 1990.
• Starhawk, *The Spiral Dance*, Harper & Row, 1979.

never mind the warlocks
xy chromosomes and the craft
Liam Cyfrin

In Julia Phillips's very chunky and nutritious history of Wicca (conveniently slipped into this very grimoire), she mentions an apocryphal story about the talented Mr Crowley that's often dug out by those wishing to make a case for a flourishing pre-Gardnerian form of 20th century Witchcraft. According to occult historian Francis King, the Beastly One once mentioned to his friend, Louis Wilkinson, that a Coven of Witches had offered him initiation, which Mr C declined on the basis that he didn't fancy being "bossed about by women." This story didn't appear in print until well after the publicizing of Gardner's form of Wicca and so is of dubious value as proof of anything much. Still, it's worth repeating not solely because it has an entertainingly Crowleyan ring to it (the old darling having been as staunch an advocate for feminism as the average Ayatollah), but because it highlights a curious imbalance in a movement that in most respects and prizes balance above all else.

influenced Craft because, it's implied, in a sense it's their turn. We've had patriarchy; we've had anathematizing of the feminine; we've had a misogynistic alpha male in the sky running the universe and not appearing to be overly fond of His own creation. It's as if the bathtub of history (and, yes, since you ask, I *am* having trouble believing that I typed that) has had a disproportionately large amount of hot water pouring in for endless ages. Now it's time to redress the balance with some cold before we all boil our tushes an unflattering shade of scarlet.

But is fair-play all that's going on here or are women simply better Witch material than men? By the mid-1970s, not a few Wiccan women were so convinced of the latter hypothesis that they were prepared not only to exclude men from their Circles but to give any semblance of a God the boot from their cosmology. By those still advocating bal-

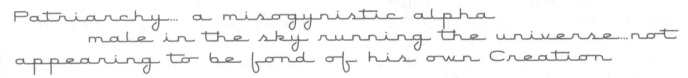

Patriarchy... a misogynistic alpha male in the sky running the universe...not appearing to be fond of his own Creation

The position of Gardnerian-influenced Witchcraft is neatly summarized by Stewart and Janet Farrar in their introduction to *Eight Sabbats for Witches* [Hale, 1981] when they discuss Wicca's seemingly contradictory emphasis on "the essential equality of man and woman … and the advisability of the High Priestess's being recognized as 'first among equals.'" This, it is often suggested, is a reaction to centuries of imbalance of the sexes, a major cause of human history's seeming such a complete pig's breakfast. Women are given a slightly preeminent place in Gardnerian-

ance, this separatism was sometimes put down to being "just a passing phase" of feminist spirituality. Most Dianic Wiccans rose above the criticism. For a certain percentage, it wasn't the first time they'd come up against the "just a passing phase" explanation for some rather central aspects of their identity.

These two branches of the Craft, the girls-only and the co-ed, coexisted relatively harmoniously for many years and continue to do so, but – phases or no phases – it eventually became noticeable that the hardcore exclusivists were becoming less common. The legacy of the promotion of the Craft as purely Women's or Goddess Religion, however, was to increase contemporary Wicca's numerical imbalance of the sexes. (As a side issue, non-supernaturally inclined feminist critics often disapprove of the "Witchcraft as religion for women" position, feeling it encourages women to lean on magic, tacitly accepting that they'll never get on in a male-dominated world by conventional means. Other critics feel the first bunch of critics might like to credit the average Witchy woman with a little more intelligence.)

Then, just when the lads felt it was safe to go back into the Circle, a new twist on the Craft developed: Wicca not so much as Women Power, as Girl Power (or, briefly, "Grrl Power" until everyone got sick of explaining that it didn't have anything to do with barbecues). The next generation of young ladies was ready to flex a little magical muscle. Many older Wiccans furrowed their brows about the youngsters' fondness for spell-books with very pink covers and worried that they were skimming past Pagan spirituality and discipline in their rush to get to the really cool conjuring bit. However, just as many other older Wiccans warmly remembered being disapproved of by their elders back in their younger days and sat back to let the younger generation work things out for themselves, just as they had.

The up-shot of all this her-story, of course, is that, from Crowley's bossy pre-Gardnerian ladies, through the no-man's-land of ultra-feminist spirituality, to 21st century Chick-Lit Books of Shadows, the role of the Wiccan male has often been a little perplexing. In the context of the Craft, the question (asked by women for centuries, no doubt) repeatedly arises: is this gender necessary?

To answer that, let's first consider whether the gender in question is necessary in the Wiccan concepts of deity. Deities are slippery critters in the Wiccan world, since different Witches have very different definitions of them. Some treat individual divinities as discrete entities, and think of their interactions with them much as a nun might her prayers to individual saints or an Enochian magician his or her contacts with angelic beings. The individual Witch may interact with a number of these more or less equally ranked powers or with a single patron, sponsor or ally. This is true polytheism, where the divinities may have a head honcho or honchette, but do not necessarily require a next-level-up Higher Power of their own. If there's no totem pole, there's no one in the top position.

In this type of Witchery, when we're dealing with individual entities, there is obviously no divine prejudice towards either gender. Many pantheons are represented as being male dominated (often more a reflection of the cultures through which the myths have passed down to us than of those who originated them), but no Witch invoking Athena, Isis or Freyja is going to be dopey enough to think they've got a second-class citizen on their hands. The polytheistic deities are really just a bunch of unusually powerful people, with idiosyncratic strengths and weaknesses. Generalizations on gender make no species of sense in this context.

An alternative, or sometimes co-existing, Wiccan view of deity is closer to Dion Fortune's slightly-too-oft-repeated dictum: "All the gods are one god and all the goddesses are one goddess." This leads to a sort of dualistic approach to divinity. This supernal She and He are considered to be conscious, more-or-less people-ish entities by some. More commonly, though, they are seen as being closer to the Yin and Yang energies of Taoism than to some sort of Mr and Mrs Jehovah who like to dress up in interesting costumes to confuse the puny Earthlings.

This approach seems to sit well with the Craft. When Wicca is thought of as a slightly wild and wooly Western equivalent of Taoism, several apparent paradoxes become less bothersome, including Janet and Stewart Farrar's stressing of the equality of opposites and simultaneous precedence of the feminine. In Taoism, neither the Yin (one of the manifestations of which is femininity) nor the Yang (which relates to masculinity) is superior. True virtue and potency comes through neither alone but through their harmonious interaction – Tao itself.

inhabits every male (black spot, white tadpole). A strictly all-female Craft would indeed make the aforesaid fundamental error of imagining humans to be pure manifestations of either Yinniness and Yangiosity.

So there's our metaphysical support for the Wiccan male. Next item: are women somehow better equipped for the Craft? Well, it's like this: more women than men do get drawn to the Craft and get very good at it, but only a very small percentage of either gender population is really Witch material. The notion,

The Craft isn't about Girl Power ...but about individual power and freedom.

However, stillness, silence and emptiness (all Yin qualities) are considered preconditions for action, speech and fullness. A cup that isn't hollow, for example, doesn't make a terribly useful beverage holder. In disciplines such as Tai Chi, a condition of stillness must be attained before the gentle flow of Yang and Yin motions begin. In Wiccan ritual, stillness, meditation and centering should precede the casting of the Circle. If we accept the correspondences between the Craft and Taoism, the value of the masculine in the former becomes a conceptual shoo-in. Just as Craft tools such as the chalice, cauldron and pentacle symbolize a Wiccan Yin and the wand, athame and boline a Yang, and so the invoking of both God and Goddess qualities invokes Tao. Having both female and male Witches in the Circle reiterates the symbolism.

But we're not going to make the fundamental error here of thinking women are all Yin and men are all Yang, are we now? Of course we're not. We're far too sensible. The symbol of the Tao hammers that point home very clearly, with its little black spot on the white tadpole-shaped thing and the white spot on the black. In doing so it also makes a clincher of an argument for the importance of both sexes in the Wiccan Circle. The Goddess

beloved of self-help publishers, of every woman being a potential Witch is about as accurate as the claim that every woman is a potential astronaut, every man a potential saxophonist and every dog a potential spokes-woofer for *Munchy Bites Dog Chow*.

It does seem as if a higher proportion of women have the right blend of intelligence, intuition and ingenuity to shine in the Craft but whether this reflects inherent capabilities or social biases is far from clear. Male weightlifters can usually brandish heavier lumps of metal than their female counterparts due to a genetic advantage; male politicians outnumber females due to cultural prejudice. My spider-sense tell me that the Wiccan situation is closer to the political in this respect, but if asked to back that up, I'm likely to change the subject quickly, pretend not to have heard or feign a sudden bout of sleeping sickness. Basically this is a very difficult issue on which to reach a verdict without raising a few generations of laboratory test Witches.

The next catch for many males drawn to the Craft is how they're meant to go about it. What's expected of them? Role models are, after all, thinner on the ground than leftover donuts at a police picnic, and there's little guidance to be found from rummaging about in the media. Dictionaries excluded men from their definitions of Witchery from day one, though we're often reminded these days that "*Wicca*" (pronounced "*Witcha*") is a masculine word in Old English, the feminine equivalent of which is "*Wicce*" (pronounced "*Witch-eh*"). The traditional fairy-tales we're brought up on generally differentiate Witches and Wizards, considering the terms to be as sexually clear-cut as mares and stallions (or possibly geldings, fictional Wizards being about as highly sexed as house-bricks). Horror fiction and movies are even less useful, frequently saddling male Witches with the highly uncomplimentary term "*Warlock*" – from the Old English "*Waerloga*" which means liar, oath-breaker or traitor. Contemporary fantasy tends to steer males into the roles of Sorcerer, Magician or Wizard, as in Hogwarts (an institution that makes Lady Thatcher look a bit of a radical) and represent Witching as a strictly girlish occupation, as in productions like *The Craft*, *Practical Magic* and the otherwise ace *Buffy*.

So, clearly your average male Wiccan needs to be a pretty independent thinker, willing to create his role in the Craft for himself. That having been said, those readers familiar with the Witchy community are probably aware of a few emerging archetypes. You've probably encountered the large, jovial, and invariably beardy type who sees himself as something of a protector of his community, the intense, androgynous young man who looks like he'd be most at home fronting a Goth band in Rivendell, or the good-natured elder who spends much of his time smiling indulgently at the bright young things enlivening the Circle but now and then startles everyone with a pronouncement or observation of such insight that thoughts of a Witchier Merlin suddenly leap to mind.

But ultimately the role of everyone, male, female or none-of-the-above, called to the Craft is to be themselves. Playing a part temporarily may help to bring out particular aspects we need to develop but the costume mustn't become a straightjacket. In the Circle we should be more truly ourselves than anywhere else, rather than reducing ourselves to a single facet of our identities. This is one of the principal reasons why, for the deeper forms of Wiccan magic, skyclad has it all over street clothes, robes, or funky Middle-Earthenware – but that's another chapter.

If you're male and feel utterly sure that the Craft is where you're meant to be, it's almost certain that you have the required qualities already: a respect for both tradition and innovation, freedom from the preconceptions that make many men view women as beings from another planet (important point: men are from Earth, women are from Earth, we have fossil evidence) and the ability to find both masculine and feminine strengths within everyone you share a Circle with.

In a mixed gender Wiccan ritual, both the differences and similarities of the sexes are celebrated, sometimes with party hats and streamers. By comparison with certain other religions which shall remain nameless, the Craft can be the gender equivalent of knocking down the Berlin Wall or dismantling apartheid. Despite the packaging it sometimes receives, the Craft isn't about Girl Power any more than the anti-racism movement in the US was about what used to get labeled *Black Power*. Both are about individual power and individual freedom. Which aren't at all bad things to be about when you come down to it.

coming out of two closets
the path of the gay witch
Christopher Penczak

When I was a young boy, my parents took me to St. Joseph's Catholic Church every week for mass. I watched intently, somewhat dazzled by what was happening up on the altar. Candles, incense, chalices, bread and wine involved in an intricate ceremony that I could only watch. Special words were chanted or sung over the Eucharist – thin, bread-like wafers that the priest said was the body of our lord and savior, Jesus – which was then given to us. It still looked like thin dry wafers to me, but I could feel magick in the air. Something special was happening.

> I could feel magick in the air.
> Something special was happening.

I went to Catholic school all my life until college, taking religion classes right along with math, science and history. At the very beginning, early in grammar school, I was a believer. I liked watching the show and singing along. In many ways weekly mass was my first musical experience. It was music, drama and religion all rolled into one. But in religion class I started asking questions that bothered my teachers. I didn't understand or like the answers I was given. I wanted to know why people couldn't participate more. Why did you need the priest to do it all? Why weren't there any women priests? Why didn't the nuns have a part in the ritual? My questions fell on deaf ears. My answers were something like "That's the way it's always been," or "That's the way God wants it." Others would quote the fall of Adam, with Eve's role in the drama being the justification for women's exclusion from the priesthood. None of this felt right to me. The dazzle of my religion started to tarnish as I entered my teen years.

It didn't have the same magick to it.

By the time I was in high school, I realized my own feelings and ideas were in direct conflict with my religion. Religion classes were intertwined with morality classes. I found being a gay boy trying to grow up in this unfriendly environment of an all boys' Catholic school very difficult. Coming out in an all boys' school is particularly tough and I remained in the closet, daring to tell no one, not even my close friends. I was told it was okay to be gay, but not to act upon it. That was a sin.

The only shining light from this school was a favorite nun who was my religion teacher. Sister said: "Talk to God everyday. I talk to HER all the time." She didn't last long in this conservative school. From her attitude, mannerisms and clothing style, I now wonder if she was a lesbian, although it didn't even cross my mind at the time. But before she left, she showed me that there were other ways to look at religion, or at least God. Until that time, I had never thought that God could be a "she." I started to ask other teachers why God was always referred to as "he" and got the same stifled answers as before. I knew I believed in something. I felt spirituality before in my life, and now I definitely knew that Catholicism was not the way for me.

I flirted with atheism for a while, but ultimately felt compelled to continue my quest for my own Holy Grail, a religion that would accept me for who I am and empower me to live my life and find happiness. I studied some

Eastern religions, and understood the philosophies of Hinduism, Buddhism and Shinto, but they didn't really click with me. My quest was long and difficult, filled with a few dark nights of the soul, but guidance came from an unexpected quarter. Little did I know it would lead back to the original myths of the actual Holy Grail and its Celtic lands.

Since I was seven, I'd hung out with a funky, fun art teacher. We had lessons in small groups every Friday afternoon. By the time I was in high school, we'd become friends outside of class, and I would hang out in her studio. Our relationship was not the typical teacher/student one. We talked for hours about art, history, myths and men. She didn't know I was gay but I felt that she would probably understand more easily than anybody else I knew. Much later in life I found out I was wrong, but that didn't stop her from being monumental in my life and spirit.

Gradually she introduced me to concepts of magick from classical mythology, talking about the pre-Christian Goddess cults, the Egyptian priesthood and magickal symbols. Finally she "came out of the broom-closet" (as I found out modern Witches like to say) and told me she was a Witch. I thought she was crazy. "Witches are fantasy. They're not real," I told her and made several *Wizard of Oz* jokes. I was a smart-ass teen, and thought she was playing a joke on me, but I had to admit the metaphysical ideas behind it fascinated me. And the parallels between the social stigma of being a Witch, and being gay intrigued me.

sexuality seemed to be equated in some trial transcripts, with victims trying to prove their innocence by showing a family with children. Although this teacher didn't know it, she had started to point out the parallels between being gay and being a Witch to me. We both had closets. I was still not out of mine. I really honored her bravery for coming out of hers and sharing such an intimate aspect of herself with me.

My friend was not trying to recruit me in any way. She knew I was searching, and thought the Craft might answer some questions. I borrowed books and eventually participated in rituals with her. She even invited my mother to rituals and discussions to show we weren't doing anything questionable. She had a little bit of a Mrs. Robinson reputation because she spent a lot of time with people younger than her, still in touch with her own youth and inner child. My mother got more interested in Witchcraft as time went on. Both of us later went on to study with her teacher, Laurie Cabot, the "official Witch of Salem, Massachusetts." I think somewhere in the back of my mother's head, she feared I was joining a cult, but once she saw the positive change in me, she became genuinely intrigued too. She eventually gave up Catholicism for the more balanced, empowering rites of Witchcraft.

In Witchcraft classes we studied a variety of topics I thought were unrelated. We surveyed world religions for the similarities and differences. I never knew that there were parallels

The parallels between the social stigma of being a Witch, and being gay intrigued me.

In later years, as I continued my studies, I found that not only were Witches persecuted in the Burning Times of the inquisitions, but gays, lesbians and transgendered people were also put to death. Witchcraft and homo-

between the Greeks, Egyptians, Norse and Celts. We studied quantum physics, Hermetic philosophy, modern psychology and European history. They all blend together in the art and science of Witchcraft. I learned the term "flaming faggot" actually came from when homosexuals were put death by the burning stake right along with accused Witches during the inquisitions. My two histories are even more intertwined.

Gays and lesbians were often considered special people in pre-Christian, Pagan societies around the world, honored for their unique balance of masculine and feminine energies. Many were psychically talented, and were considered healers and counsellors. Witchcraft honors the divine through both the masculine and feminine, through the God and Goddess. Sexual union through these divine beings creates all life. Their union is symbolized through a sacred Witchcraft ritual called the Great Rite, where Witches plunge the sacred blade/athame (masculine) into the sacred chalice (feminine) and then drink from the chalice – now containing blessed waters of life – and share cakes of grain.

Some Witchcraft groups focus more on the Goddess energies, some on the God. Gays, lesbians, bisexuals and transgender people are often welcomed with open arms, and some ritual groups, or Covens, are exclusively gay or lesbian. I was taught that "all acts of love" are acts of worship to the Goddess. Sexual preference did not matter. There are some traditions of Witchcraft, however, which are less than welcoming, being based rigidly in concepts of heterosexual fertility, since the ancient Witch cults were most concerned

music, dance, theater and ultimately spirit. These are the classic parishes of gay culture, where collectively so much of our energy is focused. It is easy to be unaware of the underlying sacredness of such acts, beyond their value as entertainment, but when understood as such they can be forms of meditation, divine communion and worship.

In both class lectures and her writing, Laurie would casually talk about gay and lesbian Witches she knew. My class of fifteen had one open lesbian and one man we all assumed to be gay. For the poor sheltered Catholic gay boy, it was mind-blowing. I had never really spent any time with anyone who was openly and honestly queer. This was in the early '90s when there were few gay images and role models on television, movies or books. Those available often turned out to be the victims of hate crimes or the chief suspect of a murder mystery. To find those in a spiritual circle who accepted it so nonchalantly was so surprising to me. In fact, in the culture of the Witchcraft class and rituals I later attended, such acceptance was expected. If my mother, myself or any of our friends attending exhibited homophobia or prejudice against anyone present, we would have been the odd and abnormal ones. It was truly the reverse of the culture I grew up in for most of my life. In seemed like a long lost queer paradise to me, yet I still didn't come out right away. I was afraid the oasis would vanish as quickly as it manifested, a figment of my imagination.

Gays and lesbians were often considered special people in pre-Christian, Pagan societies around the world, honored for their unique balance of masculine and feminine energies.

about the fertility of the crops and of the tribe. While in modern times that is still important, present day teachers of the Craft look also to the fertility of the creative mind, through art,

Unfortunately, the general populace and mainstream media still mostly misunderstand Witchcraft. The centuries of misinformation might be thought of as starting with Saint

Augustine's propaganda campaign shortly after the fall of Rome and was continued by the Church's persecution of European Paganism. Again, I found pain in the form of the traditional Church! All the same, I decided that it was time to come out of the broom-closet, and tested the waters with my friends. Most of them were from Catholic school, and while many were not planning on being practicing Catholics, the concept of Witchcraft was still too far out of their reality.

I tried to explain that my new practice was an exploration of pre-Christian spirituality, with roots in our Palaeolithic past, when the Earth Mother was honored, along with her consort, the Animal-Grain Lord. Sadly my friends were intent on thinking that a Satanic cult had brainwashed me, and that I'd become crazy and delusional. I explained that Witchcraft has nothing to do with Satanism,

friends, both straight and gay, who understood my path. With their support and my new path, I continued my training in Witchcraft and eventually pursued other healing arts as well. During these initial classes, I had life-changing experiences involving psychic healing, astral travel and spell-work. They opened me up to the interconnectedness of all things. At first I was just looking for a philosophy, an armchair spirituality. I understood the concepts, but thought this whole magick thing was self-delusion. I had many doubts. When first being taught about this aspect of Witchcraft, it seemed like I was learning relaxation techniques and pop psychology. Ritual was almost too similar to the Catholic mass to me. I wanted to escape my past religious associations for something new. (I was later to discover that much of the Christian mass was actually borrowed from Pagan traditions.)

My friends and family knew I was a Witch before they knew I was gay.

that Satan is a relatively modern Christian mythological concept, combining images of fallen angels, Biblical adversaries and popular Pagan deities like the Horned Gods, Cernunnos and Pan. The Gods of the Old Religion had been literally demonized by the conquering one. The Church had tried to sway Pagan believers to the new faith by telling them that their Gods were really devils. Witches don't believe in a devil. We are responsible for our own actions. The harder I tried to explain that my path was essentially positive and life affirming, the more difficult it became. I lost a lot of friends and, looking back, I understand. If I hadn't had a positive experience with Witchcraft, and if I hadn't been gay and open to seeing things differently, with my schooling, I might easily have assumed the Craft was Satanic too.

Luckily, in college, the Goddess and God sent me more artistic, musical and creative

I expected to fail many of my tests in the magickal disciplines of the Craft, but surprisingly passed with flying colors. Other experiences as I continued to learn included meeting spirit guides, experiencing past-life regression and performing spells. My initial experiences seemed almost incredible – but now that I am an experienced Witch I have come to always expect the incredible in every moment of my life. I always appreciate it, but have decided to live a magickal life all the time. In doing so I have found my Holy Grail.

After my extensive period of training, I was initiated as a Witch. All my family and friends knew I was a Witch before they knew I was gay. One of the tenets of Witchcraft is to develop self-esteem. To do magick successfully, you need to be confident. I wanted to do more magick, so I had to get my head together. By becoming a Witch, you are your own priest or priestess – exactly what I longed for when I looked at the Catholic altars of my youth. As a Witch you need no intermediary to connect with the Divine – to Be Divine – but this responsibility requires a lot of soul-searching and introspection. My decision to follow the path of the Craft took me out of a spiral of doubt and fear about my sexuality, happiness and future.

After my initiation, in college, I felt it was time to come out of my gay closet and openly be myself. All my fears were dashed, as for the most part, friends and family greeted me with open arms. It was a wonderful, life-affirming process for me, and I don't know if I ever would have found the courage without the spiritual support I found in Witchcraft. The experience of coming out of the broom-closet, a trial in itself, prepared me to come out as a gay man. Coming out is much like a magickal ritual of initiation. Once you do it, you are never quite the same again. You can't go back to being who you were. Your worldview is shifted.

I later found my life-mate through a love spell designed to find the person I meant to be with for this life. Imagine my surprise to find he is not a Witch, but comes from another very similar Pagan tradition. Our shared spiritual life, doing rituals together often, only deepens our love and commitment to each other. We are very happy together.

Coming out of the broom-closet helped me come out of all my other closets and be true to myself. My life's calling is now teaching and healing using these principles. The two deepest most intimate parts of myself are now also the most public, because I want people to know they are not alone. Most of my own students come from a questioning background. They are searching for something and are unsure if Witchcraft is it, just like I once was.

Many are queer too. At times it's like looking into a reflection of my past. I am proud to aid in their empowerment, regardless of whether they choose the path of the Witch or not. I want to share all the blessings I've received with anyone who wants to discover their own empowerment and walk the spiral path of healing and wisdom.

a queer situation
queering the craft the wiccan way
Mitchell Coombes

My Wiccan way

I can still remember the first spell I cast. It was a love spell that I found it in one of my mother's lifestyle magazines. On a full moon I had to pour some sand out on a flat surface and draw a stick figure of myself with my index finger. Then I had to close my eyes and wrap a piece of string around my finger. As I was doing this I had to envision the person I had a crush on being pulled towards me. *"Bring to me what my destiny shall be – so mote it be."* I was twelve when I first cast that spell and now at the age of sixteen I look back at some of the things I did thinking I was an experienced Witch. In four short years I have learned so much and yet I am still at the very beginning of my Craft.

What I like about Wicca is that in today's modern society any mainstream Australian or American can pick up a book on Witchcraft or Wicca and learn. I know it wasn't always this way. Wicca is also a positive, spiritually enlightening and accepting religion of choice, and being a gay Witch I feel happy and proud knowing my religion does not force an individual to have certain sexual preferences or beliefs. In Witchcraft you are free to be who you want to be and practice the way you want to practice. Growing up as a Catholic I did not feel happy and satisfied with what I was being told to believe and I also did not like the structure of this religion. I'm not trying to say that the Catholic faith is wrong – for some it's perfect. But when I was being brought up in the faith it didn't help me to feel fulfilled, spiritually, mentally and psychically, so I started looking for alternatives. I wanted to find a religion that was accepting, loving, acknowledged that males and females are equal, and worshipped male and female deities, recognizing they are inside us and around us, not just in the sky out of our reach. For me Wicca was and is perfect.

The Craft has shown me a way to feel whole and as such offers me a much brighter future. Wicca helps me feel confident within myself. There was once a stage in my life when I couldn't read or write and now I am a writer working on books and articles for magazines. I also had a very unhappy schooling life during my early school years and Wicca really did help me pull myself though all the negativity that was being sent towards me from my school peers who would send me home in tears everyday. I guess the bottom line is that Wicca may not be right for everyone but it feels right for me. I feel balanced and grounded in life, and I feel I can connect to the God and Goddess. And once you have experienced the true magick of Witchcraft, when you allow the Earth's energies to empower you and you tangibly experience the natural high and the *love* of it all, then you will yearn for more and Witchcraft becomes not just magick and spells but a profound way of life.

So where does queer fit into Wicca?

There are some people out there who feel that queer people *cannot* work Wiccan magick successfully. Most of this problem comes from the magick concept of raising energy through polarity. TM Luhrman explains the principle behind this prejudice:

"… ritual tries to create a human 'battery' for magical force, and it uses the 'inevitable' attraction between male and female to provide the 'opposite charges'…'You can't work magick with a homosexual … [the author was told] … Homosexuals just can't create a current.' " (TM Luhrman, *Persuasions of the Witch's Craft*, Harvard University Press, 1989; p.64. Note that Luhrman isn't stating her own opinion here, but reporting that of some Wiccans she had encountered.)

I personally don't think this theory is true. As I see it, deity is neither male nor female. Deity is just a higher power and I believe that the images of the Goddess and God are inner reflections of our subconscious. Witchcraft focuses on balance, as, for example, in the equality of males and females. But that doesn't mean a queer Witch can't achieve successful results from their workings. Everyone has masculine and feminine characteristics in them, and a queer Witch can work magick and the "opposite charges" will still be there.

Being a gay Witch I feel happy and proud knowing my religion does not force an individual to have certain sexual preferences or beliefs.

Today we live in the information age and people are being educated to become more accepting and tolerant of Witches and the practice of Witchcraft, and also of the gay, lesbian, bi and transgender communities. My concept of Wicca is that it is accepting and frankly the Gods and Goddess don't care who we sleep with as long as we "do what we will and harm none." They are happy, and so we are – it's a win/win situation, people! So don't be afraid to identify yourself as a queer Witch, don't let anyone tell you your magick is not going to work because of your sexual identity, and as Aleister Crowley once said: "To pagans … Sexuality is a positive force. It is the force of creation which brings all things into being."

Queer fits into the Craft perfectly and there are literally thousands of queer Witches practicing their Wiccan ways around the world. I'm a queer Witch and Wicca works for me, my spells work, my beliefs are strong, my personal relationship with the Goddess and God, within and without, is healthy and positive. I am living evidence that queer Witches can "create the current" and turn onto the magick of nature, love and Witchy blessings. And never forget: "All acts of love and pleasure are sacred to the Goddess."

Some basic tips for queer Witches

Ideas for lesbian and bisexual women

• Emeralds, cowry shells, roses and oysters are sacred to lesbians and are very good ingredients to incorporate into lesbian love/relationship and sex magick rituals and spells.

• You and your partner could wear cowry shells around your necks (or carry them with you) to signify your commitment and love for each other. You could also exchange rose quartz rings in a ritual of commitment or dedication.

Ideas for gay and bisexual men

• Place a hyacinth flower on your altar as this flower is sacred to gay men because of its relationship to Apollo. You may also like to place a hyacinth stone with the flower to add to the power of your magick. Carrying the stone can add to a gay man's safety.

• Carry an obsidian crystal with you so it can absorb any negativity that may be directed at you. You may also like to buy your partner a cypress flower instead of a rose. Cypress flowers represent love and compassion of the same sex. You can also wear cypress in oil form or burn it as incense.

Ideas for transgender and intersex people

• On your altar place almonds and pomegranates as these items are sacred to transgender and intersex people. These items can help empower your spell work bringing your intent into action and power.

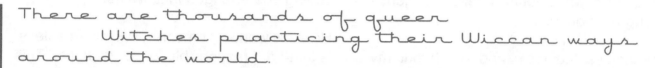

There are thousands of queer Witches practicing their Wiccan ways around the world.

• Make a wand out of an almond tree branch to help you focus and channel energies more efficiently. You can decorate the wand with meaningful symbols, such as runes, your magickal name/s, etc. You can bind leather and maybe add a clear quartz crystal to the top and bottom of the wand to enhance its energetic conductivity.

It's Saturday afternoon, we've done the morning chores and eaten a delectable brunch of sun-dried tomato, goat cheese and prosciutto frittata, a pot of blackberry sage tea, and homemade crescent rolls filled with pesto, freshly grated Parmesan and Boursin cheese. The world beat CD *Voodoo Roux* is playing, and white lotus incense is gently scenting the house.

I look across the table and reach out my hand. My beloved looks into my eyes and smiles knowingly as I playfully half drag, half guide his way to our bedroom. Indonesian lounging pants and my Balinese sarong are dropped to the carpet along the way. Beneath a multi-colored batik of the Hindu Gods Shakti and Shiva in Tantric Yab Yum embrace, I lay him down and look lovingly into his eyes. We both quiet our minds and begin to deepen and lengthen our breathing.

As we breathe and slow down, we will leave linear time aside along with the cares and concerns of our day-to-day lives. For the next several hours or minutes we will be between the worlds of *have to*'s, *should*'s and schedules. Like the Gods we will engage in the oldest magical act of Creation – the weaving of masculine and feminine energy through hormonal arousal and intercourse. In this Sacred Space of our own, we will call one another by our own names and the names of the Gods. We will remember that I am field and fruit and that He is seed and plow. We will intentionally focus our thoughts on love and on healing. It is our ritual.

What is Sacred? What is Magick? What is Sex?

When I ask my students from around the country, they say that Sacred is special, set apart, holy. What is Magick? Aleister Crowley once said, "Magic is the art of changing Consciousness at Will." What is Sex? A friend told me, "If your boyfriend or parents would be upset by walking into a room and seeing you engaged in it, it's sex."

How this works, for me as a Wiccan Priestess, is that I am responsible for my thoughts. This is the first gift of Initiation I received. Quantum physics currently teaches that the smallest unit of matter in the universe is thought. Modern Science has finally caught up with what shamans, priests/priestesses, Witches and magicians have known for thousands of years. Before anything exists, it is first a thought. Our thoughts create our reality.

Sexuality and Eros are the life-force itself. Sexuality is woven into our blood, breath and bones. It is primed and programmed into our most fundamental mating instincts. In states of arousal, our hearts beat faster, we take in more oxygen, and our bodily systems are flooded with euphoric chemicals like phenylethylalamine, oxytocin, and endorphins. When sexuality is combined with joy, love, pleasure and laughter, it substantially raises our immune system.

Sex is much more than penis in vagina. As any jealous sweetheart can tell you, sex takes place anytime we engage in thoughts, touch or the exchange of energy with the intent to raise feelings of sexual arousal. When we consciously use our thoughts and intentionally combine them with touch, the exchange of energy and/or intercourse we create a powerful force that can be applied to healing, creating vision, enhancing intuition, or deepening intimacy. This practice, ritual or yoga (means practice) can be done alone, with a friend or with a beloved.

Imagine: It is 10,000 years ago on the eve of Solstice. Depending on whether you are above or below the equator, it is either the longest night or longest day of the year. Let your mind's eye travel north and south, east and west. Everywhere you go the people are gathered, they are drumming, chanting, singing, and dancing. Their movements are rhythmic. Their hips sway and thrust. Men leap. Women undulate. Their breathing is long and deep. Their eyes are bright. Their bodies shine with sweat. They are all participating in a celebration and honoring of the turning of the seasons and the cycle of life. Their dance is a prayer, an invocation and enticement to fertility itself.

7,000 years, the healing forces of sexuality will be studied throughout the world, by healers, teachers, priests/priestesses, shamans and magi. One of the foundations of Chinese Medicine and the Tao is the effectiveness of sexuality's healing properties for the body's energy, hormonal and emotional systems. These healing properties will become integral in Hindu and Buddhist Tantra and Native American Quidoshka, as well as being core to the Temples of Love throughout the Middle East and Europe.

Depending on where in the world you live today, the knowledge of the Divine Power of Sexuality became public enemy number one some 200 to 5,000 years ago. The driving unstoppable power of sexuality, its healing properties, its veneration of women as divine, and its immediate and personal access to God/Goddess had to be demonized, subverted and controlled for the hier-

> *Fertility and the sexuality that fuels it are the sacred forces that bring life to the world.*

Fertility and the sexuality that fuels it are the sacred forces that bring life to the world. All the people know that without the Sun and the Moon, the seed and the earth, the man and the woman, the God and the Goddess, there would be no new life, no food to eat, no children to carry on the life of their people. The most special, sacred and beautiful woman is filled with new life. She is pregnant. She is as the Goddess, giving forth new life. Children born nine months after the festival take the last name of the Gods. These children born belong to the Gods and to the community.

As the evening continues people of childbearing years will pair off and mate. Their act of sex will inspire the Earth and its animals to be fruitful. It will also give more precious children to the community. In the ensuing 5,000 to

archical, warrior based, sky God religions to prevail. Layne Redmond in her book *When the Drummers Were Women*, which chronicles the rise and fall of women's divinity and musical creativity, puts it very well:

"[Because] this male god is asexual in essence. Because the goddess (and the fertilizing god) is denied there can be no sacred marriage rite. There can be no sexuality. In fact, sexuality, because it is excluded from the nature of deity, is considered wrong. The power to arouse a man sexually is no longer divine. It becomes original sin. Eve's body became not the means to sacred communion with the divine, but the source of evil released into the world. The underworld, shadowy cave and sacred womb of holy initiation, becomes hell."

Not only did women lose their power and divinity in this huge worldwide cultural paradigm shift, men also lost the divine power of their own sexuality, the sacredness of their emotions, and both lost the easeful access to sex as a harmonizing, healing force. What we are left with is the "battle of the sexes" – virgins and whores, wimps and bastards.

bodies and hearts; and

• Are able to choose who we love, how much and when.

Then we become the Magician of the Tarot channeling energy from Earth to Heavens and back again. And let's remember joy, laughter and pleasure. In the Wiccan Charge

Choose who we love, how much and when...pleasure without love is off the mark.

Who practices Sex Magick? We all do. Sex Magick and Sacred Sexuality are our birthright. Sex Magick takes place each time we make love and wish for a child. Each time we engage in sex with the desire for trance or blissful expansion. Every time we hope that making love will bring us closer to our beloved. Every time we touch our lover with the intent of bringing nurturing and healing through our caresses. Sacred Sexuality and Sex Magick are on the rise (so to speak) all over the world today. Sacred Love, Sacred Sex and Tantra are being talked about by celebrities, spiritual seekers and the folks next door.

Although I recommend taking workshops, watching videos and reading books on subjects listed as Tantra, Sacred Sexuality, and Sex Magick, I personally recommend coming from your heart and best intentions for the highest good and trusting your intuition. Sex Magick is encoded into our DNA.

Researching, experimenting and reclaiming sex, attraction, seduction, enticement, and pleasure as Sacred is subversive, beautiful, radical, empowering, rebellious, peaceful and holistic. I believe that we become an adept Wiccan Priest or Priestess of Sex Magick when we consciously:

• Focus and choose what we think in lovemaking;
• Set our intentions;
• Breathe, slow down and get present in our

of the Goddess, She says, " All acts of Love AND Pleasure are my rituals." Self-sacrificing, co-dependent love without pleasure, is not a rite of the Goddess. Pleasure for its own sake without heartfelt, compassionate Love, is also off the mark. Joining Love AND Pleasure is the key. Offering up a sacred orgasm to the Universe for the good of all can be a prayer and filled with fun. Enjoy!

Readings and Research Suggestions:

Fiction:
• Cerridwen FallingStar, *The Fire Within*, Cauldron, 1990.
• Whitley Strieber, *Cat Magick*, Doherty, 1986; Grafton, 1987.

Non-Fiction:
• Margo Anand, *The Art of Sexual Ecstasy*, JP Tarcher, 1991.
• Jalaja Bonheim, *Aphrodite's Daughters*. Fireside, 1997.
• Nik Douglas, *Spiritual Sex*, Pocket Books, 1997.
• M Francesca Gentille, *Sacred Sexuality and Dance* (Published online by the author - see also: www.lifedancecenter.com)
• Bonnie L Johnston and Peter L Schuerman, *Sex, Magick and Spirit*, Llewellyn, 1998.
• Thomas Moore, *The Soul of Sex*, Perennial, 1999.
• Zaihong Shen, *Sexual Healing Through Yin and Yang*, DK Publishing, 2000.

Witchcraft is a fertility religion and spiritual path. Sex is sacred, magick is sensual, and if you have any major hang-ups about sex and sensuality, you may have trouble being an adept Witch. Whether as Witches we incorporate our sexual practices into our rituals (be it solitary, with a partner, or even in a Coven situation) or whether we just insist on treating sexuality as one of life's great treasures instead of something debased or somehow impure, the magick of our physical selves is a matter of reverence and respect. This often causes those who have a vested interest in either repressing or exploiting sexuality to claim that Witches and Pagans have an attitude to matters of the flesh that would make Austin Powers look like a celibate monk!

In fact, although Witches see a positive virtue in the blending of physical and spiritual happiness, the way this is expressed in individual lives varies widely. You'll find no shortage of monogamous, polygamous, gay, straight, bisexual and even celibate Witches. Where the Craft differs from many other spiritual paths is in refusing to claim that any one of these expressions is the One, True, Right and Only Way to live our lives.

Is it true to say that Witches are less prone to sexual jealousy and possessiveness than most people? Well, it's probably true to say that we try a lot harder to keep that sort of negativity at bay and maximize our happiness and that of the people we love. Like everyone else with a functional conscience, though, we do try to find a balance between our own needs and those of our lovers.

Conventional sexual attitudes can be hard to shift. Many of us have them drummed into us at very tender ages, and despite our quests for freedom the indoctrination clings on. How, for example, would you feel if you had a partner and they took part in a magickal sex ritual to honor Beltane by enacting the Great Rite (lovemaking as religious sacrament) with someone other than yourself? Speaking for myself, I would celebrate and honor the symbolic significance of the act and not be threatened in any way (also I would probably be off doing it with someone else). To me and to many other Witches and Pagans (but – and I stress this – not *all*), there is a big difference between sex in ritual, and sex with someone you love and who is your life partner.

Having said that, I will add that in reality, rituals involving actual sex are much less common than certain sensationalistic journalists like to tell the non-Witchy world, and there are absolutely no obligations for Witches who are in Covens or in any other situations to have ritual sex with each other. It is utterly a matter of choice, and whether or not your magick involves any form of sexual expression has no bearing on your right to be a Witch. If you enjoy raising power through your sexuality, your magick will benefit from it, but if it's simply not in your nature to do this, forcing yourself can only have a negative effect on your workings.

Powerful sex magick occurs when the participants are mature, experienced and grounded in matters of life, love and love-making. This rules out teenagers, the emotionally fragile, egocentrics and power-trippers. Inside the Circle and outside, *never* allow anyone to persuade you into doing anything sexually that you really do not want to do. By allowing this, you undermine your self-respect and your magick.

Really great rites

I have never had sex with a stranger as part of a Witchcraft ritual. But let's not forget that some of the tribal practices that are our Witchy origins involved fertility festivals where it was seen as essential to mate with others who were either not necessarily well known to you or were masked to conceal their identities. The sexual rites of Beltane – basically sex in the fields to ensure the fertility of the next season's crops – were very holy events. Genetics weren't really understood at the time but our ancestors had enough savvy to realize that the survival of our species depended on the diversity of the tribe. Although these archaic rituals aren't an integral part of modern Witchcraft, they still resonate within the practices and attitudes of modern Witches today.

In general practice, the uniting of a Wiccan Circle's High Priestess and High Priest's bodies doesn't take place in the ritual but is represented by the symbolic union of female and male – the chalice and the athame, "that which is female and that which is male – conjoined you are the forces that shape all creation," are united to represent the act of sex. It's as simple as that. Simple in its magnificence, the passion of love on all levels, matter through to spirit in this world and all the worlds above, below and in between, is at the heart of what we do and who we are.

However, most Witches know a thing or two about how to raise magickal power and its similarity and interrelationship with raising sexual power. As a mature Witch, however, I find all Witchcraft ritual profoundly sensual and rooted (excuse the pun – actually you'll probably only get it if you're Aussie!) in the ecstatic experience that is orgasm. When I raise energy in a Cone of Power, I find that it reflects the pattern of energy conjuring and release of orgasm. Energy builds up to an ecstatic peak that explodes – floating over, in, throughout and around all things, and then there is the gentle settling of the spark that started it all until it is anchored to the earthly realm again. All this is a mirror of the build up/release/wind-down expression of energy that is orgasm.

The good news is that if you're drowning in hormones, certain Witchy rituals will have you on cloud nine! As I suggested in my book, *Magickal Sex – A Witch's Guide to Beds, Knobs and Broomsticks*, rather than saying a prayer at night, have an orgasm (alone or with your partner) and offer the energy to the Universe where it can be put to even more good use. In any solitary magickal working, I find virtually nothing beats using the energy of orgasm to fuel a spell to fruition or to seal the intent of a ritual. Also, when the orgasmic energy is forged in the act of lovemaking between two committed, loving partners, it is utterly mind-blowing and a sure-fire recipe for success.

Nothing beats using the energy of orgasm to fuel a spell to fruition or to seal the intent of a ritual.

In both cases, though, remember to treat the raising of sexual pleasure and power reverently. That doesn't mean you can't go absolutely wild with passion (you'd never catch a Witch saying that was a bad thing!), but it does mean that you shouldn't make the working a pretext for having sex. Some people still come out with tired clichés about Witches only getting involved with the Craft as an excuse for sexual indulgence. Frankly, Witches don't feel there's anything to excuse. If you want to do something warm, naked and snuggly, great! Knock yourselves out and have fun. There's no need to wrap it in ritual first to legitimize it.

If, however, you want to perform a seasonal celebration, spellcasting or other working empowered by the magic of your body, then you don't want a half-hearted quickie, followed by a shower to wash it all away. Raise the power slowly, don't rush towards the orgasm, and don't be in a hurry to wind up the Circle and clean up afterwards.

Don't push yourself too hard when trying to dispel areas of sexual repression. For example, many of us are taught to be very shy about nakedness, so if working skyclad with friends seems daunting, get used to it by being naked at home alone or with your partner to help normalize it. Perhaps progress to other non-sexually threatening situations like skinnydipping at a nude beach or being naked at a Pagan festival before trying the strange intimacy of a Coven Circle. Discuss any nervousness with the group (for instance, some guys, especially younger ones, might be embarrassed at the thought of inadvertently conjuring up an erection mid-ritual, and would need reassurance that it's perfectly fine if they do).

A lot of people have an ingrained sense of negativity about masturbation too, so when considering using it in ritual, get a lot of practice in first! Learn to enjoy it and erode any attitudes of guilt or embarrassment before attempting it to empower a spell. Similarly, if you're trying sexual magick with a partner, first have lots of non-ritual sex! Nervousness and awkwardness aren't going to help your magick so get very comfortable with each other's bodies before hitting the Circle. Take it in turns to pamper each other, to watch each other masturbating (a powerful way to learn what your partner most enjoys), and most especially to communicate.

Of course, the beauty of studying sexual magick is the fact that the homework is a whole lot more pleasant than most! I don't *really* have to urge you to study hard, do I?

the words of the witches
some individual voices from the craft

After countless years of oppression and obscurity, Witchcraft, in all of its many forms and traditions, both ancient and recent, is the fastest growing religion in America, England, Canada and Australia. Academic surveys estimate that there are about 4.5 million practitioners in America alone.

Since I began practicing about 25 years ago, I've witnessed enormous changes within the movement. I've also seen huge changes as Witchcraft has emerged from the broom-closet and gained real visibility, and even acceptance, within mainstream culture. There are TV shows with lots of adorable good Witches, and there's Harry Potter, and even Oprah Winfrey and Gillette razors referring to "the Goddess." And certainly the coverage in the mainstream press has undergone a sea-change with respectful coverage on television and in newspapers all across America. But are we having an impact on that broader culture? Does our visibility make any difference in the world? And is it even possible for us to make a difference?

with disregard to the consequences. Living in New York City, I am keenly aware of the very immediate and hideous consequences of this very distorted perspective.

There is a deep and ancient wound at the heart of Western civilization, a terrible suffering caused by this mistaken notion that the Divine is not present in the world. And this suffering has led to a madness that makes men fly planes into buildings in order to get to God, madness that makes men justify pre-emptive military strikes in order to assert their power, madness that threatens the very life of this planet and its inhabitants.

But what difference can our relatively small movement make in the face of such a deeply entrenched idea accepted by billions of adherents to the Biblical religions? As always, I look to my spiritual teacher for answers – and in Nature we find an answer. It is called the Theory of the Hundred Monkeys, and it applies not only to social groups, but to ecosystems, crystals, and atomic particles as

> There is a deep and ancient wound at the heart of Western civilization ... caused by this mistaken notion that the Divine is not present in the world.

I believe that it is not only possible but critical. We are confronted by a world at enormous risk, largely due to problems that have emerged from the dominant theological view that says God is not present in the world. The Biblical models argue that the Divine is exclusively male, that we are born in sin, that the world is nothing but inanimate matter to be used up as we see fit, and disposed of

well. Briefly, Nature shows us that even a small minority can have a profound impact on the vast and surrounding majority, or environment, when a sufficient number of that minority engages in new, creative, and particularly life-enhancing behavior.

In other words, we do not need to convert the world to our viewpoint to have an impact. Nor would we want to convert everyone to Witchcraft since Nature also teaches us that a healthy ecosystem requires diversity. But we can have a deep, positive and lasting impact on the world around us. We need only reach a size and visibility great enough for our values and perspective to begin to resonate within the larger global community. And we need only reach such a size for the common effort of our magickal/spiritual work to have a profound impact on that global community.

But if we are to make a contribution to changing the world, we need to ask ourselves what that contribution will be. We need to know who we really are and what we bring to the world in order to make a difference. What are our core values? What is the central precept that we all share, no matter what our tradition or manner of practice? There are those that argue that all that Neopagan groups have in common are their differences, that "organizing Pagans is like organizing cats." But I disagree. I think it is time for us to come together like a pride of lions. I think there is a profound spiritual wisdom that actually unites us. And it is this shared wisdom that can transform the world from dis-spirited violence to fertile creativity.

There is an emerging view, shared by myself and many others, that the single most important spiritual precept that unites most Neopagan groups and most Witches is the *experience* of immanent divinity as a daily reality, not an abstract concept or belief. We all share the knowledge, derived from our experiences using magickal/spiritual practices, *that the Divine is everywhere present in the world, and within ourselves.* This is a radically different worldview than the one that currently dominates global culture, both Western and Eastern. It is also the very truth that can make all the difference in our personal futures, and the future of the Earth.

And it is a truth that requires us to reconsider and possibly change some of our ideas about Witchcraft and how we practice it. The shift in perspective when we view Witchcraft through the lens of immanent divinity can be subtle and it can be absolutely profound. While investigating these questions, I began to discover that we were not as free from the old Biblical models as we would like to be. There is a great deal of residual "stuff" that permeates much of our thinking, our language, and our practices. Witchcraft has now been around long enough to develop its own dogma, and interestingly it seems that a lot of that dogma reflects old models of Biblical thought that are completely inconsistent with our core spiritual principles.

I try to explore some of these thoughts in my book *WitchCrafting* and in my talks, but I'd like to propose just a few items for you to consider now. It's a radical revisioning intended to provoke our thinking and re-empower our practices, and maybe help us to make the difference that can transform the world. My hope is that you will find this a valuable exploration that stimulates our thinking in a more critical and creative way. We don't necessarily need all the right answers, but we do need to be asking ourselves the right questions.

So here are some thoughts about just what we can contribute in the way of important values that will resonate through and transform the broader culture in which we live. Let the magick begin within each of us and radiate outward into the world:

1. The Divine is within you and is everywhere present in the natural world. And everything is interconnected by this sacred energy. This is the principle of immanent divinity at the center of our spirituality. It is not something we believe – it is something *we know because we experience it* with the use of our practices, and through our relationship

with Nature. Witches do not have faith in the Divine; they have experience with the Divine.

2. Maybe it's time for a new definition of magick that goes beyond the idea of changing consciousness at will and changing reality in conformity to your will. I'd like to propose that magick is also what happens when you open yourself to the Divine. All real magick is a manifestation of the Divine – it is how you commune with and co-create reality with deity. Magick is not about commanding and controlling, but about communing and co-creating.

3. Witchcraft is not about information – it's about transformation. It is not about believing, but about experiencing. So practice, practice, practice, and do it as much as possible in Nature! Witchcraft enables you to commune with divinity and to manifest your destiny, your desires and your highest and sacred self because you have tapped into the power that makes magick real.

Witchcraft is not about information – it's about transformation. You are living and making magick within a divine, living reality.

4. The real ethics of how Witches live and practice are simple: Witches live in a sacred manner because we live in a sacred world. We therefore treat all of life with reverence and respect. The Witches' Threefold Law (i.e., "That which you send out, returns threefold") is simply not appropriate for Witches because it reflects a Biblical model of punishment. What it is actually saying is that I will not hex or harm because if I do the harm will return to me three times over. In other words, I'll be punished. That's not ethics; that's expediency. If you truly experience the world as sacred, you do not need to be threatened with punishment in order to know the difference between right and wrong.

5. Because all magick flows from our con-

nection to the Sacred, our lives and our magick must be guided by the sacred nature of the energy with which we work.

6. The energy Witches work with is not neutral – it is divine love, even when it manifests in its "destructive capacity." Nature teaches us that death serves life, and life proceeds from the union that is love. And Nature teaches us that the Divine is both masculine and feminine, as well as being beyond gender.

7. Magick often works in unexpected ways because it is *not* a mechanical process, and the Universe is *not* a machine. You are living and making magick within a divine, organic, living reality.

8. The real secret of successful spellcasting, as with all of magick, is your connection to the Divine power within you and surrounding you. It is not in a formula, a tool, a potion, or something external. There is power in everything, but it is not unleashed until you interact with it. Immanent divinity means the power is, ultimately, always within you.

9. Nature makes the Divine tangible. By working, living, and practicing your magick in harmony with Nature, you are in harmony with the Divine. It is wise for Witches to spend time on a regular basis in real wilderness where Nature is most fully and powerfully itself as an unadulterated and undamaged expression of the Divine.

10. The ultimate teacher is the God/dess inside you and the world of Nature all around you. You are the awakened and empowered self-awareness of a sacred universe.

Those who practice this beautiful religion know that timing is everything – and just when we most need to know ourselves, like anyone coming of age, this powerful and growing movement is engaging in self-examination. We are looking at what we really believe and why we believe it, what we do and why we do it. We are growing, maturing, and changing. We are coming to a clearer understanding of our core principles and practices. We want to understand and experience Witchcraft, not just as a means towards an end, but also as a meaningful and powerful religion – a spirituality that can make a difference not only in our personal lives, but in the life of this extraordinary planet. Understanding the *why* behind the *how* unlocks the real power of Witchcraft as a profound religion.

The following interview was originally published in my first book, *Witch – A Personal Journey* (Random House Australia, 1998). At the time of this interview, Ly was known as Ly Warren-Clarke, and her book, *The Way of the Goddess* (recently re-edited and re-published in an international edition by Llewellyn, entitled *Witchcraft in Theory and Practice*), was the first I ever bought about Witchcraft.

It was unique because it was the only book I could find at the time about practicing the Craft in the Southern Hemisphere as everything else on the shelves was written in the Northern Hemisphere. Because Witchcraft's rituals and observances are based around events in the cycles of Nature, it's important when you're starting out to have some kind of guidance pertaining to your unique experience of these cycles. Ly's book was a wonderful guide for a fledgling Aussie book Witch! Ideas on meditation and visualization (both essential for casting spells) as well as introductions to Tarot and the Qabalah (an ancient Hebrew occult philosophy that has had a big impact on Witchcraft) plus suggested rituals to celebrate different Sabbats were all there for me to formally get started on the path. A year down the track and my well-worn and oft-thumbed copy had done its job and I had initiated myself as a solitary practicing Witch.

So, imagine my excitement when I bumped into Ly one day about six years later in the Australian Mecca for all that's spiritual, Byron Bay. My band, Def FX, were doing a show in town that night and every time we came through I would make a beeline for the fantastic book and esoteric supplies shop called *Pendragon*. I was looking at some ritual swords and daggers when a woman walked in whose intense presence gave me goosebumps. At the time I didn't know who she was, but with her flaming red hair, strong posture and powerful face she made a big impact on me. She started talking to David, the owner of the shop, and I overheard him call her Ly a few times. I hung around listening in on their conversation and trying to get up the courage to introduce myself – I mean, this woman was my original High Priestess! However, eventually David called me over to introduce me to Ly, explaining I was in a band and often visited the shop.

I was so nervous that I didn't initially tell her what an impact her book had made on my life. This meeting was one of the first of a series that eventually brought me "out of the broom-closet" so I was a bit scared of coming across as a slightly inept and ill-informed Witch-pretender in front of someone so established and accomplished. But Ly was really friendly, warm and, dressed in her hand-dyed local threads, up close she looked more like an enthusiastic teenager than some aloof ceremonial Witch Queen. She seemed pleased that I'd stuck with the Craft after so many years, because when the New Age explosion happened in the early 1980s, Witchcraft got swept up in all the commercial packaging of alternative spirituality. A lot of people read a book on the Craft one week and then ran around calling themselves Witches or magicians, only to become reincarnated American Indians the next on purchasing another book. I told her that her book had given me a definition to a previously nameless "something" that I'd felt inside for a long time.

We chatted for a while and she gave me a few more pointers and tips, and invited me to attend a gathering the next night. Unfortunately, Def FX was heading up to Brisbane (a city two hours north) for another show and so we parted, saying maybe we'd bump into each other again next time I was in town.

Three years on I found myself writing my first book, and of course the first person I wanted to speak to was Ly. Tracking her down wasn't hard; I presumed she'd still be in the Byron area, though I hadn't seen her on the subsequent trips there. I went into a couple of "New

appeared, dressed in black – but it wasn't a Witch's robe she wore, just workout gear!

Ly's voice is deep, gruff even, with a strong, no-nonsense edge. As she talks it sails from an eerie whisper to exultant shouts and her hands fly around, emphasizing everything with sweeping expansive gestures. Her body is phenomenal in its streamlined muscularity and striking tattoos adorn much of her exposed skin. Over the next several hours I was to hear an incredible tale: the story of a unique woman – a loner – yet a friend to many, a mother, a leader, a visionary and a very powerful Witch.

A unique woman – a loner – yet friend to many, a mother, a leader, a visionary and a very powerful Witch

Agey" shops and asked if Ly was still doing any Tarot readings in the area. The first two weren't sure, but the third said that Ly was reading privately but didn't have her number. However, I could surely find her at the local gym the next morning as apparently she'd become a fitness junkie! I was there bright and early and spotted her straight away, doing some stretches at the other end of the room. Her hair was blonde now, and she looked even fitter than before – really remarkable for a woman who would have to be in her forties. I introduced myself again, and she gave me her phone number so that we could organize to spend some time together.

Ly lived (at the time of writing) in a rambling, ramshackle house just outside the main township of Byron. At first I couldn't find a way in – the only door at the front of the house had a little sign on it saying: "Only people under 14 allowed." So, I made my way around the back and into the overgrown and huge flourishing garden, promptly collecting a spider web right in the face. "Hello! Anyone home?" I called out. Just as I came to the back door, Ly

Ly grew up in Mosman, a suburb on Sydney's North Shore. Both she and her sister were adopted. Her parents separated when she was eleven, marking a turning point in her life.

I have hardly any memories at all before age eleven. I can remember my first day at kindergarten and that's it. At age eleven I woke up to my feelings about life, about myself. Perhaps seeing my mother get rid of my father had something to do with it. My mother's ability to handle any situation and to be determined impressed me – I mean, she would rather raise two daughters single-handedly than have to cater to any man's whims or ideas on child raising. The individuality of the women in my family really had a big impact on me. They made me think for myself.

When Ly's father left, her grandmother came to live with the family. She was an enigmatic woman who read Tarot cards and tea leaves, and became a bit of a mentor to Ly.

She didn't tell me if she was a Witch or not;

that wasn't my business. She was a very private lady. I remember once she took off – just disappeared for a few days! My mother finally came to me in a spin of panic saying, "She's gone, no one knows where Nan is" – but a few days later she walked back in as if nothing was wrong. I said to her, "Where have you been? I've been worried stupid," and she said, "I'm an adult, I go, I come – I don't have to explain myself to you or anybody else." That was her way.

In The Way of the Goddess *there is a section on numerology. Here Ly talks of the powerful spiritual significance of the number eleven. The key phrase in understanding the power of this number is: "I accept" – and it was in her eleventh year that Ly accepted that her life was traveling down a profound spiritual path, and that she had a direct link to a world that most never experience until perhaps death. In fact, a bizarre dream followed by two near-death experiences in one week made her realize her life was going to be anything but normal.*

I have never forgotten this dream: I was running, running, running. Whoever had been following me was long gone, and as I turned around to look where they'd been, I saw that the entrance that I had come through was closed. I was standing in a chimney of white, chalk-like crevices and striated rock. In one of these clefts of rock was a Being sitting there – you could call it angel. I couldn't tell if it was a man or a woman, and all night long it talked to me in rhyme about life, the universe, everything. I kept thinking "I've got to wake up and write this down" over and over again, but I woke at dawn with only a memory.

The next week I was at Balmoral Beach swimming, and one of the guys I'd been playing with came and held me under the water. I remember thinking, "I'll put my hand over my nose and make an air-pocket so I can breathe." So I did that, breathing away, and

that's all I remember until I came to with someone on top of me pumping the water out of my lungs. Within the same week, I was helping my mother wash up and she said to me, "Bring the toaster over and I'll shake the crumbs out of it." It was plugged in and I remember picking it up with my fingers wet from washing up and laughing myself silly because it tickled so much! I came to hours later with severe burns.

The following week was when my grandmother disappeared. It was all happening – bang, bang, bang! So much strange phenomena! I mean I was living at 666 Military Road, Mosman! Things were going bump in the night, and once, all these rocks rained on the roof … it was wild! And it wasn't just me that noticed it: my family, my animals, everyone was affected.

It was at this time that Ly entered her first formal religious training – her mother enrolled her in a Roman Catholic Girls' School.

Oh, I fell into the hole beautifully, I must admit! I was baptized, had my first communion, got the confirmation, the whole thing. But it was the passion of it all that hooked me, not the dogma, not the scriptures. It was the feeling. The wonder of being in a cathedral prior to dawn when there was nobody else around and lighting the votive candles there. I would dress in blue robes and carry candles down the aisle and think of myself as a "child of Mary." I loved the Trinity, but it wasn't the Father, Son and Holy Ghost. It was my Lady, being Mary, on one side and my Lord on the other. The passion and tension all coincided with the awakening of my sexuality. Anyway, about a year or so later I saw through all that and went into my Jewish phase – off to the synagogue!

But the synagogue just wasn't as interesting as the séances Ly was having at home with her grandmother!

I was doing séances from the age of thirteen with my grandmother. It was very experimental, but she encouraged me to explore the supernatural. She'd say, "The only thing that will hurt you in life is a man with a knife! Anything else, go for it! Explore, experiment, know your exits and know your way in." I knew I was psychic, especially when I was young. I backed off a bit from it in my teens due to peer pressure and boy distractions. But there's nothing that esoteric about being psychic – intuition, that's it: knowing when someone is lying or telling the truth. If you listen and look you'll hear and see.

One of the things Ly was hearing and seeing that definitely no one else could was an entity name Binah.

"Explore, experiment, know your exits and know your way in"

I've been clairaudient for as long as I can remember, though this particular force didn't give me her name until much later in my life. She used to take the name of any particular archetype of Our Lady – there's only one but she shows many faces. Sometimes she presents herself as male, and she's been with me the whole way through. I've written down much of what she's told me – I've got three grimoires (records of magickal work) full of the most incredible, prophetic stuff. The force that she is can be as frightening as it is magnificent; it's a part of me and outside of me.

The traditional accoutrements of the Craft, Tarot cards, were something Ly became very familiar with long before the word "Witchcraft" had become part of her vocabulary.

I only started using them in my late teens and early twenties, but I was familiar with them much earlier because my grandmother used them. She even predicted her own death! She could give names, times, dates and places. In my teen years I would be ready for

a date and if the guy hadn't turned up I'd be woefully saying, "Oh, he's stood me up." She would swill her tealeaves around in her cup and throw her cards on the table and say, "Darling, just stay calm. He's had a bugger of a day and he'll ring you at eleven." And the guy would call! She was that good.

But this was never called Witchcraft. I was just always surrounded by magick. It's funny how you come into a knowing of what you are, and you haven't got a name for it so you go searching. I would look in libraries and bookshops and find books by Aleister Crowley hidden away, but there were no books on the Craft except coffee-table ones, and Dennis Wheatley novels, which were rubbish. I would read them and think, "This is not the truth" – and inside there would be this burning, twisting feeling, because I knew how to make things happen. I knew there was a force working inside me.

It wasn't until Ly was seventeen that she actually came into contact with other bona fide Witches who agreed to initiate her into their Coven.

I was introduced to a group who were working in (the Sydney suburb) Edgecliff by a friend of the family who knew about me and what I was looking for. I was initiated and stayed with them for two years but then I took off. At first it was a relief to be with like-minded people; it was a very well established group and we worked some powerful magick. I learned fast, but I started getting annoyed because there was a lot of arrogance in the group and they were very tempted to play around with what, at that stage in time, I considered to be dark forces. At the time, a man ran the Coven and women weren't afforded equal status. I realized, ultimately, that the whole thing was quite manipulative. At this time I was pregnant, so after I had my first child as a single parent in 1972, I moved back with my mother and worked as a freelance computer analyst. At the same time I was doing Tarot readings for people and getting lots of experience.

It was in her late twenties that Ly felt it was time to get involved with other people of the Craft again.

I had to find a group to finish what had begun. I found a fairly well-known group in Sydney who were quite upfront about what they were doing; in fact they were putting out the *Wiccan Newsletter* and were easily contacted. They agreed to initiate me and I went along to meet the Coven. It was a Sunday afternoon and we were all sitting around chatting and drinking cups of tea; it was all very nice and I was thinking, "What do we have here? Either they are very, very secretive or there's nothing here." I had a dead feeling inside me that this was more about show than real magick. Unfortunately my instincts were right – it was all quite superfluous and shallow. They had all these ideas about rank and title. It was incredibly hierarchical. People had to wear different colored robes to denote rank and they refused to acknowledge my previous training insisting that it was worth nothing – their way was the only way.

Inside there would be this burning, twisting feeling, because I knew how to make things happen.

But the urge to work with others was very strong and I stayed with them for a short journey through first, second and third degree initiation rites all within a year. Then I left and took the Coven with me setting up the Coven of the Crystal Glade. It was at this time that I decided to go full-on into magick. I knew I needed to spend more time with my child; my mother had been babysitting him for long

enough! I had a Coven to train, Tarot to read and a child to raise, so I left my job. I started teaching Qabalah at the New Awareness Center in Sydney, writing articles for various publications and running the Coven. If I wasn't getting paid cash, I would barter my services, though I was always taught to "have your hand crossed with silver" and "you have to pay the piper." To this day I stand by this, and even though most of the time I receive money, I will accept vegetables, clothing … sometimes I'm given really wonderful and interesting things of the kind that I'd never get myself.

In 1982 Ly was invited to the now famous first Mount Franklin Gatherings. Witches from all over Australia came and gathered at a property in the Victorian Midlands to exchange experiences and ideas – which they've continued to do once a year to this day. The inaugural Gathering was to be a pivotal time for Ly.

People had come from all over the place, Western Australia, South Australia, it was like a Who's Who of Witches and the first of its kind. Prior to this there were a lot of people hanging around in closets. Everyone had been coming out a little before that. I guess Nevill Drury was very responsible for that – his book about the occult in Australia, *Other Temples, Other Gods* [co-written with Gregory Tillet (Methuen, 1980)] and the television show that went with it made a big impact on a lot of people.

Anyway, after the gathering I went back home to Sydney and one week later birthed my second child. A week after that I shrugged my shoulders, packed everything up, said goodbye to everyone, loaded up the truck and moved to Victoria! I guess destiny leads

It's not the words that matter – it's the feeling behind that's the most important part of ritual. It's the dance, the movement, the song, the harmony, the energy that's raised.

you and my destiny led me back there.

Ly lived in the picturesque Victorian Midlands for the next ten years, bringing up her children, running Tarot workshops and reading for people, as well as starting up a Coven, which she named Order of Stellar Fire.

I ceased using the word Coven because it had become whitewashed all over the place. I set up the Order with a High Priest I had worked with in Sydney. I created a bit of controversy on the scene at this time by initiating a young, brilliant magickian, who was twenty-four. I had complaints from a group I used to work with because he was homosexual, and the same happened when I initiated another very gifted person who was a lesbian. In my mind there is no room for this kind of prejudice. Both were fabulous, exciting and powerful people and the work we did together was phenomenal.

Over the years Ly has initiated at least 30 people into the mysteries of Witchcraft with a dozen going on to take High Priest/esshood from there. She does not initiate into a particular tradition like Alexandrian or Gardnerian, preferring instead to draw from various sources and letting individuals uncover their path for themselves.

They're initiated into the challenge of working with magick and part of that is understanding discipline as well as passion. So initially they are trained to know rituals and spells word for word and then they are taught that it's not the words that matter – it's the feeling behind that's the most important part of ritual. It's the dance, the movement, the song, the harmony, the energy that's raised.

I teach my initiates about protection and about waking up to the forces – letting these blow through them. We get in touch with the Earth magick itself, we call it God and Goddess and we get close to it and explore it. We also explore new ideas and we build trust and power between us.

Initiation is a journey and a process, and what is required of a High Priest or Priestess is that you're there with them throughout. There is an external power or a power other than the limitation of self that makes itself known to an initiate and it usually gives three years of hell! It's like the dance of Persephone with Lord Hades in the underworld – it's tough! The initiates go through really tough times, exploring and confronting their deepest fears and desires. Talk about waking up to yourself! The ones that see it through, who don't say, "I can't handle this – you've introduced me to the dark side," are the ones who understand that for light to exist there has to be dark. They're the ones that I can point my sword at and say, "I hand this to you."

During her time in Victoria Ly also wrote The Way of the Goddess.

It took me two weeks to write. It was my first book and it actually stemmed from a training program I'd been working on for some time, a series of twenty-six lessons over twenty-six weeks. Nevill Drury, who was then an editor at Harper and Rowe, visited me while I was pregnant with my daughter, Serenity, and saw these lessons laid out on my dining room table. He read them and said, "This is good, it's a book. When you've written the second half send it to me." I said, "Never!" I wasn't into coming out at the time and I thought there was no way I would write a book. I birthed my daughter and started running a workshop through a local bookstore and getting on with life.

One evening after I'd shut up shop I sat down and went into meditation to balance myself before the workshop started that night. I was sitting there with a couple of candles and unraveling my mind when all of a sudden in huge big italics, like neon lights across my mind, came Binah, loud and clear, screaming at me, "You deny me!" I'm not kidding – the way this force communicates is full on!

That night I did a very intense workshop talking about the spiral dance, weaving the web of life, the whole lot. The following evening I was sitting at my typewriter to write up the notes on the workshop and out came the second part of my book. It literally poured out of me, chapter by chapter, and two weeks later I'd finished it. I freaked a bit – it was so personal, my voyage, the way I travel. I thought, "Am I game enough to send this to Nevill?" But I did, and didn't hear from him for two weeks. In that time he sent it off to Britain, where they'd written up the contracts and sent them back. I didn't think getting published could be that easy!

Ly's book was a success right from the start, and the interest it generated, specifically in women, spurred her to write a second book with Cathy Magus.

We initially wrote *The Way of Merlin* for men. Everyone said The Way of the Goddess was written for women, but I would say, "I'm a woman! That's the reason it sounds the way it does – I'm doing the talk!" So Cathy and I started from the premise of a man's magick-

al aid book, but ultimately threw that away because the book is for everyone. They key lesson in the book is the value of legend, the power in symbolism, the fact that legend can be the greatest teacher of all.

One of the most significant experiences during the ten years in Victoria was what Ly calls the "Great Work."

The late 1980s and early 1990s were an incredible time for me. I was being overwhelmed by people who wanted Tarot readings. The word had got around that I was very accurate and clients were flooding in. I also had people climbing through the windows asking to be initiated – seriously! A friend of mine said she didn't know how I handled living in such a remote place and having at least thirty-five people pass through the living room every day! It was like a magickal tide rising to a point where I'd never known such an incredible force – a huge crest – the most brilliant people to work with, the most amazing Qabalistic work. The Great Work was the peak of all this. Four women, myself a Sagittarian/fire sign and three other women who were water, air and earth signs committed ourselves to the task. We devoted ten weeks of our lives, six nights a week, to this particular work. The others in the group we left to their individual studies as they were not prepared to make such a sacrifice at that time.

The impetus for the Great Work came from an incredibly strong sensation that the pattern of balance of life itself was being threatened on Earth. In fact in the middle of this work, Saddam Hussein invaded Kuwait. We would sit at our altars in our individual temples purely and simply to give everything that we possibly could to the forces that protect

We were going across the abyss where time, space, energy and matter converge and anything could happen.

life, to stop that sensation that the balance was being tipped against the powers of life. That's all we were there for, because anyone who is working magick is there for the giving, not the taking. The receiving is a side pleasure. We women did ritual and meditated alone and would only come together at the main Temple on Fridays to discuss the progress so as to remain as objective as possible. It was in the second week that we all received psychic communications from an entity … "Bang!" Like white light! That Friday we met and compared notes and found we had all, virtually word for word, got the same information. One through her dreams after the rituals and the other two through the written word – automatic writing, where you just write what you're hearing as fast as you can and you stop to figure out what it says later.

We were being told that the world was being unclogged from the bottom up, meaning the world will know tragedy and there was little that our magick could do to stop the tide. A pulse had started that was going to shake things up to a point where we humans would be at a new level of evolution. We were told that in an evolutionary scene we are going across the abyss where time, space, energy and matter converge and anything could happen.

There were predictions and information about the nuclear testing on Mururoa Atoll – "Fire will rain down on Mother Mountain underground and there will be earthquakes …" – that sort of thing. Some of the communication was terrifying but the work went on. When it finally came to a close, everything stayed really intense for another year but ultimately I started to feel like I was suffocating with people. I went into a major crisis of self. My body weight went up enormously – it was like I was trying to buffer myself – the man I was with was trying to manipulate me, everything was coming down. Exactly a year to the day after the initial rituals of the Great Work, I kept waking up in the morning with this

severe adrenalin attack and at weird times like 2:22, 3:33, 4:44. It was always the same game – get up, make a cup of coffee and sit down and go over everything that was happening in my life.

One morning Binah came through and said, "You are going to Byron Bay." I said, "How am I supposed to get rid of this house, and organize this? There's so much to do." The next Saturday I was teaching Tarot and I said to my group, "I'm out of here, I'm going to Byron Bay," and one of the students said, "Oh that's interesting, I've got a property up there, you can have it if you like." Just like that! I had somewhere to go and within the month I was gone. At the same time I continued having the adrenalin attacks and everything started to change, my body went from ten stone to eight-and-a-half stone in a matter of three weeks. It just shrank! And not through trying or ill health – everything just lightened up and got easier.

At the time of this interview, Ly had lived in Byron for five years. She'd established the Temple of Bethasaherh and the three women who took part in the Great Work had all moved up to join her.

Initiates tend to follow each other around, though at the moment I mainly work solitary and sometimes with a couple of initiates. I'm still doing Tarot and a lot of my time is spent writing. Within a month of moving here I started another book, *Infinity's Web* and now I'm working on the second part, *The Quest of Veils*. I'm also writing a book called *Body Language* which is about a Zen influenced weight training regime I've developed; and I'm doing an anthology of all my private magickal work. Some of the dialogues that have gone down from Goddess to Priestess, like the Binah papers, are really amazing.

Ly has some definite opinions about where Witchcraft in Australia is heading given that it is receiving a lot of relatively decent publicity these days.

Witches are who you are and magick is what you do. It's not heading anywhere – it's going to remain what it's always been: occult, hidden. Occult is the whole principle of it. We work between the worlds, not up on stage in a position. Individuals may make themselves known publicly, but not the magick. The whole principle is that it's a path of hidden wisdom. As such, Witchcraft will be where it has always been, which is between the worlds.

Witchcraft is not New Age, not "popular" and not somebody else's idea of acceptability. Witchcraft is not a thing that will ever be acceptable because the truth of it is that Witches are individuals and they can't be stereotyped or typecast. As soon as you think you know them they change. Change is the way.

There's something inside that I call the "green." You look inside and you think of self, but nobody is at home, and you can only see the Universe as far as you look: endless

> No illusion and no lies, just perfect grace, joyous simplicity and brilliance – that's where you dwell

A lot of the time people are what I call "players." They play with Witchcraft – they're putting up fronts and dressing up. What they're seeking is identity. The minute they realize that they've got one and don't need to put on masks to prove it, they find themselves and might find they were Witches all along. I always know kind. I can feel it – something comes off a person who's been there, who's felt it. It isn't linear and "heading" anywhere. It's where it's always been which is practicing the Craft of magick. It seeks to alter, if you like, that which is crushing at any level, anything that is restraining energy. Now, energy can be restrained in matter, but to be able to weave, to never accept the limitations that others set up for you and to be able to change them at will – that's where Crowley had it right. Change in accordance to will, but first you must know your will, and your will may have nothing to do with what you want. Understanding the difference between information and knowledge is important. Knowledge is gained through personal experience, internally and externally. Knowledge is pure, it is the essence of life itself. Witchcraft is knowledge and the people that "play" with the information of Witchcraft can't maintain what they set up and ultimately it is just superficial.

space. A quiet place with plenty of power where there is no illusion and no lies, just absolutely perfect grace, joyous simplicity and brilliance – that's where you dwell. You find that place and then you know how to make any parking space turn up, how to banish any stop signs in your life, how to banish any limitations others set up for you. Find the "green" and stay there.

My contact with the Craft, and eventual entry into it, really began when I was about twelve years old. At that time my uncle lent me a book on Spiritualism and, being an avid reader, I devoured it and went back for more. I quickly read all the books he had and then had to go to the local library where, for the next several years, I worked my way along the shelves from Spiritualism into ghosts, ESP, magic, Witchcraft, Voodoo, folklore, and so on. From studying the bibliographies contained in the books I liked, I was directed to further reading and so it just snowballed.

It was some years later that I read two of Margaret Murray's books, *The Witch Cult in Western Europe* (1921) and *The God of the Witches* (1933). These impressed me but, at that time, I had no idea that the Old Religion still existed. It was a few more years before I finally came across Gerald Gardner's works, *Witchcraft Today* (1954) and *The Meaning of Witchcraft* (1959). These affected me strongly, for here was a living (if, perhaps, re-born) Pagan religion that struck a great many chords with me. This was about 1960. I got in touch with Gardner and began a correspondence with him. This developed to where he put me in touch with his High Priestess, Monique Wilson (Lady Olwen), and this in turn led to her initiating me. Gardner then encouraged me to introduce the Craft to America, which I did in the very early 1960s. I later became Gardner's spokesman in the United States, having immigrated here in February 1962.

The early years of establishing Wicca in the US were satisfying, trying, pleasurable, horrendous, and truly worthwhile! But on the first Samhain after Gerald's death, he visited our Circle – and was clearly seen by all present – and that was a definite high point and for me endorsed that I was doing the right thing.

There was a big interest in Witchcraft in America in the early 1960s, and my wife and I were not short of Coven candidates. But, as taught, we were cautious and did not initiate anyone without due process. Such was the demand for Wicca entry at that time, however, that we received a great deal of criticism for this caution. But even today I feel that we did the right thing, having seen so many problems resulting from indiscriminate initiations. Many people at that time, however, impatient and without Coven contacts, decided to start their own Covens without proper training or initiation. This resulted in a number of pseudo-Wiccan groups based solely on misinformation gleaned from such sources as Ira Levin's novel *Rosemary's Baby* (1967), from ceremonial magic, and other non-traditional sources.

I dedicated myself to straightening popular misconceptions about Witchcraft, through the press, radio, and television, but tried to remain anonymous in so doing. Betrayal, by a journalist with the *New York Sunday News*, resulted in my name's eventually being published. This, in turn, led to a great deal of persecution, for myself, my wife, and for our two children. I went through much the same sort of thing that Gardner had gone through when he first tried to show what Witches really believe and practice. I had rocks thrown through my windows, my car set on fire, my children verbally abused, and so on. However, I continued my self-appointed task of correcting misconceptions of Witchcraft. Gardner's books had, by this time, gone out of print so I wrote *Witchcraft From the Inside* (Llewellyn, 1971) to fill the gap. This was to be the first of many such books.

I found my life paralleled Gardner's in many ways. One such parallel was the building of a collection of artifacts which grew into a museum. Gardner had a Museum of Magic and Witchcraft on the Isle of Man, the first of its kind in the world. My collection became the first of its kind in the United States, formally opened in 1968. Originally the collection was housed in the basement of my Long Island home, and was open by appointment only, but in 1973 we moved into an old Victorian house in Bay Shore. There it was reviewed in many major newspapers and periodicals and was the subject of a television documentary. Artifacts from the collection were loaned, for a special exhibit, to the Metropolitan Museum of Art and to the New York Museum of Folk Art.

I was not totally happy with the Gardnerian form of Wicca. It no longer met my religious needs and, also, I was dismayed at the blatant ego trips and power plays displayed by many of its later practitioners. After much thought and research I founded the Seax-Wica Tradition, based on a Saxon background. It was more democratically organized than the Gardnerian degree system tradition. Although originally written for my own personal use, I found there was a great deal of interest in it and was persuaded to publish the rituals in *The Tree: Complete Book of Saxon Witchcraft* (Weiser, 1974). Some irresponsible writers later suggested that the tradition was written as a joke, but that is far from the truth since it is a form of the religion to which I felt very strongly drawn.

While later living in Virginia, I founded the Seax-Wica Seminary and published the *Seax-Wica Voys*, a Wiccan magazine. The

> I think the Craft is changing to be more relevant, and I believe that it does have to do that practice. I had rocks thrown through my windows, my car set on fire, my children verbally abused ...

Other Covens eventually hived off from the original New York one, slowly spreading the Gardnerian branch of the Craft throughout the United States. Gradually other traditions began to appear, joining with the various spurious ones to establish the Craft as a viable alternative religion in America. My writing continued. In 1969, just prior to my Witchcraft book, *A Pocket Guide to the Supernatural* had been published by Ace Books. This was followed by *Practical Candleburning* (Llewellyn, 1970), *Witchcraft Ancient and Modern* (HC, 1970) and many more. I have now been averaging approximately one book a year since 1969.

Moving to New Hampshire after my first wife and I divorced, I finally admitted to myself that

seminary, as a correspondence school, grew to over 1,000 students worldwide. Eventually, however, I found it took too much of my precious writing time and had to terminate it.

In 1983, married to my third wife, I moved to San Diego, California, where I worked for a few years for a theatrical and film casting company and became very close friends with the actor John Carradine, working with him for the last few years of the actor's life. Over the years I've also worked with Orson Welles (as Technical Consultant for *Necromancy*), William Friedkin, and other movie actors and directors. I played a few character parts in movies, appearing as a crazy psychiatrist in the cult movie *Mutants in Paradise*! While in San Diego, I also turned to writing full time, became good friends with Scott Cunningham, a fellow author and Wiccan, and made the video *Witchcraft Yesterday and Today*, shortly to be reissued – up-dated and expanded – as a DVD.

Finally my wife Tara and I decided that we had had enough of Coven Witchcraft and became Solitaries. In 1992, also having had enough of living in a condominium, we moved to Ohio (Tara's home state) and bought a small farm from where I continue my writing, which now takes the form of fiction as well as non-fiction.

I think I've written close to forty books now, though I'm not certain of the exact number. As to which I'm most proud of, the publication of "Big Blue" – aka *Buckland's Complete Book of Witchcraft* (Llewellyn, 1986) – was most certainly a highlight for me (with a new, revised, enlarged version now out and available). After that, perhaps my encyclopedia *The Witch Book* (Visible Ink Press, 2002) and the encyclopedia of divination, *The Fortune-Telling Book* (Omnigraphics, Inc, 2003), are ones I'm also proud of. But really I still get a thrill at the appearance of *every* new book! I have special thoughts for my *Romani Tarot* (Llewellyn, 2001) and the new *Cards of Alchemy* (Llewellyn, 2003), as cards rather than books, though they both do have books to accompany them.

I've just finished writing *Wicca For One*, a sort of companion volume for *Wicca For Life* (Citadel, 2002), and, at the time of writing this chapter, I'm working on a complete expansion and update of *Doors To Other Worlds*, which will be retitled *Buckland's Book Of*

Spirit Communications and will be out in March 2004. There are many more projects in the works, and at the moment I'm trying to work exclusively on a fantasy novel I've been doing off and on for some time. It's a Tolkienesque work which I'm really enjoying writing. I have to admit that I prefer to write fiction to non-fiction – see my novels *The Committee* (Llewellyn, 1993) and *Cardinal's Sin* (Llewellyn, 1996).

In recent years I've been somewhat out of touch with the general Pagan/Wicca scene, sticking closer to home and doing far fewer public appearances than in the past, yet I'm fully aware that Wicca and Paganism continue to expand and make tremendous headway in the fields of public relations and public opinion. The small and large screens used to be notorious for depicting us in the totally inaccurate black-magic-devil-worshipping mode, but Hollywood has finally realized the errors of its ways. With movies and television programs like *Charmed*, *Buffy* and *The Craft*, Witches are being depicted, if not totally accurately, at least with some semblance of truth.

There is a much greater acceptance of Wicca as an alternate religious path today. The advance in public acceptance was evident – to me at least – on a recent US national network newscast (NBC) when there was a report on something pertaining to religion. There was a cut-away to a Wiccan to get her comments, followed by a cut-back to the newscaster, who behaved as he always does after any particular expert has made comment. I thought this a wonderful demonstration of the acceptance of Wicca as "just another religion." This represent as a vast differ-

I went through much the same sort of thing that Gardner had gone through when he first tried to show what Witches really believe and practice. I had rocks thrown through my windows, my car set on fire, my children verbally abused ...

ence from when I first started forty years ago. I think the Craft *is* changing to be more relevant, and I believe that it does have to do that. I don't know that it necessarily follows that the "archaic" language has to go, as some have suggested. For many that's part of the attraction. Happily there are sufficient "traditions" – and the potential for more – for the Craft to continue in a large number of guises, including the original Gardnerian. One of the attractions is that the "Old" Religion is essentially a New Religion, which is why it's growing so rapidly.

For many years yet, more public relations work will be needed for Witches and Pagans, and every opportunity should be taken to correct misconceptions. Perhaps more importantly than that, there is need for an end to the petty squabbling that still pervades the movement. It has been going on for decades now, and I doubt it will ever end completely. But we do need to keep reminding ourselves that what is right for one is not necessarily right for another. And what is right for another is not WRONG, because it's not right for you! There needs to be an end to the competition that some seem to feel they must indulge in, including the competition of Covens and Solitaries (I have much to say on that in my new book *Wicca For One*). Live and let live. If you really can't love your neighboring Witch, at least let him or her get on without your criticism.

The Craft has been a most important part of my life. Shortly after the initial publication of this book I'll be 70, so it's been a part of me for much more than half my life. I know it will continue to be part of me, for however long I may last (and I keep telling my wife: "I'm not going!").

The following interview was originally published in my second book, *Witch – A Magickal Year* (Random House Australia, 1999). Since then Wendy has done numerous tours in the US and the UK, gaining international fans, both Witches and non-Witches alike, with her evocative music and magickal lyrics.

I first met Wendy Rule in Melbourne's Social Security office in 1997. We were both standing in line waiting to hand in our welfare forms. We'd heard a lot about each other but had never actually met. I'd recently moved to Melbourne from my hometown of Sydney after the breakup of my band, Def FX, and I

> I see the Goddess/God being given form through the human psyche.

was looking forward to seeing a performance from Melbourne-based Witchy music Goddess, Wendy Rule. We both spotted each other at about the same time and after a couple of fairly hesitant and wry smiles we burst out laughing! She'd heard great and huge things about me and I about her. How appropriate it was then that we meet as struggling artists in the dole queue!

We exchanged phone numbers, agreed to catch up and so began a friendship. It is with great pleasure that I feature Wendy in this book – she is an astonishingly talented performer, who sends me into a trance every time I see her perform her dark, mystic songs that express perfectly the essence of one who is called by the Goddess.

Wendy, as a Witch you have such a significant affinity with the Goddess, do you consider that the Goddess, or Goddesses, exist in their own right, or do we imagine them into being?

I actually believe that they do exist in their own right, but not actually as Artemis or Selene. I do believe there is a Universal female entity and male entity; you can call them Goddess and God, or Yin and Yang. There is energy polarization, and in this I am deeply interested – I find Wicca a great way to explore this. I certainly see the God/Goddess being given form through the human psyche. I think if there were no humans on earth, there would still be a sense of spirituality, because there would still be the cycles of nature – of life and death, of birth and rebirth.

What is your history as an artist and musician?

I have a teaching degree in drama and literature. Originally I wanted to be an actor and I always loved singing, but I didn't see it as a career thing. I went to University and studied literature, which was my greatest love, and the more I studied literature, the more I dropped out of drama classes.

When did you start performing in public?

I started doing school plays at high school, and that's when I became addicted to applause! When I was nineteen and halfway through college, I connected up with a guy musically and did jazz gigs. They were quite grueling but good training. Then I got my own jazz trip up and happening for a while, before joining a really tacky rock group called The Mistress.

Were you the Mistress … ha ha?!

Ha! Well, I suppose I was! But as the years went on and I became a practicing Witch, my spirituality emerged very present in my music and that continues now.

The underworld is a very valid place to be. We are born in the Dark and we return there.

What is your religious background?

I remember when I was about thirteen I became really spiritual. I ended up deciding I wanted to go to Sunday School to learn more about Christianity. I was considered quite strange by my family and this led me to bury my spiritual yearnings for quite some time. I went into a kind of humanistic period, got involved in the human rights movement, feminism and socialism. It wasn't until something much greater than me touched my life (which was falling in love and giving birth to my child) that I thought, wow! There's something much bigger.

Tell me about giving birth.

The biggest revelation that I am a Witch came when I became pregnant with my son. All of a sudden the world opened up to me like it never had before. The riper I became, the more aware I was of female power. I read everything I could about ancient birthing practices and healing and herbalism. It was an incredibly nurturing time for me. I am very grateful to my son for giving me that time. Before I had Reuben, I had a miscarriage. As a Scorpio and an awakening Witch, to have to deal with death before I could actually embody life sent me on a huge underworld journey. Being four months pregnant and then losing my child was very full on. I was grieving so heavily, but what I was grieving was the essence of life moving into death because, as I didn't know this child, I couldn't grieve for the

individual. I had to learn that for every life there is death in a very profound way.

A year after having Reuben, I had another miscarriage which again catapulted me into the dark. I have three planets in Scorpio and it seems that the cycle of death-life-death-life plays itself out within me. That's what I try to convey through my music, the underworld of potential and growth – the seed that hasn't been brought to the light yet. If there's one thing that I'm meant to do using mythology and music, it is to make people aware that the underworld is a very valid place to be – not in staying down there, but going there and accessing the Dark and not having a sense of fear. We are born in the Dark and we return there.

I guess it's relevant here to bring up the theory that Witches are either dark or light. Personally, I don't think there is any such thing as a "white" or "black" Witch – you don't have to attach morality to these states. However, given that we've been discussing your attraction to the dark, how do you relate to the concept of hexing?

I'm pretty hardline actually – with hexing, I just don't! I think if I started I might like it too much! I really am fully aware of the three-fold law, in that what you send out comes back. As a Scorpio, I have a tendency to fall into my personal abyss, to go into that vicious and self-destructive side of my nature, so it's much safer for me to say, "I am the Eagle – I can rise above this," rather than be vindictive.

It's funny as you and I sit here, we look like the archetypal "white" or "black" Witches – me all blonde and bright, you all dark and mysterious! How do you relate to the light?

Very well now, actually. I think I had a problem embodying it for a while there, but I can access the underworld more safely now and rise to the surface again. I'm much more open to solar energy now rather than just lunar. I still lean much more strongly to Goddess worship, but I think I have a more holistic understanding of the polarity of female and male.

Speaking of the masculine, which God figures do you particularly relate to?

Mercury is one, though he is very androgynous. I have a very strong affinity with him, maybe because I have a Gemini moon. I relate very strongly to his mental energy. Also the Horned God, Cernunnos and Pan – all that lusty, masculine energy! As God of the Forest and Animals, he can be an important part of a Witch's world. However, my connection with the Earth is more on an Artemis level; it tends to be much more chaste and free and virginal.

separate my Witchcraft and my music, but even a song that isn't openly about Witchcraft is going to be colored by my worldview, which is that of a Witch. I don't like to be didactic; it's not like I want everyone else to join up and become a Witch. I'm not going door-knocking! I just see my role as one that makes the Craft accessible, as it is incredibly nurturing, especially for women.

Do you bring Reuben up as a Witch? How does he relate to his mother being a Witch?

He relates very well actually. He's a complex little thing – Taurus with a Sagittarius moon. With Reuben, I think it's important to give some guidance. We talk a lot and he certainly sees the Earth as sacred. He'll talk about the Goddess and Mother Earth, and at this stage that's enough, I think. For example, he would never harm a tree because that would be harming the Goddess. I hear him telling his friends, "Don't do that," if they're going to

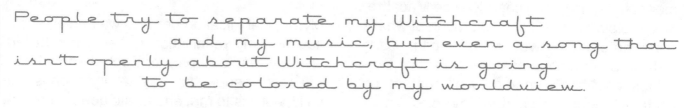

People try to separate my Witchcraft and my music, but even a song that isn't openly about Witchcraft is going to be colored by my worldview.

I'm often asked by men if a guy can be a Witch. I always say yes, most definitely.

I believe the solar and lunar energy can be embodied by both sexes. Intrinsically, the sun does represent a masculine energy, but it doesn't mean that a female can't tap into it. Goddesses like Athena have a very solar vibe to them. Men can embody lunar energy even though it is intrinsically female. In any kind of union – heterosexual, gay and lesbian – you're talking about an attraction of polarities, masculine and feminine, regardless of gender. *You are very open about your Witchcraft and you have a very public profile. Do you feel you were called to do this?*

Absolutely. I see it as a calling. People try to

squash an insect or something. We go down to the river together and make little offerings to the fairies. Fairies are a really nice way of explaining nature's spirits, and also I expose him to a lot of mythology, too. On a full moon, we go down to the river and put our little moon biscuits and flowers for the Goddess and the fairies.

How do you practice Witchcraft in an everyday sense?

In general, I tend to be a little less ritualistic than some Witches. I don't do spells by working with colors and herbs pedantically – I just use what's around at the time. [At the time of this interview] I'm in my third year of an astrology degree so I tend to work magically with aspects of astrology. It has greatly enhanced my understanding of Witchcraft. Also, of course, my musical performances are very magical and transformational. My everyday practices as a Witch are basically the way I live my life. I cast Circle with my wand on stage, and sometimes with salt and water when I'm at home. But if I'm down by the river, I'll open Circle simply by calling in the four elements. I use a lot of singing and chanting which feels comfortable and natural to me.

No – but I think there are many that will be drawn to it, but ritual is very much a female thing. Men can get into it but women are naturally much more ritualistic. We bleed every month and that's a ritual. One thing that is going to take off as a huge thing for men and women is Paganism, which is an aspect of Witchcraft. Worshipping and revering nature is going to make more and more sense to people as the planet continues to suffer environmentally. But it is to women that Witchcraft

> *Worshipping and revering nature is going to make more sense as the planet continues to suffer environmentally.*

When you do this, do you feel you are tapping into something that has been established for thousands of years, or do you think we are creating our modern Craft of Wicca?

I think we're tapping into it, but I think we are making it our own – we're creating it how it is meant to be now. The song "Danse Macabre" on my album *Deity* is an exploration of what's gone before that we are now connecting with. In a Jungian sense, the collective consciousness that is shared by all humans on Earth at this given point in time on a linear level has gone back through time. We all share the same gene pool: women who were burned at the stake, the Crusades, right back through time to the person that carved the Goddess of Willendorf. Witches share this essence and we are unified in that.

Do you envisage a time when Witchcraft could be a major world religion?

Definitely. If not mainstream, then definitely popularized to the point that we will no longer have to explain that we don't worship Satan and have orgies.

Can you see men embracing Witchcraft as much as women?

calls most loudly and this is timely – as now, more than ever, it is our time.

Although you have been practicing Witchcraft for a long time, you have [again, at the time of this interview] recently decided to embark on a period of re-initiation.

My original initiation process was a self-initiation and my re-initiation is being conducted with my magickal partner Zeph. I know there are some people that say self-initiation is not valid, but it is to me, and as life goes in seven-year cycles, I think it's time to acknowledge that and go back to basics for a while. So Zeph and I have been spending a month on exploring each element – really going in depth. At the moment we are focusing on Earth and Water.

What does "spending time on each element" incorporate?

Well, recently, for Earth I went to Zeph's little cottage in the forest where she lives. We went for a walk to silently and deeply connect with the elements around us. There are kangaroos around and it is a really earthy environment. Afterwards we did drawings and then went into a meditative trance – sometimes we dance and just really feel our bodies.

There was one ritual we did where it was pretty much a healing ritual for the Earth. We hadn't baked any cakes for the libations at the end, but we did bring some chocolate! Towards the end of the ritual Zeph had left her backdoor open. Into the magickal space we had created walked a possum and grabbed the chocolate! The little furry Goddess took our offerings!

Part of the re-initiation into the elements is to embrace them literally and symbolically. When Zeph and I delved into Water, I found that I was swimming all the time. Reuben and I went camping by the river and we swam naked together. I was gulping clean water as I swam – immersed inside and out.

The funny thing about initiation is you can't plan it too much. We just have the basic ideas of what we'll do – we have the four elements and then we spend a certain amount of time working with the Goddess essence and then the God. We're trying to lose everything we've "learned" and get instinctual.

I'm only eating organic food. Doing a lot more menstrual rituals and that sort of thing. I've gone back to using cloth pads; and trying to make every single part of my life sacred.

I focus on a sense of the sacred when I set up my altar with the basic tools and "props." For example, with herbs and crystals, I think that consciously putting them on your altar is like untangling them and acknowledging each for the glory of what it is. I don't know if they have an inherent power but they certainly have a psychological power, especially because you are working on a symbolic level anyway. It's all about correspondences, and what goes on in your mind affects the astral planes and manifests back on Earth. In ritual I often go into a trance where I begin to see the elemental forces as being alive. They're always these sort of morphing, humanoid forms – in the cascading fountain of a waterfall, in the leaping flames of a fire, in the mist of incense smoke, in the granite rocks by the beach.

So, given you have such an instinctual and spontaneous relationship with Witchcraft, have you never felt drawn to be initiated into an established group?

I've had a problem with the hierarchy of the whole Wiccan scene. You get certain camps attaching a lot of relevance to grandiose titles, and I like standing outside all that. It's not part of my trip to be climbing any sort of ladder. I was offered the opportunity to be initiated as a Priestess into the Church of Wicca and I opted out because I thought I don't want that to be the essence of what Witchcraft is for me. Some people need that sort of structure but I just don't.

I see myself more as a Universal Witch. I must break so many "rules" but I really don't give a damn. I just do what I must and what feels right. I don't see myself as a black or white Witch. I actually see myself as a green Witch – to do what I do as a Mother, Lover, Artist, Teacher, "and it harms none." I go where my heart leads me, following my bliss.

How do you integrate your Witchcraft privately and publicly?

I had been feeling a split between my private and public life, though now I find I am marrying both of these a lot more now. I think the way that my music's going is a lot more ritualistic. I've decided not to attempt to cater to a pop market and I am going to let my music be as Witchy and perhaps kooky as I like.

The music is now becoming a really necessary part of the Witchcraft process. I sing a lot in ritual anyway. The way that Witchcraft can be so healing, like many other things, is the way you can integrate all aspects of what makes you special – the different aspects of what I am are now coming into a whole.

Motherhood is considered a very sacred act of magic by Witches, and you have obviously committed yourself to it.

Yes, I have decided to bring Reuben up overtly Wiccan now, because [at the time of writing] he is seven this year and I think he is ready for it. Every mealtime we treat much more ritualistically now. It's fun and exciting for him. One of us says a "grace" of sorts, which is thanking the Earth for her bounty. He's embracing it fully. The cooking and preparation of food which was once a chore is now an act of ritual. It's much, much better for him and for me.

I'm no longer thinking, "I have to be successful musician." I can be that and much more. I'm thinking, "Work on yourself, work on your own personal growth and everything will fall into place." I'm just not worried anymore. I just go with it, whichever way it leads.

So in many ways you are starting over, tapping into a sense of wonder that a novice would feel.

When I first started doing Witchcraft so many things that interested me I didn't know were linked, like crystals, Tarots, astrology, mythology, herbs, loving nature. I didn't know there was this thing called "Wicca." Suddenly this huge aspect of what I was became coherent. Now I feel, "Okay, my Witchiness is very coherent and everything else in my life is held in this huge, lush, cauldron," and it's like I feel like I am shedding a skin, re-initiating, letting go of my ego layer. I think ego's great – I'm not against it – but I also think it can be a barrier for you. Just to let go and trust that what I am is intrinsically okay is a huge achievement.

I see that my work, what I do, is about becoming whole, healing myself and then sharing that healing energy with the Universe. So now I put aside at least half an hour a day to meditate and I never used to do

that! I'm usually so manic – having a Gemini moon I'm always rushing around! But now I'm not just "vagueing out," I'm not just "doing the washing" – everything I do is valid and has meaning and is ultimately healing.

Some people might say, "Duh! That's no revelation!" But it is to me. I want to be whole, sane, in touch with my emotions and in touch with my Goddess and God, and honor that within me that makes me unique, regardless of what people think or what the pressure of my public career has made me feel in the past.

I spend a lot of time in worship, much more than I do in magick, with a freshness and trust in the flow of things. I'm finding that I'm doing some really intense spells. Like when you first start out, all your spells work. Just when the Universe goes, "Well, this is real, honey!" and you trust it, it throws you into the abyss of test and trials! Certainly in the last seven years I've gone into the Underworld.

What's your favorite spell?

My favorite spell is one of transformation. Being a Scorpio I often work with that. I feel it's unhealthy to be stuck in one place. Everything else in life is growing and changing, and so must I.

I basically connect with the energies of the Universe and acknowledge openly that I'm part of the transformational process. I grab my wand and I go outside and sing to myself. I dance. I sing a really repetitious line and whirl myself into a trance. I actually don't use many props except my wand. I just sing and dance and open the four Quarters and welcome in the energies of the Universe.

The mindset that makes me most connected to magick is really understanding that we are the union of the four elements plus spirit/ether. *Really* knowing that on the deepest level – then you're always at the center of the crossroads, the union of the four elements, wherever you stand is the center of the world.

Lyrics

Following are some lyrics Wendy has provided from some of her favorite compositions.

DISSOLVE (from *World Between Worlds*, released 2000)

It is Samhain and the veils are thin
We cannot force them
To dissolve to your power
It is Samhain and the veils are thin
There is a madness
To the reason within

What will it take to cross over?
(Thought beyond mind)
What will it take to cross over?
(Will beyond fear)
What will it take to cross over?
(Faith beyond will)
What will it take to cross over?
(A mirror that dissolves me)

It is Samhain and the veils are thin
They are the weavings
Of the soul of the spider
It is Samhain and the veils are thin
There is a reason
To the madness within

What will it take to cross over?

DEITY (from *Deity*, released 1998)

When the moon is lit
On her Eastern side
And I slowly am centering, centering
When my blood is pulled

With the waning tide
And I fall and am willingly entering
Night
The Dark
The Womb that's hollow
It's here I've found a voice to follow

I am the Maiden
I am the Mother
I am the Crone
I am the sea
I am the sky
I am the blood
I am the Moon
Never alone
Never alone
Never alone

When the moon is lit
On her western side
And she slowly is brightening, brightening
When the Earth is full
With the waxing tide
And I breathe with it, ripening, ripening

See, reflected in the water
The older moon held by her daughter

CIRCLE SONG

(Used in ritual to open Circle in the Southern Hemisphere)

The East, the Air, the sword, the mind
The gate that leaves the night behind

The North, the sun, the flame, the fire
The gateway to our souls' desire

The West, the womb, the waters flow
The gateway to the world below

The South, the star, the silent Earth
The gateway to our souls' rebirth.

HORSES (from *The Lotus Eaters*, released 2003)

See all the waves' white horses
Wind in their hair
See all the waves' white horses
Calling me to
Ocean
The waves' white horses
Wind in their hair
See all the waves' white horses calling me to

All that is wild
All that is free
All that is wild
All that is free
Feel the waves' white horses liberate me

Oh, I long to fly like a migrating bird
Oh, I long to fly
Over the sea
Over the sea
Some day I'll fly like a migrating bird
Far far away
On wings that are wide

To all that is wild
All that is free
All that is wild
All that is free
See the waves' white horses
Dancing below me

Before Z Budapest and Starhawk, before Margot Adler and Janet Farrar, there was Rosaleen Norton …

Most people knew Rosaleen Norton simply as Roie. The Roie I remember was slight in build, with dark and rather untidy curly hair, quick darting eyes and mysterious arched eyebrows. During the 1950s she had become famous in Australia – perhaps one should say notorious – as an eccentric and bohemian practitioner of Witchcraft. She wore flamboyant blouses, puffed on an engraved cigarette holder, and produced bizarre fantasy paintings which had a distinct touch of the Pagan and demonic about them.

This was of course a time when a rather prudish and puritanical mentality prevailed in Australia and when society in general was by no means as culturally diverse or as tolerant as it is today. The public at large was astounded by Rosaleen's risqué paintings and had frivolous, happy natures, whereas her compositions invariably focused on figures of the night – phantasms from the darker recesses of the soul.

Roie originally presented herself as a trance artist. From an early age she had a remarkable capacity to explore the visionary depths of her subconscious mind, and the archetypal beings she encountered on those occasions became the focus of her art. It was only later that Roie was labeled a Witch, was described as such in the popular press, and began to develop the persona which accompanied that description. As this process gathered momentum, Roie in turn became intent on trying to demonstrate that she had been *born* a Witch. After all, she had somewhat pointed ears, small blue markings on her left knee, and also a long strand of flesh which hung from underneath her armpit to her waist – a variant on the extra nipple sometimes ascribed to Witches in the Middle Ages.

> The public was astounded by Rosaleen's risqué paintings and drawings... phalluses into serpents, passionate encounters with black panthers.

and drawings which depicted naked hermaphroditic beings, phalluses transforming into serpents, and passionate encounters with black panthers. And while the work of fellow erotic artist Norman Lindsay was halfway to becoming respectable – a type of tempered voyeurism made it possible to admire the naked frolics depicted in his paintings and drawings and call them "art" – it was by no means as easy for Rosaleen to be accepted. As she herself would say, Lindsay's figures were creatures of the day

However, I feel that much of this was simply the development of her mystique. From her earliest childhood, Rosaleen wanted to be different. She reveled in being the odd one out, purporting to despise her schoolmates. She argued continuously with her mother. She "hated" authority figures like headmistresses, policemen, politicians and priests. She had no time at all for organized religion, and the Gods she embraced – a cluster of ancient Gods centered around Pan – were, of course, Pagan to the hilt. She regarded Pan as the God of Infinite Being. Traditionally, Pan is known as the God of flocks and shepherds in ancient Greece. Depicted as half-man, half-goat, he played a pipe with seven reeds and was considered the Lord of Nature and all forms of wildlife. He was also rather lecherous, having numerous love affairs with the nymphs, especially Echo, Syrinx and Pithys.

Pan was undoubtedly a rather unusual God for a young woman to be worshipping in Australia. But then Roie was different. And she was different in an age when it was quite a lot harder to be different than it is now. She was bohemian, bisexual, outspoken, rebel-

"I came into this world bravely. I'll go out bravely." Pagan to the end, she departed this life

lious and thoroughly independent in an era when most young ladies growing up on Sydney's North Shore would be thinking simply of staying home, happily married with a husband and children. Roie was not afraid to say what she thought, draw her Pagan images on city pavements, or flaunt her occult beliefs in the pages of the tabloids. To most people who read about her in newspapers and magazines she was simply outrageous.

I met Roie towards the end of her life, in 1977. She had already become a recluse but a friend of mine, Barry Salkilld, and I had tracked down a person called Danny who knew her. Danny worked in a jeweler's shop in Sydney's Kings Cross and we explained to him that we were genuinely interested in magical techniques and practices and wanted to discuss both her personal view of magic and her perceptions of the world at large. The message filtered through and we were granted an interview.

Roie was living then in a rather dark basement flat at the end of a long corridor in an old building in Roslyn Gardens, just down from Kings Cross in the direction of Rushcutters Bay. She was somewhat frail but still extremely mentally alert, with expressive eyes and a hearty laugh. She even invited us to share an L.S.D. trip with her, but in the gloomy recesses of her basement flat we shuddered to think of the shadowy beings we might unleash through this powerful psychedelic, and we both politely declined. I later found out that Roie periodically used L.S.D. to induce visionary states and that this was all about enhancing her awareness as an artist. She did not, however, use the drug simply for recreation, for she was well aware of its potency.

We talked at that meeting about the Gods Roie encountered in trance, about her view that Pan was alive in the "back-to-Nature" movement supported by the counterculture, and we also discussed her strong personal bond with animals. Roie told us that she believed most animals had much more integrity than human beings and she also felt that cats, especially, could operate both in the world of normal waking consciousness and in the inner psychic world simultaneously. She even remembered a time which may have been a previous incarnation in England. She believed she had once lived in a past century in a rickety wooden house in a field of yellow grass, somewhere near Beachy Head in Sussex. There were several farm animals there – cows, horses and so on – and she herself was a poltergeist, a disembodied spirit. She recalled that when "normal" people came near the house they were frightened by her presence and could not accept the existence of poltergeists or any other "supernatural" beings. But the animals accepted her as she was – as part of the natural order.

For Roie this went some way towards explaining her love for her own pet animals, and throughout her life she lived surrounded by creatures of all kinds, from pet lizards and spiders through to mice, turtles and cats. In her dark and very private Kings Cross living room, she still had her animal friends to comfort her, and she related to them more positively than to her human neighbors in the daylight world outside. One couldn't help feeling that here in the twilight realm of her basement flat she felt thoroughly at home. She no longer felt any strong desire for regular contact with the external world.

Roie's personal beliefs were a strange mix of magic, mythology and fantasy, but derived substantially from mystical experiences which, for her, were completely real. She was no theoretician. Part of her disdain for the public at large, I believe, derived from the fact that she felt she had access to a wondrous visionary universe, while most people lived lives that were narrow, bigoted and based on fear. Roie was very much an adventurer – a free spirit – and she liked to fly through the worlds opened to her by her imagination.

Roie's art reflected this. It was her main passion, her main reason for living. She had no career ambitions other than to reflect on the forces within her essential being, and to manifest these psychic and magical energies in the only way she knew how. As Roie's older sister Cecily later told me, art was the very center of her life, and Roie took great pride in the brief recognition she received when the English critic and landscape artist John Sackville-West described her in 1970 as one of Australia's finest artists, alongside Norman Lindsay. (Sackville-West was a tra-

ditional artist who had two works accepted by the Royal Academy in London. As reported in the *Sun Herald* (October 25, 1970), he specifically named Norman Lindsay and Rosaleen Norton as "two of Australia's finest artists.") It was praise from an unexpected quarter, and it heartened Roie considerably because she felt that at last someone had understood her art and had responded to it positively. All too often her critics had responded only to her outer veneer – the bizarre and often distorted persona created by the media – and this was not the "real" Roie at all.

Roie is long gone now.

Late in November 1979 Roie was taken to the Roman Catholic Sacred Heart Hospice for the Dying at Sydney's St Vincent's Hospital. Shortly before she died she told her friend Victor Wain: "I came into this world bravely. I'll go out bravely." And she was true to her word. Unrepentant in her worship of Pan, unfazed by all the crucifixes around her at the hospice, and a Pagan to the end, she departed this life on December 5, 1979.

There is no doubt in my mind that Rosaleen Norton would have flourished in the company of Starhawk, Z Budapest and Margot Adler if she were alive today, but sadly she was ahead of her time. Such frameworks of thinking simply did not exist in her day. While Rosaleen emphasized Pan as the universal life-principle, rather than worshipping the Mother Goddess as a giver of life and sustenance, there was nevertheless a comparable feeling in her approach to life. As Rosaleen told me in 1977, Pan was very much a deity for the present day, not simply an archetypal figure from antiquity. For her, Pan was the

Roie's personal beliefs were a strange mix of magic, mythology and fantasy, but derived substantially from mystical experiences which, for her, were completely real.

creative force in the universe who protected the natural beauty of the planet and conserved the resources of the environment. And like Starhawk, Rosaleen believed that magic had a political consequence – Pan was alive and well in the anti-pollution lobbies, and among the Friends of the Earth!

Like her contemporary Wiccan counterparts, Rosaleen shared a vision of magic as a way of re-sacralizing the world, of finding divinity in Nature. In a sense we can say that Rosaleen was a feminist in a time when there were no feminists, a Witch at a time when Witchcraft was still widely misunderstood. But more than anything else, she was a free spirit and an independent venturer in the magical cosmos. Her visions of the night – those eerie phantasms which haunted her imagination and opened doorways to other realms of mythic consciousness – serve as a reminder that there are always greater realities in the universe which we can acknowledge and explore. This, I feel sure, is the single message she would have wished to leave behind, for others to pursue.

Dry ashes and a parchment hand
Behold the iron man
Gone still.
He's sleeping now, his cancer cough
Receding to a wheeze;
Transported off to dream again
Where shores are paved with steel

I cannot follow
So I wait
And summon up a prayer:
"Our Father, who art in Heaven
"Hallowed be thy name …"

Irony
Such words should fall from Pagan lips,
But compassion knows no creed.
It's time for bridges now, not steel.
And need drops pallors on the feet of Mars

Sleep, old man, and after dusk I'll
Call the Corners my own way.
Fair dreaming, rest
Till Silence calls
To raise his weather-beaten hands
And welcome your new day.

In the spring of 2000, my Mom's husband Warren, an ironworker, died at home. Disease stole his vitality, his strength, and his ability to speak. It did not, however, take his dignity. Nothing on Earth could have robbed him of that.

Deathbeds are crossroads ...

Warren was an iron man, rough and often tactless. He was my Mother's soulmate, too. I had issues with the man himself, but he was good to my Mom and that's all that mattered.

I was present when he passed on, and offered prayers for his safekeeping. Unlike a certain minister (whom Warren had kicked out when he began to preach), I just made a point of being there when needed. My place was not to wave a flag but to hold space and provide comfort.

There's a lot to be learned from such simplicity.

Deathbeds are crossroads, and not only for the people in them. Our greatest lessons ride shotgun with the shadows and they aren't always clear.

It took time and tears, the wreckage of my marriage and reconciliation with my family to understand some of the lessons I learned that spring.

In hindsight, I see forgiveness, focus, family and the universality of prayer.

Warren's still at home today, turning on the lights and watching over Mom.

Rest well, you tough old bastard.

Blessings and fair dreamings. You earned them all.

the unbroken circle

making contact

with much assistance from Anna Korn and Don Frew
(Covenant of the Goddess)
Constance De Binero (The Index)

Updated for 2004 by Liam Cyfrin and Fiona Horne
(with special thanks to Julia Phillips and Hiraeth
MacDonald)

ALEXANDRIAN

Founded in England during the 1960s by Alexander Sanders (1926-1988), self-proclaimed "King of the Witches," and his wife Maxine. Originally Alex claimed to have been initiated by his grandmother when he was seven years old, but later admitted that this was untrue. In fact, he was initiated into a regular Gardnerian Coven. Alexandrian Covens focus strongly upon training, emphasizing areas more generally associated with ceremonial magic, such as Qabalah and Angelic and Enochian Magic. The typical Alexandrian Coven has an hierarchical structure, and generally meets weekly, or at least on Full Moons, New Moons and Sabbats. Rituals are usually done skyclad.

Most Alexandrian Covens will allow non-initiates to attend circles, usually as "neophytes" who undergo basic training in circle craft prior to being accepted for first degree initiation. Alexandrian Wicca uses essentially the same tools and rituals as Gardnerian Wicca, although in some cases the tools are used differently and the rituals have been adapted. Another frequent change is to be found in the names of deities and guardians of the Quarters. In some ways these differences are merely cosmetic, but in others, there are fundamental differences in philosophy. Over the last 30 years, the two traditions have moved slowly towards each other, and the differences which marked lines of demarcation are slowly fading away.

See:
• Stewart Farrar, *What Witches Do* (Davies, 1971).
• June Johns, *King of the Witches* (Davies, 1969).
• Maxine Sanders, *Maxine the Witch Queen* (Star, 1976).

Contact:
• Vivianne Crowley:
BM Deosil, London WC1N 3XX England.
• Arion Rhys: Los Angeles, California;
arion@starkindler.org
•Hiraeth MacDonald: Australia;
hiraeth_macdonald@yahoo.com.au

AMYTHYSTIAN

Founded in 1968 by Lady Amythyst (the tradition took its first students then; previously it was just family). Amythystian Craft is rooted in the Order of the Garter and the Order of the Royal Oak, is traditional with lots of Hermetic beliefs, and is dedicated to preserving old traditions while growing into a new generation of enlightened ones. It teaches by example in daily life, at home and at work, as well as when among our own. It believes in a strict code of ethics exemplified by one's actions and lives by the Wiccan Rede.

Contact:
• Lady Amythyst: Order of the Royal Oak,
PO Box 6006, Athens, GA 30604;
avalon@mindspring.com

See:
• www.mindspring.com/~avalon

AQUARIAN TABERNACLE CHURCH

An American tradition of Wicca based on

English Traditional Wicca and focused on service to the larger Wiccan and Pagan community through open worship gatherings. The ATC was founded in 1979 by Pierre "Pete Pathfinder" Davis, who received training and initiation on the Wiccan path first in New Jersey and then in Washington state. The Church is based in Index, WA, where it owns the Retreat House and the central Church offices, as well as an outdoor sanctuary with a ring of standing menhirs set in an old-growth cedar forest.

The ATC is a fully tax-exempt legal Wiccan church in the USA, Canada and Australia, with over 30 congregations in these countries. The ATC provides regular, open worship circles, sponsors several annual festivals, and functions as an umbrella organization, accepting affiliations by Wiccan groups wishing to become recognized, open and public Wiccan churches.

Contacts:
• Pete Pathfinder: ATC,
POB 409, Index, WA 998256;
(360) 793-1945;
atc@aquatabch.org
See www.AquaTabCh.org

• Michele Favarger:
ATC-Canada, PO Box 20048,
Duncan Mall Stn, Duncan, BC Canada;
ATCcanada@seaside.net

Publication:
Panegyria:
see www.aquatabch.org/panegyria/index.php

BRITISH TRADITIONAL

The term "British Traditional" refers to a variety of traditions which originated in the British Isles and which have certain characteristics in common. There is a mix of Celtic and Gardnerian beliefs, mostly based on the Farrar studies. Worship of the God and Goddess is balanced, Covens are co-ed, and there is a degree system. The New Wiccan Church is a federation of British Traditions (Gardnerian, Alexandrian, Mohsian, and Central Valley Wicca-Kingstone, Majestic Order and Silver Crescent). NWC is dedicated to preserving initiatory Craft.

Contact:
• Allyn Wolfe: New Wiccan Church,
PO Box 162046, Sacramento, CA 95816.
See www.angelfire.com/ca/redgarters/

Publication:
• *Red Garters International*:
see: www.angelfire.com/ca/redgarters/redgarters.html

CABOT TRADITION

Based in Salem, MA, the Cabot Tradition of Witchcraft has grown and developed through the more than 40 years its founder, Laurie Cabot, has been a practicing Witch. She has taught "Witchcraft as a Science" for the past 25 years. The Cabot Tradition is based on the teaching she received in the Kent Tradition of England, in addition to 50 years of research and practice in Egyptian and Celtic religions. Rituals are eclectic, and practitioners wear black robes and gold pentacles. Students begin by learning the scientific foundations of magic and the principles of light and energy. They learn to unlock the window of their "third eye" and tap into their own psychic abilities as well as diagnose and send healing energies.

Students are introduced to the laws that govern life and the practice of Witchcraft. They learn divination, astrology, herbal techniques and ritual magic. Finally, they make the transition from the practice to the religion of Witchcraft, where they learn to apply the magic-filled mythology of the Celts in their life as a Witch. The Cabot Tradition Witch ultimately claims their sovereignty and adds their own energy to the tribe.

See:
• Laurie Cabot (with Tom Cowan), *Power of the Witch* (1989).
• Laurie Cabot (with Jean Mills), *Celebrate the Earth* (1994).

Contact:
• Witchcraft as a Science:
PO Box 8736, Salem, MA 01450;
(978) 744-6274. See www.lauriecabot.com

CELTIC

The Celtic path is really many traditions under the general heading of "Celtic." It encompasses Druidism, Celtic Shamanism, Celtic Wicca or Witta, the Grail Religion, and Celtic Christianity (the Culdees). Each path is unique and can stand alone or meld together with another and still be part of the Celtic tradition. It is primarily derived from the ancient pre-Christian Celtic religion of Gaul and the British Isles.

As they are practiced today, most of the Celtic paths are part of the Neopagan revival, focusing on Nature, healing with group and individual rituals that honor the Ancient Shining Ones and the Earth. Most are very eclectic, but hold to the Celtic myths, divinities, magic and rituals. Celtic paths are among the more popular traditions.

Contacts:
• Wiccan Temple of the Celtic Way:
PO Box 112, Park Forest, IL 60466;
(708) 747-9273.
• Celtic Studies Center:
27013 Pacific Hwy, W #315,
Des Moines, WA 98198.
• Ár nDraíocht Féin (ADF):
PO Box 17874, Tucson, AZ 85731-7874. See www.adf.org
• The Henge of Keltria:
PO Box 4305, Clarksburg, WV 26302.
See www.keltria.org

Publication:
• Keltria:
PO Box 4305, Clarksburg, WV 26302.
See www.keltria.org/journal/index.html

CEREMONIAL

Uses a great deal of Ceremonial Magick in practices, mostly derived from the works of Aleister Crowley. Detailed rituals with a flavor of Egyptian magick are popular, as are Qabalistic ritual forms.

Contact:
• College of Thelema:
PO Box 415, Oroville, CA 95965;
gr-cs@thelema.org

CHURCH AND SCHOOL OF WICCA

Founded in 1968 by Gavin and Yvonne Frost, with two stated aims: (1) to improve to image of Witchcraft worldwide; and (2) to promote green areas throughout the world. The Church has enrolled almost 40,000 students in its correspondence courses, and had as many as 14 subsidiary churches and schools as part of its structure. The very word "Wicca" was popularized by the Church through its use of the word. In 1983, a Federal appeals court ruling made the Church of Wicca the only fully recognized church of Witchcraft.

The Frosts employ a Celtic pantheon, but they encourage their students to choose their own gods and goddesses, all within a structure of syncretic monotheism. Key beliefs are in: the Wiccan Rede, progressive reincarnation, the law of attraction, power through knowledge, and harmony. The philosophy of the Church – sometimes called "spiritual libertarianism" – is ever-developing and eclectic, and leadership is egalitarian or horizontal.

Their influence is incalculable. Certain of the Frosts' 22 books have been translated into at least five languages and many groups have formed around leaders who were originally students of the School.

See:
• Gavin and Yvonne Frost, *A Good Witch's Guide to Life*.

• Gavin and Yvonne Frost, *Good Witch's Bible*.

Contact:
Gavin and Yvonne Frost:
Church and School of Wicca,
PO Box 297, Hinton, WV 25951-0297,
(800) 407-6660; school@citynet.net
See www.wicca.org

Publication:
• *Survival:*
see www.wicca.org/godolphin/pubs.html

CIRCLE OF SALGION, CHURCH OF WICCA

The Salgion Tradition is a Celtic tradition of Witchcraft that honors the deities of the Celtic Ray and recognizes the divinity within nature and ourselves. Reverend Cheryl Sulyma-Masson founded the Circle of Salgion in 1987 with the birth of her Coven.

As the single Coven grew into several under the main Salgion Coven, the tradition embarked upon the next phase of its growth when it decided to pursue both state and federal recognition as an organized church. Both goals were accomplished in 1995. Since that time, the Circle of Salgion, Church of Wicca has held open Sabbat rituals that include both grove members and the general public. The Salgion Tradition has always felt the community is an essential part of one's spiritual life and strives to be a place for that community to grow. The tradition also feels that opening their Sabbat rituals to the public allows non-Wiccans to become more respectful and sympathetic toward their religious practices.

Contact:
• The Circle of Salgion, Church of Wicca: PO Box 574, Rehoboth, MA 02769.
See www.circleofsalgion.org

DIANIC

This is the most feminist Craft tradition. Most Dianic Covens worship the Goddess exclusively (Diana and Artemis being the most common manifestations), and most today are women-only. Rituals are eclectic – some are derived from Gardnerian and Faerie Traditions, while others have been created anew. Emphasis is on rediscovering and reclaiming female power and divinity, consciousness-raising, and combining politics with spirituality.

The Dianic Craft includes two distinct branches. The first of these derives from the initial Dianic Coven in the US, which was formed in the late 1960s by Morgan McFarland and Mark Roberts, in Dallas, Texas. This branch gives primacy to the Goddess in its theology, but honors the Horned God as her beloved consort. Covens include both women and men. This branch is sometimes called "Old Dianic" and there are still Covens of this tradition, especially in Texas. Other Covens, similar in theology but not directly descended from the McFarland/Roberts line, are sprinkled around the country.

The second branch, Feminist Dianic Witchcraft, focuses exclusively on the Goddess and consists of women-only Covens, often with strong lesbian presence. These tend to be loosely structured and non-hierarchical, using consensus decision-making and simple, creative, experimental ritual. They are politically feminist groups, usually very supportive, personal and emotionally intimate. The major network is Re-Formed Congregation of the Goddess, which publishes *Of a Like Mind* newspaper and sponsors conferences on Dianic Craft.

Z Budapest founded the Susan B Anthony Coven in 1971, declaring Dianic Witchcraft to be "Wimmin's Religion" and publishing a *Feminist Book of Lights & Shadows*. The Women's Spirituality Forum was founded by Z in 1986, and is dedicated to bringing Goddess consciousness to the mainstream of feminist consciousness through lectures, retreats, classes, cable TV shows, and rituals in the effort to achieve spiritual and social liberation.

See:
• Z Budapest, *The Holy Book of Women's Mysteries* (1980; 1986).

Contacts:
• Re-formed Congregation of the Goddess: PO Box 6677, Madison, WI 53716. See www.rcgi.org

• Z Budapest: Women's Spirituality Forum, PO Box 11363, Oakland, CA 94611; silverZB@aol.com

See www.zbudapest.com/index.shtml

ECLECTIC

This term refers to groups and individuals not following any one particular tradition or mythos, but incorporating elements of several, according to the training, preferences and experiences of the practitioners. Deities from several pantheons may be invoked, (sometimes even within the same ritual), particularly when a working is being created for a specific cause. In such a case, Eclectics may call upon, for example, an assortment of Love Goddesses, etc, from many different cultures.

Contact:
Elsa Die Löwin: See
www.draigsffau.org/Folk/Elsa.html

ECUMENICAL PAGAN

The Ecumenical Pagan Tradition is two Pagan churches: SummerLand, ATC, and Church of the Ancient Sacred Mother, CAW (defined in 1997, "founded" over 19 years). Presiding Elder, Jacque Omi Zaleski, was trained Shaman Pagan, English, Alexandrian, and Egyptian Traditions Wiccan, and Renzi Zen Buddhist; Don Mackenzie was trained Church of All Worlds

Pagan. They practice a very broad-based Paganism which is Earth-honoring, life-affirming spirituality, matrifocal, sex-positive, non-exclusivist faith dedicated to healing Mother Earth through positive actions.

Ritual is a blend of Shamanism, Wicca, and Deep Ecology, with active participation through impromptu expressions of love and honesty to bring out the best of human potential: self-esteem, not ego.

Contact:
WindTree Ranch:
Rural Route 2 Box 1, Douglas, AZ 85607-9802; windtree@AOL.com See
www.spiralpath.dm.net/windtree

FAERY/FAERIE/FAIRY/FERI

Created by Victor Anderson (1917-2001) in the 1960s and further developed by Gwydion Pendderwen (1946-1982). Victor tells of antecedents of the present tradition in the Coven in which he was involved in the 1920s and '30s in Oregon.

It is an ecstatic, rather than a fertility, tradition, emphasizing polytheism, practical magic, self-development and theurgy. Strong emphasis is placed on sensual experience and awareness, including sexual mysticism, which is not limited to heterosexual expression. This is a mystery tradition of power, mystery, danger, ecstasy, and direct communication with divinity. Most initiates are in the arts and incorporate their own poetry, music and invocations into rituals. The tradition is gender-equal, and all sexual orientations seem able to find a niche.

According to Francesca de Grandis, founder of the Third Road branch: "Faerie power is not about a liturgy but about one's body: a Fey shaman's blood and bones are made of stars and Faerie dust. A legitimate branch of Faerie is about a personal vision that is the Fey Folks' gift to a shaman."

Initially small and secretive, many of the fundamentals of the tradition have reached a large audience through writings of Starhawk, the most famous initiate. Some secret branches remain. While only a few hundred initiates can trace their lineage directly to Victor Anderson, many thousands are estimated to practice neo-Faery Traditions.

See:

Cora Anderson, *Fifty Years in the Feri Tradition* (1994).
Victor Anderson, *Thorns of the Blood Rose* (1970).
Francesca de Grandis, *Be a Goddess*, (Harper, 1998). See also Francesca's *Wiccan and Faerie Grimoire*, an on-line Book of Shadows: www.well.com/user/zthirdrd/WiccanMiscellany.html

Contact:

Francesca de Grandis: The Third Road, PO Box 210307, San Francisco, CA 94121.
See www.well.com/~zthirdrd
Alison Harlow: PO Box 67273, Scotts Valley, CA 95067; aharlow@ix.netcom.com

GARDNERIAN

This is a closed initiatory tradition which was founded in England circa 1953 by Gerald Gardner (1884-1964) and further developed by Doreen Valiente and others. Gardner was initiated into a Coven of Witches in the New Forest region of England in 1939 by a High Priestess named "Old Dorothy" Clutterbuck. 1949 saw the publication of *High Magic's Aid*, a novel about medieval Witchcraft in which elements of the Craft as practiced by that Coven was used. In 1951 the last of the English laws against Witchcraft were repealed (primarily due to the pressure of Spiritualists) and Gardner published *Witchcraft Today*, which set forth a version of the rituals and traditions of the Coven.

Gardner gave his tradition a ritual framework strongly influenced by Freemasonry and Crowleyan ceremonial magic, as well as traditional folk magic and Tantric Hinduism. The tradition was brought to the USA in 1965 by Raymond Buckland (who was initiated in 1964 by Gardner's High Priestess, Lady Olwen) and his wife, Rosemary. They established a Coven and museum on Long Island, which was turned over to Theos and Phoenix after the Bucklands' divorce in 1973.

Gardnerian Covens are always headed by a High Priestess and have three degrees of initiation, closely paralleling the Masonic degrees. Worship is centered on the Goddess and the Horned God. The tradition emphasizes polarity in all things, fertility, and the cycle of birth-death-rebirth. Eight seasonal Sabbats are observed, and the Wiccan Rede is the guiding principle. Power is raised meditation, chanting, astral projection, and dancing. Gardner also advocated the use of scourging and sex magick ("The Great Rite"), though in practice these are rarely used by contemporary Gardnerians. Designed for group/Coven work, though solitary workings have been created. Covens typically work skyclad.

See:

Gerald Gardner, *Witchcraft Today*, (Rider 1954).
Gerald Gardner, *The Meaning of Witchcraft* (Aquarian 1959).
Philip Heselton, *Wiccan Roots: Gerald Gardner and the Modern Witchcraft Revival* (Capall Bann, 2000).
Philip Heselton, *Gerald Gardner and the Cauldron of Inspiration: An Investigation into the Sources of Gardnerian Witchcraft* (Capall Bann, 2003).
Ronald Hutton, *The Triumph of the Moon* (OUP, 1999).

Contacts:

Lady Brita: PO Box 934, Kenosha, WI 53141; thpmag@execpc.com
Vivianne Crowley:
BM Deosil, London WC1N 3XX, England.
Merlyn and Epona: Children of Artemis,
BM Artemis, London, WC1N 3XX, UK. (The Children of Artemis offers a Coven-finding service to its members in the UK. They do have many contacts in the Gardnerian tradition, but also with people involved in most other forms of Wicca and Witchcraft.)
Julia Phillips: Australia;
wyrd@ozemail.com.au

Publications:
The Hidden Path:
PO Box 934, Kenosha, WI 53141-0934.

The New Wiccan:
see www.strega.fsworld.co.uk/nwmag.htm
Note: Both of these publications are restricted to vouched-for initiated Witches only.

Witchcraft & Wicca Magazine:
See www.witchcraft.org

Note: While many respected Gardnerian initiates amongst others write articles for Witchcraft & Wicca, it contains no Book of Shadows material and is available to the general public.

GEORGIAN

Founded by George "Pat" Patterson. If one word could best describe the Georgian Tradition, it would be "eclectic." Even though the material provided to students was nominally Alexandrian, there was never any imperative to follow that path blindly. Pat always said that: "If it works use it; if it doesn't, don't." The newsletter was always full of contributions from people of many traditions. Pat's intent was to provide jumping off points for students and members.

Contact:
Church of Wicca of Bakersfield.
See www.georgianwicca.org

GLAINN SIDHE ORDER OF WITCHES

Founded in 1975 by Andras Corben-Arthen, this is a traditional Witchcraft Order based on the teachings of a hereditary family of Scottish Witches. Focus is on Witchcraft not as a religion, but as a form of European shamanistic magic. Nine initiatory levels are used, each involving completion of specific physical, mental and psychic training. The EarthSpirit Community is the public face of the Glainn Sidhe Order.

Contact:
Andras Corben-Arthen:
PO Box 723-N Williamsburg, MA 01096.
See www.earthspirit.com

HEREDITARY/TRADITIONAL

These are secretive forms of Witchcraft which predate the Gardnerian revival. While many claims were made by people in the 1960s and '70s that their Pagan roots stretched back to the dawn of time, this seems to have been more fancy than fact. Frequently Hereditary Witches are those whose families practice herbology or folk magic traditions, and may claim an ancestor or lineage of ancestors who were initiated Witches. A typical example was Sybil Leek (1923-1983), whose Diary of a Witch (1968) claimed that true Witches could only be born, not made. Most Hereditary and Traditional Witches are found in the British Isles and Europe, though Covens following those traditions have been established elsewhere.

HOLY ORDER OF MOTHER EARTH (HOME)

Founded by Morning Glory and Oberon Zell, Anna Korn, and Alison Harlow, HOME was chartered in 1978 as a Magickal Order of the Church of All Worlds. Rituals have been developed over 20 years of living and working on sacred lands in Northern California, and threads were woven in from the various other traditions that members of the rural homesteading community had been trained in: CAW, Faerie, Dianic, Strega, Shamanic, Celtic, NROOGD, Mohsian, etc.

Most of the rituals are designed for large groups (30-100), and tend towards Mystery Pageants, all-night vigils and "bardics" (much HOME liturgy takes the form of songs and chants). Practices are basically shamanic (see "Shamanic Witchcraft"). Thealogy is

CAW/Gaian. Mythological basis is primarily British and Greek (although particular rituals may encompass other mythologies as well, such as Sumerian, Egyptian or Welsh), and HOME's Eight-Sabbat Wheel of the Year combines the May Cycle and the Eleusinia. Rituals are seldom repeated, usually being created freshly for each occasion. A basic liturgy, however, has been compiled in a "Magick 101" course and an intended three-volume *HOME Cooking,* of which only one volume has been completed.

Contact:
HOME:
PO Box 688, Penngrove, CA 94951;
Oberon@mcn.org
See www.caw.org and, particularly, www.caw.org/home

MINOAN BROTHERHOOD

A gay men's tradition of Witchcraft established in New York by the late Lord Gwydion (Eddie Buczynski) in the mid-1970s, at the same time as the Minoan Sisterhood was being established by Lady Miw, also in New York. The Brotherhood remains exclusively a venue for gay men to explore a traditional ritual Witchcraft, one which can foster a similar, though gay, sexual mysticism and sense of personal empowerment as in some British traditions of Wicca.

As the founder was a Gardnerian initiate, the rituals are roughly Gardnerian, with changes to accommodate a different core mythology and ritual custom. Imagery and deities are those of Ancient Crete and Mycenae. Working tools and their uses are virtually identical to those of British Traditional Wicca.

There are three degrees of initiation, tracing a line back to Lord Gwydion. Covens are secretive, and do not generally proselytize for new members. Worship centers on the Great Mother of all Living, as well as Her Divine Son, the Starry One, and His consort,

the Earth-Shaker. Skyclad meetings are held at the Full Moon and Sabbats. Invocatory practices (to encourage divine possession by the Gods) are common, and one of the aims is the recognition of each brother's inherent divinity. The Brotherhood does magic together in Covens, in couples or alone.

Contact:
Temenos Drakontos:
PO Box 191522, San Francisco, CA 94119;
Taliesin39@aol.com

NEW REFORMED ORTHODOX ORDER OF THE GOLDEN DAWN (NROOGD)

The NROOGD was initially a group of San Franciscans interested in the occult who banded together to perform an archetypal Witches' Sabbat for a class at a San Francisco university in 1968-69. Using published sources from Robert Graves, Margaret Murray and Gerald Gardner, a ritual was composed that has served as the basis of NROOGD practice ever since. After repeat performances of this rite yielded results, a decision was made to create a group identity and train others in its performance. The name New Reformed Orthodox Order of the Golden Dawn was coined since it was a wholly new tradition, it was Orthodox since it took its beliefs from the ancients, and it was a Magical Order as was the Hermetic Order of the Golden Dawn.

Esbats in NROOGD Covens usually focus on the working of magic, or on celebration of the divinity of each participant, recognizing a usually triply aspected Goddess and God. The magickal workings often include charms and simple poetry. There are three degrees of initiation. NROOGD continues to hold large public ritual celebrations at each of the eight Sabbats for the benefit of the greater Pagan community, and periodic meetings of area Covens are held to decide responsibilities for the coming year. Perhaps the most unique of these celebrations is the annual Autumn re-enactment of the Eleusinian Mysteries.

Contact:
Rowan Fairgrove: NROOGD,
PO Box 90304, San Jose, CA 95109;
nroogd@conjure.com
See www.nroogd.org

Publication:
The Witches' Trine:
PO 48 Page Street, San Francisco, CA 94102.
See www.conjure.com/TRINE/trine.html

PAGAN WAY

Developed in 1969 by Joseph Wilson, Tony Kelley, Ed Fitch, John Score, and a few others, for the purpose of providing an accessible Wiccan tradition and liturgy that had no formal initiation or membership requirements. Through round-robin correspondence among 15-20 different Wiccan groups, basic principles and ideas for rituals were developed. Ed Fitch composed group and solitary rituals based on Celtic and European folk traditions, with some Gardnerian influence, and Tony Kelley wrote introductory materials. These were first printed in *The Waxing Moon* magazine. These materials were never copyrighted, but deliberately placed in the public domain to gain the widest possible distribution. They were released by various occult publishing houses as *The Rituals of the Pagan Way* and *A Book of Pagan Rituals*.

Donna Cole and Herman Enderly adapted this material and formed the first formal Pagan Way Grove in Chicago in 1970. Though no central organization was ever formed, Pagan Way Groves thrived during the 1970s. By 1980, few remained, although the materials continue to be widely used, and have greatly influenced the development of many groups.

In the British Isles, the movement evolved separately with the founding in 1971 of the Pagan Front, which later became the Pagan Federation.

Contacts:
Joseph Wilson:
bearwalker@netonecome.net
See users.cwnet.com/season/neighbor/ntrvewjw.htm

Pagan Federation:
BM Box 7097, London WC1N 3XX, England.
See www.paganfed.demon.co.uk

PECTIWITA

Religion of the Picts, the indigenous people of Scotland. Transmitted in early 1980s by Raymond Buckland from Aidan Breac. A tradition for solitary Witches, PectiWita emphasizes natural magic and the Craft as a way of life rather than worship of the Gods (though that does exist). The Craft is passed through families, practicing herbalism and divination.

RECLAIMING

Reclaiming began in San Francisco in 1980 when Diane Baker and Miriam Simos (Starhawk) offered a class in ritual work. New teachers were recruited from these classes, and the "bud" of Reclaiming's teaching cell was begun. In 1982, while a Spiral Dance ritual was being planned by several of these people, a blockade was called at Diablo Canyon nuclear power plant. Many of the planners of the ritual went off to the blockade, and when they returned, they brought with them new models of non-hierarchical group structure. Folks started meeting under the name Reclaiming Collective, working to unify spirit and politics. Soon a new tradition of Witchcraft was emerging. The Reclaiming Tradition is eclectic and based on personal empowerment, structurally non-hierarchical, and engenders in most of its initiates a strong commitment to the work of the Goddess in the world.

In 1991, Reclaiming incorporated as a

California non-profit organization. Its objective and purpose are: "to worship the Goddess and the Old Gods; to celebrate the ancient sacred holidays of the Wheel of the Year and the Cycles of nature; to provide religious education" with a consensus-based process for decision-making. Their vision is rooted in the religion and magic of the Goddess – the Immanent Life Force. They see their work as teaching, making magic and "the art of empowering ourselves and each other to deepen our strength, both as individuals and as community; to voice our concerns about the world in which we live; and to bring to birth a vision of the new culture."

See:
Starhawk, *The Spiral Dance* (Harper and Row, 1979; updated 20th anniversary edition also available).

Contact:
Reclaiming Collective: (415) 339-8150.
See www.reclaiming.org

Publication:
Reclaiming Newsletter:
see www.reclaiming.org/newsletter

SEAX-WICA

This tradition was founded on Samhain 1973 by Raymond Buckland when he was living in New Hampshire. It was a result of his growing dissatisfaction with Gardnerian Craft (after more than ten years in that tradition) due partly to the prevalence of ego-trips and power plays then unsettling the community. Contrary to statements from some misinformed people, the new tradition was *not* started as a joke but as a very serious attempt at a Wiccan tradition that could overcome some of the faults of degree systems. Buckland started it for his own personal practice but was soon swamped with people who had heard of his new version of the Craft and found it to be the type of path they had been looking for. Because of this, he finally had the rituals published (it is a non-secret tradition).

In Samhain 1975 the first edition of the *Seax-Wica Voys* appeared; a magazine for Seax-Wicans worldwide, published eight times a year. Also in 1975 the Church of Seax-Wica was established, later to become a part of the Universal Life Church and, as such, to obtain official legal recognition. By this time the headquarters was situated in Virginia. To provide instruction in Wicca to those in geographically "challenging" places, a correspondence course was established, which grew into the Seax-Wica Seminary, one of the first of its kind. This grew to have over a thousand students worldwide, all of whom were dealt with personally by Buckland.

The Seax-Wica remains active around the world, with much activity in Great Britain and Australia, and even with Saxon Witches in Russia and Japan. The tradition centers around the deities Woden and Freya. It is a non-degree system with a democratic form of Coven leadership. Its Witches can celebrate in a Coven situation or as Solitaries. Covens can be led by male and/or female. The Manifesto of Seax-Wica, as originally published in 1974, is as follows:

"The aims of Seax-Wica are (i) To worship the God and Goddess of the Old Religion, whether as part of a group (Coven) or as an individual. (ii) To aid others in learning of that worship. (iii) To combat the untruths and straighten the misconceptions of the Craft held by many outsiders. (iv) To work for harmony among the different traditions of the Craft. (v) To work for a happier relationship between Man/Woman and other aspects of Nature (for we are all a part of Nature). (vi) To help members progress and improve themselves mentally, physically, and spiritually."

See:
Raymond Buckland, *The Tree: Complete Book of Saxon Witchcraft*
(Red Wheel/Weiser, 1974).

1734 TRADITION

This is a name that has been applied to the practice of Witchcraft based on the philosophy and work of Robert Cochrane (1931-1966), a British Witch active during the 1950s and early '60s. While Cochrane claimed to be a hereditary Witch, this claim is difficult to substantiate. What is known is that he found a teacher (non-Gardernerian), formed a Coven he called The Clan of Tubal Cain, researched the Craft and did the best he could to recreate what he believed to be the Old Religion. The earliest his Craft connection can be documented is 1953. During the mid-1960s, a correspondence developed between Cochrane and an American, Joseph Wilson. Cochrane's letters to Wilson and others form the basis for the tradition practiced today.

Cochrane was a poet and a philosopher who loved to write in a cryptic and mystical manner. He delivered poetry, riddles and folksongs more often than facts and he inspired research and evolution rather than a strict adherence to dogma. The tradition fosters the evolution of the Witch working in it: a continual quest for knowledge and experience. Most Covens work in a shamanic manner to a large degree. It is an oath-bound tradition, and adherence to the ethic is paramount. "1734" is not a date, but a cryptogram for the name of the Goddess. Many of today's Covens rely heavily on meditation and vision. Most work out of doors whenever possible, use dance and chant to raise energy and use aspecting (a form of channeling) regularly.

See:
Justine Glass, *Witchcraft, The Sixth Sense – and Us* (Spearman, 1965).
William Gray, *Western Inner Workings* (Weiser, 1983).
Doreen Valiente, *The Rebirth of Witchcraft* (Hale, 1989).

Contact:
Joseph Wilson:
bearwalker@netonecome.net

SHAMANIC WITCHCRAFT

First articulated as such in April 1974 by Morning Glory Zell in a paper called "Whither Wicca?" presented at the Gnostic Aquarian Festival in Minneapolis, MN, Shamanic Witchcraft refers to practices associated with those of tribal shamans in traditional Pagan cultures throughout the world. A Shaman combines the roles of healer, priest(ess), diviner, magician, teacher and psychopomp (spirit guide), utilizing altered states of consciousness to produce and control psychic phenomena and travel to and from the spirit realm.

Followers of this path believe that historical Witchcraft was the Shamanic practice of European Pagans; and Mediæval Witches actually functioned more as village Shamans than as priests and priestess of "the Old Religion." Shamanic Witchcraft emphasizes serving the wider community through rituals, herbalism, spellcraft, healings, counseling, rites of passage, handfasting, Mystery initiations, etc.

A distinguishing element of Shamanic Witchcraft is the knowledge and sacramental use of psychotropic plants to effect transitions between the worlds. The theory and practice of Shamanic Witchcraft has permeated widely throughout many other established traditions.

STREGHERIA

Stregheria is the Craft of the Italian Witches. It is an ancient system, steeped with history that dates back to at least the fourteenth century. Strega are the descendents of an ancient people who used moonlore, nature, symbolism, and spirits (Faeries) to work their magick. Strega accept the duality of both a female and male God, known by different names in different traditions. Stregheria also recognizes a spiritual teacher and wise woman, Aradia, known as the Holy Strega. The message of Aradia, called the Covenant, offered her followers the path to freedom and personal empowerment. Aradia also taught that the traditional powers of a Witch would belong to any who adhered to the way of the Old Religion. Aradia called these Gifts and Beliefs. The Charges of Aradia is the message she left her followers.

The Tools of the Stregheria are likened to the armor and weapons of a knight: any true Witch must be to some degree a spiritual warrior. The magickal focus is largely upon spells, omens and natural objects. These are used in amulets, talismans and charm bags. Nature is viewed as the manifestation of spiritual forces. Magick is the art of understanding the interplay between these forces and the ways in which they can be influenced. Ritual circles are seldom used for spellcasting or other works of magick. Stregheria and Wicca celebrate many of the same seasonal Festivals even though the names and some of the dates are different.

See:
CG Leland,
Aradia: The Gospel of Witches (1899).

Contacts:
Lori Bruno: Sacred Paths Alliance,
33 Everlyn Ave, Medford, MA 02155,
(781) 395-9297,
lorib1818@aol.com

Fabrisia's Boschetto:
-Fabrisia@Fabrisia.com
See also www.fabrisia.com
The Church of the Equinox: (201) 450-4696

TEMPLE OF ARA

The Ara Tradition is a non-dogmatic, innovative and progressive tradition of Wiccan spirituality based on the central principle, and experience, of immanent divinity. It reflects years of shamanic Wiccan practice and is intended to help us discover the Divine that dwells within, and all around us, and to rejoice in the ecstasy of that communion. The tradition was founded in 1983 by High Priestess Phyllis Curott with the birth of her Coven, the Circle of Ara.

The Ara Tradition traces its roots to the Minoan and Gardnerian Traditions in New York City; at the same time that she was training in the Minoan Sisterhood, Phyllis was studying core shamanism and actively participating in the first shamanic drumming circle based on the work of Dr. Michael Harner. As high priestess of the Circle of Ara, now one of the oldest and longest running Wiccan congregations in the United States, Phyllis deconstructed traditional and often patriarchal Wiccan teachings to distill a system of core practices and principles, then blended these with core shamanic practices. It is this model of teachings, referred to as core shamanic Wicca, that she has passed on to her students.

After numerous daughter and granddaughter circles, lectures, workshops, and books, Curott and the Elders realized that their tradition has grown and evolved into an international movement, and so the Temple of Ara was formed in order to formalize and maintain the Ara Tradition across the globe. It is in the process of incorporating under New York State law as a religious nonprofit organization so that it can continue to expand its various international training programs and community services.

See:
Phyllis Curott, *Book of Shadows: A Modern Woman's Journey into the Wisdom of Witchcraft and the Magic of the Goddess* (Broadway Books, 1998).
See also www.bookofshadows.net/
Phyllis Curott, *Witch Crafting: A Spiritual Guide to Making Magic* (Broadway Books, 2001). See also www.witchcrafting.com

Contact:
The Temple of Ara, 350 Third Ave., # 707, New York, NY 10010-2310;

www.templeofara.org

Publications:
ARA News: the official electronic announcement list of the Temple of Ara: groups.yahoo.com/group/AraNews
Ara Quarterly: the official newsletter of the Temple of Ara: www.templeofara.org/newsletter

WICCAN SHAMANISM

Founded by Selena Fox in the 1980s, this tradition has an ecumenical and multicultural focus. It is a combination of Wicca, humanistic psychology and a variety of shamanistic techniques to change consciousness, such as drumming and ecstatic dancing.

Contact:
Circle Sanctuary:
PO Box 219, Mt Horeb, WI 53572;
(608) 924-2216,
circle@circlesanctuary.org
See www.circlesanctuary.org

Publication:
Circle Network News:
see www.circlesanctuary.org/circle

OTHER TRADITIONS include regional/ethnic, based on mythology and practices of various cultures, such as Baltic, Greco-Roman, Sumerian, Egyptian, Welsh, and Norse.

SOME WICCAN NETWORKS

Covenant of the Goddess:
PO Box 1226, Berkeley, CA 94701.
See www.cog.org

Pagan Educational Network:
PO Box 586, Portage, IN 46368.
See -www.bloomington.in.us/~pen/

Note that further US and international contacts can be found in the "Additional Websites, Contacts and Resources" chapter of this book.

Here are some more resources for you relating to some of the subject matter covered in *POP!* Remember there are extensive contacts and websites recommended by the authors within their articles in this book also.

Witchy Publications

newWitch Magazine
www.newWitch.com

The newest, coolest and most informative magickal magazine in the US. The mag features up-to-the-minute articles and is an exciting reflection of the growth in popularity of the Craft in the US.

Sage Woman
www.sagewoman.com

newWitch's big sister and long established as the premium magazine of Goddess consciousness in the US.

Witchcraft Magazine
Australia's best mag! Informative, extremely well-produced and relevant whether you are in Oz or on the Moon. I urge international readers to subscribe for quality articles, great pictures and inspiration.

You can order internationally through www.whitemagic.com.au/wcraft.

US Witchy Supplies Online

Panpipes Magickal Market Place
www.panpipes.com

Absolutely anything you can imagine is available here at the oldest Occult Supply store in California. My good friend Jymie Darling is in charge and does a superb job of procuring anything your Witchy heart desires and gets it to you in the blink of an eye – or the wiggle of a nose?

Psychic Eye
www.pebooks.com

A well-established and respected supplier of New Age, Witchcraft and other related products.

Raven's Flight
www.ravensflight.net

Raven's store is one of the most interesting around with its elaborate and enchanting entrance on a busy street in North Hollywood that opens into an extensively stocked Witchcraft Supply store. They have an excellent online store too.

Witchy Contacts

The Witches' Voice
www.witchvox.com

An exciting and reliable educational network dedicated to correcting misinformation about Witches and Witchcraft. *The Witches' Voice* includes hundreds of articles, up-to-the-minute news reports of interest to the Pagan/Witchcraft community, book reviews, shopping network and is comprehensively linked to international contacts. An amazing hub of activity in the Witchy Universe.

The African American Wiccan Society
www.aawiccans.org

This excellent site is maintained by African Americans, other minorities and Pagan communities who practice Wicca and other Earth-based religions. They have created this organization for the purpose of giving information, support, mutual worship and resources to their members who range from Wiccans, Yorubian-based, Shamans, Kemetics, Kush, to Native, and others. It is their belief that there are many people of color who are of an Earth-based tradition and who seek community with people of like minds.

Oh – and There's Me!

Please note also that at my website www.fionahorne.com there are many links to Witchy websites as well as addresses of international suppliers both in the "About Witchcraft" section and the "Spellbook" sections.

Raw Vegan Organic Food and Raw Living

Contacts for evolved magickal living – spiritually, mentally, emotionally and physically.

LifeForce Foods
www.livingintheraw.com

This hot new company – created by master culinary artists, Burke Bryant and Leo Miller – is dedicated to creating delicious gourmet raw vegan organic food and has product placement in supermarkets in Los Angeles (soon to be national) as well as offering in-house food preparation, weekly meal planners and delivery services. Their Raw Personal Pan Pizza and the Great Fraudulent Tuna Sandwich have to be eaten to be believed! The company philosophy of LifeForce Foods is:

"to support health, environmental awareness, personal growth, spiritual evolution and positive social change through raw, vegan, organic foods. Our foods model a new sustainable way of community living, while inspiring individuals to achieve a greater experience of wellness, physically, emotionally and spiritually. Through market distribution, restaurants and personal delivery services, LifeForce Foods' mission is to positively influence the lives of our customers and make a meaningful contribution to the health of our society and the planet."

Living and Raw Foods
www.living-foods.com

The largest community on the Internet dedicated to educating the world about the power of the living and raw vegan/vegetarian food diet. The site provides information to let you make an informed choice on how you wish to live. Contained within the many pages of this website, you will find recipes, articles, resources, links, testimonials, information and support.

Just Eat An Apple
www.justeatanapple.com

The leading magazine on the Raw Food Diet, JEAA is a fantastic resource on the subject of raw foods and natural living. Do yourself a favor and invest in a subscription to JEAA.

Rhios Raw Energy
www.rawfoodinfo.com

Rhio is a leading proponent of the raw/living foods lifestyle, through her Raw Energy Telephone Hotline and this very comprehensive and entertaining website provides information about health-related issues and raw and living foods events as well as up to the minute reports of the raw revolution happening around America.

Jurlique – The Purest Skincare on Earth
www.jurlique.com

This Australian-born company, now internationally established, makes the most divine and effective organic plant-based, animal cruelty free skin care in the world. I bought my first Jurlique product over thirteen years ago at the tiny, South Australian organic herb farm that housed its inception, and now I can visit their Beverly Hills Spa for a facial! Their Eye Gel is the only thing that gets rid of the bags under my eyes after a late night writing on my laptop! The company philosophy is to support organic industry and create a global awareness of the importance of treading lightly on our precious Earth in order to continue to enjoy the beauty and bounty she offers. There are no chemicals, artificial fragrances or animal contents: only the purest skincare in the world – truly.

Animal Rights

Animal Rights Resource Site
www.animalconcerns.org

The Animal Concerns Community is a project of the Enviro Link Network (www.envirolink.org), a non-profit organization which has been providing access to thousands of online environmental and animal rights/welfare resources since 1991. This community serves as a clearinghouse for information on the Internet related to animal rights and welfare.

People Rights

Amnesty International
www.amnesty.org

People need saving too. Amnesty International (AI) is a worldwide movement of people who campaign for internationally recognized human rights.

AI's vision is of a world in which every person enjoys all of the human rights enshrined in the Universal Declaration of Human Rights and other international human rights standards.

In pursuit of this vision, AI undertakes research and action focused on preventing and ending grave abuses of the rights to physical and mental integrity, freedom of conscience and expression, and freedom from discrimination, within the context of its work to promote all human rights.

True Majority

www.truemajority.org

Ben Cohen – the ice cream guy from Ben and Jerry's (we just *have* to get him making vegan raw ice treats!) – started True Majority in order to compound the power of all those who believe in social justice, giving children a decent start in life, protecting the environment, and America working in cooperation with the world community. I am a member and greatly appreciate the regular newsletters and positive action suggestions and opportunities this site proposes and makes available.

Earth Rights

Green Cross International

www.gci.ch

The mission of Green Cross is to help ensure a just, sustainable and secure future for all by fostering a value shift and cultivating a new sense of global interdependence and shared responsibility in humanity's relationship with nature.

Global Green USA

www.globalgreen.org

Global Green USA, the United States affiliate of Green Cross International, fosters a global value shift toward a sustainable and secure world through education, advocacy, partnerships, and programs focused on the safe elimination of weapons of mass destruction, stemming climate change, reducing resource use, and preventing conflicts over fresh water.

Acting as a catalyst, facilitator, and mediator, Global Green encourages collaborative approaches and crosscutting solutions to environmental challenges.

Planet Ark

www.planetark.com

Planet Ark is an Australian not-for-profit organization that was set up by the tennis player Pat Cash and (my friend!) international charity campaigner Jon Dee back in June 1991. Planet Ark also has offices in the UK, and its impact and initiatives are international.

Planet Ark's aim is to show people and business the many ways that they can reduce their day-to-day impact on the environment.

Planet Ark is largely funded by corporate sponsorship. They work in partnership with businesses and organizations that want to help bring about real environmental change. They are also funded through the sales of a limited range of environmentally responsible products and a small number of government grants.

Features of Planet Ark's website include: Up-to-the-minute World Environment News from the Reuters news agency and fact sheets, media releases, info and pictures on international issues where Planet Ark is currently campaigning, and details of how you can help.

Since *POP!* is pretty well packed with further reading suggestions, as are my other books, I have kept the titles fairly select here, listing only my absolute personal faves, some I've referred to earlier in this book and some newer titles!

Non-Fiction

I guess I should start first with my other books …

Witch – A Magickal Journey (HarperCollins, 2000)

Seven Days to a Magickal New You (Thorsons/HarperCollins, 2001)

Magickal Sex – A Witch's Guide to Beds, Knobs and Broomsticks (Thorsons/HarperCollins, 2002)

Witchin' A Handbook for Teen Witches (Element/HarperCollins, 2003)

Next, though they've been mentioned elsewhere in *POP!* I can't help myself again recommending those written by my good friend, Phyllis Curott. She is a remarkable woman, a powerful Witch and one of the most sincere and fabulous people I have ever met.

Phyllis Curott, *Book of Shadows: A Modern Woman's Journey into the Wisdom of Witchcraft and the Magic of the Goddess* (Broadway Books, 1998)

Phyllis Curott, *Witchcrafting: A Spiritual Guide to Making Magic* (Broadway Books, 2001)

An important and thorough title that will assist you in forming a Coven is:

Amber K, *Covencraft – Witchcraft for Three or More* (Llewellyn Publications, 1998)

If I haven't yet convinced you to look into raw food, this lovely book is about understanding how to cook not only with sight, scent and taste in mind but also with magick:

Scott Cunningham, *Cunningham's Encyclopedia of Wicca in the Kitchen* (Llewellyn, 2000)

Janet and Stewart Farrar are two very knowledgeable and respected Witches (as is Janet's new fella, Gavin Bone). I highly recommend all their books including:

Janet and Stewart Farrar, *A Witches' Bible* (Phoenix, 1996)

Janet and Stewart Farrar, *The Witches' God, The Witches' Goddess* (Phoenix, 1998)

Anything written by Nevill Drury is an enlightening read. One of his more recent titles that I love is a complete guide to magick making with a smart and analytical approach:

Nevill Drury, *Everyday Magick* (Simon and Schuster, 2002)

I know you all want lots of spells and Antonia Beattie is a champ at coming up with some of the best! Check out her titles, such as:

Antonia Beattie, *Power Spells: Magic for*

Personal Power and Inner Peace (Barnes and Noble Books, 2002)

Antonia Beattie with Amargi Wolf, *Girl's Guide to Spells* (Barnes and Noble Books, 2001)

Antonia Beattie, *Spells to Attract Wealth and Abundance* (Barnes and Noble Books, 2000)

Antonia Beattie, *Love Magic* (Barnes and Noble Books, 2000)

Jessica Adams is an amazing astrologer/living Goddess and I always enjoy her work. She has teamed up with two other Goddesses to write one of the ultimate guides to modern living in:

Jessica Adams, Jelena Glisic and Anthea Paul, *21st Century Goddess: The Modern Girl's Guide to the Universe* (Allen & Unwin, 2002)

This is a beautifully presented book and will enchant you with its comprehensive information and advice on astrology, dreams, crystals, energy clearing, numerology, rituals and psychic power.

The following book is a classic read and the title says it all really. It is an enjoyable insight into pre-patriarchal times when Goddesses ruled the Earth:

Merlin Stone, *When God was a Woman* (Barnes and Noble Books, 1976)

A brilliant and groundbreaking book that suggests that the development of literacy in humans initiated the decline of the feminine (Goddess) in society and led to patriarchal dominance and misogyny. If that sounds heavy, don't let it put you off this book – it is a smart and beautifully inspiring read:

Leonard Shlain, *The Alphabet versus the Goddess* (Penguin, 1998)

A big book with a brief history of *everything*. In this very readable book, Jared weaves history and biology together to help comprehend what it is to be human:

Jared Diamond, *Guns, Germs and Steel* (Norton, 1999)

Now to Fiction!

William Tevelein is an Australian marvel, and his first novel is a perfect one to enjoy as part of a Coven reading circle. It's a wild and Witchy mysterious fantasy that's funny too. If you have trouble finding it in the US, www.amazon.com should help.

William Tevelein, *The Visitants: Book One of The Casting of the Golden Dice* (Penguin, 2002)

Another great and prolific Oz fiction author, particularly for young adult readers, is Kim Wilkins. Her "Gina Champion" series is fun, fear and magic woven into delicious stories. Her latest is:

Kim Wilkins, *Moonstorm – A Gina Champion Mystery* (HarperCollins, 2003)

An amazing interpretation of the life of the Wicked Witch of the West from *The Wizard of Oz*. In this book she is a much misunderstood creature who is actually a brilliant revolutionary and heroine:

Gregory Maguire, *Wicked, The Life and Times of the Wicked Witch of the West* (Regan/HarperCollins,1995)

Anton and Mina Adams produce a wide variety of literature, esoteric and otherwise, under numerous noms de plume. In their Adams family incarnation, they tend towards wizardry, having produced two historical overviews – *The Learned Arts of Witches & Wizards* (Lansdowne, 1998) and *The World of Wizards* (Lansdowne, 2002) – and *The Wizards' Handbook* (Lansdowne, 2002), an introduction to magic for youngsters who are, as it were, Potter-ing about with spellcraft.

They live in suitably strange and comfortably cluttered rural house, with a most amusing pair of dogs and enough books to sink a reasonably large ocean liner.

Phil "Satyrblade" Brucato has been a professional author for nearly fifteen years, and is best-known as the driving force behind three award-winning series of books: *Deliria: Faerie Tales for a New Millennium, Mage: The Ascension* and *Mage: The Sorcerers Crusade*. Beyond those credits, though, he has worked on everything from newspaper and magazine columns to comic strips, short stories, webzines, computer games, market copy, and whatever else captures his attention.

An eclectic priest and healer, Phil has spent over 20 years working in theatre, music, publishing, bodywork, and alternative spirituality. Vigorous, curious and eternally fascinated with life, he also teaches workshops in the Bay Area in connection with the Lifedance Center, Celebrations of Love, and his own personal practice. A recent transplant to the Bay Area, Phil favors hope, chivalry and passionate intensity. He has a satyr tattooed on his shoulder blade, and it's there for a reason.

For more information about Phil Brucato and *Deliria*, check out www.laughingpan.com.

In addition to his extensive back catalogue, **Raymond Buckland** has recently published two encyclopedias, *The Witch Book* and *The Fortune-Telling Book*, created the *Cards of Alchemy* set and has two upcoming books: *Buckland's Book of Spirit Communications* and *Wicca For One*.

Lucy Cavendish is the author/creator of *The Oracle Tarot* and *Magical Spellcards*, both published by Hay House. In 1991 she created *Witchcraft magazine*. Lucy first connected with spirits and deities when she was a little girl, and is devoted to helping people discover the healing power and pure joy of magic.

Please visit her at www.lucycavendish.com

Gabrielle Cleary is a practicing Witch and Wiccan High Priestess of Applegrove Coven, Sydney, Australia. She has worked both as a solitary and in groups, conducts teaching circles, public and private gatherings and rituals, both large and small, as well as presenting workshops at events such as the Australian Wiccan Conference, Gateway, Gathering Of All Tribes, the Pagan Summer Gathering and Magick Happens.

She was a contributing author to Doug Ezzy's *Practising the Witch's Craft* (Allen & Unwin, 2003) – writing on training in the Craft. She is also the producer and presenter of a Sydney Pagan Radio program, *The Cauldron*, and a past committee member of the Pagan Awareness Network Inc. Gabby is passionate about Kitchen Witchery, Magical Herbalism and the experiential aspects of her path.

Her chapter in *POP!* was originally published as part of the Conference Papers of the Australian Wiccan Conference 2002 and is based upon a workshop of the same name. Gabby invites you to surf by the home of Applegrove Coven on the web: www.fortunecity.com/bally/westmeath/24/homepage.htm.

Serene Conneeley is a writer, healer and Witch. She lives in the city but is most alive when her bare feet are on the dew-soaked grass of Glastonbury Tor, dancing through the stone circles of Ireland, following vampires in New Orleans, wandering the windswept beaches of Iona or hiking across the Camino in northern Spain. But through all her searching she has come to know that the divine is within not without, and it doesn't matter where you are.

She is currently writing spiritual stories for *New Idea* magazine and slowly working on her first book.

Mitchell Coombes is sixteen years old (as this book goes to print) and has been a practicing Witch since the age of twelve when he cast his first spell and began to educate himself on "real Witchcraft."

He now has a regular radio segment "Witchy Wednesdays" on Australia's New FM 105.3 where he talks about Witchcraft and answers callers needing a Witchy fix. He writes about Witchcraft for various publications and is the author of the self-published *Wicca* (Independent Books).

Mitchell has recently become known as "Australia's Homopsychic" with a Gay Witchcraft/psychic section on Australia's most successful queer website, www.queerplanet.com.au/homopsychic.

Visit Mitchell at www.mitchellcoombes.com and email: admin@mitchellcoombes.com.

High Priestess **Phyllis Curott** is a lawyer; and author of *Book of Shadows* (Broadway, 1999) and *Witch Crafting* (Broadway, 2001).

She is also the founder of the Temple of Ara (one of the oldest Wiccan congregations in the US) and the Temple of the Sacred Earth; president emerita of the Covenant of the Goddess; and co-founder of the Religious Liberties Lawyers Network.

Visit her site, www.phylliscurott.com.

Liam Cyfrin (pronounced "Kivrin") has been a permanent fixture in Australian magical writing for over twenty years but, due to a habit of shedding pen-names the way snakes shed skins, has managed to keep this a deep dark Craft secret revealed only to those who can impress him with a really innovative new pronunciation of the word *athame*.

For most of its ten-year run, he was co-editor (with Rhea Loader) of the Australian esoteric magazine *Shadowplay*, for which he mainly wrote peculiar fiction and "filk" follies such as the oddly ubiquitous "Model of a Modern Esotericist." He has also been a contributor and consultant on nearly all Fiona's books to date (but somehow missed the sex magic one, an oversight that he feels does his public image no good at all).

He lives with his honey in the Blue Mountains in Australia, and spends much of his spare time staring into the misty distance and inventing new and increasingly abstruse pseudonyms.

Kayt Davies (BA (Psych), MPhil (Lit)) is a Scorpio firehorse journalist counselor and has just completed a Master's thesis delving into the psychological richness of the Persephone and Narcissus myths, positing that they can help contemporary mothers and daughters to compassionately negotiate the minefield of adolescence. Part of this project was an interweaving and retelling of the two myths into a new novel called *Pomegranate Flesh*. To find out more visit: www.kayt.info.

Kayt is also the editor of *Australian Vital Magazine*, a national glossy publication all about health, vitality, well-being and enjoying life.

Nevill Drury was born in Hastings, England, in 1947 but has lived most of his life in Australia. He has been interested in western magic and consciousness research for over thirty years and has written widely on shamanism and the Western esoteric tradition, as well as on contemporary art.

He holds a Master's degree in anthropology from Macquarie University in Sydney and is the author of over fifty books, including *Exploring the Labyrinth*, *Sacred Encounters*, *The Elements of Shamanism*, *The Shaman's Quest* and *The Dictionary of the Esoteric*. His most recent publication is *Magic and Witchcraft: from Shamanism to the Technopagans* (Thames & Hudson, London and New York 2003). His work has been published in fifteen languages.

Taylor Ellwood is the co-author of the recently published *Creating Magickal Entities* from Egregore Publishers (www.egregorepublishing.com) and the author of *Pop Culture Magick*, which will be published in 2004 by Immanion Press (www.immanionpress.wox.org). He is the author of a number of articles on occultism, having been an active practitioner of magick for ten years. He is currently pursuing his Ph.D. in Literacy, Rhetoric, and Social Practice at Kent State University in Ohio.

He is also writing a super hero novel and his next book on the occult, *Space/Time Magick*. This essay is excerpted from a chapter on divination and space/time. Taylor can be reached at ashmage@hotmail.com, and those interested in the space/time magick work should check out the following links:

www.gnostica.net/timemachines
www.livejournal.com/users/teriel *or*
www.livejournal.com/users/timemagick

Scaerie Faerie (no, it's not her Magickal name!) is a twenty-something Veterinary Nurse from the UK. She is very interested in all matters occult and spiritual, but Pagan and Witch are the only labels she finds fit her comfortably. She is a devoted mum to her family of animals, and reads as if her life depended on it (she holds a special love for the works of Kim Wilkins).

She also loves writing, listening to music, watching

films (in fact she insists you all watch *Heavenly Creatures* and *The Green Mile* if you haven't already done so), the comedy of Eddie Izzard, Ben Elton and Billy Connolly, astrology and drawing with her limited skill. She's a double Scorpio, so don't mind her too much! More of her writing can be found on her personal website: www.devoted.to/scaeriefaerie.

Janet Farrar and Gavin Bone are practicing Wiccans and authors who publish books on the subjects of Paganism, Magick and Witchcraft. Prior to **Stewart Farrar's** death on February 7, 2000, Janet and Stewart had been publishing their works since 1971, and are recognized as experts on Witchcraft and the Occult. Gavin joined them in 1993, and worked with them on *The Pagan Path*, a study of Paganism worldwide, *The Healing Craft*, a healer's workbook for Pagans, and their recent publication *The Complete Dictionary of European Gods and Goddesses*. To date, between them they have had eleven books, on the subjects mentioned, published in the United States, Britain and as far afield as Brazil, Japan and the Czech Republic.

Janet and Gavin are active members in The Aquarian Tabernacle Church Ireland and have links with several covens in the United States and Europe. They also regularly do lecture and workshop tours in Europe, the United States, and just recently, in Australia and New Zealand. They are also active with Ancient Ceremonies Theatre (ACT) within the Republic of Ireland. This is not a Druid Grove but a ceremonial theatre group which re-creates Druidic Ritual for Public Ceremonial Occassions. This group came about because of the need locally for ceremony, initially at the twinning of Athboy in Co. Meath and L'Autonne in France. They have since performed several other times, which has included "performing" for the Chamber of Commerce of their home town of Kells.

They live in the Republic of Ireland, in a small cottage with an influx of field mice, eight lazy cats, a goat called Fanny and poor plumbing!

Brenna Fey is the Pagan pen name of Ally Peltier, who lives in New York City. Her writing has appeared in *Circle* magazine, *Cauldrons and Broomsticks* e-zine, and other non-Pagan venues. She served for several years as the Assistant Editor of *Cauldrons and Broomsticks* e-zine and is now Editor of the *Ara Quarterly* newsletter.

Francesca Gentille has a BA in Psychology and has completed Advanced Training and Graduate Study in Non-Violent Communication. She is the co-founder/co-director of the Nevada Center for Cultural and Martial Arts.

Francesca is also a second degree Wiccan Priestess, an initiated daughter of Yemaja, an initiate of Ishtar, a professional life coach, a nationally recognized relationship coach, a Neo-American Tantrika and a Sacred Sensual Dancer. She has been following the Pagan Path for eighteen years.

Websites:
www.lifedancecenter.com
    – her virtual Center for Passionate Living Courses and Coaching.

www.ishtartemple.org
    – an ongoing project to Integrate, Sexuality, Healing, Transformation and Relationship (Ishtar).

www.nvcama.org
    – The Nevada Center for Cultural and Martial Arts.

Philip Johnson is a graduate of the University of Sydney in both Religious Studies and Theology, and a media consultant on alternate spiritualities. He lectured on the subject of alternative religious movements at the Presbyterian Theological Centre in Sydney for fourteen years. In 1991 he co-founded the Community of Hope, which is a Jesus-centered spirituality movement, and under its auspices co-ordinates an exhibitor's booth in alternate spiritual gatherings like the international Mind Body Spirit Festivals.

He has co-written several books including *Beyond Prediction: The Tarot and Your Spirituality* (Lion), and *Riding the Rollercoaster: How the Risen Christ Empowers Life* (Strand).

Websites recommended by the author:
www.jesus.com.au
www.sojo.net
www.cstone.tv

His chapter in *POP!* contains excerpts from "Wiccans and Christians: Some Mutual Challenges" by Philip Johnson (©1999), reproduced with kind permission of the author. The complete text is located on-line at www.jesus.com.au.

Tri Johns reveres life as a multitalented artist. She expresses her creative passion in her profession as a Makeup Artist for the Entertainment Industry and is also a promising expressionist writer who believes experience exposes the core of artistic creation. As an abstract painter she liberates her insatiable need for peculiar exploits.

Tri has been practicing Witchcraft for several years as

a Solitary Witch and for one year in a Coven with Fiona Horne.

Iya Ta'Shia Asanti Karade is a Yoruba Priestess in the Ifa Tradition of the Karade order. Iya Ta'Shia is also an award-winning writer and journalist, and is the author of the acclaimed book, *The Sacred Door*.

For more information about Iya Ta'Shia's work visit her web site: www.sacreddoor.com.

Odyle Knight is the author of *Bali Moon – A Spiritual Odyssey*. She is currently working on her second book, *Bali Magic – In the Shadow of Stars*. Odyle has a BA in History and Psychology and Diplomas in Education and Educational Studies – Counseling. She has always been interested in the metaphysical and has completed a Diploma in Astrological Studies from the Royal College of Astrological Studies, London and worked as an astrologer for a number of years. Odyle has given lectures and workshops pertaining to spiritual topics in numerous organizations around the world including the Spiritual Society of Great Britain, the Theosophical Society of Australia and the Freemason Society. She has traveled extensively visiting many countries but has made her home in Bali.

As partner to a Balinese priest and mystic for nearly ten years, Odyle gained an insight into the magical practices and customs of this timeless culture, which as one of the last remaining Hindu kingdoms retains its place within the largest Moslem country in the world, Indonesia. She has traveled extensively throughout the islands of Indonesia in order to gain a broader perspective of this vast dynamic country. A seeker of knowledge and believer of destiny, Odyle was captivated from the first by the island of Bali and was driven to share her incredible experiences with others.

Bali Moon – A Spiritual Odyssey can be purchased online from Adyar Books, Sydney, Australia; www.adyar.com.au. The author may be contacted at odyleknight@hotmail.com.

Carmela Leone was born in Brisbane, Australia, in 1964. A child of Sicilian parents, she was baptized a Roman Catholic. As a child, Carmela attended church every Sunday until, at the age of thirteen, she informed the local priest that she had discovered her own personal dialogue with "God" and that she was "cutting out the middle man." Carmela left the church and soon after, discovered she was a Pantheist; she took to visiting forests and parks on Sundays instead.

In 1991, Carmela met Fiona Horne, who introduced her to Wicca and Paganism. Since then she has been a practicing Witch and a dedicated Pagan. Carmela has featured in two of Fiona's books, and is currently a member of a Coven in southwest England, where she now lives. Carmela has one child, a boy named Galen.

Rhea Loader is a Feri Witch. Her interests include writing, web design, aromancy, art, crafts, jewelry making and belly dancing.

She has been a Feri initiate since 1987, a Trad High Priestess since 1983, and the editor of *Shadowplay* magazine/e-zine since 1984 (www.shadowplayzine.com).

She likes to remind people that all she wants from life is a little bit of everything on a big plate. Rhea is part of Nightwing, a Feri and Alexandrian circle in Seattle. Email her at rhealoader@hotmail.com.

Dylan Masson is High Priest of the Circle of Salgion, Church of Wicca and manager/webmaster for The Witches' League for Public Awareness, a proactive educational network dedicated to correcting misinformation about Witches and Witchcraft, founded in Salem, Massachusetts, in May 1986 by Rev. Laurie Cabot.

He can be emailed at dylan@circleofsalgion.org. You might also like to visit the Church of Salgion website: www.circleofsalgion.org. There you'll find a full history of the tradition, as well as Coven descriptions and contacts.

Christopher Penczak is an eclectic Witch, teacher and healing practitioner who encourages all to find and create their own traditions of spirituality. Formerly based in the entertainment industry, Christopher left to pursue a magickal life helping to empower others through his writing, readings and healing sessions. His work combines age-old traditional teachings and the natural wisdom found across the world with the flexibility to forge new traditions in modern society.

He is the author of several books, including *City Magick* (Weiser, 2001), *Gay Witchcraft* (Weiser, 2003), *The Inner Temple of Witchcraft* book and CD set (Llewellyn, 2002), *The Outer Temple of Witchcraft* book and CD set (Llewellyn, 2002) and the forthcoming *Sons of the Goddess: A Young Man's Guide to Wicca* (Llewellyn, 2005). More on his work can be found at www.christopherpenczak.com.

Julia Phillips is a Wiccan High Priestess whose experience includes running both Covens and magical lodges in London, Sydney, and Melbourne. Her formal study of the occult began in 1971, when she began to attend lectures at the Society of Psychical Research in London. In 1975 she obtained her first Tarot deck, and it was through the study of the Tarot that she met the

High Priestess of the London Coven into which she was initiated. She immigrated to Australia in 1988 and currently lives in Melbourne.

Julia edited and published *Children of Sekhmet* (1986-1990) and *Web of Wyrd* (1990-1993), and in 1991 founded the Australian Pagan Alliance and its magazine, *Pagan Times*, which is now in its twelfth year of continuous publication. She is the author of *The Witches of Oz* (Capall Bann, 1994), a guide to the practice of Wicca in the Southern Hemisphere. She also wrote the chapter "The Magical Universe" for *Practising the Witch's Craft* (edited by Douglas Ezzy, Allen & Unwin, 2003), and was a contributor to *Bast and Sekhmet: Eyes of Ra* by Storm Constantine and Eloise Coquio (Hale, 1999) and *The Encyclopedia of Modern Witchcraft and Neo-Paganism* (edited by Shelley Rabinovitch and James Lewis, Citadel Press, 2002).

For more information on the Australian Pagan Alliance, contact: Pagan Alliance Inc, PO Box 26, North Hobart, Tasmania, Australia 7002; pagantimeseditor@neogenesis.com.au. The Alliance is Australia's oldest and largest organization for Pagans. Each State has its own coordinator, newsletter and activities for members. Most States also run gatherings for members and other Pagans in the local community.

Janine Roberts (who also writes under the pen-name Jani Farrell-Roberts) worked for Aboriginal-run landrights organizations for many years. She was appointed Mining Advisor to the National Federation of Aboriginal Land Councils, her job being to research the mining corporations that wanted entry to Aboriginal lands. She authored a number of books, all well received within the Aboriginal community, including *From Massacres to Mining: the colonisation of Aboriginal Australia*. She co-produced with Aboriginal Elder, Robert Bropho, the film *Munda Nyuringu: He's taken the land, believes it is his and won't give it back*. This won a national Best Documentary Nomination. She is also the author of the critically acclaimed *Glitter & Greed: The Secret World of the Diamond Cartel* (The Disinformation Company, 2003).

Janine now works as a priestess, shaman and Witch – and as an investigative journalist and producer, with her documentaries shown on US, UK and Australian television. She also teaches a nature-centered spirituality, writes against war and on medical issues, and organizes Witchcamps – one of which was attended by Starhawk.

Her chapter in *Pop!* is based on her new book, *The Seven Days of My Creation: Tales of Magic, Sex and Gender*, in which she tells more about Aboriginal magic as well as of her extraordinary Orlando-like journey. Her story is interwoven with much of original research into patriarchy, magic and Witchcraft. She writes of finding an alchemic balance between the male and female aspects we all possess, of working with pain and fear, listening to instincts, of the sacred aspects of sex and gender, magic and gnosticism, powerful women and Witch-trials, and of hermaphrodite Goddesses. The book is published internationally by iUniverse Inc, and can be purchased from the publisher's website – www.iuniverse.com – where it can be browsed, and from all major online bookshops such as Amazon.com. The author can be contacted at Janine@sparkle.plus.com.

2001 saw **Wendy Rule** finally take her talents overseas from Australia, touring initially to the UK, Europe and the USA. In October she returned to New York just after September 11, a city still beautiful but deeply grieving. It was during this trip that she wrote the material for her latest album *The Lotus Eaters* in a process of meditation and sorrow.

"… an extraordinary evening of mystical mastery interwoven with threads of timeless myths. Wendy's voice and skilled songwriting touched our deepest selves and got us in touch with feelings often suppressed be over-worldly cares. The audience was moved, mesmerized, delighted." (Concert review, New Mexico.)

The response of audiences was so strong that she returned again in 2002 to tour the West Coast of the US as well as Europe and Britain. May 2003 brought the long awaited release of Wendy's fourth album, *The Lotus Eaters*, and Wendy is now sharing her Odyssey with the world.

For more information on international touring dates and how to purchase Wendy's music visit: www.wendyrule.com.

Releases:

2003	*Lotus Eaters* Shock Records
2000	*World Between Worlds* Shock Records
May 2000	Video release of the musical play *An Underworld Journey* Independent release
1998	*Deity* Shock Records
1997	*Live* album Independent release
1996	*Continental Isolation*

(three track CD single)
Shock Records

1996   *Zero*
Shock Records

Caroline Tully is a Witch, writer and artist who spends a lot of her time being torn between Hellenic Reconstructionist Paganism on the one hand, and Scottish Witchcraft and faerie lore on the other. She subsequently wishes she had two heads.

Caroline is a feature writer and reviewer for several Pagan publications, including *Witchcraft* magazine, and has also contributed a chapter on the Sabbats to an anthology of Wiccan and Pagan writing, *Practising the Witch's Craft*, edited by Douglas Ezzy (Allen & Unwin, 2003). She has one child, a magical little boy named Jasper.

David Wolfe (born August 6, 1970) is the author of the best-selling books *Eating For Beauty* and *The Sunfood Diet Success System*. He is considered by peers to be the world authority on raw-food nutrition. He is also CEO of Nature's First Law Inc., the world's largest distributor of books, juicers, audio/videotapes, organic beauty products, bulk organic foods and exotic raw foods to assist people in adopting, maintaining, and enjoying raw-plant-food-based lifestyles.

David conducts nearly 100 health lectures, seminars, and hosts at least five raw adventure retreats each year in the United States, Canada, Europe, and the South Pacific. You may view his current schedule in the Events section of www.rawfood.com. David is also the founder of the Hawaiian-based non-profit Fruit Tree Planting Foundation whose mission is to plant 18 billion fruit trees on Earth.

In addition to his action-packed lecture schedule, David plays the drums in his all-raw rock and roll group, the Healing Waters Band, and in 2004, he promoted another form of Pagan-friendly raw living, co-starring as "Avocado" the house naturist, with Fiona Horne in SCI FI Channel's *Mad Mad House*.

David's websites include:
www.rawfood.com
www.davidwolfe.com
www.thebestdayever.com
www.fruittreefoundation.org
www.thehealingwatersband.com

Anatha Wolfkeepe is Acting High Priestess of the Covenant of Earthgate; feature writer and columnist for popular Australian magazine *Witchcraft*. The Founder and Director of Studies of the Church of the Ancient Mysteries, Anatha has 26 years' experience in Magickal Religion. Involved with ongoing research and practice in the techniques of Energy Healing and Core-Shamanism, she has extensive experience in the Native Traditions of ancient Britain and Europe.

Through Dedicated Seed-Houses, the CAM promotes the transformation of "congregation" into Priest/esshood. "Our mission is to teach Teachers and heal Healers. To seed positive evolutionary change we must first awaken our individual Nature-Intelligence by moving as Hedge Witches into the "wildstream" of Nature behind and beyond human society. Without effective individuals there can be no effective community."

She can be reached through the Church of the Ancient Mysteries, PO Box Q223, QVB Post Office, Sydney, NSW, Australia, 1230; +61 414 774 358; or wolfkeepe@AncientMysteriesNet.org. See also www.AncientMysteriesNet.org.

Courses and Training: *Training in Magickal Religion for Solitary and Coven* (available in workshop form or experience-based correspondence) includes: The Circle Gate; Sacred Arts and Guilds of Esbat and Sabbat; Holding Sacred Hearth; Healing and Blessing Body, House and Land; Magick of Storytelling; Healing our Lost Rites of Passage. *Natural Magick and Witchcraft Traditions*: Newsletter; Natural Magick and Divinity Correspondence Training and Membership Program; Priest/esshood Apprenticeship Concessions. *Healing Spiritual Emergency/Spirit Emerging:* supporting initiatory self-healing through the transitional states of the magickal path (the Sacred Dark); distance healing and clearing. *In-Person Women's Sessions:* Bodywork; Energy-Healing; Core-Shamanism; Tarot and Oracles; Dreamwork and Story Magick; Past/Other Lives; Residential Healing/Training Intensives available.

Morning Glory Zell-Ravenheart (born 1948) is a Witch, Priestess, Loremistress and Goddess historian—famous for her rituals, songs, poetry, and her Goddess Collection of over 150 votive figurines. She undertook her first vision quest and self-initiation in 1968 at Big Sur in California. She met her soulmate, Oberon, at the 1973 Gnostic Aquarian Festival in Minneapolis, and they were married the following Spring.

She helped produce *Green Egg* magazine and the Living Unicorns, and founded Mythic Images (www.MythicImages.com), producing museum quality replicas and original visionary interpretations of ancient Goddesses and Gods, by Oberon and herself.

Morning Glory has created ceremonies of every kind and scale, from simple rites of passage, to spectacular events such as the 1979 Solar eclipse at the

Stonehenge replica in the Oregon Dalles. Her journeys have taken her to the Australian Blue Mountains, the depths of the Coral Sea, the jungles of New Guinea, the ruins of ancient Greece, the caves of Crete and the Taoist Goddess Temples of China.

Oberon Zell-Ravenheart, born in 1942, is a modern-day Wizard, and an Elder in the worldwide Magickal Community. In 1962, he co-founded the Church of All Worlds, a Pagan church with a futuristic vision. Through his publication of *Green Egg* magazine, Oberon was instrumental in the founding of the modern Pagan movement. In 1970, he had a profound vision of the Living Earth which he published as an early version of "*The Gaia Thesis*."

Oberon is an initiate in several magickal traditions, and has been involved in many interfaith projects. He is a theologian (and thealogian) and ritualist, creating and conducting rites of passage, seasonal celebrations, Mystery initiations, Earth-healings, and other large rituals. Oberon has traveled throughout the world, celebrated solar eclipses at ancient stone circles, raised Unicorns, and swam with Mermaids (it's a long story – or several!). He sculpts altar statues of Gods and Goddesses, and his first book is *Grimoire for the Apprentice Wizard,* a "Boy Scout Manual" of Wizardry for the Harry Potter generation. Living in Northern California, Oberon is lifemate to Morning Glory, and senior member of the Ravenheart Family.

He cordially invites you to visit:
www.MythicImages.com.

alter

A table or similar surface upon which the working tools of a Witch, representations of the Goddess and God, and articles used in spellcraft are placed. A Witch's altar generally faces the Earth Quarter (south in the southern hemisphere and north in the northern) and is positioned either in the center of the working space or close to the Circle's perimeter in the Earth Quarter. Altars may either be permanently set up or prepared only when required. In outdoor rituals, stones, tree stumps, and the like are often used as makeshift altars.

astral realm/plane

Terms popularized by Theosophy to describe the lower levels of existence, subtler than the physical plane but resembling it closely, all physical objects being believed to have astral equivalents. While Theosophy describes the various levels or planes very specifically, the term "astral" is typically used less precisely in Wicca (and many other magical traditions) to describe a variety of realms of being made of energies subtler than matter though still apparently retaining form. It is widely believed that changes made on the astral bring about changes in physical reality, this principle being used in many forms of magic (such as astral projection, in which the astral equivalent of the body of the Witch or magician is set free to explore and modify that plane).

athame

A knife, traditionally but not necessarily double-edged and black-handled, used by a Witch to delineate sacred space, astrally inscribe pentagrams and other symbols, and direct energy in consecrations (e.g., in spells and the charging of wine). It also represents the power of Air (or, less typically, Fire) and a Witch's identity as a Priest/ess of the Craft. The word "athame" was popularized by *Gerald Gardner* and appears to be derived from *The Key of Solomon*. The usual pronunciation is either "ath-*arm*-ay" or "*ath*-aym-ee."

bind

(1) To bind a spell is to complete its casting, releasing it to do its work independently of the weaver of the spell. The spell is bound to its desired result and should henceforth only be thought of in terms of its completion, not the manner in which it will work. Some spells incorporate the actual tying of a knot to bind the spell. (2) To bind an individual magically is to use spellcraft to prevent them from behaving in a certain fashion. Some Witches never use such spells, feeling them to be overly manipulative, while others feel they have a duty to do all they can to prevent, for example, a rapist or child molester from repeating their crimes. A binding is very different from a curse since it only prevents specific behavior, rather than harming an individual. The caster of the spell can, therefore, safely accept the spell's "return."

book of shadows

A book of spells, rituals and lore, either assembled by the individual Witch according to his or her own tastes and requirements or deriving from one of several Books of Shadows compiled by *Gerald Gardner* and associates in the 1940s and 50s. The individually assembled Book of Shadows (BOS) is the more widely used type now and their contents may contain everything from magical diaries, recipes and picture collections to transcriptions from grimoires and other magical texts.

celtic

Relating to a particular Indo-European race thriving in the pre-Roman era in Britain, France and other regions of Western Europe. The remaining strongholds of Celtic culture include Ireland, Scotland, Wales and Brittany. Wicca is strongly influenced by ancient and contemporary Celtic culture and magical traditions but, contrary to many superficial books and articles on the subject, it isn't a Celtic religion or movement but, rather, one of the most multicultural of all spiritual paths. Some traditions, however, do emphasize the Celtic aspects of the Craft, just as others might the Scandinavian, Italian or Jewish aspects.

chakra

One of seven centers of spiritual energy positioned along the spine and skull of the human body which, when activated through meditation and visualization allows the flow of a current of energy, enhancing magical and spiritual workings. An Eastern concept, popularized in the West by Theosophy and related organizations, chakra workings are now commonly used by Wiccans of many traditions.

chalice

A drinking vessel, generally handle-less and comprising a bowl, stem and base, used in Wicca to represent the element of Water. The principal use of the chalice in Wiccan ritual is to contain wine (or mead, water, juice or whatever is preferred) to be blessed by the Goddess and God, before being drunk to take that blessing into the body. Where more than one person is in the Circle the chalice is passed, with a kiss, around those assembled to deepen the bonds between them. A chalice may also be used in spellcraft to hold an item of jewelry, etc., being consecrated.

church

In a Wiccan context, generally a reference to the many forms of Christian Church or, historically, either the Roman Catholic or a significantly powerful Protestant Church. Though occasionally used disparagingly (generally by those viewing it as an historically oppressive force), the Christian Church is afforded by most Witches the same respect they accord all religions. Wiccans in general have no grievance with any religious organization or individuals except those who revile and seek to demonize the Craft or any other equally worthy faith.

circle

A space delineated and sanctified by a Witch or Witches for the purposes of protection or a ritual. A Wiccan Circle may be visibly represented or simply astrally inscribed. The Circle is actually better visualized as a sphere than a boundary on the ground, and as a field of energy rather than a bubble – through which, presumably, one's head would poke out when near the edge!

coven

A small group of three or more Witches who regularly join together for Circles. Though the term is often loosely used to describe any group practicing the Craft, the Coven should ideally be united by a strong level of commitment to both Witchcraft and the group itself. Bonds between Coven members are typically those of very close friends or even family members, and groups of casual acquaintances getting together for an occasional Sabbat or spellcasting are more properly referred to as "Groves" or simply "Open Circles" or working groups. The traditional ideal number of members is thirteen, although in practice this is more like a maximum number of members. Many of the most durable Covens only comprise three to six members.

collective unconscious

A term from Jungian psychology descriptive of a deep stratum of shared knowledge and insight available to all members of the human race. This shared wealth of information is believed to be encoded in symbols rather than verbal language. The concept was coined to provide a hypothetical explanation for the way in which distantly located cultures with no apparent means of communicating ideas and mythologies often seemed to generate very similar grammars of symbolism.

correspondences

In magical theory, the kinship of certain sets of ideas or qualities. A keystone of contemporary magical lore is the concept that a deeply encoded unity may be found in superficially different substances, so that, for example, a particular color, perfume, herb, element, magical tool, planet, zodiacal constellation and day of the week share an inherent quality. Hence, the color red relates to the planet Mars, and the color green to Venus; the scent of frankincense relates to Jupiter and myrrh to Saturn; and so on. In ritual, a particular energy can be magnified by concentrating as many different related substances and influences together as possible.

craft, the
One of the terms used loosely to describe either **Wicca** (see below) or Witchcraft of all varieties. The term was used to describe Freemasonry long before Witchcraft adopted it, suggesting that it is one of many Masonic phrases adopted by Gerald Gardner in his reformulation of the Craft in the 1940s and 50s.

deosil
Movement in the direction of the sun, hence clockwise in the northern hemisphere (where the sun rises in the east, veers to the south (i.e., the direction of the Equator), before setting in the west) and anti-clockwise in the southern hemisphere. In Wiccan ritual, sunwise motion tends to be used to draw power in, and counter-sunwise movement to banish or cast energy out. See also **Widdershins**.

druidic
Pertaining to the faith of the early Celtic priest and priesthood or their modern day counterparts. In Britain, Druidry is the second largest Pagan movement after the Craft, with which it shares many beliefs and practices.

etheric plane
A term popularized through Theosophy to describe the energy field interconnecting the physical and **astral** (see above) planes. The etheric is often referred to as "life force" (and a host of other names) and is the most commonly perceived portion of the aura.

familiar
A spirit assistant to a Witch. A familiar may be either an elemental or a formerly human spirit, often taking the form of, or actually inhabiting the body of, an animal. It should be stressed, however, that not all Witches' pets are necessarily familiars. Witches enjoy the company of animals for their own sake as much as any intelligent member of the human race does!

gardner, gerald
An Englishman who, in the 1940s through to his death in 1964 was instrumental in popularizing modern **Wicca** (see below).

guardian
Generally short for "Guardian of the Watchtower" – one of many images used to personify the elemental powers of each of the four **Quarters** (see below). Guardians may also be spirits, elemental or otherwise, called to protect a Witch, other individual or even a location from harm.

hex/hexing
A word derived from a German word for Witch describing the casting of a spell. Although the word itself has no connotation of either positive or negative spellcasting, in common usage the word is used synonymously with "curse."

intuition
A form of perception or thinking not apparently connected to rational structuring of thought. Witches tend to give this form of mental activity equal (or sometimes even superior) status to logical thought, on the basis that the brain comprises two sides, each with its own mode of coming to conclusions.

invoke
To call a spirit or deity into oneself or one's **Circle** (see above).

laity
Laypeople considered as a group. All those persons who are not members of a given profession or other specialized field.

libations
In Wicca, an offering to the Goddess and God of wine (or another beverage) blessed within the Circle. In an outdoor ritual, the offering may be poured during the Circle; in indoor Circles, the offering is taken out after the closing of the ritual. Though libation literally means an offering of drink, Wiccans frequently extend the meaning to include the offering of whatever food was shared during the Circle as well.

magick
An archaic spelling of "Magic" popularized by Aleister Crowley, largely to differentiate it

from stage magic. The term has been repeatedly redefined by modern occultists and Witches but essentially refers to the manipulation of reality by apparently supernatural means by the will of an individual or group. In *POP!* "magick" is spelled by some writers without the "k" (i.e., "magic") but they are always referring to metaphysical and spiritual phenomenan.

metaphysical

Strictly, abstractly philosophical, but in general usage synonymous with "supernatural." Most Witches find both terms of limited usefulness, interpreting both to mean "pertaining to matters not yet understood by science."

occult/occultist

The "occult" is another term for that which is hidden, i.e., that which is not yet understood by conventional wisdom. An occultist is, therefore, one who studies those subjects that exist within human experience but outside established understanding.

ouija board

A board on which alphabetical (and related) characters are marked out and upon which an indicator (traditionally an inverted glass or a planchette – a small board on wheels) is held by the fingertips of two or more people in the hopes that disincarnate spirits will be able to communicate. Popularized by Spiritualism, Ouija boards are rarely used by Witches, who tend to feel that inviting any passing spirit into their bodies or homes is slightly more dangerous than leaving the front door open in a high-crime neighborhood.

pentacle

A disc or stone inscribed with a *pentagram* (see below) and possibly other esoteric symbols representing the element of Earth. The pentacle can be used to hold objects being consecrated, to act as a shield against unwanted energy or to help ground energy. An alternative to the pentacle as a Craft tool symbolizing Earth in some Wiccan traditions is a stone (often polished into a spherical shape). The word "pentacle" is often also casually used to mean a pendant, ring or earring inscribed or molded into the shape of a pentagram.

pentagram

A regular five-pointed star used as a symbol of blessing and power in many magical traditions, including the Craft. The five points are often said to represent the four elements giving rise to the fifth – the element of spirit. For this reason, the pentagram is generally shown with one point uppermost, representing the ascent of spirit through balanced matter, while the inverted pentagram is often seen as a symbol of the spirit in decline (hence its use in negative magic and Satanism). However, in Gardnerian Craft, the inverted pentagram is used as a symbol of their second degree and in that context shouldn't be mistaken for a malevolent symbol.

quarter

Within a Witch's **Circle**, one of the cardinal points of the compass, each of which corresponds to one of the four Elements. Correspondences will vary from tradition to tradition and place to place but the quartered **Circle** is one of the most common features of Wiccan ritual.

runes

Alphabetical characters used by Germanic and Scandinavian people up until the Middle Ages. The original runes were associated with a number of magical **correspondences** (see above) and have recently been revived as a tool for divination. A rune may also be a short poem used as a spell or invocation.

satanism

A form of inverted Christianity where the vices of the Christian faith are held to be virtues and vice versa. Despite some superficial similarity in magical tools and trappings, there is no theological or philosophical connection between **Wicca** (a form of Pagan religion/spirituality) and Satanism.

sigil

A sign or symbol supposedly possessed of an inherent magical power.

skyclad

A term borrowed from Jainism by **Gerald**

Gardner to describe nakedness as a state of power and sacredness rather than vulnerability. While some Wiccan traditions work clothed in robes, costumes or even street clothes, the tradition of skyclad working remains popular since it emphasizes several qualities necessary to the Craft: self-acceptance, individuality, freedom and mutual trust. In recent years, the word has also gained popularity in non-Wiccan contexts.

solitary (or solitaire)

A Witch who practices the Craft alone most of the time, whether by choice or circumstance. Most Witches who are part of Covens or other working groups still work solitary at least some of the time. While the Gardnerian **Book of Shadows** stated one couldn't be "a Witch alone," contemporary thinking is of the opinion that a Witch needs to do just that periodically to avoid becoming dependant on group energy.

taoism

A Chinese religion/ philosophy with a number of similarities to the Craft, notably an emphasis on spiritual polarity (in Taoism conceived of as Yin and Yang; in Wicca, as the God and Goddess) and the interconnectedness of all things. Traditional Taoism also has a strong pantheistic and magical element, and recommends alignment with the natural flow of life's energy.

third eye

One of the **chakras** (see above), positioned in the center of the forehead and associated with the pineal gland. The chakra is related to the power of inner vision, both active visualization and the ability to see between the worlds.

wand

A length of wood, often decorated with carvings and tipped with crystals, used in Witchcraft to represent the element of Fire (or, less typically, Air). The wand was originally conceived as a symbol of authority in magic and is frequently described as being used in commanding spirits and the like. In the Craft, it is more often used to direct energy either into an object or – in the case of healing energy, for example – out of the Circle and towards a spell's target. Since Fire also relates to the Will, the wand is often held aloft in the making of oaths or the proclaiming of an intention. Some traditions use a staff or a forked-headed staff called a stang, instead of the shorter wand.

western magick

The magical practices associated with the Western Mystery tradition, an array of systems given the collective name to differentiate them from Indian and Far Eastern esoteric magical practices. Many influential occult organizations such as the Theosophical Society have had eras in which they championed Eastern traditions but showed little interest in ancient European esoteric traditions. While much of value was imported to Europe by these organizations, many occultists felt their own cultures were being dangerously neglected, hence the emphasis on the West.

wicca

A contemporary form of Pagan Witchcraft owing much to the mid-20th century work of **Gerald Gardner**. While Gardner represented Wicca as being a magical tradition existing for centuries in much the form he described in his books, it's now clear that he was much more like the innovative, creative Wiccans of today, formulating his own vision of Witchcraft from a wide range of influences. Wicca wasn't Gardner's invention any more than rock and roll was Elvis Presley's. Both, however, were enormously influential in changing and popularizing their chosen fields. Using the word "Wicca" in this sense is useful in differentiating modern Pagan Witchcraft from the many other species of Witchcraft around the world.

widdershings

Movement in the opposite direction to that of the sun, hence anti-clockwise in the northern hemisphere and clockwise in the southern hemisphere. See also **Deosil**.